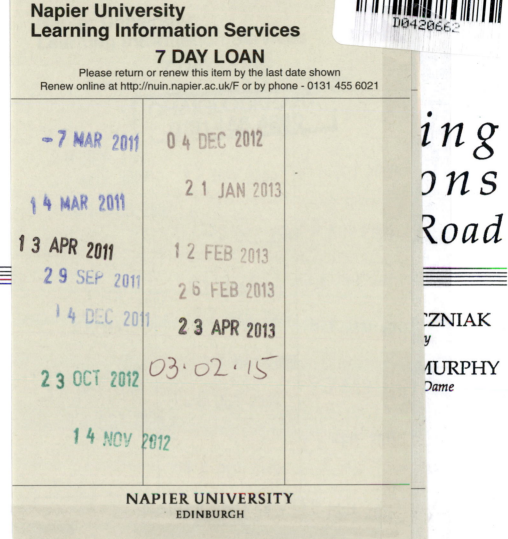

ing
ons
Road

CZNIAK
y

MURPHY
Dame

PRENTICE HALL, UPPER SADDLE RIVER, NEW JERSEY

Library of Congress Cataloging-in-Publication Data

Laczniak, Eugene R.
   Ethical marketing decisions : the higher road / Gene R. Laczniak,
Patrick E. Murphy.
      p.   cm.
   Includes bibliographical references and index.
   1. Business ethics. 2. Marketing—Moral and ethical aspects.
I. Murphy, Patrick E., 1948–   . II. Title.
   HF5387.L333 1993
   174′.4—dc20   92-29935
                                                                          CIP

Series Editorial Assistant: Sarah Carter
Production Administrator: Elaine Ober
Editorial-Production Service: Spectrum Publisher Services
Cover Designer: Suzanne Harbison
Manufacturing Buyer: Louise Richardson

© 1993 by Prentice-Hall, Inc.
A Pearson Education Company
Upper Saddle River, NJ 07458

Transferred to digital print on demand 2002

Printed & bound by Antony Rowe Ltd, Eastbourne

ISBN 0-205-13627-3

Prentice-Hall International (UK) Limited,London
Prentice-Hall of Australia Pty. Limited, Sydney
Prentice-Hall Canada Inc., Toronto
Prentice-Hall Hispanoamericana, S.A., Mexico
Prentice-Hall of India Private Limited, New Delhi
Prentice-Hall of Japan, Inc., Tokyo
Pearson Education Asia Pte. Ltd., Singapore
Editora Prentice-Hall do Brasil, Ltda., Rio de Janeiro

To our parents
Ray and Jean Laczniak
and
John and Betty Murphy
who guided us along the road with their
encouragement, example, and love

Contents

Preface   ix

Chapter 1   **Analyzing Marketing Ethics**   1
             Some Questions About Marketing Ethics   3
             Different Types of Managers and Their Approaches to
                 Ethics   11
             An Organizational View of Ethics   13
             Frameworks for Ethical Decision Making   17
             Ideas for Ethical Action   21
             Conclusion   22

Chapter 2   **Ethical Reasoning and Marketing Decisions**   25
             The Importance of Ethical Theory   27
             Comprehensive Ethical Theories   28
             Models of Marketing Ethics   42
             Ideas for Ethical Action   48
             Conclusion   51

Chapter 3   **Ethics in Marketing Research**   53
             What Researchers Owe Respondents   56
             What Researchers and Clients Owe One Another   62
             What Researchers Owe the Public   66
             Corporate Intelligence Gathering   68
             Ideas for Ethical Action   72
             Conclusion   75
             Appendix 3A   Marketing Research Code of Ethics of the
                 American Marketing Association   76

Chapter 4   **Product Management Ethics**   81
             Product Safety   84
             Product Counterfeiting   89
             The Ethics of Product Management   91

	How to Evaluate Ethics in Product Management	102
	Ideas for Ethical Action	103
	Conclusion	106
Chapter 5	**Ethical Issues in Distribution, Retailing and Pricing**	**109**
	Channel of Distribution Issues	110
	Pricing Issues	125
	Ideas for Ethical Action	134
	Conclusion	136
	Appendix 5A NAPM Code	137
	Appendix 5B Dayton Hudson Corporate Principles	138
	Appendix 5C Ralphs Credo	139
Chapter 6	**Ethical Concerns in Advertising**	**143**
	The Power and Complexity of Advertising	144
	Advertising and Society	145
	How Advertisers Use Moral Philosophy	151
	Ethical Questions Facing Advertising	153
	Positive Developments and Future Challenges for Ethics in Advertising	167
	Ideas for Ethical Action	170
	Conclusion	172
	Appendix 6A BBB Children's Advertising Review Unit Advertising Policies	173
	Appendix 6B American Advertising Federation Principles	174
	Appendix 6C American Association of Advertising Agencies Policies	175
	Advertising Examples	179
Chapter 7	**Personal Selling Ethics**	**185**
	Consumer Irritation with Sales Efforts and Salespeople	185
	Why Personal Selling Presents Particularly Difficult Ethical Questions	188
	Sales and the Law	189
	The Gray Areas of Selling	191
	Gifts and Entertainment: Areas That Are Not Unethical Per Se	194
	When Are Salesreps Most Pressured to Compromise Their Ethics?	196
	Sales Management Ethics	197
	Ideas for Ethical Action	199
	A Simple Framework to Evaluate Sales Ethics	203
	Conclusion	204
	Appendix 7A The Ethics of Selling for Xerox	205

Chapter 8	**International Marketing Ethics**	**209**
	Motivations for Expanded Global Marketing	210
	Causes of Ethical Problems in International Marketing	211
	World-Wide Codes of Ethics	218
	Strategic Planning and International Marketing Ethics	221
	Ideas for Ethical Action	225
	Conclusion	228
	Appendix 8A Caterpillar's Code of Worldwide Business Conduct and Operating Principles	229
Chapter 9	**The Ethics of Social, Professional, and Political Marketing**	**239**
	Social Marketing	241
	Marketing by Professionals	250
	Political Marketing	260
	Conclusion	269
	Appendix 9A Graduate Management Admission Council Code	270
	Appendix 9B American Bar Association Model Rules of Professional Conduct	271
	Appendix 9C Advertising Guidelines of the Council of Medical Specialty Societies (CMSS)	272
Chapter 10	**Implementing and Auditing Marketing Ethics**	**277**
	Organizing for Marketing Ethics Implementation	278
	Enacting Ethical Marketing Policies	288
	The Concept of an Ethical Audit	292
	An Ethical Audit for Marketing	295
	Ideas for Ethical Action	297
	Closing Comments	299
	Appendix 10A The Security Pacific Credo and Guidelines for Gifts	302
	Appendix 10B Ethical Audit Questions for Marketing	303
About the Authors		**312**
Name Index		**313**
Subject Index		**319**

P r e f a c e

Mark Twain once remarked, "Always try to do the right thing, it will surprise a lot of people. And it will astonish the rest." Trying to do the right thing is what ethics is all about. The behavior of marketing managers, like many other professionals in our society, is increasingly questioned. For instance, shortsighted treatment of the environment came into focus on Earth Day 1990. (We remember the first Earth Day in 1970, when we were university students.) It brought to mind the abuse of the physical environment by various sectors of society, including business, government, and consumers. Other recent scandals, such as defense contractor cost overruns, the rampant insider trading in the financial sector, government frauds in housing, as well as cheating and racial discrimination, have lifted ethics to the front pages of newspapers. All of these events have come together to raise questions about where we as a society, and marketers as significant actors in society, get our values about what is "right," "just," and "good."

Certainly, ethics is a tough, complex area that raises difficult questions. Marketing ethics is no different. When we set out to write a book on the topic of marketing ethics, a few of our associates offered their snide remarks: "Marketing ethics is an oxymoron—like a square circle." "It must be a very thin book; everybody knows that marketers do not have ethics." "It won't take you long to complete that project; any business person realizes that marketing is about persuasion and efficiency, not about ethics and value judgments."

We don't believe these comments to be even remotely true. While being ethical sometimes reduces short-term profits, it should enhance long-range shareholder value. We contend that good marketing strategies and good ethics are inextricably and positively linked. In the pages that follow, we hope to persuasively illustrate why taking the higher ethical road is most often good business strategy, provides for long term organizational profitability, and stands resolutely as the "proper" thing to do.

Ethics as a Field of Study

Ethics is a word commonly used by many individuals but with different meanings and interpretations. Most often, *ethics* deals with the morality of human conduct. What do we mean by *marketing ethics*? We define marketing ethics as *the systematic study of how moral standards are applied to marketing decisions, behaviors, and institutions*. It is a subset of business ethics. It is also important to recognize that many of the transgressions that critics of business consider to be "unethical" are outright violations of the law. While legal transgressions often overlap with ethical discussions—and we will deal with these from time to time—our view is that ethics is superordinate to most legal considerations. In other words, ethical responsibility places demands on managerial behavior that go above and beyond the law.

This is where the difficulty arises. Because ethics sometimes deals with subjective moral choices, the question becomes *what* moral standards ought to be applied to *which* ethical questions in marketing. For example, is it proper for an advertising copywriter to use a blatant (but legal) sexual appeal, which some see as exploitative and demeaning of women, when the agency has demonstrated that such appeals sell more of a client's cosmetics products? Cynics claim that arguable issues like these are likely to generate much disagreement and illustrate the futility of dealing with the "always subjective" ethics area. However, as we shall show repeatedly in the pages that follow, in many industries and in many situations, there is more of a consensus about what is accepted by the majority as "proper" than many casual observers might suspect.

The Two Aspects of Ethics

We see ethics, or the study of moral choice, as having two dimensions. First, ethics, via its foundation in moral philosophy, provides various models and frameworks for handling ethical situations. That is, there are various approaches to ethical reasoning. For instance, ethics leads us to consider whether we should judge the moral appropriateness of business decisions based on the *consequences* for various stakeholders or on the basis of the *intentions* held by the decision-maker when a particular action is selected. Often, differing approaches lead us to similar conclusions about the "ethicalness" of a particular action. Unfortunately, different approaches can sometimes lead to divergent conclusions. Early in this book, we set out to discuss the fundamental approaches to analyzing marketing ethics, and we explain what rationale lies behind the different perspectives people use to deal with ethical problems.

The second dimension of ethics has to do with ethics as the "right" thing to do. This is the *normative* aspect of marketing ethics. When people say that someone is acting ethically, they usually mean individuals are doing what is *morally correct*. The underpinnings for having a feeling about what one ought to do comes mostly from our individual values. These are shaped by our family, religious training and personal feelings about how we should treat other people. A prominent manager once remarked that perhaps some of the elusiveness about what constitutes an ethical person could be overcome if people substituted the word *trust* for ethics; that is, ethical marketing managers are *trustworthy* in that they can always be counted on to try to do the right thing.

It is also true that ethics is one of those subjects where people cannot say anything of substance without revealing quite a bit about their own values. Throughout this book, we will make normative judgments about various aspects of marketing practice. While some of our evaluations will undoubtedly cause debate and disagreement, our major purpose is to increase managers' sensitivity to the ethical questions which regularly occur in the practice of marketing and to assist them in making more consistently ethical decisions.

Organizational Ethics

The field of ethics has usually focused on the individual and the choices that are made by people. However, most marketing managers work within the context of an organization. Therefore, the *corporate culture* in which they operate can shape, enforce, and at times override the individual ethical dispositions that managers have about a particular situation. Some academics and business people contend that the individual values of mature managers are firmly fixed by the time that they assume organizational responsibility. We do *not* believe this is true. As we discuss in Chapter 2, we think that the values of a manager can evolve over time. However, even if individual values were relatively "fixed," numerous case studies (including some discussed in this book) have clearly shown that the ethics of managers can be overridden by *organizational* pressures for increased profit, performance, or prestige. Throughout this book, we attempt to take into account the interplay between organizational and individual values in discussing the various issues within the domain of marketing ethics. Our managerial suggestions and implications are thus geared to the *organizational* adjustments that can be made to impel ethical behavior.

Ethics Versus the Law

As we shall observe on several occasions, ethics typically deals with moral responsibilities that go beyond the requirements of the law. For example, it is *not* a *legal* requirement for a seller to provide an extension to a financially struggling (but loyal) buyer, when that buyer requests some additional time beyond a payment deadline. This situation, however, may evoke an *ethical* obligation. Alternatively, certain business practices, such as bribery payments in international markets, may be illegal but *not necessarily* unethical. And at many times, ethics and the law can be co-extensive. This is because part of the function of law is to formalize the basic and widely shared moral expectations about behavior that a society demands. For example, much of civil law is an attempt to codify the fundamental duties that society believes that various parties (including corporations) owe one another as transactional relationships occur. Hence, sometimes, what is illegal is not unethical. More often, what is legal, might be unethical. And there are a great many things, appropriately so, that are both illegal and unethical.

Ethics within Marketing

In business firms, marketing is the most visible functional area because of its interface with consumers. Communicating with and satisfying customers is the essence of marketing. Selling and advertising are especially noticeable and essential activities in achieving the marketing mission. Since marketing is so close to the public view, it should not be surprising that it is the subject of considerable societal analysis and scrutiny. One 1980s public-opinion poll ranked advertising practitioners and sales representatives among the lowest of occupations in terms of perceived ethics. Taken together, these factors mean that marketing is an area of business commonly identified with questionable practices.

In this book, we examine a range of ethical issues facing marketing managers. Certain issues, like those in pricing and purchasing, are long-standing ones that have been debated for some time. Others, such as slotting fees, marketing by professionals, and computerized telephone-sales solicitations are emerging concerns that managers must increasingly face.

How This Book Is Organized

The chapters of this book are ordered in such a way that the ethical concerns facing the marketing manager are treated systematically. We begin in Chapter 1 with an elaboration of basic perspectives and frameworks for studying ethical issues in marketing, including *the costs of unethical behavior* and several often-asked questions about marketing ethics. Chapter 2 covers the foundations of ethical reasoning—utilitarianism, duty-based theories, and virtue ethics—as they pertain to marketing decisions. Chapter 3 then moves to the subject of marketing research, which is commonly used as a basis for marketing decisions. Such ethical considerations deal with researcher responsibilities to respondents, clients, and the general public.

Chapters 4 through 7 cover the marketing mix variables of product, price, distribution channels, and promotion. Chapter 4 examines the many ethical issues that arise in development and management of products, including issues such as product safety. Chapter 5 discusses ethical concerns within distribution channels as well as ethical issues that arise in connection with pricing. Chapter 6 analyzes the many and varied ethical questions that occur in the process of advertising products. Chapter 7 then turns to the personal selling function and its concomitant ethical responsibilities as buyers and sellers negotiate exchange.

The final chapters examine several emerging areas of ethical concern to marketing managers. Chapter 8 pertains to international issues facing marketing managers as business organizations expand their operations to new markets and cultures. Chapter 9 discusses three separate topics: social marketing, marketing by professionals, and political marketing. All of these issues have received increasing attention as generators of possible ethical conflicts for marketers. Chapter 10 examines organizational mechanisms (e.g., corporate codes and ethics training programs) to formally and informally instill ethical values into the marketing organization. The book concludes with several new ethical challenges to marketing managers as they face tomorrow's tough marketing decisions.

Managerial Approach to the Subject

Our approach has a distinct managerial flavor. We believe that if ethical decisions are to occur within organizations, managers must shape an organizational culture hospitable to such outcomes. Therefore, our method uses ethical theories and reasoning as a foundation for managerial decision-making. In each chapter, we identify several key issues, and then move to providing guidance for resolving them. Every chapter concludes with an "Ideas for Ethical Action" section outlining the organizational options available for overcoming ethical obstacles. Managers can use these ideas as guideposts for moving their companies toward more consistently ethical decisions. We believe that the professional practice of marketing is *self-actualized* only when marketing strategy and tactics are tempered with an underlying and abiding concern for high ethical principles.

Acknowledgments

Several organizations and individuals deserve acknowledgment as well as our heartfelt gratitude in assisting with the publication of this book. First, we want to thank our universities for supporting this project by allowing us to work full-time on the arduous task of developing the first drafts of each chapter. Professor Laczniak was granted a sabbatical at Marquette University for the second semester of the 1989–90 year for the primary purpose of working on this book. Dean Thomas A. Bausch of Marquette University deserves recognition for his assistance. Professor Murphy was on leave from his teaching duties at the University of Notre Dame for the same time period. Joseph P. Guiltinan, then Chairman of the Department of Marketing, was instrumental in granting the leave.

Second, this book received substantial scrutiny by a number of extremely knowledgeable individuals familiar with ethics in marketing. Three reviewers read and commented on the entire manuscript. Professor Thomas Klein of the University of Toledo merits our everlasting debt for his meticulous and thoughtful annotations on virtually every page of the book. T. R. Martin and J. Howard Westing, emeritus faculty from Marquette University and the University of Wisconsin—Madison and senior scholars in the business ethics field, provided many helpful insights on the next-to-final draft of the manuscript.

Each chapter was also reviewed by an expert in the particular topical area, and we are appreciative of the many useful comments provided by this cadre of reviewers. They are (in alphabetical order): Roy Adler of Pepperdine University, Joseph Bellizzi of Arizona State University—West, Clarke Caywood of Northwestern University, Warren French of the University of Georgia, David Fritszche of the University of Portland, Joel Huber of Duke University, William Kehoe of the University of Virginia, Thomas Klein of the University of Toledo, Russell Laczniak of Iowa State University, and James Weber of Marquette University.

Third, our secretaries and student assistants provided many hours of labor to this project. At Marquette University, Jane Gray was involved in this effort from the very beginning. Her patience and dedication to all of the clerical aspects of this project are greatly appreciated. At the University of Notre Dame, Greta Hoisington provided much helpful assistance in copying and correspondence matters. A number of students from both institutions did considerable library and exhibit development work. At Marquette University, Gary Brunswick and Jeff Stanislawski helped gather materials instrumental to the launching of the book. And Jeanne Simmons, in particular, worked on all aspects of the manuscript "fact checking" and pulling all the details together. To her, a special *thank you* is in order. At the University of Notre Dame, Megan Moran and Greg Pelligrino, who served as summer research-assistants, were especially helpful in the early stages; in addition, Vladimir Mendoza and David Neidell performed a number of assignments in various phases of the book; during the final stages, Elizabeth Wholihan and Tonya Callahan provided invaluable assistance in getting the manuscript ready for production. To all these individuals, we say thanks.

Fourth, many individuals at Allyn & Bacon assisted in our work. To our first editor, Henry Reece, who supported and signed the book, we are thankful for his confidence and vision in making this book a reality. Susan Nelle Barcomb and Rich Wohl picked up the project in its latter phases. The assistants to the marketing editor, Katherine Grubbs and Sarah Carter, followed the important details of the project to their completion. Carol Alper persistently performed the mundane job of securing the many permissions for the book. We also wish to thank Kelly Ricci and the staff at Spectrum Publisher Services for helping make this a better product.

Finally, we want to thank our wives (Monica and Kate) and sons (Andrew and Stephen; Bobby, Brendan, and Jamie) for providing the needed emotional support and for allowing us the time, often at their expense, to complete the book. We also acknowledge the efforts of one another. This was truly a joint effort and each contributed equally to the entire project. The order of authorship is, thus, alphabetical and not reflective of differential output.

Despite all this assistance, there are undoubtedly some omissions and errors that remain. We take full responsibility for them.

G. R. L.
P. E. M.

C h a p t e r *1*

Analyzing Marketing Ethics

Scenario 1

Recently, a large consumer products company knowingly sold a water purification system whose filtration mechanisms were contaminated with methylene chloride—a probable carcinogen.[1] Basically, the so-called Clean Water Machine contained a carbonated filtration system that was sealed with a methylene chloride-based glue that seeped into the water. Company engineers quickly spotted the problem, but the judgment of the firm was that the risk to individual consumers was slight, because the leakage was minimal. At least, this was the company's public posture after questions about the product began to emerge. One wonders whether this organization hoped to continue sales while it redesigned the filter, thereby eliminating the negative publicity stemming from the public disclosure of this (possibly) toxic, clean water machine. **Is it ethical for an organization to continue selling a product when some parties have raised major questions concerning its safety?**

Scenario 2

The glut of new products and the limited amounts of shelf space has caused large supermarket chains to demand up-front payments called *slotting fees* for stocking some new products. Supermarket chains justify this practice primarily because they have very narrow profit margins and because unsuccessful new products are costly to stock and to remove from the shelves. Some firms claim that such practices discriminate against small manufacturers who are without the ability to pay the large amounts that are demanded. For example, one supermarket chain asked $25,000 from a small Montana specialty foods producer to have its pizzas placed in freezer cases in its California stores. Other manufacturers complain of the practice because many of the slotting fees are privately negotiated and as they are often made in cash, they become especially subject to abuse.[2] **Are such practices fair to smaller food manufacturers?**

Scenario 3

Because tobacco manufacturers have been heavily criticized in the United States and other developed countries about the safety of cigarette smoking, they have looked to the Third World as the major source of their growth. Developing countries now consume about one-third of the $200 billion worth of all cigarettes sold. Moreover, some of these countries have been targeted for major tobacco promotion campaigns in the immediate future. Often, tobacco companies develop relationships with the local government, which collects a substantial proportion of the product's price in the form of a sales tax. To make matters worse, several tobacco companies admit that many of the brands sold to developing countries contain more tar and nicotine than cigarette brands marketed in developed countries.[3] **Are such practices ethically justifiable?**

Scenario 4

Travel agents are sometimes accused of not keeping the best interest of their clients in mind. In some cases, they have attempted to capture frequent flyer points that have not been credited to existing customer files for their own accounts. In other instances, the travel agents participated in sweepstakes sponsored by airline or rental-car companies. These sweepstakes allow for an improved chance of "winning the game" based on the amount of business directed toward a particular airline, hotel, or rental-car company.[4] The net result is that, without the customer knowing it, clients might be steered into higher cost travel options, as this is in the best interest of the travel agent. **Are such practices acceptable if clients are not significantly penalized in terms of higher costs or greater inconvenience?**

Scenario 5

As Americans become increasingly health conscious, advertising stresses the health and nutrition benefits of various food products. This has led to numerous cases of misleading or exaggerated claims. For example, ads running in several women's magazines are urging women to drink more milk in order to prevent osteoporosis (the development of brittle bones that can fracture easily). What the ads do *not* say is that many dairy products (e.g., whole milk) are high in fat content and can contribute to high cholesterol levels and, as a result, heart disease. Similarly, many cereal manufacturers have now promoted the supposed health benefits of consuming high-fiber cereals. One recent headline screamed, "Grab a weapon in the war against cancer."[5] The weapon was a cereal spoon. This advertising appeal was used because of the statistical linkage of the consumption of certain bran and fibrous material to low rates of intestinal cancer. Yet, what the advertising omits to say is that the medical community is still debating what the proper level of fiber consumption should be. Also an overconsumption of fiber—a mistake uninformed consumers might make—can lead to a neglect in one's diet of other sources of nutrition.[6] **Are such promotions inherently unfair?**

Marketing ethics deals with the study of how moral standards are applied to marketing decisions, behaviors, and institutions. It is important, because most marketing decisions have ethical ramifications, whether business executives realize it or not. When the actions taken are *proper*, the ethical dimensions go unnoticed and attention centers upon the economic efficiencies and managerial astuteness of the decisions. But such is not always the case. If a marketing decision is ethically troublesome, it can have highly visible outcomes that become a public embarrassment or worse. Consider the specific situations presented at the beginning of this chapter.

These examples are only the tip of the iceberg and are meant to be illustrative of the various areas of marketing (including product management, international issues, retailing, service distribution, and advertising) that can raise ethical questions about appropriate marketing practice. The recent spate of general business ethics scandals, including the Savings and Loan debacle, Wall Street insider-trading scams, the price gouging by several defense contractors, the check overdraft scheme by the former E.F. Hutton brokerage firm, and the collapse of junk bond dealer Drexel–Burnham, has only heightened the skepticism of the American public toward business and marketing practices.

Some Questions About Marketing Ethics

How Does the Public Feel About Business?

Analysts who track the public pulse have established a perception of business and marketing that is less than flattering. Consider the following statistics that seem to show that Americans generally distrust business and marketing people.[7]

- A *Business Week/Harris* poll indicated that white-collar crime is thought to be very common (49 percent) or somewhat common (41 percent) and that 46 percent of the public believe that the ethical standards of business executives are only average.
- A *U.S. News & World Report* survey points out that the majority of the American public believes that many business people regularly participate in unethical transgressions, such as taking home office supplies, padding expense accounts, and using small amounts of organizational funds for personal purposes.
- A *Time* magazine study suggests that 76 percent of the American public saw a lack of business ethics in business managers as contributing to the decline of U.S. moral standards.

EXHIBIT 1–1   Executives Think Managers Are Sometimes Unethical

An article in *The Wall Street Journal* reports that 66 percent of senior executives believe that managers will "occasionally" act unethically in their respective business dealings. Fifteen percent characterized the incidence of unethical behavior by managers as "often."

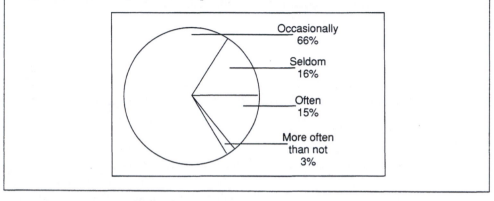

Occasionally
66%

Seldom
16%

Often
15%

More often
than not
3%

Source: *The Wall Street Journal* (September 18, 1987), 31.

• A *Touche Ross* survey of the business community (see Exhibit 1–1) reported that the general feeling (even among business executives) is that the problems concerning business ethics portrayed in the media have *not* been overblown or exaggerated.

From a marketing standpoint, it is even more distressing to realize that among various categories of business professionals, those holding marketing positions are viewed to be among the *least* ethical. For example, in a 1983 Gallup poll judging the ethics of various occupations, the categories of *salespeople* and *advertising practitioners* were ranked at the bottom of the "honesty and ethical standards" scale.[8] This disturbing public opinion probably developed because of the unethical practices of a few marketers. Yet, because of a minority of highly publicized incidents, all marketers are too often construed as hawkers, pitchmen, con-artists, and cheats.

Does the Typical Marketing Manager Face Ethical Problems?

Some marketing managers contend that they are relatively exempt from ethical dilemmas or that moral pressures do not generally affect them. In reality, most studies confirm that between 65 and 75 percent of all managers do indeed face major ethical dilemmas at some point in their careers.[9] An ethical dilemma is defined, for our purposes, as a manager confronting a decision that involves the trade-off between lowering one's personal values in exchange for increased organizational or personal profit. In other words, marketing managers sometimes feel compelled to do things that they feel ought not be done. Based upon the reports of practicing managers, most marketing executives are *not* free from dealing with ethical concerns. If anything, the percentages referenced above underestimate the number of marketers who face an ethical dilemma, because they may not recognize one when confronted by it. Judging from the questions being raised about the propriety of marketing practices, many marketing decisions clearly have significant moral consequences.

Can Emphasizing Ethics Make a Difference?

The point has sometimes been made that preaching ethics in an organization does not have an effect upon the behavior of managers. This view was captured in an old adage which states, "Scruples, either you got 'em or you don't." For years, the Harvard Business School and other colleges of business did not bother to teach business ethics on the supposition that efforts along these lines would most likely prove fruitless. Underlying this approach is a stream of research that indicates moral development occurs at a rather early age and by the time an individual enters a business organization, his or her moral sensibilities are established and somewhat immutable.[10] There is also strong evidence that this viewpoint is probably in error, as various case studies have consistently shown that the ethical gyroscopes of managers can be spun about by organizational actions and economic pressures.[11] Sometimes managers do take actions they feel are *wrong* according to the values that they hold. This happens because of organizational pressures to keep costs down, expand sales, or improve short-term profitability.

Do Ethics Affect Profitability?

The general response to the question, "Do ethics affect profitability?" has to be "Yes." The magnitude of that effect and its direction depends on the circumstances at issue, as well as the time frame upon which management would like to focus. In the short run, it seems fair to say that in many situations taking the higher ethical road will depress profits. If this were not the case, the cost of being an ethical organization would be little and the debate about having good ethics would be far more muted than it is. Some of the time good ethics are in fact traded for reduced profits. Consider, for example, the organization that after public pressure voluntarily changes its product packaging, because it is not bio-degradable at the landfill site. Suppose further that the product packaging leaves behind certain residues that eventually could be damaging to the underground water table. Investing in new packaging and retooling the product process to accommodate that change will result in a cost of several million dollars. In a situation such as this, doing the ethical thing (i.e., being a good environmental citizen) adds to the cost curve of the organization and, at least temporarily, makes the organization less competitive in the marketplace.

In the long run, we contend that the relationship between good ethics and profitability is most likely positive. Consumers over time will normally recognize the organizations that attempt to be responsive to various ethical and social factors in the marketplace. In our packaging example, shifting public expectations may eventually dictate environmentally friendly packaging for all products. The organization that has already made the packaging adjustments benefits from the goodwill of its progressive gesture, and can capitalize in the market by such a change in public expectations, because it is already in place. We believe that situations where good ethics lead to enhanced customer respect and profitability are fairly common. One example is Giant Foods Inc. of the Washington DC area, which was the first supermarket chain with unit pricing, nutritional labeling, freshness dating, and various other innovations that show it to always be on the cutting edge of consumer responsiveness. This has resulted in substantial positive publicity and most likely contributed to the steady sales volume they experienced.

Significantly, the Business Roundtable, a group composed of the chief executive officers of the 100 largest US-headquartered organizations, recently released a report titled, "Corporate Ethics: A Prime Business Asset." In that report, the Roundtable makes the following observation:

> *One of the myths about business is that there is a contradiction between ethics and profit. The myth is thoroughly debunked by the attitudes and actions of top managers. There is a deep conviction that a good reputation for fair and honest business is a prime corporate asset that all employees should nurture with the greatest care.*[12]

Exhibit 1–2 presents a listing of nine companies, each a leader in its respective industry. All have made a public commitment to the higher ethical road as a key component to their overall business strategy.

Why Should Marketing Organizations Attempt to Foster Ethical Decisions?

Besides the obvious answer that being ethical is simply the proper thing to do—a point to be developed later—marketers should be ethical because *not* to be so, would likely generate significant personal, organizational, and societal costs.[13] Consider first the *personal costs.* When unethical actions become known, the outcome for the managers who engaged in the transgression is a reprimand or (for serious violations) job termination. Even when superiors concede privately that organizational pressures may have contributed to a manager's unethical action, they will not admit this publicly. Managers who believe that their companies will support them when ethical violations become public are typically mistaken.

If an action is illegal as well as unethical (as many such actions are), the manager who makes the questionable ethical decision can be held personally liable. The Foreign Corrupt Practices Act of 1977 (which applies to US-based organizations) prohibits the bribery of foreign officials to obtain overseas con-

EXHIBIT 1–2   Corporate Ethics: Nine Companies Meeting the Challenge

Information from 100 member companies of The Business Roundtable shows that major US corporations have stressed ethical behavior for a long time and are addressing the recent challenges with vigor, skill, and determination. Nine organizations, each a leader in their industry, are profiled below. Collectively, they represent strong evidence that profitability and a commitment to high ethics not only can co-exist but can reinforce one another.

Boeing

In a company with a long tradition of commitment to ethics and values by top management, experience shows that every new chief executive must recreate the ethical culture of the corporation and that it is necessary to win the active support and involvement of divisional or operating company executives.

Champion International

The Champion Way as a statement of corporate culture and values has proved to be a helpful guide for management through a period of turmoil as well as the basis for action to ensure survival and profitability.

Chemical Bank

The Decision Making and Corporate Values Seminar and the Streetbankers program underscore Chemical's emphasis on ethical management decision-making and its commitment to corporate responsibility.

General Mills

A high-performance company sustains ethical, traditional, and successful consumer marketing by attracting and developing compatible persons of talent who must demonstrate they subscribe to the belief that high-quality products and services and comparable business practices are the best route to consumer preference.

GTE

A $15 billion telecommunications, electrical products, and electronic defense systems company develops explicit policies in response to deregulation, intensified international competition, ethical problems reported in the defense industry, and the need to change the corporate climate to evaluate quality of product and service.

Hewlett–Packard

Particular values, defining ethical and human concerns, have driven all the company's relationships with its employees, its customers, its suppliers, and the communities in which it has operated. These values have been integrated into and are central to the company's strategy, its objectives, and its self-image.

Johnson & Johnson

An in-depth portrait of the company's forty-year-old credo shows how one of the best-known ethics efforts works and the profound effect that it has on the way the entire company thinks about its responsibilities. The evolving credo programs, the company culture, and representative decisions by management demonstrate the variety of ways in which leadership can influence the moral climate of a large organization.

Continued

EXHIBIT 1–2   *Continued*

Norton

An Ethics Committee of the board of directors and an annual Ethics Review are only two features of the broad and successful attempts to institutionalize a process for ensuring ethical standards of conduct throughout this multinational organization. Other policies and the Norton culture reinforce these programs.

Xerox

A well-written code of conduct, a proactive approach to affirmative action, innovative programs to benefit the local community, and a tradition of CEOs with a strong ethical sense are the main components of Xerox Corporation's commitment to corporate ethics.

Source: "Corporate Ethics: A Prime Business Asset," *A Report on Policy and Practice in Business Conduct* James Keogh, (ed.) (Business Roundtable, February 1988), 2.

tracts and illustrates this point.[14] For each violation—that is, the payment of a bribe—the organization is subject to a $1 million fine. More significant however, the manager responsible for this payment is personally subject to a $10,000 fine per violation and a maximum of five years in prison. Relatedly, the courts are increasingly disposed to incarcerate executives shown to be responsible for violations of the law which endanger consumers.[15] For instance, a manager who premeditatedly decides to market an unsafe product (the managers responsible for the clean water product decision in scenario 1 come to mind), are subject to criminal and personal liability. Criminal liability, of course, is the harshest of penalties (see Exhibit 1–3), but there are other negative outcomes.

Companies that take their ethical reputation seriously will not hesitate to terminate employees who violate ethical and professional norms. This obvious gesture communicates an organization's *seriousness of purpose* concerning the maintenance of an ethical culture. Such terminations affect the career prospects of these individuals, not to mention the personal embarrassment that goes along with being fired in this way. In summary, from a personal standpoint, unethical behavior does not pay, because it can lead to a loss of personal integrity, possible reprimand, potential dismissal from the organization and even jail.

Substantial *organizational* costs also result from unethical behavior when ethical transgressions by a company become public. Typically, these take the form of reduced sales and a loss of goodwill. A classic case is the experience of the Nestlé Company with their marketing of infant formula in Third World countries.[16] In that well-known situation, Nestlé attempted to aggressively market infant formula, as a substitute for mothers' breast milk, in less developed countries. Nestlé seemed to pay little attention to the fact that the proper use of infant formula requires sanitary conditions and a fairly high literacy rate on the part of the users, who have to follow *written* instructions. Because these conditions were not present, infants incurred a substantially higher rate of malnutrition than if they had been fed mothers' milk. As these circumstances became known, the result was a public-relations nightmare, as well as a balance sheet catastrophe for Nestlé. The

---

EXHIBIT 1–3   Paying Off Itchy Palms Is a Great Idea—If You Like Jail

Virtually all US states prohibit a vendor from trying to influence another company's employee by paying, or even offering to pay, certain sums of money without the knowledge and consent of that person's employer.

Federal law bars payoffs made through the mail or in interstate commerce. And federal rules specifically prohibit other types of commercial bribery—from paying a bank officer to obtain a loan approval to giving kickbacks in connection with government contracts.

Things could get so bad that a zealous prosecutor or civil plaintiff could apply the Racketeer Influenced and Corrupt Organizations Act (RICO). That federal racketeering statute potentially opens the defendant to triple damages, fines, and imprisonment.

Suppliers face three major problems if they bribe a purchaser's employee or agent: The courts could render a large damage award in favor of the purchaser. They also might void a sales contract. If those aren't sufficient incentives, there's also a significant chance that the supplier could face criminal charges.

Criminal statutes forbidding commercial bribery contain rather significant penalties. In fact, many states have toughened those penalties. For example, in 1983, New York raised commercial bribery in the second degree from a Class B to a Class A misdemeanor. The state also raised commercial bribery in the first degree—which occurs when the employee's benefit exceeds $1,000 and causes economic harm of more than $250 to the recipient's employer—from a misdemeanor to a felony.

And in 1986, Congress increased penalties under the federal Anti-Kickback Act, which prohibits kickbacks in connection with government contracts. Violators now are subject to a ten-year prison term and a $250,000 fine.

Source: Quoted from, Steven A. Meyerowitz, *Business Marketing* (October 1988), 60–62. Reprinted with permission. Copyright Crain Communications, Inc. All rights reserved.

derogatory publicity caused various worldwide consumer boycotts of Nestlé products that resulted in a substantial loss of sales.

A similar case involves the Beech Nut Company (now a Nestlé subsidiary), which continued to sell a cheap, chemical-based substitute juice as *real* apple juice for babies. The motive was primarily to maintain company cash flow.[17] The firm denied any wrongdoing, even after the evidence plainly indicated the company was guilty of hundreds of counts of premeditated product fraud. In this situation, the reputation of Beech Nut—a company marketing to children and dependent upon fostering an image of safety and care—has probably become irreconcilably besmirched because of the actions of a few unscrupulous managers.

E.F. Hutton represents still another case. The once proud stockbrokerage house was involved in an elaborate check-kiting scheme whereby Hutton earned interest daily on millions of dollars of nonexistent cash. When the scandal became public, hundreds of E.F. Hutton brokers took their client lists elsewhere. The once famous slogan, "When E.F. Hutton talks, people listen," was sarcastically rephrased by Wall Street wags to read, "When E.F. Hutton speaks, people lose interest." The end result of this mess was that a much scaled down E.F. Hutton was merged into another brokerage house. Some Hutton officials continued to maintain that the scandal had nothing to do with the company's financial woes. The point is that when unethical dirty laundry is aired, the organizational costs can, and regularly do, take the form of legal penalties and substantial revenue losses. As E.F. Hutton painfully learned, the loss sometimes can mean the elimination of an organization's greatest asset—its good name.

Another case history that illustrates the point that poor ethical choices can mean big punishment has to do with the fall of junk bond traders Drexel-Burnham. Crossing the boundaries of good ethical practice, Drexel employees participated in the dissemination of insider information, self-dealing among its clients and subsidiaries to prop up the market, and putting companies "into play" (i.e., spreading rumors that they are take-over targets) in order to collect fees to mount a take-over defense.[18] In short, Drexel played the business game "hard ball" style and was a ruthless competitor. They made hundreds of millions of dollars in profit—for a while. But when they ran afoul of the law and various protective requirements necessitated that they raise liquid capital quickly, the major commercial banks turned their backs and refused to extend Drexel a further credit line. As *Fortune* magazine characterized it: "Greed and mismanagement destroyed the innovative, aggressive firm."[19] Drexel, the Wall Street symbol of the "high flyer" during the 1980s, was grounded and went bankrupt.

Finally, there are enormous *external costs* that are generated by the unethical behavior of organizations. First, consumers who are tricked into buying a product that they do not need or who end up paying substantially more for a product or service than is justified, incur an excess economic cost and will start to resent the marketing system. Some groups, like the poor, the old, the handicapped, the mentally feeble, children, and recent immigrants, are particularly vulnerable to unethical marketing practices. These groups can least afford the extra cost. Sometimes when businesses run aground, such as in the recent spate of S&L bankruptcies, the government is forced to pick up the tab. Similarly, when certain industries pollute the environment by utilizing materials that are hard to dispose of, the taxpayer bears the social costs of these questionable business practices.

Besides the economic or ecological costs suffered by victims of unethical marketing practices, there is a general damage to the credibility of the existing economic system—a system which requires a high level of trust to operate smoothly. Whether one believes in a free market economy or a partly planned economy, most of us would agree that it is the efficient firm with the superior product that should be rewarded, rather than the dishonest firm, which gains a perceived advantage via misrepresentation. Yet, when a competitive situation exists wherein an unethical marketing practice generates a short-term benefit for less efficient firms that take moral short-cuts, the advantages of the supposedly efficient marketplace are shortcircuited. If questionable marketing practices continue to happen, further erosion of the confidence of the American public in the marketing system will occur. Thus, the costs of unethical marketing involves social and economic costs that all consumers and innocent marketers must pay.

Different Types of Managers and Their Approaches to Ethics

One way to establish how ethical concerns might be of value to an organization is to visualize the archetypal ways in which managers might confront an ethical issue.[20] We believe that there are several fundamentally different managerial styles that account for the divergent ways that various managers treat ethical questions (see Exhibit 1–4).

First, there is the *crook*. This type of manager looks at a particular marketing situation and realizes it has negative ethical consequences. The crook *knows* that certain actions are morally wrong but consistently goes ahead with unethical actions—presumably for personal reward and perhaps the (short-term) economic gain of the organization in terms of enhanced profit. Such unethical, and often criminal activity, exists in only a minority of the population. Most companies will attempt to purge such individuals from the organization when their pattern of action becomes evident. Others, however, may tolerate such behavior if the actions lead to economic rewards for the organization. In any event, concern for ethical issues by the organization will probably not greatly influence the behavior of this type of individual.

A second type of manager is the *legalist*. A legalist, as the name implies, seldom thinks of issues in a moral context but rather according to the law. For such managers, the law is not only the lowest common denominator concerning whether or not a particular action is acceptable behavior, it is the only denominator. Often, the legalist manager believes that the ethical beliefs of others represent merely "opinion." To the extent that public opinion about what is "right" has been codified, such prevailing notions of propriety are to be found in the law and

---

EXHIBIT 1–4 Types of Managers and the Ways They Face Ethical Issues

Different kinds of managers will resolve ethical problems in different ways.

- *The Crook* Knows what's right, but will very often act unethically.
- *The Legalist* Has little use for theories of business ethics or professional morality. If it's legal, it's acceptable.
- *The Moralist* Always tries to do the right thing: a person of principle.
- *The Seeker* Wants to do the right thing. Doesn't always recognize ethical problems; doesn't fully understand ethical consequences.
- *The Rationalizer* Recognizes ethical problems, but will often rationalize to the economically expedient solution.

Source: Expanded upon from: T.R. Martin, "Ethics in Marketing: Problems and Prospects." In *Marketing Ethics: Guidelines for Managers*, ed. Gene R. Laczniak and Patrick E. Murphy, 3–5 (Lexington, MA: D.C. Heath and Company, 1986).

the system of jurisprudence which underlies the law. Unfortunately, the prevalence of this minimalist and litigious approach to business morality has been increasing in popularity, especially in the United States.

A third kind of manager might be called the *moralist*. This manager looks at a decision with potential ethical consequences and, based upon some method of moral reasoning and personal principles, generally arrives at what is arguably a fair and just resolution of the issue. Such highly principled moralists, who almost always recognize the potential ethical consequences of their actions, and then are able to arrive at appropriate judgments regardless of organizational pressures, are relatively rare.

The fourth type of manager might be called the *seeker*. This manager genuinely wants to do the right thing but doesn't always have the appropriate information or moral awareness. Seekers may be required to make decisions that have ethical consequences, but they may not always recognize an ethical choice. This type of manager can clearly benefit from ethical education as well as a greater degree of stated ethical concern by the organization. Such managers need to be made aware of the potential ethical ramifications of marketing decisions as well as of the trade-offs that exist among the alternative actions. We suspect the number of managers falling into the seeker classification is fairly large. This category probably best describes younger and/or less experienced marketing managers, because they have had less time to cultivate their moral sensitivities in the marketplace.

The fifth type of manager, the *rationalizer*, presents the most difficult situation. The rationalizer recognizes that certain decisions have an ethical impact, but they generally will find a way to justify the most economically expedient solution whether it is ethical or not. That is, they have the ability to recognize that there are moral consequences to particular decisions, but they can find reasons why in their situation the normal moral cautions do not apply (see, for example, the reasons depicted in Exhibit 1–5). The statement, "I wrestled with my conscience and won," comes to mind. Obviously, this sort of manager can benefit from heightened ethical concern in the organization. This is particularly true, when that concern takes the form of teaching a method of moral reasoning that can be applied to marketing decisions or when it compels managers to act ethically because they fear organizational sanctions. Some of the company programs described in Exhibit 1–3 represent good illustrations of how a concerned approach shapes ethical behavior.

The upshot of this discussion is that corporate efforts to stimulate ethical concern will not change managerial behavior at the extremes. Certain managers (i.e., crooks) will be predisposed to act unethically, and others (i.e., moralists) will try to do the right thing regardless of the organizational posture. However, in the middle ranges, where we probably find most managers, there would appear to be a sufficiently large number either looking for moral guidance (i.e., seekers), preoccupied with the law (i.e., legalists), or not possessing the necessary determination (i.e., the rationalizers) to reason through morally difficult problems.

For organizations concerned with improving their ethical climate, the ability to influence seeker-, legalist-, or rationalizer-type managers becomes a valuable

---

EXHIBIT 1–5   Four Rationalizations for Unethical Conduct

A belief that the activity is within reasonable ethical and legal limits—that is, that it is "not really" illegal or immoral.

▶ A belief that the activity is in the individual's or the corporation's best interests—that the individual would somehow be *expected* to undertake the activity.

▶ A belief that the activity is "safe" because it will never be found out or publicized; this is the classic crime-and-punishment issue of discovery.

▶ A belief that because the activity "helps the company," the company will condone it and even protect the person who engages in it.

Source: Reprinted by permission of the *Harvard Business Review*. Excerpt from "Why *Good* Managers Make Bad Ethical Choices," by Saul W. Gellerman (July–August 1986). Copyright © 1986 by the President and Fellows of Harvard College. All rights reserved.

strategic window of opportunity. Those managers who do not regularly recognize the ethical implications of their decisions, are in need of heightening or raising their ethical sensitivities by *ethics education*. Those who recognize situations with moral consequences but cannot properly deal with them are in need of education which concentrates upon *ethical reasoning* (i.e., knowing how to think through ethical problems). Those who see only a legalist response to a problem may benefit from a knowledge of *ethical theory*. Organizations might learn what percentage of their managers most likely fall into each category via ethics seminars or even some customized "paper and pencil" tests. Then, codes, seminars, or other forms of education can be tailored to fit the ethical needs of a company's executives. How to design, implement, and evaluate such programs is discussed in Chapter 10.

An Organizational View of Ethics

Organizational Versus Individual Ethics: Is There a Difference?

As noted previously, the ethics of the organization and the values held by the individual manager may not be the same. When they are not compatible, there can be a conflict between the organizational pressure that impels a particular action and what the manager believes *ought* to be done. The typical conflict in such cases involves the manager who holds a higher standard of behavior than that utilized by the organization (although in the case of crooks and possibly rationalizers the opposite is also possible). In such situations, the manager is often confronted with a decision option that, if taken, involves lowering personal values in exchange for increased organizational gain. These dealings produce "moral stress" in the manager, because the core values of the organization, as embodied in the corporate culture, seem to imply a choice different from that which would be selected by the manager based upon personal values. As discussed earlier, surveys of managers show that such ethical dilemmas are not uncommon. Many managers report wrestling with ethical conflicts at some point in their career.

Organizations that have an organizational climate that causes managers to act contrary to their individual values need to understand the *costs* of unethical behavior that have been articulated in this chapter. Sometimes managers who choose to follow organizational pressures rather than their own conscience rationalize their decisions by maintaining that they are simply *agents* of the corporation. In other words, as company agent, the manager assumes the duty to do exactly what the organization most desires—often translated to mean maximizing return on investment.

The weaknesses of such a rationalization are several, including:

1. Managers can never fully abdicate their personal responsibility in making certain business decisions. The defense of being an agent of the corporation sounds suspiciously like the defense given by certain war criminals that they were only following orders.
2. It is quite possible that the manager does not fully understand what is in the best interest of the organization. Short-term profits, even if advocated by the manager's immediate supervisor, may not be the most important consideration for the organization. The earlier discussion of the relationship of ethics to costs and profitability illustrated why this is the case.
3. The manager has an irrevocable responsibility to parties other than his organization. This moves us to the *stakeholder concept* which makes clear that there are other publics to which organizations owe duties and obligations.

The Stakeholder Concept

A perspective that now must be considered, because marketing is usually undertaken in the context of an organization, is the *stakeholder concept*. A *stakeholder* is any group or individual who is (or can be) affected by the achievement of a firm's objectives.[21] For example, a large organization's typical stakeholders include stockholders, customers, suppliers, employees, the host communities (or countries), and various other parties. The stakeholder concept is useful in ethical analysis, because it allows managers to gauge the impact of their decision on several affected groups.

At times it is useful to distinguish between the *primary stakeholders* and the *secondary stakeholders*. Primary stakeholders are those that have a formal, official, or contractual relationship with the firm; all others are classified as secondary stakeholders.[22] Primary stakeholders are the owners, suppliers, employees, and customers of the organization. Secondary stakeholders encompass public-interest groups, the media, consumer advocates, and local community organizations that have occasional interest in the various corporate activities. For example, the amount of paper and plastic packaging generated by fast-food chains is a concern of local environmental groups, while the media may be more interested in the firm's treatment of its minority employees.

Although it is true that by definition primary stakeholders have a direct relationship with the firm, they should not necessarily receive the greatest weight when determining which particular strategic option a manager should choose. For example, an action that may be in the best interest of stockholders and customers—building a distribution center on recreational parkland—may be villainized by the media (a stakeholder group) to the local community (another stakeholder group) generating overall public opinion (a third stakeholder) against the project. Organizations that subscribe to the stakeholder concept try to see that its primary stakeholders attain their objectives, while at the same time keeping other stakeholders satisfied. One management expert characterizes the goal of stakeholder management as creating the classic "win-win" situation for all stakeholders.[23] In other words, the task of management is to seek solutions that will ideally achieve the goals of all stakeholders. Failing that, management must at least select options which generally optimize net stakeholder benefits.

One example of an organization that has apparently internalized this approach is Johnson & Johnson (J&J).[24] Its corporate credo—an embodiment of the stakeholder concept—is shown in Exhibit 1–6. This document focuses on their perceived responsibilities to consumers, employees, communities, and stockholders. The first version of this credo was instituted in 1945. Between 1975 and 1978, former J&J chairman James Burke held a series of meetings with the firm's 1,200 top managers; they were encouraged to challenge the credo. What emerged from the meetings was agreement that the document functioned as it was intended; a slightly reworded but substantially unchanged credo was introduced in 1979.

In recent years, the company has surveyed all employees about how well the company meets its responsibilities to its four principal stakeholders. The survey questions employees from all fifty-three countries where J&J operates about every line in the credo. The tabulation and reporting of results is confidential. (Department and division managers receive only information pertaining to their units and composite numbers for the entire firm.) The interaction at meetings devoted to discussing these findings is reportedly very good.

Does J&J's credo work? Top management feels strongly that it does. The credo is often mentioned as an important contributing factor in the company's exemplary handling of the Tylenol product recall several years ago when some of that product was tampered with. It appears that the firm's commitment to the credo makes ethical business practice a high priority.

Increasingly, more and more organizations like J&J are accepting the stakeholder concept. They are beginning to develop procedures for linking stakeholder concerns to the strategies they conceive. In order to implement a stakeholder management approach, organizations need to do several things including:[25]

- Delineate who their stakeholders are.
- Determine which ones are primary and secondary and exactly what stakes each group holds in the organization.
- Establish what responsibilities (economic, ethical, legal, or philanthropic) the organization has to each stakeholder group.

EXHIBIT 1–6

Our Credo

We believe our first responsibility is to the doctors, nurses and patients,
to mothers and fathers and all others who use our products and services.
In meeting their needs everything we do must be of high quality.
We must constantly strive to reduce our costs
in order to maintain reasonable prices.
Customers' orders must be serviced promptly and accurately.
Our suppliers and distributors must have an opportunity
to make a fair profit.

We are responsible to our employees,
the men and women who work with us throughout the world.
Everyone must be considered as an individual.
We must respect their dignity and recognize their merit.
They must have a sense of security in their jobs.
Compensation must be fair and adequate,
and working conditions clean, orderly and safe.
We must be mindful of ways to help our employees fulfill
their family responsibilities.
Employees must feel free to make suggestions and complaints.
There must be equal opportunity for employment, development
and advancement for those qualified.
We must provide competent management,
and their actions must be just and ethical.

We are responsible to the communities in which we live and work
and to the world community as well.
We must be good citizens — support good works and charities
and bear our fair share of taxes.
We must encourage civic improvements and better health and education.
We must maintain in good order
the property we are privileged to use,
protecting the environment and natural resources.

Our final responsibility is to our stockholders.
Business must make a sound profit.
We must experiment with new ideas.
Research must be carried on, innovative programs developed
and mistakes paid for.
New equipment must be purchased, new facilities provided
and new products launched.
Reserves must be created to provide for adverse times.
When we operate according to these principles,
the stockholders should realize a fair return.

Johnson & Johnson

Source: Johnson & Johnson, New Brunswick, New Jersey.

• Decide how the organization can best respond with planned strategy to the
opportunities and threats inherent in sometimes conflicting stakeholder
claims.

Again, the rights and claims of various stakeholders are important, because they become the objects to which the different theories or frameworks of ethics are applied. Since a large part of ethics is *deciding what is properly owed to whom*, determining stakeholders and their claims is analogous to establishing the facts of a legal case. For example, consider the situation faced by a public-relations firm that is asked to take on a foreign country as a client. Suppose the country has acceptable diplomatic relations with the United States, but is also accused of violating human rights. The stakeholders are, in part, the employees of the public-relations agency, the US government, the client country, the stockholders of the public relations firm, other customers, the media, and the general public. Each group might very well view the ethical stakes involved in this controversy from a different perspective. The employees are concerned with their right to earn a living; the US government may be preoccupied with maintaining cordial relations with the developing country; the stockholders may be motivated by the prospect of a client willing to sign a lucrative long-term contract; the media may be fueled by the apparent hypocrisy of helping a government that most of the US general public finds to be abhorrent. The complexity of stakeholder analysis is apparent from this example.

Frameworks for Ethical Decision Making

What standards do marketers use to grapple with questions that have ethical implications? Historically, marketing managers and business executives have gravitated toward a utilitarian or consequence-based method of problem solving. More will be said about utilitarianism in Chapter 2. However, applied to an ethical situation in a marketing context, the utilitarian reasoning employed by many managers would take the form of a cost/benefit analysis. Businesspeople, because of their economics training, are naturally prone to talk about concepts such as "maximizing profitability" and "concern for the bottom line." Profitability essentially translates into the excess of revenue over cost. It does not require a great stretch of the marketing manager's imagination to apply similar thinking to an ethical context. Thus, managers often operate with a rule that essentially says to make decisions in such a way that the benefits to the firm exceed the costs incurred by the firm to the greatest extent possible. Depending upon how a manager defines *benefits* and *costs* one might arrive at different conclusions. If the emphasis is mostly upon *economic* criteria (e.g., short-term profits) it is easy to see how a fair amount of the ethical analysis conducted by business executives gives great weight to financial outcomes. Such a perspective often focuses on how various action alternatives would benefit stockholders in the short run.

There are other shorthand decision rules besides cost/benefit analysis that are used by business people. Certain expeditious frameworks for ethical decision making have been postulated as useful. The extent to which these thumbnail frameworks have been utilized by marketers has not been systematically studied. Some of the maxims which might aid a marketer facing an ethical dilemma are the following:[26]

The Golden Rule act in a way that you would hope others would act toward you.

The Professional Ethic take only actions which would be viewed as proper by an objective panel of your professional colleagues.
   (See The Code of Ethics of the American Marketing Association presented
   in Exhibit 1–7 for an example of standards that professionals might apply.)

The TV Test a manager should always ask, "Would I feel comfortable explaining this action on TV to the general public?"

When in Doubt, Don't if a manager feels uneasy about a decision there is probably reason to question it. The individual should probably seek guidance from a trusted person before proceeding with the decision.[27]

Some thumbnail rules are difficult to apply in specific situations. At times, the application of different rules of thumb to the same situation seems to suggest entirely different solutions. For example, if all salespeople pad their expense accounts 15 percent because customary gratuities (i.e., tips) are not technically reimbursable, the *professional ethic* might dictate the practice is okay despite its variance from the letter of company policy. Why? Because this is the only mechanism to recover a legitimate cost. In contrast, the *when in doubt, don't* rule questions whether padding expense accounts is acceptable.

Despite this ambiguity, such short maxims can have considerable value. One wonders whether the product manager who permitted the controversial Clean Air Machine (scenario 1) to continue to be sold—knowing that methylene chloride might be leaking into the carbon filtration system—could feel comfortable explaining those actions to the general public on television (i.e., pass the *TV test*). Similarly, the *professional ethic* can be extremely useful for those subspecialties in business that have a code of professional conduct that covers certain recurring situations. For example, various groups of professional marketing researchers have developed detailed codes of ethics that cover situations commonly encountered by their peer group (see Chapter 3). Included, for instance, in many marketing research codes of ethics would be dictums that stipulate that respondent confidentiality should be protected when it is promised, that data which do not confirm the hypothesized findings of the researcher are not suppressed, that the limitations of various statistical methods are identified in the research report, and so forth.

Whatever frameworks are used, the consensus regarding what constitutes proper ethical behavior in a decisionmaking situation tends to diminish as the level of analysis proceeds from the abstract to the specific. Put another way, it is easy to get a group of managers to agree *in general* that a practice is improper, however, casting that practice in a very specific set of circumstances usually reduces consensus. For example, most managers would agree with the proposition that business has the obligation to provide consumers with facts relevant to the informed purchase of a product or a service. However, let's test this proposition in a specific situation.

EXHIBIT 1–7 American Marketing Association Code of Ethics

Members of the American Marketing Association (AMA) are committed to ethical professional conduct. They have joined together in subscribing to this Code of Ethics embracing the following topics:

Responsibilities of the Marketer

Marketers must accept responsibility for the consequences of their activities and make every effort to ensure that their decisions, recommendations, and actions function to identify, serve, and satisfy all relevant publics: customers, organizations and society. Marketers' professional conduct must be guided by

1. The basic rule of professional ethics: not knowingly to do harm.
2. The adherence to all applicable laws and regulations.
3. The accurate representation of their education, training, and experience.
4. The active support, practice, and promotion of this Code of Ethics.

Honesty and Fairness

Marketers shall uphold and advance the integrity, honor and dignity of the marketing profession by

1. Being honest in serving consumers, clients, employees, suppliers, distributors and the public.
2. Not knowingly participating in conflict of interest without prior notice to all parties involved.
3. Establishing equitable fee schedules including the payment or receipt of usual, customary and/or legal compensation for marketing exchanges.

Rights and Duties of Parties in the Marketing Exchange Process

Participants in the marketing exchange process should be able to expect that

1. Products and services offered are safe and fit for their intended use.
2. Communications about offered products and services are not deceptive.
3. All parties intend to discharge their obligations, financial and otherwise, in good faith.
4. Appropriate internal methods exist for equitable adjustment and/or redress of grievances concerning purchases.

It is understood that the above would include, but not limited to, the following responsibilities of the marketers:

In the area of product development and management:

- Disclosure of all substantial risks associated with product or service usage.
- Identification of any product component substitution that might materially change the product or impact on the buyer's purchase decision.
- Identification of extra-cost added features.

In the area of promotions:

- Avoidance of false and misleading advertising.
- Rejection of high-pressure manipulations or misleading sales tactics.
- Avoidance of sales promotions that use deception or manipulation.

In the area of distribution:

- Not manipulating the availability of a product for purpose of exploitation.
- Not using coercion in the marketing channel.

Continued

EXHIBIT 1–7 *Continued*

- Not exerting undue influence over the reseller's choice to handle the product.

In the area of pricing:

- Not engaging in price fixing.
- Not practicing predatory pricing.
- Disclosing the full price associated with any purchase.

In the area of marketing research:

- Prohibiting selling of fundraising under the guise of conducting research.
- Maintaining research integrity by avoiding misrepresentation and omission of pertinent research data.
- Treating outside clients and suppliers fairly.

Organizational Relationships

Marketers should be aware of how their behavior may influence or impact on the behavior of others in organizational relationships. They should not demand, encourage, or apply coercion to obtain unethical behavior in their relationships with others, such as employees, suppliers, or customers. Marketers should

1. Apply confidentiality and anonymity in professional relationships with regard to privileged information.
2. Meet their obligations and responsibilities in contracts and mutual agreements in a timely manner.
3. Avoid taking the work of others, in whole or in part, and represent this work as their own or directly benefit from it without compensation for or consent of the originator or owner.
4. Avoid manipulation to take advantage of situations to maximize personal welfare in a way that unfairly deprives or damages their organization or others.

Any AMA member found to be in violation of any provision of this Code of Ethics may have his or her association membership suspended or revoked.

Source: Reprinted from *Marketing Educator* (Fall 1987), published by the American Marketing Association, Chicago, IL 60606.

Suppose we have a manufacturer of cleaning concentrate whose directions call for mixing one part of the concentrate with four parts of water; suppose further that this cleaning concentrate has been sold in this manner for twenty-five years. Now, assume that an issue of *Consumer Reports* indicates that the product will clean just as effectively in many instances if mixed with one part concentrate to eight parts water. Thus, consumers need only use one half as much concentrate. **Does the company have an ethical responsibility to inform customers of this fact?**

Again, most managers *agree* that business has the obligation to provide consumers with facts relevant to an informed purchase. But does such an informed purchase include full disclosure of this *new information*, especially if further product testing in different cleaning situations might produce different results?

Ideas for Ethical Action

The organization that is interested in *improving* rather than simply *understanding* ethical decisions needs (a) an organizationally mandated sequence of steps to determine who the stakeholders are, what the firm's responsibilities toward them should be, and (b) an organizational commitment by top management to an ethical culture. Chapter 10 details many of the specific steps an organization can take to help shape ethical behavior. However, some of these mechanisms are previewed below.

Specifically, *any organization can take steps that shape the behavior of managers by virtue of controlling the corporate environment in which they operate.* Several possible steps are addressed here. These actions can influence the organizational culture in the long run.[28]

Identification of Stakeholders As specified earlier, management's first step when encountering an ethical problem should be to delineate which stakeholders might be affected by the decision and what responsibilities management owes to each relevant group.

Top Management Leadership A primary factor in setting a firm's ethical tone is the posture and seriousness of purpose communicated by top managers toward this issue. Most studies of business and marketing ethics make this quite clear.[29] As Deal and Kennedy point out in their book, *Corporate Culture*, managers give extraordinary attention to those matters stressed in the corporate value system. These values are personified more often than not by the top executive in the organization.[30]

Codes of Ethics These statements are ideally the articulation of corporate values in a moral context. One recent report indicated that 75 to 80 percent of all major corporations have established codes of ethics.[31] Such codes can help vitalize the organization, but some are simply public-relations boilerplate or "motherhood and apple pie" statements. Unfortunately, many existing codes are primarily legalistic in orientation.[32] Chapter 10 will discuss how codes of ethics can become an important force for ethical concern in the organization.

Ethics Seminars/Programs Several organizations choose to hold periodic seminars for marketing managers that deal with the question of ethics. Each manager might be required to attend one seminar every several years. The purpose of such educational modules is not so much to provide exact answers to particular questions as to sensitize managers to potential ethical problems that fall within their responsibilities. The programs or seminars may take the form of helping managers develop their capacity for moral reasoning or may involve the discussion of hypothetical situations that treat circumstances that managers might face.

Ethical Audits Increasingly, firms are finding that unless they monitor their ethical performance, it will be taken for granted. As a result, some companies have developed systematic procedures that allow the organization to determine whether its employees, suppliers, and vendors are taking the commitment to ethical and social responsibility seriously. This process can involve the utilization of an outside consultant or a special ethics committee of the board of directors empowered to periodically evaluate operations against a prescribed set of standards.

Conclusion

Some managers, when given the opportunity to act unethically, especially when that action will lead to *personal gain*, will choose to be unethical. All marketing managers will not behave like saints anymore than one could expect ethical behavior from *all* doctors, lawyers, or college professors. Such moral shortcomings will also often lead to organizational and social costs. Nevertheless, for the organization that takes its ethical duties seriously, the provision of mechanisms to aid managers to better morally reason through ethical problems is essential. In addition, the establishment of a corporate culture that will help direct managerial actions toward beneficial ends goes far in creating an ethically enlightened marketing organization. The question of what is necessary to help marketing managers reason through an ethical problem is taken up in Chapter 2.

Endnotes

1. "Norelco Sold Water Purifier That It Knew Could Be Hazardous," *Milwaukee Journal* (October 9, 1988), A13.

2. Richard Gibson, "Space War: Supermarkets Demand Food Firms' Payments Just to Get on the Shelf," *The Wall Street Journal* (November 1, 1988), A1.

3. Steve Mulson, "Smoking Section: Cigarette Companies Develop Third World As a Growth Market," *The Wall Street Journal* (July 5, 1985), 1.

4. Robert L. Rose, "Travel Agents' Games Raise Ethics Issues," *The Wall Street Journal* (November 23, 1988), B1.

5. "The Food/Health Supplement," *New York Times Magazine* (April 16, 1989), Part 2.

6. Betsy Morris, "Rise In Health Claims in Food Ads Can Help and Mislead Shoppers," *The Wall Street Journal* (April 2, 1985), 33.

7. Reported in Donald P. Robin and R.E. Reidenbach, *Business Ethics: Where Profits Meet Value Systems* (Englewood Cliffs, NJ: Prentice-Hall, 1989), 4.

8. Gallup Poll, "Honesty and Ethical Standards," Report No. 214 (July 1983).

9. Archie B. Carroll, "A Survey of Managerial Ethics: Is Business Morality Watergate Morality?," *Business and Society Review* (Spring 1975).

10. L. Kohlberg, "Stage and Sequence: The Cognitive Developmental Approach to Socialization." In *Handbook of Socializations Theory and Research*, ed. D.A. Goslin, (Chicago: Rand McNally, 1969), 347–480.

11. Steve Brenner and Earl Molander, "Is The Ethics of Business Changing?," *Harvard Business Review* (January/February 1977), 52–71.

12. James Keogh, ed. "Corporate Ethics: A Prime Business Asset," *A Report on Policy and Practice in Business Conduct* (Business Roundtable, February 1988), 2.

13. Based upon Gene R. Laczniak and Patrick E. Murphy, "Incorporating Marketing Ethics into the Organization." In *Marketing Ethics: Guidelines for Managers,* ed. Gene R. Laczniak and Patrick E. Murphy, (Lexington, MA: D.C. Heath and Company 1986), 98–100.

14. Jack G. Kaikati and Wayne A. Label, "American Bribery Legislation: An Obstacle to International Marketing," *Journal of Marketing* (Fall 1980), 38–43.

15. See note 13 above.

16. S. Prakash Sethi and James E. Post, "The Marketing of Infant Formula in Less Developed Countries," *California Management Review* (1979), 21:35–48.

17. James Trauk, "Into The Mouths of Babes," *New York Times Magazine* (July 24, 1988), 17.

18. "After Drexel," *Business Week* (February 26, 1990), 37–40.

19. B.D. Fromson, "Did Drexel Get What It Deserved?," *Fortune* (March 12, 1990), 47–50.

20. Adapted from T.R. Martin, "Ethics in Marketing: Problems and Prospects." In *Marketing Ethics: Guidelines for Managers,* ed. Gene R. Laczniak and Patrick E. Murphy, (Lexington, MA: D.C. Heath and Company, 1986), 3–5.

21. Edward R. Freeman, *Strategic Management: A Stakeholder Approach* (Boston, MA: Pitman Publishing, 1984), 25. See also Kenneth E. Goodpaster, "Business Ethics and Stakeholder Analysis," *Business Ethics Quarterly* (January 1991), 53–73.

22. Archie B. Carroll, *Business & Society: Ethics and Stakeholder Management* (Cincinnati, OH: Southwestern Publishing, 1989), 58.

23. See note 22 above.

24. The following discussion is drawn from Patrick E. Murphy, "Creating Ethical Corporate Structures," *Sloan Management Review* (Winter 1989), 81–86.

25. See note 22 above.

26. Gene R. Laczniak, "Business Ethics: A Manager's Primer," *Business* (January–March 1983), 23–29.

27. Saul W. Gellerman, "Why *Good* Managers Make Bad Ethical Choices," *Harvard Business Review* (July–August 1986), 85–90.

28. Partially adapted from note 13.

29. See note 26 above.

30. Terrence E. Deal and Allen A. Kennedy, *Corporate Culture: The Risks and Rituals of Corporate Life* (Reading, MA: Addison Wesley Publishing, 1982).

31. W. Mathews, "Codes of Ethics: Organizational Behavior and Misbehavior." In *Research in Corporate Social Performance and Policy,* ed. William C. Frederick, (Greenwich, CT: JAI Press, 1987), 107–130.

32. Donald P. Robin et al., "A Different Look at Codes of Ethics," *Business Horizons* (January–February 1989), 66–73.

Chapter 2

Ethical Reasoning and Marketing Decisions

Scenario 1
The Thrifty Supermarket Chain has twelve stores in the city of Gotham, USA. The company's policy is to maintain the same prices for all items at all stores. However, the distribution manager knowingly sends the poorest cuts of meat and the lowest quality produce to the store located in the low-income section of town. His justification for this action is based on the fact that this store has the highest overhead, due to factors such as employee turnover, pilferage, and vandalism. **Is the distribution manager's economic rationale sufficient justification for his allocation method?**

Scenario 2
The Independent Chevy Dealers of Metropolis, USA have undertaken an advertising campaign headlined by the slogan: "Is your family's life worth 45 MPG?" The ads emphasize that while Chevy subcompacts are not as fuel-efficient as foreign imports and cost more to maintain, they are safer according to government-sponsored crash tests. The ads explicitly ask if responsible parents, when purchasing a car, should trade off fuel-efficiency for safety? **Is it ethical for the dealers association to use a fear appeal to offset an economic disadvantage?**

Scenario 3
A few recent studies have linked the presence of the artificial sweetener, subsugural, to cancer in laboratory rats. While the validity of these findings has been hotly debated by medical experts, the Food and Drug Administration has ordered products containing the ingredient banned from sale in the United States. The

Jones Company sends all of its sugar-free JC Cola (which contains subsugural) to European supermarkets, because the sweetener has not been banned there. **Is it acceptable for the Jones Company to send an arguably unsafe product to another market without waiting for further evidence?**

Scenario 4

The Acme Company sells industrial supplies through its own sales force that calls on company purchasing agents. Acme has found that providing the purchasing agent with small gifts helps cement a cordial relationship and creates goodwill. Acme follows the incentive policy that the bigger the order, the bigger the gift to the purchasing agent. The gifts range from a pair of tickets to a sporting event to outboard motors and snowmobiles. Acme does not give gifts to personnel at companies that they know have an explicit policy prohibiting the acceptance of such gifts. **Assuming no laws are violated, is Acme's policy of providing gifts to purchasing agents morally proper?**

Scenario 5

The Buy American Electronics Company has been selling its highly rated System X Color TV sets (21″, 19″, 12″) for $700, $500 and $300 respectively. These prices have been relatively uncompetitive in the market. After some study, Buy American substitutes several cheaper components (which engineering says may reduce the quality of performance slightly) and passes on the savings to the consumer in the form of a $100 price reduction on each model. Buy American institutes a price-oriented promotional campaign that neglects to mention that the second generation System X sets are different from the first. **Is the company's competitive strategy ethical?**

Scenario 6

The Smith and Smith advertising agency has been struggling financially. Mr. Smith is approached by the representative of a small South American country that is on good terms with the US Department of State. He wants S and S to create a multimillion dollar advertising and public-relations campaign that will bolster the image of the country and increase the likelihood that it will receive US foreign aid assistance and attract investment capital. Smith knows the country is a dictatorship that has been accused of numerous human rights violations. **Is it ethical for the Smith and Smith agency to undertake the proposed campaign?**

In order to resolve ethical issues, managers must know something about ethical reasoning. These fictional scenarios reflect events that culminate in ethical problems requiring managerial reasoning.[1] They are typical of the kind that marketing managers face in the course of their day-to-day activities. Some of the fundamental questions raised are

- Are fear appeals ethical when utilized as part of a promotional strategy (scenario 2)?

- Is gift giving, if not specifically prohibited by the buying organization, an appropriate and ethical selling strategy (scenario 4)?
- Does the manufacturer have the ethical right to switch performance-related components in a *branded* product without informing consumers (scenario 5)?

These and other situations (see also the scenarios heading Chapter 1), are representative of the ethical dilemmas that marketing managers wrestle with. The purpose of this chapter is to illustrate how ethical theory, applied through moral reasoning, can be used to clarify such questions and aid managers in developing solutions to ethical problems.

The Importance of Ethical Theory

In order to bring some structure to ethical questions, managers need to enhance their ability to reason ethically. What is meant by *ethical reasoning*? It is **the process of systematically analyzing an ethical issue and applying to it some ethical standard.** This process will generally consist of three steps.

1. *Definition of ethical problem* This first step necessitates establishing whether a marketing decision has an ethical impact. And it requires determining the nature and consequences of the action involved. The result of this step is to frame a marketing situation as an ethical question. For example, is it acceptable to use controversial medical information as a major selling point in an advertising campaign? (In the chapters that follow, we will highlight the areas of marketing practice where questions of this kind might most logically be posed.)

2. *Selection of an ethical standard* There are various theories of recommended moral behavior. While many will lead managers to the same solution given a similar circumstance, different standards will sometimes lead to different solutions. The existence of competing moral theories is one reason why well-intentioned managers disagree about what is ethically *proper*. (A goal of this chapter is to elaborate on some of the major *theories* of ethical behavior.)

3. *Application of the ethical standard* Once an ethical standard has been chosen, it still must be applied to the specific situation. The application of a standard to a particular scenario and the subsequent determination of an ethical choice is the process of ethical reasoning mentioned earlier. (Throughout this book we describe various kinds of rationales that marketing managers use to reason ethically to solutions for ethical problems.)

If marketing managers do not follow this or a similar procedure, ethical discussions too easily degenerate into a clash of personal opinion or preference. For the most part, ethical reasoning ability is grounded in a knowledge of ethical theory. If managers understand ethical theory, they can draw upon certain frameworks that include ethical principles of decision making. Those principles can then be applied to determine the appropriate choices emanating from an ethical problem. For example, in the case of scenario 3 (dealing with the possibility of sending to another country a soft drink that has been banned in the United States because of health questions) the *options* a manager might consider are

1. Sending the product to the foreign market where it can be legally sold.
2. Waiting for additional research information that might further validate or invalidate the danger of the substance.
3. Exporting the product with a warning label.
4. Disposing of the product to a wholesaler at a severely discounted price and letting that independent business firm make its own determination as to what to do with the controversial product.

As these alternatives indicate, ethical questions are inherent in each option.

How *should* a marketing manager go about deciding what to do? How does one go about reasoning to an ethical solution? The answer lies partly in understanding different ethical theories. This response is not without its problems. As noted, the difficulty in choosing among various theories is that different ethical theories may lead to different conclusions. However, this realization should not be sufficient to dismiss the study of ethical reasoning as a fruitless exercise. Ethical issues regularly stem from "tough cases." Few people maintain that ethics is an easily understood subject. The existence of ethical dilemmas, where different approaches lead to different solutions, should not be a cause of cynicism. Some ambiguity is inherent in grappling with tough ethical problems, whether in marketing or other realms. The fact that different principles sometimes generate different decisions opens up more options than may have been considered initially. A more optimistic view is that managers should take some satisfaction from knowing that the application of various ethical theories to a particular situation will often lead to consensus. Clearly, the use of ethical theories will not usually generate unethical solutions.

In this chapter, we briefly present four general categories of ethical theory. Our summation includes brief overviews of egoism, utilitarianism (i.e., consequence-based theories), duty-based approaches (i.e., deontological theories), and virtue ethics. These approaches are also applied in the context of the scenarios at the beginning of this chapter and are summarized in Exhibit 2–1.

Comprehensive Ethical Theories

Unless a manager operates in a completely intuitive manner (and some do), the ability to reason about ethical questions requires some knowledge of ethical theory. Four major ethical theories are now presented along with a discussion of how they relate to marketing decisions.

EXHIBIT 2–1   Summary of Normative Ethical Theory

	Egoism	Utilitarianism	Duty-Based Theories	Virtue Ethics
Focus of the Moral Decisions	The morality of self-worship	The morality of consequences	The morality of duty	The morality of aspiration
Operational Criteria of the Theory	Personal or organizational gain	Costs and benefits	Absolute standards of conduct tempered with penalties	The attempt to vitalize classic ideals

Managerial Egoism

Egoism is a philosophy that asserts that individuals act exclusively in their own self interest. Thus, *managerial egoism* holds that executives should take steps which most efficiently advance the exclusive self interest of themselves or their firm. An example of individual egoism might be the product manager who postpones making needed improvements to a mature product, because she knows already that she will be promoted in six months and she is interested only in next quarter's financial performance. Another example—this one illustrating organizational egoism—would be the firm that has been ordered to install pollution abatement equipment because of illegal discharges but waits until the deadline date so that interest earned from cash-on-hand can be maximized. An obvious problem with such a philosophy arises when the pursuit of an organization's goal conflicts with the duties owed to other stakeholders. Often managerial egoism is used in conjunction with a legalistic approach. It then becomes a variant of the notion that managers have a responsibility only to obey the law; otherwise they should exclusively focus on maximizing return on investment. This theory often serves as an extension of the old adage that managerial fiduciary duties boil down to "obey the law" and beyond that to the notion that "the business of business is to maximize profits." Presumably, other required controls upon unacceptable behavior will be provided by the invisible mechanisms of the marketplace.

There are several problems with managerial egoism. First, some moral philosophers do not see egoism as a philosophy at all. Why? Because an egoist has problems "universalizing" egoism as a guiding philosophy for others, because if ·

the egoist advocated that everybody act in their own self interest that prescription itself would *not* be in the self interest of the egoist. However, philosophical semantics aside, managerial egoism does not stand up to scrutiny for other reasons.

There are many instances of questionable marketing practices that seem to illustrate the egoistic approach. For example, the defense industries' enthusiastic efforts at developing codes of ethics might only be motivated by their belief that such efforts will allow them to continue to bid on defense contracts despite past scandals. It has become clear that the marketplace does not always provide the necessary control to ensure a fair and level playing field for business organizations and consumers. Responsibilities are owed to stakeholder groups other than shareholders, and these groups may not hold a primary interest in seeing the maximization of return on investment. Because the long-term goals of the managerial egoist are very often only economic, the long-term interests of the organization are not necessarily best served using this approach.[2]

Utilitarianism

Probably the most widely understood and commonly applied ethical theory is *utilitarianism*. In an organizational context, utilitarianism basically states that a decision concerning corporate conduct is proper if and only if that decision produces the greatest *good* for the greatest number of individuals. Good is usually defined as the *net benefits* that accrue to those parties affected by the choice. Thus, most utilitarians hold the position that moral choices must be evaluated by somehow calculating the net benefits of each available alternative action. Importantly, *all* of the stakeholders affected by the decision should be given their just consideration.[3] Philosophers call the utilitarian approach to ethical problem solving a *teleological* theory, because the act is judged by the *consequences* it produces. Teleological theories deal with outcomes or end goals, as the word comes from *telos*, the Greek word meaning "end."[4] The often-used line, "the end justifies the means," is the classic application of *some* forms of utilitarian thinking.

Several different formulations of utilitarianism exist. These differences harken back to the original writers on the topic, such luminary nineteenth century philosophers as Jeremy Bentham and John Stuart Mill.[5] One major school of thought (*act utilitarianism*) focuses on the *action* which has been taken, analyzing it along the lines of whether the selected action produces more good than bad. For example, a pharmaceutical company may operate by the principle that it will release any Federal Drug Administration approved drug with some side-effects, *as long as* it helps more persons combat a particular disease than the number troubled by the (minor) side effect. A second perspective (*rule utilitarianism*) looks at whether the option or choice selected conforms to a *rule* which attempts to maximize the overall utility of the particular act. That is, does the action (when compared to other possible actions) produce the greatest good for the greatest number. In this case, the pharmaceutical company might operate according to a principle whereby it must also calculate the cost and benefits of another option that calls for additional product development to reduce side effects.

Business executives explicitly or implicitly tend to accept such consequentialist approaches to ethical problems, because they are often quite compatible with traditional business ideology. Why? Just as this theory seeks to maximize happiness or *the good,* business people often wish to maximize profit or return on investment or share price. If a businessperson then draws the conclusion that the greatest good usually equals the highest profitability, it is easy to see how the two systems (utilitarianism and business ideology) are philosophically compatible.

Consequence-Oriented Philosophy and Marketing Management

A strong appeal of the utilitarian approach has to do with its similarity to *cost-benefit analysis.* Marketing managers regularly need to conduct such analysis; this approach of weighing the pros and cons of alternative economic and managerial actions is a staple of most MBA programs and therefore is ingrained in the psyche of many administrators. Business executives appreciate the fact that most utilitarians recognize that not everyone will benefit from a particular action—hence the emphasis in utilitarianism is upon the *net* utility of particular outcomes. Marketing managers, of course, also realize that their business decisions must often be placed in the context of a "win–lose" situation. That is, consequences of a business action are seldom singular; they are multiple and typically cut both ways. For instance, in mature markets the only way to *gain* market share might be to take it away from competition. Or the only way to long-term shareholder value might be by trading off profits (and perhaps management bonuses) in the short-run. Similarly, the effort of developing a new market segment, such as an untapped international market, will require substantial expenditures in the short run, most likely reducing immediate profits. Japanese companies have long recognized this reality when entering the US market. Firms such as Toyota, Fuji, and Mitsubishi have been willing to trade off profitability in order to build customer reputation and increase market share. Ideally, the eventual cash flow and long-term profits from the new market will make this short-term sacrifice worthwhile.

Still another reason why marketing managers are so accepting of a utilitarian approach lies in its flexibility. Utilitarianism accommodates complex situations more easily than other, more absolute philosophical approaches. In short, the factors considered within the utilitarian framework can be conveniently varied from the short term to the long term, from a few to many stakeholder groups, or from financial to nonfinancial criteria. While conflicting stakeholder claims *can* be recognized, many managers often weigh the goals of stockholders (i.e., owners) with direct ties to organizational profitability as more important than the goals of other groups.

For example, in scenario 1 at the beginning of this chapter, involving the distribution manager of the supermarket chain sending lower quality cuts of meat and vegetables to lower profitability stores in disadvantaged neighborhoods, one can see how this approach *might* be defended using economic utilitarianism. The manager rationalizes that as long as the meats and vegetables are above some minimally acceptable quality level, it is in the best financial interest of the super-market chain to take whatever action it can to enhance overall operations. As the less financially important units happen to be located in the least affluent areas of the city, economic advantage is maximized by systematically discriminating against these less profitable units. Alternatively, management may also calculate (quite reasonably) that the marginal value of the inner city store can only be maintained by offsetting the impact of higher insurance and security costs and lower sales volume per square foot with other cost-cutting measures. When compared to the alternative of closing the store (with the external costs of lower employment and less service to that neighborhood), the current practice may be the most ethical in a utilitarian sense.

Limitations of Utilitarianism

Consequentialist approaches to ethical reasoning are obviously not without their problems. Perhaps the most evident concern, which applies to almost any formu-lation of utilitarianism, is the question of who decides what "the good" is. Indeed, there are usually many opinions as to what constitutes the nature of the actual benefits of a particular action. When this is the case, *who* is it that decides which perception of what "good" shall prevail? Is it the CEO, the VP-Marketing, the product managers, or a panel of customers? Second, it appears that utilitarianism is a philosophy where sometimes the ends can justify the means. That is, just because the outcome of a particular action produces a "net good" for a corpora-tion, or for that matter the society, does that necessitate that such an outcome should be attained at the expense of lost benefits to other parties? For example, a pharmaceutical firm may make considerable profit marketing a particular contra-ceptive device. Moreover, the product may benefit the needs of many women. However, should this item be permitted in the market if it causes a significant and lasting health problem for a minority of users? Those who practice most forms of utilitarianism recognize that one *cannot* cause great harm to certain others in order to achieve a desirable or noble end. This seems to be the point that animal-rights activists are stressing in advocating a ban on the use of animals in safety testing various products such as cosmetics. In fact, one of the greatest ethical precepts is *never knowingly do harm*. But, the definition of what constitutes "a harm" or a significant harm is subject to debate.

Third, those marketing managers who adopt a primarily economic interpre-tation of utilitarianism must answer whether such an approach is compatible with the concept of justice. The transformation of utilitarian theory into economic utilitarianism is somewhat understandable, in the sense that a business organiza-tion is primarily an *economic* enterprise. But because an action is economically beneficial does this mean it is just and proper? For instance, because the market demands sexually explicit pornographic material—and pornography is profitable to most of the parties involved in the production and consumption—is it ethical to market such material? Even though a particular action has produced the greatest economic good for the greatest number, that still does not *prove* that the

EXHIBIT 2–2   Lunch Box Ethics*

Michael Moriarity is the director of marketing research for the Kiddie Container Corporation, a firm which controls 60 percent of children's plastic lunch-box sales in the US market. Moriarity has just completed a market research study, and the final report has been turned over to Ms. Jeanne Reeder, vice president of marketing for Kiddie Corp. The study findings have confirmed some of the suspicions that she has had all along. Specifically, the highlights of the report suggest the following:

1. Eighty-four percent of childrens' lunch-box purchases are determined predominantly by the desires of the child.
2. Eighty percent of lunch box purchases are strongly influenced by the character or design pasted on the side of the lunch box (for example, *Mickey Mouse, My Little Pony, Fred Flintstone,* etc.).
3. Having a "current" or "trendy" character sticker on the lunch box is "extremely important" to the *majority* of first to third grade children (especially boys).
4. Not having a current or trendy character on one's lunch box can contribute to social rejection or ridicule. One teacher who was interviewed as part of the study stated, "It could be social suicide for a youngster to show up two years in a row lugging an *Alf* lunch box or toting *Roger Rabbit* when *Batman* is America's current star." And another noted, "What you carry gives you status in the blackboard jungle...adults have their BMWs and kids have their lunch boxes."
5. Children will often make "a scene" at the point of a purchase station where lunch boxes are displayed, crying or arguing with their parents for a particular lunch-box design. Retailers have sometimes called the area where lunch boxes are sold the "whine sign."

This particular selling season Kiddie Corp. was in the very fortunate position of having the licensing rights to three of the absolutely hottest (lunchbox) characters on the current children's scene: (1) *The Simpson's,* (2) *Teenage Mutant Ninja Turtles,* (3) *Super Mario Brothers* (from the popular Nintendo game).

As a result of the strong share of market that Kiddie Corp. controlled and because of the conclusions contained in the market research report, Ms. Reeder recommended increasing the price of the lunch boxes that had the currently fashionable characters from $3.99 to $7.99. Because of the social status involved in trendy lunch boxes, it was believed that price would be relatively inelastic. In addition, Reeder recommended removing as many of last year's models from the shelves as possible and replacing the paste-ups with up-to-date stickers. Simultaneously, Reeder instructed that an advertising campaign be quickly developed that included a series of ten-second segments featuring each of the "hot" characters that Kiddie Corp. held licensing rights to. The TV advertising campaign was to run on Saturday morning children's programming and would conclude with the slogan, "Don't be a geek, snack with a 1990s model lunch box."

Were the actions taken by Vice President Reeder of the Kiddie Container Corporation ethical?

*The Kiddie Container Corporation is a fictional organization. The events described in this case are not intended to depict the operations of any existing organization. This exhibit is original to the authors. The overall situation is loosely based on N.R. Kleinfield, "Another August under the 'Whine Sign,'" *New York Times* (August 6, 1989), F4.

action is just and proper. Exhibit 2–2 presents a marketing scenario that raises some of these utilitarian trade-offs.

In short, the utilitarian principle to act in a way that results in a greatest good for the greatest number is a popular method of ethical reasoning that is explicitly, or implicitly, used by many managers.

Duty-Based Theories

A second category of ethical theories are classified by philosophers as *deontological*—the term coming from the Greek word *deon* meaning "duty." This impressive sounding word basically indicates that actions are best judged as "good," standing alone and without regard to consequences. Thus, the inherent rightness of an act is *not* decided by correctly analyzing and choosing the act that produces the best consequences, but rather upon the premise that certain actions are "correct" in and of themselves because they stem from fundamental obligations.[6]

Many duty-based theories take the form of listing rules or obligations that must be followed in all, or almost all, circumstances. Typical of such a list is the one that was developed by English philosopher William David Ross.[7] Ross sought to assemble what he called *prima facie* duties. That is, certain actions are self-evident in that persons of sufficient intellectual maturity would recognize that they *ought* to be done. The duties delineated by Ross, and how they might be applied to the scenarios mentioned at the beginning of this chapter, are presented in Exhibit 2–3.

Perhaps the most famous duty-based theory was developed by the Prussian philosopher Emmanuel Kant.[8] Kant contended that moral laws took the form of *categorical imperatives*—principles which defined behavior appropriate in all situations and that should be followed by all persons as a matter of duty. Kant formulated the categorical imperative as follows: *Act in such a way that the action taken could be a universal rule of behavior for everyone.* He elaborated at length on this principle. One important amplification was that actions taken should always treat other persons as an end and never solely as a means. Thus, this moral imperative suggests that it is unethical for salespeople to manipulate consumers or pressure them into buying something, because they would be treated as merely a means to an end.

For business, such duty-based approaches to ethics have important implications. This theory suggests, among other things, that the cost–benefit analysis is inappropriate to the evaluation of some situations. Why? Decisions that produce a good outcome but significantly hurt other stakeholders in the process are not morally acceptable using this line of reasoning. Also, it suggests that the goal of seeking the maximum *net* consequences of an action may include intermediate steps which could be judged as morally inappropriate. Why is this so? Because *means* as well as *ends* should be morally evaluated. Thus, an implication flowing from duty-based theories is that sometimes business executives must take actions which do not produce the best economic consequences. *Not* to do so could be

EXHIBIT 2–3   One List of Basic Obligations That Are Binding on Everyone

1. **Duties of fidelity** stem from previous actions that have been taken. These would include (to name a few) the duty to remain faithful to contracts, to keep promises, to tell the truth, and to redress wrongful acts. In a marketing context, this might include conducting all the quality and safety testing that has been promised consumers, maintaining a rigorous warranty/servicing program, and refraining from deceptive or misleading promotional campaigns. For example, in scenario 2 at the beginning of this chapter, the dealer's association may decide that the heavy-handed fear appeal is in bad taste because of the implicit duty of fidelity they have to potential auto buyers.

2. **Duties of gratitude** are rooted in acts other persons have taken toward the person or organization under focus. This usually means that a special obligation exists between relatives, friends, partners, cohorts, and so forth. In a marketing context, this might mean retaining an advertising agency a while longer, because it has rendered meritorious service for several years or extending extra credit to a historically special customer who is experiencing a cash-flow problem. In scenario 4 heading this chapter, Acme management may conclude that the duty of gratitude would allow the provision of a small gift, if such a practice is not explicitly forbidden by the client organization.

3. **Duties of justice** are based on the obligation to distribute rewards based on merit. The justice referred to here is justice beyond the letter of

the law. For example, an organization using sealed-bid purchasing to secure services should award the contract according to procedure rather than by allowing the second or third lowest bidder to rebid. Or in scenario 1 at the outset of this chapter, the distribution manager might reason that the managerial problems caused by a few shoplifting or troublemaking customers is not a sufficient reason to discriminate against all the store's buyers.

4. **Duties of beneficence** rest on the notion that certain actions can improve the intelligence, virtue, or happiness of others. Basically, this is the obligation to do good, if a person has the opportunity. In scenario 6 at the beginning of this chapter, this might mean that the Smith and Smith agency turn down the public-relations contract, albeit financially attractive, because of the duty to support the human rights of others.

5. **Duties of self-improvement** reside in the concept that actions should be taken to improve our personal virtue, intelligence, or happiness. This seems to represent a modified restatement of moral egoism: Act in a way that will promote one's self-interest. In a marketing context, this might justify a manager's attempt to maximize the return on investment (ROI) of his profit center, because such performance may lead to pay increases and organizational promotion. In scenario 6 heading this chapter, this might mean that Smith and Smith undertakes the public relations (PR) contract to survive because, after all, the charges against the client country have not been proven, and the country's gov-

Continued

EXHIBIT 2–3   *Continued*

ernment is officially recognized by the US Department of State.

6. **Duties of nonmaleficence** (noninjury) consists of duties not to injure others. In a marketing context, this might involve doing the utmost to insure product safety, providing adequate information to enable consumers to use the products they purchase properly, and refraining from coercive tactics when managing a channel of distribution. For example, in scenario 3 at the beginning of this chapter, Jones Company may decide against exporting the controversial soft drinks to maximize consumer safety, even though it believes the government's data are invalid.

Source: Adapted from William D. Ross, *The Right and the Good* (Oxford, UK: Clarendon Press, 1930).

morally wrong. That is, some actions might violate the basic duty to treat everyone fairly. Scenario 1, dealing with the hypothetical Thrifty Supermarket chain is such a case. The action taken by the distribution manager probably produces the best economic results for the supermarket chain. However, reflection indicates that the customers of the low income stores, where the poorest cuts of meat and vegetables are sent, have been used merely as a *means* to obtain a satisfactory economic *end* for Thrifty Supermarkets. In other words, certain consumers have been unjustly discriminated against to the benefit of others (see also Exhibit 2–4).

A modern theory which is duty-based in its approach has been formulated by Harvard professor John Rawls.[9] Rawls derives two principles of justice, which, like Kant's categorical imperative, are never to be violated. These principles are the *liberty principle* and the *difference principle.*

- The liberty principle states that each person is to have an equal right to the most extensive basic liberty compatible with a similar liberty for others.

- The difference principle states that social and economic equalities are to be arranged so that they are to the greatest benefit of the least disadvantaged.

The liberty principle is fairly understandable in light of the American political tradition. Basically, it argues that people have inherent rights, such as the freedom of speech, the right to vote, the right to due process of law, the ownership of property, and that they have a right to exercise these liberties to the extent that they do not infringe upon the fundamental liberties of others. In a marketplace context, Chrysler Motors has developed a six-point Car Buyers' Bill of Rights (see Exhibit 2–5) that represents a good corporate illustration of the liberty principle.

The difference principle is a bit more complicated. Basically, it states that actions should not be taken that will further disadvantage those groups in society which are currently the least well-off. In other words, corporate actions should be

---

EXHIBIT 2–4   Cicero on Profit and Moral Responsibility

Two thousand years ago, Cicero posed a question about the conduct of an Alexandrian trader who had arrived in Rhodes during a famine with a ship laden with corn. Should the trader tell merchants that other vessels were on their way—or say nothing, and let them bid up the price of his corn? Cicero declared that a businessman's responsibility to the starving people outweighed his responsibility to make a profit.

Cicero on Moral Philosophy

To everyone who proposes to have a good career, moral philosophy is indispensible.

De Officiis, 44BC

formulated in such a way that the social and economic inequalities are arranged so that they benefit the least advantaged the most. This principle—a somewhat controversial one—is basically an *affirmative action* principle for the poor and politically underrepresented groups in society. Over time, it is an egalitarian principle that should make those least well-off, better off. The difference principle also emphasizes that it would be unethical to exploit one group for the benefit of others. In scenario 6 heading this chapter, the difference principle would probably suggest that the Smith and Smith agency forego the public relations program, because its implementation could add legitimacy to the (corrupt) ruling foreign government. Furthermore, it might exacerbate the position of a worse off group, namely, the citizens of a country where human rights are systematically violated. Similarly, it seems to suggest that marketers may have superordinate duties to certain groups which are illiterate in the workings of the marketplace. (In Chapter 6 we discuss the responsibilities that marketers may have when communicating with groups demanding special consideration.)

Like utilitarianism, duty-based theories are controversial in part because there are many kinds of deontological theories. Various moral philosophers have compiled different lists of basic obligations or duties. While the lists overlap, they are not identical. Second, duty-based theories represent the antithesis of modern relativism (i.e., the notion that moral decisions can only be made in the context of particular situations). Hence, they are viewed by some as not being well-suited to our complex, multicultural, and global marketplace, because they emphasize the development of *universal* rules. The very nature of such absolute approaches includes certain problems that are inherent in the development of categorical imperatives. Among them are the following:[10]

1. There are always contingencies that seem to complicate real-world situations. For example, regarding scenario 4, which raises the question of gift-giving, suppose the selling organization has an absolute rule against this practice.

EXHIBIT 2-5

CHRYSLER MOTORS ANNOUNCES

THE CAR BUYER'S BILL OF RIGHTS.

1. EVERY AMERICAN HAS THE RIGHT TO A QUALITY CAR

You want a car that will start every morning.

You want a car that will age well. And give you years of satisfaction.

You want quality. It's your right. Undisputed right.

Quality is also the first commitment of the carmaker. Without it he becomes morally and fiscally bankrupt. Chrysler has no intentions of breaking this commitment.

Since 1980, Chrysler—with new leadership and a new resolve—initiated **Five Key Quality Programs** involving every member of the work force, every level of management. Chrysler has completed 5 million hours of worker training, enrolled 26,000 employees in quality schools and put 560 quality teams in place.

The goal: top the quality of the imports. It's an ambitious goal, but results are already showing it is within reach. Corporate quality indicators show that, over the last 8 years, Chrysler-built car and truck quality has improved 43%.

Lowest recalls. During the same 8-year period, Government records show that Chrysler has the lowest average safety recall record of any American car company for passenger cars registered for the '80 through '87 model years.

And over the last 5 years, lower than such prominent imports as BMW, Porsche and Volvo.

2. EVERY AMERICAN HAS THE RIGHT TO LONG-TERM PROTECTION

Chrysler has consistently led the industry in long-term quality protection.

In 1980, Chrysler introduced the innovative 5/50 Protection Plan. In 1987, Chrysler extended this coverage substantially on the most important part of your car, the engine and powertrain, to 7 years or 70,000 miles. It's the **longest powertrain protection** in the industry. And you also get 7-year or 100,000-mile protection against

outer body rust-through.* The plan covers every car, truck and minivan Chrysler builds in North America, and now it includes '89 Jeep vehicles. 7/70, unprecedented when introduced.

Now, Chrysler breaks new ground again. With its new **Crystal Key Owner Care Program** that comes with the Chrysler New Yorker. It is a remarkable warranty. It protects the entire car for 5 years or 50,000 miles. It covers engine, powertrain, air conditioning, steering, rust, suspension, electrical—everything right down to the door handles.† All you have to do is take care of normal maintenance, adjustments and wear items.

Not even Rolls or Mercedes match this warranty.

3. EVERY AMERICAN HAS THE RIGHT TO FRIENDLY TREATMENT, HONEST SERVICE AND COMPETENT REPAIRS

Dealer service is the key link—be the most fragile link—between the car buyer and the carmaker. It can make or break a relationship.

Chrysler understands this, better than most. And (under the direction of Lee Iacocca) has taken specific action to strengthen and revitalize this relationship. Results are gratifying.

Highest satisfaction. Chrysler owners have the highest level of satisfaction of any buyers of American cars. Higher than GM owners. And significantly higher than Ford owners.**

As Lee Iacocca says: "The next great leap forward in the car industry isn't going to happen in Detroit. It's going to happen at the dealership." One telling example: training. Last year, 542,184 hours. That's an increase of almost 300%.

Chrysler is also giving tangible rewards to the Dodge, Chrysler, Plymouth, Jeep and Eagle dealers and their technicians for improving customer service. Because when they do, we achieve one of the highest goals in the auto industry, a satisfied customer.

4. THE RIGHT TO A SAFE VEHICLE

Safety is a right we all desire, not just for ourselves, but for our families, too. That's why Chrysler has committed enormous resources and talents to building you a safe car. And that commitment has taken hold:

...Chrysler Motors is the first American car company to offer **air bags as standard equipment.** And by 1990, Chrysler will feature driver-side air bags on every car it builds in the United States.

...Every Chrysler-built passenger car has over 30 safety features standard for '88.

...By 1992, Chrysler will have spent 440 million dollars on testing to learn how to enhance your safety.

...Chrysler Motors has a **Safety Shield Program** from design through assembly. Safety components are identified by a safety shield, so everyone at the factory knows its importance to safety.

This program guards against the malfunction of critical items such as brakes, wipers, steering systems and starters. And is one of the prime reasons why Chrysler Motors has the lowest average percentage of safety-related recalls for any American car company.

5. THE RIGHT TO ADDRESS GRIEVANCES

If you have a warranty-related problem with your dealer, you have an impartial ear ready and willing to listen to your side of the story, and this comes at no cost to you: **The Customer Arbitration Board.**

This Arbitration Board consists of three voting members: a local customer advocate, a technical expert and a person from the general public. And not one of them is affiliated with Chrysler in any way.

All decisions made by the Board include the action to be taken by the dealer or Chrysler and the time by which the action must be taken.

All decisions are binding on the dealer and Chrysler, but not on you, unless you accept the decision. The whole process normally takes no longer than 40 days.

6. THE RIGHT TO SATISFACTION

Chrysler believes there's no secret to satisfying customers. Build them a quality product. A safe product. Protect it right—with the largest powertrain warranty in the business. Service it right. And treat them with respect. It's that simple.

And Chrysler is doing exactly that. The proof is coming from you, the customer.

J.D. Power and Associates, one of the most respected research organizations in the industry, surveyed over 25,000 owners of 1987 passenger cars for product quality and dealer service. The results: Chrysler Motors has the **highest customer satisfaction** of any American car company—**two years running**—for overall product quality and dealer service.**

As good as that is, it's not good enough. If we don't satisfy you better than the next guy...you have every right to go to the next guy. So, we're never going to stop improving present programs, and creating new ones.

Because Chrysler believes it's our job to satisfy your needs. We have the obligations...you have the rights.

"QUALITY IS YOUR RIGHT. AND WE INTEND TO SEE THAT YOU GET IT."

Lee Iacocca

CHRYSLER MOTORS

CHRYSLER · PLYMOUTH · DODGE
DODGE TRUCKS · JEEP · EAGLE

Now suppose further they enter a new international market where such gift-giving is a common and expected practice. Consider further that success in this market will determine whether the firm can economically survive. Should the universal rule be violated or changed to accommodate these contingencies?

2. Universals also do not take into account the ethical character of the formulator of the universal principle. That is, if the morality of the person formulating the principle is flawed, it is possible that the principle itself will be deficient. For example, one might take issue with the universal maxims formulated by egoistic managers who see business as merely a game the sole purpose of which is the accumulation of personal wealth.

3. There may not be a mechanism for resolving conflicts among two absolute moral duties. Managers clearly have a fiduciary responsibility to their shareholders and a duty of fidelity to their employees. What happens when one action requires a trade-off for another? Which duty takes precedence? Is one universal more absolute than another?

Virtue Ethics

Another comprehensive theory of ethics is referred to as *virtue ethics*. It has a long tradition and is currently receiving renewed support. In part, virtue ethics is a contemporary reaction to the rampant relativism wherein society seems to lack a way of reaching moral agreement about ethical problems. The relativistic approach to morality seems to be based on the strength of emotional appeals and intuitionism, whereby one person's opinion is as good as another's. It is almost a one–person, one–vote method to establishing what is ethical. Virtue ethics has been resurrected to counteract modern relativism.

What exactly is virtue ethics? Its key criterion is seeking to live a virtuous life. In many ways, it is a renaissance of the Greek ideal suggesting that the guiding purpose of life should be the quest for goodness and virtue. In philosophical circles, one of the most prominent proponents of this position is Alasdair MacIntyre of the University of Notre Dame. MacIntyre basically defines virtue as acquired human qualities that enable persons to achieve "the good" in their chosen vocations.[11]

Advocates of virtue ethics suggest that one problem with contemporary organizations is that when they do look at situations with ethical implications, they are preoccupied with what the public thinks. Put another way, today's corporations may be entirely too reactive, wondering at times whether their actions will be perceived as "opportunistic," "exploitative," or in "bad taste" by the general public. This may be a misdirected effort that can be rectified through virtue ethics. Thus, organizations should instead focus on normative questions, such as "What kind of organization *should* we be?" and "What constitutes the ideally ethical organization?" Companies that know what they stand for and then embody these beliefs in a company credo, are following this approach to ethics. In short, the virtue ethics perspective seems to imply that the question of *understanding* virtue precedes the discussion and development of rules of conduct.

Once management understands the nature of a virtuous organization, ethical decision-rules will be much easier to develop.

Believers in this approach find much value in the writings of Aristotle.[12] While the essence of the virtue ethics approach cannot easily be captured in a few sentences, there are some key elements that reflect this mode of thinking. *First*, virtues are essentially good habits. In order to flourish, these habits must be practiced (see Exhibit 2–6) and the uninitiated managers in the organization must learn these virtues. This point has powerful implications for managers, including the notion that (a) organizations can only become virtuous by engaging in ethical activities and (b) organizations have to teach managers precisely what the appropriate virtues are. In other words, organizations have the responsibility to foster ethical behavior.

The *second* dimension of virtue ethics is that admirable characteristics are most readily discovered by witnessing and imitating widely acclaimed behavior. Aristotle, while focusing on the individual rather than the organization, listed such deducible virtues as truthfulness, justice, generosity, and self-control as characteristics to which the noble person should aspire. In the theory of virtue, much attention is placed on role models. The insight here is that to be an ethical person is not simply an analytical and rational matter. It takes virtuous people to make right decisions, and virtue is learned by doing. Put another way, the ultimate test and source of ethical conduct is the character of the actor. Aristotle often discussed the lives of obviously good Athenians in order to teach ethics. One learned the right thing to do by observing good people and by doing what they did. Such lessons reinforce the importance of top management serving as role models in the formation of an ethical corporate climate.

Companies that are acclaimed for their ethical corporate culture most often can trace their heritage back to founders intent on developing an organization that respected human dignity and insisted on a humane way of life. Founders of such companies as Johnson & Johnson and Hewlett–Packard (HP) shaped their organization so that they embodied the values and virtues that proved personally rewarding. The way of life in the company was not a result of an abstract code of

---

EXHIBIT 2–6   On the Importance of Habit in Cultivating Virtue

Your intellect is the seat of knowledge; your will, the seat of virtue. Your intellect sets up targets; your will shoots the arrows of your choices and acts. Ethics can be taught, but ethical conduct cannot, it must be practiced. All the theoretical knowledge in the world about music will not make you a good pianist unless you practice. All the theoretical knowledge in the world about ethics will not make you a virtuous manager unless you practice.

Source: William Oleksak, "Letter to the Editor" (paraphrasing Msgr. Fulton J. Sheen), *New York Times* (February 26, 1989), E6.

conduct, but rather such codes were later used to spell out exactly what was at the heart of the existing corporate culture.[13] For example, William Hewlett and David Packard did not formulate their company values in writing until after twenty years of operation. Only then, in order to ensure that the culture not be lost as the founders became more removed from the expanding workforce, did top management draw up a statement of corporate values, initiate training seminars in the "HP Way," and install accountability procedures.

Third, a key to understanding virtue ethics and the discipline it requires, is found in the *ethic of the mean*. Applied to virtue ethics, the *mean* is an optimal balance of a quality that one should seek. An excess or deficiency of any of the key virtues can be troublesome, as Aristotle effectively argued. For example, an excess of truthfulness is boastfulness. A deficiency of truthfulness is deception. Both of these outcomes (the excess or the deficiency) are unacceptable. The virtuous marketing manager, then, strives for a *balance* among the qualities it takes to be an effective manager. For example, she should not be so directive as to be authoritarian, nor so easy-going as to abdicate her leadership role.

Obviously, there is disagreement about exactly which characteristics should appear on a list of virtues to which an organization should aspire. Over the years, different philosophers have compiled many different lists. The one by William David Ross (recall Exhibit 2–3) is an example. Business executives are also quite capable of ranking the values that they feel are most important as well as least important (see Exhibit 2–7 for such a list). Whether or not a particular corporation elects to foster those values is another issue.

However, let's assume for a moment that an organization accepts the virtue ethics approach to corporate conduct. In other words, they subscribe to the belief that an organization should be "all that it can be" in an ethical sense. Then, with regard to the scenarios discussed earlier, one might conclude that (a) the virtuous organization has no need to provide gifts to purchasing agents in order to secure product orders (scenario 4), (b) the virtuous organization should be totally truthful; therefore it has no problem in disclosing a change of components as well as updating consumers with regard to the reliability of all their brands (scenario 5), and (c) the virtuous organization will not stoop to fear generating, emotional appeals to sell its products; manipulation is wrong; thus, almost all fear appeals would be inappropriate (scenario 2).

One logical objection to the application of virtue ethics in an organizational context is that it would sometimes be very difficult to agree on what, in fact, constitutes "the good." What virtues should an organization emulate and how should those virtues be operationalized in company policy? The contemporary philosopher MacIntyre and other recent proponents of virtue ethics seem to deal with this situation in the following way. First, they recognize a great diversity of values exists in society. However, in many cases, particular organizations are self-contained. It is within the context of individual companies that the notion of appropriate virtues should be explored. Second, consistent with Aristotle, they assume that these virtues will be "other directed" (i.e., undertaken for the good of the community rather than in a self-serving manner).

EXHIBIT 2–7   How Managers Rank Personal Values

Here's how 220 Pittsburgh-area managers ranked a set of eighteen values most important in their lives and, similarly, ranked a set of eighteen attributes they most admire.

Important Values

Top Five	*Bottom Five*
Self-respect	Pleasure
Family security	World of beauty
Freedom	Salvation
Accomplishment	Social recognition
Happiness	Equality

Attributes Admired

Top Five	*Bottom Five*
Honesty	Obedience
Responsibility	Cleanliness
Capability	Cheerfulness
Ambition	Politeness
Independence	Helpfulness

Source: Abstracted from William C. Frederick and James Weber, "The Values of Corporate Managers and Their Critics: An Empirical Description and Normative Implications." In *Research in Corporate Social Performance and Policy*, vol. 9, ed. W. Frederick, 131–152 (Greenwich, CT: JAI Press, 1987).

It is important to note that we find the corporation among the more controlled communities in modern society. Each corporation has its own *corporate culture*, often rooted in religious values (see Exhibit 2–8). It is within the context of corporate culture that a particular firm can seek the virtues that are appropriate for that organization. All of this, of course, underscores the importance of developing an ethical corporate culture that will facilitate appropriate managerial behavior. The steps necessary to do this are a topic of this book's concluding chapter.

Models of Marketing Ethics

Because of the difficulty of applying such general theories and principles to specific case situations, a number of scholars have begun to investigate what particular factors account for ethical marketing decisions. In an effort to aid their investigations, some of these researchers have begun to formulate *models* that stipulate the factors contributing to an *ethical* decision.

EXHIBIT 2–8　The Religious Roots of Ethics

There is little doubt that organized religion provides managers with a major source of their ethics. In one recent poll of 2000 business executives, approximately 50 percent claimed that religious values significantly influence their business decisions.[1] Interestingly, that same study found that the higher the organizational rank of the executive, the greater the influence of religion.

On many occasions, various religious leaders have preached that the answers to the majority of moral questions, business-related or otherwise, could be found in the Bible. There has also been considerable debate about the level of guidance generated by religious principles. On the one hand, prescriptions like "thou shalt not steal" are fairly unambiguous. On the other hand, many situations that the contemporary corporate manager is faced with are exceedingly complex and defy the application of biblical precepts.

One ambitious and controversial attempt to interject moral values into the economic marketplace involved the so-called pastoral letter on economics authored by the American Catholic bishops.[2] Drawing upon Scripture and Catholic social teaching, this document attempted to derive propositions with useful current applications. For example, among the ethical precepts implied by this document are the following:

When considering trade-offs between labor and technology, managers have the responsibility to give special weight to human resources because of the *primacy of labor over capital* doctrine.

When making strategic marketing decisions, managers have a special duty to consider the effect of those actions upon economically vulnerable members of the community because of the *preferential option for the poor* doctrine.

When making business decisions that may negatively impact the physical environment, managers have a special obligation to strongly consider possible external costs upon the ecological environment because of the *stewardship* doctrine.

---

[1] Thomas F. McMahon, "Religion and Business: Concepts and Data," *Chicago Studies* (1989), 3–15.
[2] US Catholic Bishops, *Economic Justice for All* (1986).

The Moral Development Model

This approach draws partly upon the analysis of educational psychologist Lawrence Kohlberg who studied the moral development of adolescents.[14] Kohlberg postulated that, over time, individuals develop moral systems that are increasingly complex, although there is no guarantee that any particular individual moves beyond the initial and most fundamental stage of moral development. Essentially, he saw three broad levels of cognitive moral development. These were:

1. *The preconventional stage* where the abiding concern of the individual would be to resolve moral situations, with the individual's own immediate interests and consequences firmly in mind. An individual at the preconventional level would give strong weight to the external rewards and punishments most likely to affect him. Normally, this stage includes a strong emphasis upon literal obedience to rules and authority.

2. *The conventional stage.* Individuals at the conventional stage have progressed to a level where their ethical decision-making mode takes into consideration the expectations of significant reference groups and society at large. What constitutes moral propriety has to do with a concern for others, however, still motivated most directly by organizational rules. Such rules are tempered by keeping loyalties and doing one's duty to society.

3. *The principled stage.* This is the highest level of moral development. Individuals who reach this level solve their ethical problems in a manner that goes beyond the norms and laws applicable to a specific situation. Proper conduct certainly includes upholding the basic rights, values, and legal contracts of society, but beyond that, such individuals seem to subscribe to universal ethical principles that they believe all members of society should follow in similar situations.

What the moral development model implies is that the ethical sophistication of managers can increase over time. The major difference among the various stages of moral development is that as the manager moves to a higher level of moral development, the individual is able to take more factors into consideration, especially those which go beyond personal self-interest. Two significant implications of the moral development model are that (1) some managers will be less sophisticated than others in terms of the considerations they bring to bear upon a decision with potentially moral consequences. At the most basic level, some managers will operate almost totally from the standpoint of egoistic self-interest. And (2) perhaps there are interventions (e.g., training programs) that organizations can bring to bear that will compel managers to higher levels of moral development—assuming this is a goal seen to be in the company's interest.

The Organizational Moral Development Model[15]

Some ethics experts have suggested that the moral development applies to organizations as well as individuals. Postulated is a hierarchy or pyramid of organizational concern that is determined by the degree to which the organization attempts to balance the drive for profits with ethical considerations (see Exhibit 2–9). At the lowest level of the hierarchy are *Stage one* organizations; they are basically *amoral.* In these organizations, owners and managers are the only important stakeholders. The prevailing philosophy is to maximize profit at almost any cost. Being *caught* doing something unethical and enduring punishment is simply a cost of conducting business.

Stage two organizations, a bit higher up the pyramid, are *legalistic* and are only slightly more ethical than the amoral organizations. For the legalistic organiza-

EXHIBIT 2–9   Organizational Ethical Development Model

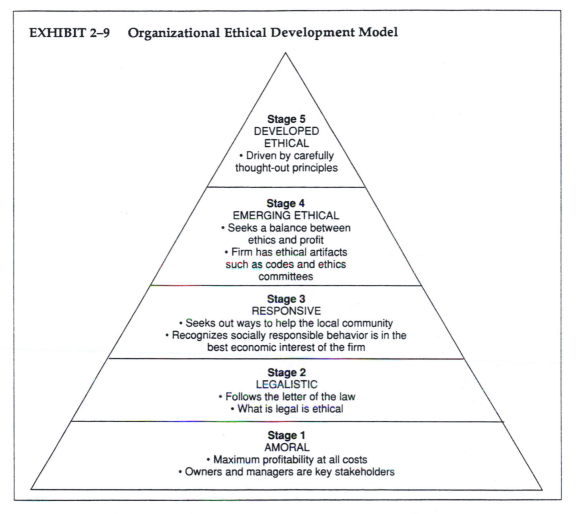

Stage 5
DEVELOPED
ETHICAL
• Driven by carefully
thought-out principles

Stage 4
EMERGING ETHICAL
• Seeks a balance between
ethics and profit
• Firm has ethical artifacts
such as codes and ethics
committees

Stage 3
RESPONSIVE
• Seeks out ways to help the local community
• Recognizes socially responsible behavior is in the
best economic interest of the firm

Stage 2
LEGALISTIC
• Follows the letter of the law
• What is legal is ethical

Stage 1
AMORAL
• Maximum profitability at all costs
• Owners and managers are key stakeholders

*Source: R.E. Reidenbach and D.P. Robin, "A Conceptual Model of Corporate Moral Development," *Journal of Business Ethics*, (April 1991), 10: 274. Reprinted by permission of Kluwer Academic Publishers.

tion, as its counterpart manager, being ethical means simply obeying the law. The only obligations that a firm of this type recognizes are legal obligations.

Further up the pyramid are *Stage three* organizations. They are characterized *responsive* because they have begun to develop a modicum of ethical concern. They recogize that a good relationship with the host community is important. Moreover, they see certain societal responsibilities (e.g., charitable giving, employee volunteerism) as duties to be performed that also happen to be expedient in providing for harmonious external relations. In short, the responsive firm usually behaves ethically, if only for self-serving reasons.

Stage four corporations are labeled *emerging ethical* because they have actually started to implement the artifacts of an ethical organization. Such artifacts include codes of ethics, ethics committees, managerial advancement partly based on socially responsible decisions, and an explicit recognition that the cost of being ethical may sometimes involve a trade-off with profits. Typically, *Stage four* organizations evidence a concern for values in the mission statement of the firm as well as in the company's planning documents. Again, the mark of an *emerging ethical* company rests in its ability to document specific actions where ethical concern has motivated an ethically responsive action.

Stage five companies are at the peak of the ethical hierarchy. These *developed ethical* organizations have clearly articulated value statements, as well as a set of agreed upon principles that can be relied upon to help the organization deal with ethical issues. Frankly, fully developed ethical organizations are rare.

As this organizational development model of ethics is only a conceptual classification, it is a matter of speculation as to how many actual firms fit into each category. Most probably, more firms are in the middle of the hierarchy than at the extremes. Totally amoral and totally ethically developed organizations are uncommon, although they are found in the marketplace.

Ideally, organizations move over time from the lower to the higher stages of ethical concern, although this is not necessarily the case. Some organizations may revert to old habits and *slip* to lower levels. Also, an organization does not necessarily pass through each stage. For example, in evolving from an *amoral* to an *emerging ethical* organization, a pause in the *legalistic* stage is not necessarily part of the development. Also, different divisions of large organizations might be at different stages.

Why is the organizational moral development model worth thinking about? This approach to ethical development underscores several important lessons:

1. The creation of an ethical orientation is the result of a managerial orientation built around moral values.
2. The approach recognizes that ethical behavior often has some economic costs associated with it—there is sometimes a trade-off between maximum short-term profit and good ethics.
3. Ethical artifacts, such as codes, ethics committees, and rewards for ethical behavior are an important aspect of organizational ethical development.

Unfortunately, the model does not specify in detail *why* an organization should strive to move up the pyramid. However, the costs of unethical behavior detailed earlier, along with the long-term benefits of maintaining an ethical culture should provide sufficient motivation for firms to want to make the ethical climb up the pyramid.

The Contingency Model

In addition to the usual factors that might influence an ethical decision, another approach suggests that there are two major intervening issues that will determine whether a manager acts ethically or not.[16] These are the *opportunity* to engage in potentially unethical action and the *relative influence* (positive or negative) *of reference groups,* especially peers and top management. With regard to the role of these reference groups, this model stipulates that when contact with peers is great, peers will have a greater degree of influence than top management upon ethical/unethical behavior. And when the interaction with top management is substantial, the attitudes communicated by top management will have a strong formulative role in shaping the behavior of subordinate managers concerning ethical decisions. For example, field salesreps often operate in fairly autonomous fashion and with limited management contact. In such cases, the attitudes of their peers regarding ethical issues would likely be more influential than the opinions of management.

With respect to the *opportunity* to engage in unethical behavior, it's not surprising that the model postulates that the greater the opportunity to engage in such behavior, the more likely an individual will do so—all other things equal. The proclivity to favor an unethical option is tempered of course by the rewards and punishments that are operating in a particular manager's environment. That is to say, ethical behavior is encouraged by codes of ethics that prohibit certain activities. Similarly, when punishments are enacted for violation of certain professional codes of conduct, unethical behavior is less likely to occur. In the absence of such deterrents, the probability of a manager acting unethically increases.

The contribution of the contingency model is that it shows individual values are not the sole arbiter of ethical behavior; peer and supervisor influence are also extremely important. With respect to the role of top management, an old organizational adage suggests that the business enterprise is but a lengthened shadow of the person at the top. In all probability, the posture of top management may be the single most important factor determining ethical behavior in an organization.[17] Similarly, the notion of "opportunity to act unethically" simply underscores the common sense thesis that given temptation, manager will sometimes succumb.

The Reasoned Action Model

Other approaches to the study of ethics have taken the *rational person* approach.[18] The basic idea is that a typical individual will approach an ethical problem from a rather calculating perspective. First, the person must perceive that a situation has ethical dimensions. At this point, several evaluations take place. One involves a judgment concerning the inherent rightness or wrongness of the ethical question at focus. Either basic or sophisticated principles are used to arrive at this judgment. A second step involves a determination of what the perceived consequences of acting ethically or unethically are. The probability that each of those consequences will occur are then subjectively calculated, taking into consideration the importance of each outcome. The ultimate ethical judgment arrived at by the manager is the result of judgment concerning the norms of behavior (i.e., the evaluation regarding the rightness or wrongness of the action) in conjunction with the evaluation of the net gain from each outcome, adjusted for the probability of its occurrence.

What all this means is that managers will systematically weigh the possible options and outcomes in light of their individual value system. One of the essential problems of the reasoned action model approach is that it never clearly specifies whether the evaluations are made from the standpoint of the self-interested individual, the manager as representing the shareholders of the organization, or the manager taking into account all the various stakeholders (i.e., consumers, employees, etc.).

Although this model may seem sophisticated upon first exposure, it is not terribly complex. Brought down to its essentials, it implies the following:

1. If managers perceive a situation which requires an action that may have ethical consequences they will attempt to *elaborate the alternative outcomes* of the options available to them to resolve the solution.
2. In coming to a decision as to which option to choose, managers will *weigh factors*, including the inherent rightness or wrongness of the act itself, the probability that acting in a particular way will lead to certain payoffs, and the value of those payoffs.
3. All of this will lead to formation of an *ethical judgment* that will culminate in the *intention* to take a particular action. Whether the action is actually taken or not can still be mitigated by various situational factors such as the likelihood of getting caught and being punished by another party.

Whether most managers facing an ethical issue possess sufficient information to make such a series of calculations is a matter for debate.

The Importance of General Models

Again, the value of models like those described above is that they elaborate important issues that bear upon ethical decision-making. These factors may deal with the moral development of the individual manager, the influence of top management or peer groups, the opportunity to engage in particular actions, or the value of various outcomes to the manager. All these organizational aspects can be adjusted to possibly improve the firm's ethical posture. Perhaps the greatest shortcoming of such models is that they are basically *descriptive*. While they articulate factors that come into play when managers might take an action with moral consequences, such approaches generally avoid making any moral judgments about the propriety of various actions.

Ideas for Ethical Action

The call to apply a specific ethical theory to a particular marketing situation is easier given than implemented. Philosophers who have studied moral theory and reasoning for many years regularly argue among themselves about what constitutes the *best* ethical resolution of an issue. (See again Exhibit 2–1 for a summary of the essential theoretical approaches.) Once again, ethics is not an easy area to understand and control. Perhaps the most marketing managers can do in attempting to vitalize ethical reasoning in their organizations is the following:

1. Develop a list of questions that reflect various ethical theories which can aid managers in determining whether a particular contemplated action or decision is unethical.
2. Recognize that there are sometimes conflicts among the various ethical principles that imply different (sometimes contradictory) decisions. Moreover, realize that these conflicts increase as the number of relevant stakeholders in a decision increases.

These two points are elaborated on in the section below.

First, a sequence of questions to improve ethical reasoning should be asked. One approach to deal more normatively with ethical issue is to require that managers proceed through a sequence of questions that tests whether the action that they are contemplating is ethical or has possible ethical consequences. A battery of such questions might include the following:[19]

Question 1 (the legal test): Does the contemplated action violate the law?

Question 2 (the duties test): Is this action contrary to widely accepted moral obligations? Such moral obligations might include *duties of fidelity*, such as the responsibility to remain faithful to contracts, to keep promises, and to tell the truth; *duties of gratitude*, which basically means that special obligations exist between relatives, friends, partners, cohorts, and employees; *duties of justice*, which basically have to do with obligations to distribute rewards based upon merit; *duties of nonmaleficence*, which consists of duties not to harm others; *duties of beneficence*, which rest upon the notion that actions should be taken that improve the situation of others—if this can be readily accomplished.[20]

Question 3 (the special obligations test): Does the proposed action violate any other special obligations that stem from the type of marketing organization at focus? (For example, the special duty of pharmaceutical firms to provide safe products, the special obligation of toy manufacturers to care for the safety of children, the inherent duty of distillers to promote responsible drinking are all special obligations.)

Question 4 (the motives test): Is the *intent* of the contemplated action harmful?

Question 5 (the consequences test): Is it likely that any major damages to people or organizations will result from the contemplated action?

Question 6 (the utilitarian test): Is there a satisfactory *alternative* action that produces equal or greater benefits to the parties affected than the proposed action?

Question 7 (the rights test): Does the contemplated action infringe upon property rights, privacy rights, or the inalienable rights of the consumer (such as the right to information, the right to be heard, the right to choice, and the right to remedy)?

Question 8 (the justice test): Does the proposed action leave another person or group less well-off? Is this person or group already a member of a relatively underprivileged class?

The questions outlined above need not be pursued in lockstep fashion. If none of the questions uncover any potential conflicts, clearly the action being contemplated is quite likely to be ethical. However, if the sequence of queries does produce a possible conflict, this does not necessarily mean that the action being proposed is unethical *per se.* There may be unusual intervening factors that would still allow the action to ethically go forward. For example, suppose it is determined that the contemplated action is a violation of the law. Perhaps the law is unjust, and thus, there could be a moral obligation for an organization to transgress the law. Similarly, suppose there is an alternative action which could be taken that would produce equal or greater good for a larger number of individuals. However, the implementation of this alternative would bankrupt the existing organization. In such a situation, taking the alternative action (rather than the contemplated action) is usually not required.

Second, the stakeholder concept should be linked to marketing ethics. As the above sections illustrate, there is no shortage of comprehensive theories that can be utilized to guide the reasoning of managers as they try to reach moral conclusions. The difficulty, of course, is applying these theories to specific marketing situations and then resolving conflicts among the principles that come up. Most typically, these conflicts will take the form of two diametrically opposed duties being owed to different stakeholder groups. For example, there is a fiduciary responsibility on the part of managers to render to stockholders a fair return. At times, this might involve taking steps that are clearly counterproductive to another stakeholder group, such as employees. For example, this may occur in the case of a plant closing. The judgmental difficulty then comes in deciding which of the two duties take precedence. Utilitarianism, and the cost–benefit analysis that it often implies, is an extremely useful tool *if* one looks at a problem only from the standpoint of one or two stakeholder groups. However, when multiple stakeholders are introduced into the situation, the use of consequence-based theories is complicated considerably.

Similarly, duty-based or virtue ethics approaches are also complex. Often, there are contradictory duties, such as in scenario 2, where management has the right to point out their truthful strategic competitive advantage (i.e., the crash worthiness of its automobiles), while at the same time perhaps violating the duty not to unfairly manipulate the receivers of their promotional messages by using fear appeals. Frequently, however, most conflicts between stakeholders are susceptible to compromise. The existence of competing claims suggests that management must face up to the challenge of creating new alternatives that result in a better balance of obligations.

Conclusion

In the end, it is weighing the concerns of multiple stakeholder groups that becomes the essence of appropriate ethical decision-making. At the same time, these multiple claims on the organization are at the root of the complexity of such decision-making. The stakeholder concept, and the multiple responsibilities that it implies, becomes the necessary reason to sensitize managers to ethical implications and to teach them to reason from the standpoint of moral theory. In the final analysis, the reality is that ethics still requires considerable prudential judgment that comes from the intuition of the manager but is tempered by a knowledge of ethical theory and standards.

Endnotes

1. Adapted from Patrick E. Murphy and Gene R. Laczniak, "Marketing Ethics: Review with Implications for Managers, Educators and Researchers." In *Review of Marketing*, eds. B. Enis and K. Roering, 251 (Chicago: American Marketing Association, 1981).

2. Norman E. Bowie, "Challenging the Egositic Paradigm," *Business Ethics Quarterly* (January 1991), 1–21.

3. Allan J. Kimmel, *Ethics and Values in Applied Social Research*, (Newbury Park, CA: Sage Publications, 1988), 45.

4. See note 3 above.

5. Jeremy Bentham, *An Introduction to the Principles of Morals and Legislation*, (New York: Hafner Publishing, 1984) and John Stuart Mill, *Utilitarianism*, (Indianapolis, IN: Hackett Publishing, 1979).

6. Robert B. Ashmore, *Building a Moral System*, (Englewood Cliffs, NJ: Prentice-Hall, 1987), 93–98.

7. William David Ross, *The Right and the Good*, (Oxford, UK: Clarendon Press, 1938).

8. Immanuel Kant, *Grounding for the Metaphysics of Morals*, (Indianapolis, IN: Hackett Publishing, 1981). [Originally published in 1785.]

9. John Rawls, *A Theory of Justice*, (Cambridge, MA: Harvard University Press, 1971).

10. See note 6 above.

11. Alasdair MacIntyre, *After Virtue*, 2nd ed., (Notre Dame, IN: University of Notre Dame Press, 1984).

12. Aristotle, *Nicomachean Ethics*, (New York: MacMillan Publishing, 1962).

13. Oliver Williams and Patrick E. Murphy, "The Ethics of Virtue: A Moral Theory for Marketing," *Journal of Macromarketing* (Spring 1990), 19–29.

14. L. Kohlberg, "Stage and Sequence: The Cognitive Development Approach to Socialization." In *Handbook of Socialization Theory and Research*, ed. D.A. Goslin, (Chicago: Rand McNally, 1969), 347–480.

15. R. Eric Reidenbach and Donald P. Robin, "A Model of Corporate Development," paper presented at DePaul University Symposium on Marketing Ethics (May 1989).

16. O.C. Ferrell and L. Gresham, "A Contingency Framework For Understanding Ethical Decision Making in Marketing," *Journal of Marketing* (Summer 1985), 87–96.

17. Raymond C. Baumhart, "How Ethical Are Businesses?," *Harvard Business Review* (July–August 1961), 6.

18. Shelby D. Hunt and S. Vitell, "A General Theory of Marketing Ethics," *Journal of Macromarketing* (Spring 1986), 5–16.

19. Adapted from Gene R. Laczniak, "Framework for *Analyzing* Marketing Ethics," *Journal of Macromarketing* (Spring 1983), 7–18.

20. See note 6 above.

$Chapter\ 3$

Ethics in Marketing Research

Scenario 1

The research director of a large corporation is convinced that using the company's name in surveys with consumers produces low response rates and distorted answers. Therefore, the firm routinely conducts surveys using the title, Public Opinion Institute.[1] **Is this an ethical practice?**

Scenario 2

A survey finds that 80 percent of the doctors responding do not recommend any particular brand of margarine to their patients who are concerned about cholesterol. Five percent recommend Brand A, 4 percent recommend Brand B, and no other brand is recommended by over 2 percent of the doctors. The company runs an advertisement that states: "More doctors recommend Brand A margarine for cholesterol control than any other brand." **Does this represent a proper usage of marketing research findings?**

Scenario 3

A research supplier estimates that a study will cost $10,000 ± 10 percent. The client agrees that this price is reasonable. But when the study is completed, the research supplier submits a bill for $15,000, claiming that the cost increased because of changes the client wanted made during the course of the study. The client, while acknowledging that certain unplanned changes were made, argues that such changes should have cost no more than an additional $2,000.[2] **How should this problem be resolved?**

Scenario 4

"We're conducting a survey," reads a letter from the XYZ Survey Research Company. The survey will be sent to 10 million homes this year. The questionnaire asks for the respondents' preferences on consumer products plus demographic and personal information such as their names, addresses, telephone numbers, occupations, and family income. To improve respondent cooperation the sponsoring company offers free samples of various consumer products. What is not said is that the personal information as well as product choices that are collected will be compiled onto data tapes and sold to other marketers so they can promote their products.[3] **Is this ethical?**

Scenario 5

A marketing research firm conducted an attitude study for a client. The data indicate that the product is not being marketed properly. This finding is ill-received by the client's product management team. They request that the damaging data be omitted from the formal report—which will be widely distributed—on the grounds that the verbal presentation was adequate for the client's needs.[4] **What should the research firm do?**

Scenario 6

Automated polling devices are often placed in malls, airports, and other locations with substantial pedestrian traffic. The hardware includes a computer, monitor, and a keyboard. Through graphics, music, and a taped message, passers-by are attracted to these devices that invite participation in a self-administered survey. The results of these "polls" regularly appear in newspaper articles that analyze upcoming elections.[5] **Is this a proper use of marketing research?**

As these six scenarios show, a range of ethical dilemmas confront marketing research practitioners. The questions posed at the end of each vignette are not easy to answer. For example,

> Is it ethical to use fictitious names of research organizations to guard against possible respondent bias?

> How should cost overruns be handled between a research supplier and the client?

> Should the public receive information about the technical details of how a widely disseminated poll was conducted?

Possible ethical difficulties flowing from market research practices involve technical, managerial, and societal issues. Reseachers must also decide how to treat the respondent, client, and the general public *fairly* in discharging their duties. We return to these particular scenarios in the course of developing the specifics of the chapter.

Professionalism and Ethics

Within the marketing profession, researchers generally receive more academic training, especially in methodological and statistical techniques, than other marketing professionals. It is also commonly believed that a higher degree of professionalism exists within the research field, because the scientific method and objectivity are two of its hallmarks.

However, ethical issues *do* come into play in marketing research for two reasons.[6] First, marketing research often involves contact with the general public, usually through the use of surveys. Because this activity relies so heavily on information from the public—often including sensitive information—marketing research is open to abuse or misuse (see scenario 4 at the beginning of this chapter). Second, most marketing research is conducted by commercial (i.e., for-profit) firms as either independent research agencies or departments within corporations. The emphasis on the profit motive may cause researchers, their managers, or clients to occasionally *compromise* the objectivity or precision of the project. Throughout the chapter, we deal with the many instances where such compromises might occur.

Concern for ethics can benefit marketing research practitioners in several ways.[7] First, and probably most important, an ethical approach enhances the profession through the increased public acceptance of the marketing research process. This is essential if marketing research is to flourish, because the research community depends on candid and time-consuming responses from the public. A second benefit is that the thoughtful study of ethical problems can help improve market researchers' sensitivity and professionalism. Third, voluntarily maintaining high ethical standards can forestall negative publicity and restrictive government regulation. For example, the expanding use of computerized, random dialing for telephone calling along with computer-assisted questioning has led some state governments to consider licensing or disclosure requirements for researchers.

Duties and Obligations of Researchers

The dominant philosophical perspective that most observers seem to use in evaluating marketing research ethics is *absolute obligations* (i.e., the duty-based approach from Chapter 2). Since marketing research ought to be built on a foundation of professional conduct, this field is rooted in a set of obligations.[8] In addition to the obvious duties to one's client and respondents, the researcher also has a professional responsibility to uphold the integrity of the research process. The American Marketing Association (AMA) has developed a code for marketing research (see Appendix 3A) that contains normative guidelines for researchers. Among others, these include the duties to avoid misrepresentation of research methods and to identify a survey's sponsor.

Other approaches focus on the *rights of subjects* in the research process and the obligations of researchers, clients, and others involved in the research process.[9]

Kant's categorical imperative holds that rules of conduct should be applied universally. Marketing researchers ideally try to implement this approach. One experienced researcher offered the following rationale for rejecting more pragmatic utilitarian theories for evaluating ethics in marketing research: "Too often, we have taken the position that if our efforts don't really damage the consumer (respondent), they aren't really all that bad.... Let's be honest with ourselves; that is merely saying that the end justifies the means."[10]

Another philosophical perspective refers to the notion of *stakeholders*. Within marketing research, there are several publics that must be considered. They include respondents, clients, research firms, employees, and the general public. If one or more of these groups is harmed by the research process, the whole field of marketing research suffers. For example, in scenario 6 heading this chapter the polling results could possibly mislead the voting public and harm the credibility of the research profession.

The balance of this chapter examines in detail researchers' duties to their various stakeholders. We begin with ethical concerns emanating from the relationship of the researcher with the respondents and then move to interactions with clients. We also examine the researcher's responsibilities to the general public. Finally, we discuss the competitive intelligence gathering process and propose several ideas for ethical action aimed at enhancing the ethical posture of marketing researchers.

What Researchers Owe Respondents

A number of ethical concerns arise in the relationship between the researcher and respondent. A respondent could be an individual answering questions via a telephone or mail survey, personal interview or be a subject in experimental research. Exhibit 3–1 lists the most prevalent activities in this context that raise ethical questions. Dubious research tactics fall into three categories: deceptive practices, invasion of privacy, and lack of concern for respondents.[11] *Deceptive practices* occur when the researcher misrepresents the purpose of the research, the investigative procedures, or the use of the results. Some of these activities are illegal as well as unethical. *Invasion of privacy* is a sensitive issue and one that is becoming more complex with the growth of sophisticated technology. The practices listed under *lack of concern for the respondent* do not raise as serious a set of ethical concerns as the other two categories, but they represent a long-term threat as they shape public opinion against marketing research.

The Duty Not to Engage in Deceptive Practices

Exhibit 3–1 lists four major types of deceptive marketing research practices. The first involves *unrealized promises of anonymity*. Most survey research is predicated on the presumption that the respondent will remain anonymous and therefore

---

EXHIBIT 3–1   Ethical Concerns in the Researcher–Respondent Relationship

Deceptive Practices
Unrealized promise of anonymity

Falsified sponsor identification

Selling under the guise of research

Misrepresenting research procedures

   Questionnaire or interview length is intrusive

   Possible follow-up contacts

   Purpose of study

   Uses made of results

   Undelivered compensation (premiums, summaries of results)

Invasion of Privacy
Observation studies without informed consent

Use of controversial qualitative research techniques

Merging data from several sources

Overly personal questions and topics

Lack of Concern for Subjects or Respondents
Contacting respondents at inconvenient times

Incompetent or insensitive interviewers

Failure to debrief after deception or disguise

Research producing a depressing effect on respondents

Too frequent use of public in research and opinion polling

Nondisclosure of research procedures (length, follow-up, purpose, use)

Source: Adapted from Kenneth C. Schneider, "Ethics and Marketing Research." In *The Practice of Marketing Research*, by James E. Nelson, 594 (Boston: Kent, 1982).

can give his or her candid opinion. The use of invisible ink and other devices to trace specific respondents is considered to be unethical and unprofessional.

A second concern revolves around *falsified sponsor identification.* This happens when the researcher believes that the respondent's knowledge of the sponsor may bias the results. For example, would the users of radar detectors respond honestly to a survey conducted by the highway patrol? What some researchers do is to create fictitious names (like US Research Inc. or Public Opinion Institute as in scenario 1) to mask the identity of the firm doing the research. In a recent survey, only 30 percent of marketing researchers and marketing executives disapproved of this practice.[12] Even though this is a common and accepted practice in industry, it does raise ethical questions. A better approach, and one that the public finds more acceptable, is to hire an external consultant to conduct the research for the sponsor using the consultant's name.

A third area of potential respondent deception is *selling or fund raising under the guise of research.* In the trade, these techniques are called "sugging" and "frugging," respectively. Such tactics have received much criticism over the years and almost 40 percent of the population has been exposed to them (see Exhibit 3–2). In the business-to-business sector, both telephone and personal interviews have been used to generate leads for follow-up sales presentations. Also, mail surveys and even focus groups (see Exhibit 3–3) are sometimes utilized for this purpose. In recent years, fund raisers for nonprofit organizations and political parties have also borrowed this technique (also discussed in Exhibit 3–3). Researchers need to be aware of this practice and help suppress it because respondent experiences with these unscrupulous practices may decrease their willingness to participate in future legitimate research studies.

The fourth type of possible ethical concern between researcher and respondent in Exhibit 3–1 falls under the general title of *misrepresenting research procedures*. Part of the research challenge is selling the idea of participation to potential

---

EXHIBIT 3–2   Image of the Marketing Research Industry

Image of the Industry

	1980	1982	1984	1986	1990
Base: Representative Sample	500	499	495	500	510
	% Agreement with the Statement				
Negative Image Attributes					
Some questions asked in polls or research surveys are too personal	47	49	51	45[1]	47
The information obtained in polls or research surveys helps manufacturers sell consumers products they don't want or need	45	43	44	43	na[2]
The term "poll or research survey" is used to disguise a sales pitch	38	38	39	41	40
Polls or research surveys are an invasion of privacy	25	26	28	24	25
Answering questions in polls or research surveys is a waste of time	18	21	22	19	18
The true purpose of some surveys is not disclosed	68	65	61	68[1]	na[2]

Source: Walker Research, *Industry Image Study*[SM], 9th ed. (1990).
[1]Denotes significant difference from 1986 to 1984 at the 95% confidence level.
[2]Denotes data not available.

EXHIBIT 3–3   Sugging and Frugging in Marketing Research

Sugging

One attempt at selling under the guise of research is being undertaken by drug companies and their marketing research consultants that hire former drug salespeople as focus group moderators. The purpose of these focus group sessions is to brief physicians on the client's product and manipulate the discussion so as to positively influence their attitudes. During the interviews the physicians' concerns about the products are also noted. These focus groups are then followed up by a letter and personal call to the participating physicians who did not know the true purpose of the focus group interview. The physicians then become unwitting participants in this sales effort.

Frugging

The American Institute for Cancer Research (AICR), a legitimate Washington-based nonprofit organization, surveyed a large sample of consumers including one of the authors in 1990. The "Survey on Diet and Cancer" contained eleven questions including some about the incidence of smoking and drinking, the use of vitamins or mineral supplements, and about the family history of cancer. Near the bottom of the one page survey in bold capital letters was the phrase **CONTRIBUTION REPLY**. The respondent was asked to make a donation for either cancer research or the compilation of a statistical profile of the eating habits of Americans. The seven categories for contributions ranged from $5 to $500.

What is your evaluation of these situations? Are they ethical practices?

Source: For more information see *Marketing News* (August 29, 1988), 4.

respondents. If deception or false pretenses are used to gain their cooperation, several problems can occur. For example, if the researcher seriously understates the time it will take to complete the interview or survey, respondents are being purposely misled. At minimum, they may get irritated or become uncooperative. Similarly, other forms of deception (e.g., false promises about follow-up contact or lying about the true purpose of the study) can undermine the integrity of the research. The researcher, who cannot disclose some of this information (because it may bias the results), should say nothing rather than lie to the respondent. And promises regarding compensation to the respondent should always be kept.

The Duty Not to Invade Privacy

The right to privacy involves the right of respondents to decide for themselves how much they will share with others their thoughts, feelings, and the facts of their personal lives.[13] Exhibit 3–1 also depicts several research practices that have privacy implications. The US Privacy Act of 1974 was designed to protect individual privacy in data collection and storage by federal agencies. Personal privacy is a right protected by the Constitution and, therefore, legislators are sensitive to researchers violating this right.

One issue that pertains to respondent privacy is *observational studies without informed consent.* The general rule of thumb is that observation studies conducted in public places (e.g., specialty stores or supermarkets) are acceptable. When the behavior is observed in private or semi-private settings, ethical problems arise. For instance, it is generally considered to be unethical to videotape someone in a department-store dressing room to prevent shoplifting. Examples of questions with less clear answers are:

Is it ethical for researchers to sort through collected trash to measure the household consumption of liquor or other products?

Should researchers use electronic monitoring vans to tabulate television viewing habits without the consent of those whose sets are being monitored?[14]

The *use of qualitative or projective research techniques* also raises privacy issues. A projective technique is an indirect method of measuring an individual's personality characteristics, underlying motivations, or basic value structure. An example of such a research method would be having consumers fill in open-ended sentences. Sometimes researchers want to seek knowledge about a respondent's purchasing behavior that can only be gained through the use of projective techniques. Why? Because some consumers have difficulty expressing the reasons why they buy some products, toiletries for instance. In this way, unconscious buying motives can be uncovered.

In the marketing research profession the following standard seems operative: if there is no psychological or physical harm to the respondent, the research is considered acceptable. This has been labeled the "no harm, no foul" approach. It does require strict attention to anonymity and confidentiality, but does not demand informed consent. Essentially the perspective is that one's privacy cannot be invaded if one is unaware of the invasion and/or it causes no harm.[15] This conclusion does not, however, extend to observational studies in dressing rooms or other private locations. Another principle is to protect privacy with confidentiality. In other words, names, addresses, and telephone numbers should never be given to clients or others.

The *merging of data from several sources* has become a more important issue because of the extensive use of computerized lists for direct marketing purposes. Some firms in this business copy lists of especially good prospects from other sources of names. The Direct Marketing Association has developed a code of conduct to cover this practice, and some of the largest mail order firms such as L.L. Bean and Lands' End subscribe to a service that detects when their lists have been surreptitiously copied.[16]

The issue of *overly personal questions and topics* remains a sensitive one. While Exhibit 3–2 shows a declining percentage of people who consider some survey questions to be "too personal," the offended group still represents almost half of all respondents. Researchers studying social problems such as drug abuse and

AIDS are caught between the right to privacy on the one hand and the need for good data and honest opinions on the other. Financial institutions and marketers of highly personal products and practices (e.g., feminine hygiene products, condoms) must also be aware that any questions about their offerings may be perceived to be too personal by some respondents.

A final privacy issue pertains to the growing use of *computerized databases.* In a cover story entitled "Is Nothing Private?," *Business Week* examined the alarming growth of computerized information about almost all US citizens. Credit bureaus were singled out as the assemblers of much of this information. Too often it was then sold to credit-card companies or other businesses. One informed observer commented, "For very little cost, anybody can learn anything about anybody."[17] Government policy makers as well as industry sources are studying this problem. (See Exhibit 3–4 for a discussion of a controversy about privacy and consumer databases.)

EXHIBIT 3–4   The Lotus Marketplace Database

A controversy regarding privacy occurred when Lotus Development Corp. teamed up with Equifax, the Atlanta-based credit reporting agency, to develop a new computer software, called Marketplace: Household. This product contained a set of eleven databases that included the names, addresses, age ranges, genders, marital status, dwelling types, and neighborhood incomes of 80 million US households. The developers contended that consumers' privacy was protected by not including telephone numbers, individual credit data, purchase history, actual income, and age.

The concern over the Lotus package resulted from its availability and affordability. The software gave small businesses information about desired demographics and specific consumers' names and addresses. This information was previously limited to the largest and most affluent corporations for one-time use only. The issue here seemed to stem, not from the level of detail, but rather the availability of this information for direct marketing usage without consumers' knowledge.

Strong public opposition, led by the American Civil Liberties Union and Computer Professionals for Social Responsibility, caused the firms to withdraw the product in early 1991. The computer group opposed the product because it "contained a great deal of information that had been obtained without the consent of the people that were listed." An additional concern was that it would not be easy enough for consumers to delete their data, or correct any inaccuracies. Lotus received 30,000 complaints and was worried about adverse publicity if Marketplace: Household were retained.

Is the collection of this type of information and development of such a database unethical?

Source: Developed by the authors from K. J. Means, "The Business of Ethics and the Ethics of Business," *AMS News* (January 1991), 6–7 and Cyndee Miller, "Lotus Forced to Cancel New Software Program," *Marketing News* (February 18, 1991), 11 and William W. Miller, "Lotus Is Likely to Abandon Consumer-Data Project," *The Wall Street Journal* (January 23, 1991), B1.

The overall issue is one of freedom of consumer information versus the right to privacy. Researchers must be more cognizant of potential privacy abuses in the future and establish and enforce acceptable marketing practices regarding privacy. One observer commented that all the discussion about privacy may:

> stir thought within the professional community about how important the respondent–researcher relationship is and how it may be jeopardized by the unethical use of information under the guise of new and better technology. And with that thought, there may come a plan for merging the miracles of modern machinery with some good old-fashioned morals if not for goodness' sakes, for business sake.[18]

The Duty to Manifest Concern for Respondents

The list of ethical concerns for this category (Exhibit 3–1) does not demand as much attention as some of the other issues examined above. Most of these areas fall under the "good business practice" rubric. The failure to debrief respondents may lead to individuals becoming suspicious of all research and, as a result, they may refuse or even attempt to subvert future research projects. Furthermore, confusing questions, poorly trained interviewers, hard-to-read questionnaires, and other factors that place an unnecessary burden on respondents should be avoided. When respondents agree to give the researcher their time and energy, it is the researcher's responsibility to minimize their burden.

As a summary point on the researcher–respondent relationship, there are usually several avenues to approaching these potential problem areas, so that the research can be conducted ethically. The choice is not to be either unethical or abandon the study. Rather, what should be done is to identify "ethical alternatives to questionable research practices and urge their immediate adoption."[19]

What Researchers and Clients Owe One Another

The relationship between the researcher and the client presents a number of potential ethical issues. Exhibit 3–5 shows three categories where ethical abuse may occur: in the research design, in the researcher's responsibility to the client, and in the client's responsibility to the researcher.[20]

Forthright Research Designs

Ethical issues may arise at any stage of the research design. Problem definition is the first stage in the process. It is often an arduous undertaking in many marketing research situations and the researcher has an ethical obligation to help clients to define precisely the problem they hope to solve. One result may be that research is unnecessary (see Exhibit 3–5). For example, the researcher may suggest to a fast-food client that a survey is needed when secondary information (like a

EXHIBIT 3–5   **Ethical Concerns in the Researcher–Client Relationship**

Abuse of Research Design or Methodology or Results

    Conducting unnecessary research

    Researching wrong or irrelevant problems

    Use of unwarranted shortcuts to secure contract or save expenses

    Misrepresenting limitations of research design

    Inappropriate analytical techniques

    Lack of sufficient expertise to conduct required research

    Overly technical language in research report

    Overstating validity or reliability of conclusions

Researcher Abuse of Researcher-Client Relationship

    Overbilling the project

Failure to maintain client confidentiality

Failure to avoid possible conflict of interest

Client Abuse of Researcher-Client Relationship

    Inappropriate use of research proposals

    Disclosure or use of the researcher's specialized techniques and models

    Cancellation of project (or refusal to pay) without cause

    Conducting research solely to support *a priori* conclusions

    Failure to act upon dangerous or damaging findings

Source: Adapted from Kenneth C. Schneider, "Ethics and Marketing Research." In *The Practice of Marketing Research*, by James E. Nelson, 608 (Boston: Kent, 1982).

simple traffic count already compiled by a regional planning authority) might suffice. For more guidance on the topic of protection from unnecessary research, see also Exhibit 3–6.

Another common problem is that the research method may cost more than the client wants to pay. Similarly, implementation of the research may be more expensive than originally proposed. What should the researcher do? Too often the researcher just scales back the design, sometimes to the point where it is methodologically suspect. In other words, the redesigned research project really doesn't meaningfully answer the necessary questions. For instance, reducing the sample size or number of interviews by one half to meet budgetary restrictions may result in findings that do not meet the accuracy requirements of the client. Similarly, not using proper respondent verification procedures or not adequately pretesting a new questionnaire are other common shortcuts.[21]

We believe that the researcher should try to convince the client to spend more in the first place or admit to the client at the earliest possible point in the study that it will cost more to do it right. Researchers should *not* wait until after the

EXHIBIT 3–6   What About Unnecessary Research?

Researchers are frequently requested to engage in a specific research project that is unrelated to the underlying problem, has been done before, or is economically unjustified. The researcher can often benefit from such an activity. This gain will frequently exceed whatever goodwill might be generated by refusing to conduct unwarranted research. **Should the researcher accept such assignments?**

This issue is not addressed in the American Marketing Association code of ethics. However, it seems to us that the researcher has a professional obligation to indicate to the client that, in his or her judgment, the research expenditure is not warranted. If, after this judgment has been clearly stated, the client still desires the research, the researcher should feel free to conduct the study. The reason for this is that the researcher can never know for certain the risk preferences and strategies that are guiding the client's behavior.

Source: Donald L. Tull and Del I. Hawkins, "Ethical Issues in Marketing Research." In *Marketing Research: Measurement and Method*, 5th ed., 730 (New York: Macmillan, 1990).

project has already been completed, as was discussed in scenario 3 at the beginning of this chapter. If the client is informed of the impact of scalebacks on validity *and* the research provides the best possible project for the price, the ethical concern is probably satisfied. Alternatively, the researcher might be prepared to sacrifice some profit to do the project right, much as physicians do when they treat low-income patients at lower rates.

Other points in the first section of Exhibit 3–5 deal with the expertise of the researcher. A client hires a researcher to secure professional expertise. Thus, issues regarding limitations of certain research designs (e.g., although experiments can best measure cause and effect, they may be too artificial) and use of sophisticated analytical techniques often present researchers with ethical dilemmas. For instance, researchers often must make judgments on how much methodological and analytical detail to share with clients. One area where researchers may let monetary considerations cloud their professional judgment pertains to a situation where they lack the expertise to conduct the required study. For example, a firm specializing in focus groups may take on a client who would best be served by telephone interviews rather than referring that client to another firm. An additional point here is that researchers should *not* try to "snow" clients with excessively technical jargon in the report and presentation. Ultimately, such tactics backfire because clients may get the impression that the researcher is trying to hide other inadequacies of the research (even if none exist).

A final ethical issue in research design is the *overstatement of conclusions*. To please the client (and possibly secure future contracts), the researcher sometimes presents conclusions in the most positive light. For example, a consumer satisfaction study might report the fact that 70 percent of the respondents viewed the product favorably, while downplaying the 20 percent of the users who were strongly dissatisfied with the product. Design and methodological abuses are not only often unethical, but also represent poor long-term marketing strategy.[22] Therefore, marketing researchers should avoid these dubious practices.

Researcher Responsibility to Clients

The second section of Exhibit 3–5 lists three areas where researchers may abuse their relationship with the client. One practice is *overbilling the client*. This can be contrasted with the two usual forms of pricing by research firms—cost-plus pricing and market pricing. Most research agencies practice the first type of pricing where the costs allocated to a particular study are determined and a percentage markup is added for administrative overhead and profit. The market-oriented method attempts to determine the market value of the research to the client; thus, more critical studies are pegged to going market price and researchers bid for these studies at a higher level. Overbilling for research, however it is done, is somewhat analogous to "price gouging" (see discussion in Chapter 5). A number of specific practices fall into this category, including building in extra overhead, charging for senior researchers' time when the work is done by junior persons, falsifying hours worked, and adding an override to subcontractors' work. These practices are unethical because overbilling is not tied to either costs or potential payoffs to the client.

Confidentiality and *conflict of interest* are two concerns that marketing researchers must commonly address. The identity of a sponsoring firm should not be divulged to respondents or other existing or potential clients, unless the firm allows it. For instance, letting a respondent or another client know who is funding the study is a breach of the researcher's professional ethics and is covered in most codes (see number 2 in the section on research practitioners of the AMA code in Appendix 3A).

Conflict of interest is a growing concern especially with the increasing specialization of some marketing research firms. Some researchers are now such specialists that they focus almost exclusively on narrow topics such as political polling, hospital-patient satisfaction surveys, or image studies for financial institutions. These specialized firms must take great care, especially in this era when there are fewer potential clients because of mergers, that they do not work for two competing companies.

There is also a temptation to inappropriately use one client's methodologies for another. We do think that similar survey instruments might be used (as long as each client is not charged for the development of the instrument), but research firms must be careful not to seek out direct competitors for their services. For example, a Northeastern advertising and research agency that worked with Lotus software solicited Microsoft with the following: "You probably haven't thought about talking to an agency in Boston. . . . But since we know your competition's plans, isn't it worth taking a flier?"[23] They went on to say that several of their employees had worked on the Lotus account at another agency and were familiar with Mirosoft's competitive software product. Microsoft shared this information with Lotus, which won a restraining order barring the agency from revealing trade secrets and pitching any other competitors.

The Client's Responsibility to the Researcher

This area represents the flip side of the previous discussion. The client also has a responsibility to act ethically in dealing with the research supplier. Soliciting proposals from several suppliers just to get free advice on how to solve a particular problem or in order to combine their approaches to develop an in-house study would constitute unethical behavior by the potential client. Exhibit 3–5 also lists other areas where clients may abuse their relationship with the researcher. Clients should obviously not disclose or try to use proprietary techniques that are not their own. Delaying payment for services or canceling standing contracts can cause serious financial and organizational problems for the research firm.

The misrepresentation of findings by the client can also lead to problems for the researcher. For example, a colleague was involved in a taste test to determine whether consumers preferred potato chips made with corn oil or vegetable shortening. The vast majority of respondents could not tell the difference. Of those who were consistent in their preferences, a small, statistically insignificant, majority chose corn oil (the product of the client). The promotional campaign based on this research stated "In a scientific test more consumers prefer potato chips made with corn oil." This claim is a clear distortion of the findings (similar to scenario 2 above). The reputation of the research firm can be damaged if its name were used in the advertising, as the message receiver would likely be misled. Situations like these can happen and have ramifications not only within the researcher–client relationship but also with the public at large.

What Researchers Owe the Public

The general public is a relevant stakeholder in the practice of marketing research. Much so-called research is disseminated to the public through advertising (e.g., through slogans such as "three out of four doctors recommend"), political polling results (e.g., exit interviews), and other "pseudo polls" (e.g., 900 number telephone voting). The inaccurate use of marketing research can lead to false impressions by the public. For example, scenario 6 (at the outset of this chapter) discusses an example of unethical marketing research, where the public is likely misled by these poll results.

Marketing research practices that deceive the public undermine the whole enterprise. The consequences of unethical research endeavors for the general public and policy makers are captured in the three points below. Such inaccurate or untrue market research:

- impairs legitimate research activities by diminishing the public's willingness to participate in survey research. This affects response rates, statistical reliability, and ultimately response quality.
- distorts policy makers' perceptions of public opinion and business-related issues. Dangerous feedback can result if policy makers misread consumer sentiment because of invalid research procedures.
- confounds the public's ability to distinguish valid from invalid research findings. Deceptive polls as well as the inconsistent and contradictory results that they provide may render the public indifferent, confused, or distrustful of what they read, see, or hear from survey research. At best, this results in widespread miseducation.[24]

Specific manifestations of these practices involve incomplete and misleading reporting, and nonobjective research.[25]

Incomplete Reporting

A problem can occur when the researcher leaves out relevant information in a report that is circulated to the general public. For example, some companies conduct test markets and publicize these results in the trade press. What is sometimes omitted is that some firms choose to conduct test markets in areas where their distribution or reputation is particularly strong. Therefore, the results of the test market are probably skewed in the favorable direction.

There are positive developments tempering these practices that may lead to less incomplete reporting in the future. For instance, we applaud the relatively recent practice of major publications such as *The Wall Street Journal* to provide, via a boxed insert, information with their polling results on how the sample was drawn and respondents contacted. Although many readers may consider this information superfluous, it provides those interested with a basis to judge the limitations and scientific validity of the poll. Furthermore, the Public Affairs Council of the Advertising Research Foundation (ARF) has published *Guidelines for the Public Use of Market and Opinion Research* that cover the origin, design, execution, and candor of the research conducted.

Misleading Reporting

This practice involves presenting research results in such a way that the intended audience will draw an unjustified conclusion. Misleading reporting sometimes happens when research findings are used in advertising campaigns. This can be a particular problem in comparative advertising. For instance, a comparative cigarette ad claimed that "an amazing 60 percent" of a sample of consumers said that Triumph cigarettes tasted "as good as or better" than Merit. This was an accurate statement of the results, but many of the respondents said that the brands tasted "as good as." Therefore, the results *also indicated* that 64 percent said that Merit tasted as good as or better than Triumph. This presentation of results likely misled a substantial portion of the public. The guidelines developed by the ARF can guard against this type of misleading reporting.

Nonobjective Research

In many instances the general public is not in a good position to judge whether research is conducted objectively. Understandably, they rely on overall percentages and often read only the headlines of an ad rather than studying how the research was undertaken. A potentially serious problem is using *leading questions* and then promoting the results to the public. For example, Burger King once used the responses to the following question to justify the claim that its method of cooking hamburgers was preferred over McDonald's: "Do you prefer your hamburgers flame-broiled or fried?" Another researcher asked a rephrased question on the same topic ("Do you prefer a hamburger that is grilled on a hot stainless-steel grill or cooked by passing the raw meat through an open gas flame?") and found McDonald's to be preferred over Burger King.[26] The upshot is that who you ask and how you phrase the question often determines the results. Viewers of commercials that make claims often assume a research objectivity that doesn't exist.

The researcher, then, has an obligation to warn management in advance of any presumed nonobjective aspects of a proposed research project, especially if the results are to be disseminated to the public. In the final report, the researcher should also clearly stipulate any effects of research bias. For instance, there may be some question about undersampling certain minority groups. Managers should then use these data cautiously, not like the cigarette and hamburger examples detailed above.

Corporate Intelligence Gathering

Corporate intelligence entails gathering information about competitors, rather than consumers. It ranges from the illegal activity of industrial espionage to the acceptable, and universally used, practice of utilizing salespeople to monitor competitors' public actions in the field. Much greater attention and emphasis was placed on intelligence gathering as competition heated up in virtually all industries during the 1980s. Furthermore, just as there are massive amounts of information about consumers stored on computerized databases, so too are there detailed computerized records of company sales, number of employees, plant dollar volume, and so forth. Companies that have instituted formal intelligence programs include many well known firms such as Digital Equipment, Eastman Kodak, General Electric, Gillette, and Wang Laboratories.

The whole area of intelligence gathering has earned a bad name because of certain dubious and even illegal tactics employed by some firms. For instance, a few companies have been known to buy their competitors' garbage from the trash hauler in order to sift through it for morsels of pungent information. Some marketers stage phony job interviews to pump information from competitors' unsuspecting employees. Others have instructed executives (using disguised names or positions) to take tours of their competitors' plants to get details of manufacturing processes and outputs. In fact, when Kelloggs ceased offering their popular public tours at the Battle Creek, Michigan plant in the late 1980s, one of the reasons they gave for abandoning the practice was that competitors were snooping on their manufacturing technology. One observer remarked that: "In the rush for competitive intelligence, business ethics are taking a beating."[27]

There are very legitimate reasons for corporate intelligence gathering. First, executives should take advantage of information that is publicly available so as not to neglect their fiduciary duty to shareholders and other stakeholders (see Exhibit 3–7). For example, Cordis Corporation, a Miami-based pacemaker manufacturer, introduced a new line of products that was superior to others available on the market. When sales did not improve and even worsened in some territories, sales reps were asked to investigate the tactics of the competition. They found that physicians were being offered cars, boats, and lavish junkets to stay with the other pacemakers. Cordis responded by increasing educational support for doctors, adding more salespeople and, in a few instances, even matching the giveaways with equipment related to pacemakers. The result was a dramatic increase in sales.[28]

EXHIBIT 3–7   Obtaining Competitive Information at Hewlett–Packard

Methods

HP must be well informed of competitive developments and is entitled to review all pertinent public information concerning competitive products (e.g., published specifications and prices and trade journal articles). However, HP may not attempt through improper means to acquire a competitor's trade secrets or other proprietary or confidential information, including information as to facilities, manufacturing capacity, technical developments, or customers. Improper means include industrial espionage, inducing a competitor's present or former personnel to disclose confidential information, and any other means that are not open and aboveboard. HP must not use consultants to acquire information by improper methods.

Confidential Material

HP employees should not receive or examine any information about competitive proposals or products submitted on a closed bid basis or under other circumstances indicating the information should be kept confidential.

HP employees must be especially alert to the risks of receiving confidential information from customers who are competitors with other HP product lines. Confidential disclosure agreements with competitors may not be signed without first consulting with HP's legal department.

Source: Hewlett–Packard, "Standards of Business Conduct," (1989), 12.

A second reason for gathering competitive intelligence is as a basis for strategic planning. Companies find, sometimes the hard way, that strategic planning cannot be conducted in a competitive vaccuum by staff people. Michael Porter, the Harvard Business School expert in strategy, popularized this notion with his acclaimed books—*Competitive Strategy* and *Competitive Advantage*.[29] Gathering accurate information about competitors is now a must for devising a good strategy. This heightened interest spawned an industry of corporate intelligence consultants and seminars. (The dirty tricks even invaded the snoopers themselves when one intelligence seminar director found a competitor who conducted similar seminars enrolled in his course under an assumed name. On another occasion his lecture notes and source book were stolen.)[30]

Third, corporate intelligence is necessary in order to be successful against global competitors. Japanese companies have long been acknowledged as expert intelligence gatherers. They have deployed "armies of engineers and marketing specialists to gather mountains of information on American manufacturing techniques, product design, and technology."[31] Many US-based firms, imitating their Japanese counterparts, are disassembling or "benchmarking" Japanese products (e.g., Xerox does it with Canon copiers), enter into joint ventures to get information on Japanese manufacturing techniques (e.g., GM and Toyota), or set up offices in Japan for the purpose of finding out what companies are doing there.

Fourth, intelligence gathering can be quite useful in the introduction of a new product. Marriott sent employees to carefully check out rival chains' rooms and services. They also interviewed competitors' executives in preparation for the launch of its Fairfield Inn economy motel unit. Coors did extensive chemical analysis on Gallo's wine coolers to determine what wine and flavorings were inside. They then went to suppliers and got the price of the ingredients. The upshot was that Coors could not compete on price.[32]

How To Discourage It

Companies cannot prevent their competitors from getting a certain amount of information about them. However, they can guard against "loose lips" and inadvertent slips that may divulge confidential data. Corporate training programs should emphasize the importance of confidentiality and specify the type of information that is considered classified. All employees, including secretaries and even summer interns, should receive such training. Furthermore, corporate codes should spell out company policies for this area. The IBM and Xerox codes explicitly deal with the unintentional disclosure of proprietary information.

Stories are legion concerning recruiters from competitors finding out valuable information from short-term or permanent workers because the current or former employees did not know they should *not* be talking about certain things. Furthermore, buyers, purchasing agents, scientists, and engineers should be instructed that certain subjects are "off limits" when they attend trade shows, seminars, and professional meetings. On the other side, employees should be advised about what *not* to do in obtaining competitor information. The watchword for companies concerned about this area is *education* of all employees.

How To Do It—Ethically

Exhibit 3–8 shows a list of eighteen sources of competitive information. They are ranked by an expert in terms of their ethical and legal ramifications. We think this is a good list for companies to follow, because it gives explicit guidance on what activities are acceptable. One source of public information not listed is help-wanted advertising. These ads can offer a wealth of information on competitors' intentions, strategies, and sometimes even planned products. For example, one major hotel chain gave advance notice of a nationwide telemarketing effort by advertising for telephone sales people. Salesreps also should be trained to seek out competitive information as part of their daily activities. One source advised companies to "be patient" in setting up a competitive intelligence system and not to expect payoffs for several years.[33]

Other technical staffers such as engineers and scientists need to be alert to publicly available competitive information at professional meetings or in scien-

---

EXHIBIT 3–8   The Wade System for Judging of Sources of Information[1]

Ethical

1. Published material and public documents such as court records.
2. Disclosures made by competitor's employees, and obtained without subterfuge.
3. Market surveys and consultant's reports.
4. Financial reports and brokers' research reports.
5. Trade fairs, exhibits, and competitor's brochures.
6. Analysis of competitor's products.
7. Legitimate employment interviews with people who worked for competitor.

Arguably Unethical

8. Camouflaged questioning and "drawing out" of competitor's employees at technical meeting.
9. Direct observation under secret conditions.

10. False job interviews with competitor's employee (i.e., where there is no real intent to hire.)
11. Hiring a professional investigator to obtain a specific piece of information.
12. Hiring an employee away from the competitor, to get specific know-how.

Illegal

13. Trespassing on competitor's property.
14. Bribing competitor's supplier or employee.
15. "Planting" your agent on competitor's payroll.
16. Eavesdropping on competitors (e.g., via wire-tapping).
17. Theft of drawings, samples, documents, and similar property.
18. Blackmail and extortion.

Source: Adapted from Worth Wade, *Industrial Espionage and Mis-Use of Trade Secrets* (Ardmore, PA: Advance House, 1965).
[1]The numbers in the list are ranked in descending degrees of ethicality or legality.

tific journals. The bottom line here is that the strategically competent organization must gather such information, but from an ethical perspective. Deception should not be part of the corporate intelligence gathering process. The practices listed in the lower two thirds of Exhibit 3–8 are definitely inappropriate.

What ethical strictures are being violated by these corporate intelligence gathering practices? We believe that the principles of honesty and fairness (discussed in Chapter 2) are two important ethical precepts that companies engaging in these practices tend to ignore. Furthermore, playing the intelligence game *fairly* is one of the absolute obligations of ethical marketing executives. We also would urge marketers to evaluate intelligence gathering efforts using a virtue ethics perspective (also discussed in Chapter 2). That is, managers should decide what their organization *should be* and whether engaging in corporate intelligence gathering is consistent with the underlying values of their firm.

Ideas For Ethical Action

First, marketing researchers should establish ground rules and let these ethical research standards be known to the people and firms with which they deal. To counteract many of the potential problems between researcher and client, it is essential that both sides understand one other. One researcher offered the following advice to maintain and increase integrity in the research profession.

> Put things in writing.
>
> Don't be afraid to face up to clients with issues and cost problems.
>
> Try to maintain open communication and promote regular feedback to the people with whom you interact.
>
> Don't be an ostrich. We are members of a profession, and we owe it to that profession to support ethical behavior by its practitioners.[34]

These sage words emphasize the necessity of researchers and clients to use formal contracts to spell out details of the research. However, the contract should not be viewed as a straightjacket; mechanisms should be put in place to alter or amend it with the agreement of both parties.

Regarding the client's responsibility to the researcher (recall Exhibit 3–5), most of the same principles hold. If clients abuse their relationship with research suppliers, it will damage their reputation in the research community and may even preclude their finding reputable research firms to work with them in the future. To guard against such abuses, the Council of American Survey Research Organizations has developed a set of guidelines that should be used to evaluate research proposals (see Exhibit 3–9). We suggest that clients inform prospective research firms that they will follow these guidelines *before* research proposals are submitted.

EXHIBIT 3–9   **Guidelines for the Selection of a Research Firm's Proposal**

If more than one research firm is asked to submit a proposal, the prospective client should indicate how the successful proposal will be determined. Factors that might be used to determine the contractor selected could include

1. Understanding of how the results of the research will be used.
2. Recognition of the types of resources that will be useful.
3. Ability to provide the necessary information, that is, personnel, facilities, equipment, and so on.

4. Relevant experience of the research firm.
5. Background/experience of individuals who will be assigned to the work.
6. Recognition of the limitations of the research.
7. Specificity, with respect to procedures to be used, can and should be outlined in detail prior to the beginning of the work.
8. Cost of services.
9. Statement of commitment to follow ethical and professional procedures at all times.

Source: Code of Business Practices, Council of American Survey Research Organizations (CASRO).

Second, researchers should treat respondents, clients, competitors, and the public using ethical, not just legal or competitive, criteria. Most marketing researchers understand that it is in their best interest to treat these stakeholders fairly. What sometimes happens in the pressures of day-to-day activities is that researchers use the "everyone else does it" excuse to condone questionable behavior (e.g., creating a fictitious research name when calling customers). Or they trot out the age old argument that "if it is legal, it is okay." We believe that researchers should be held to high, professional standards. Therefore, ethical criteria should be used in evaluating researchers. For instance, in focus group research a mutual trust should exist between the moderator, the client and research facility. Furthermore, the moderator and participants should treat each other in an honest and straightforward manner.[35]

A recent study examined the frequency of stated moral values in the codes of five large marketing research professional organizations.[36] (See Exhibit 3–10.) What is surprising is that some values, like not harming others, justice and non-discrimination, are *not* mentioned in several of these codes. There does seem to be some consensus, however, that non-deception of others and promise keeping are universally important.

Not all researchers may be that interested or familiar with the moral values shown in Exhibit 3–10. They may say that they don't have the time to understand the nuances of moral philosophy or determine the sometimes subtle differences in these values. What we would say to them is that there are thumbnail rules (covered in Chapter 1) that could be easily used by researchers to evaluate the ethical dimension of any decision. One we would recommend is the TV test. That

EXHIBIT 3–10   Core Moral Values As Ranked in Research Associations' Codes

Values*	Advertising Research Foundation	American Marketing Association	Council of American Survey Research Organizations	Marketing Research Association	Qualitative Research Council of America
Non-deception	1	1	2	2	
Keeping promises	2		1	1	2
Serving others		2**	3	3**	1
Not harming others				3**	3
Justice		2**			
Other values	3				

Source: Stephen B. Castleberry and Warren French, "The Ethical Framework of Advertising/Marketing Research Practitioners: A Moral Development Perspective," working paper, (August 1991), Figure 2.
*An adoption of the values proposed by G. J. Warnock, *The Object of Morality* (London: Methuen & Co., 1971) and W. D. Ross, *The Right and the Good* (Oxford: The Clarendon Press, 1930).
**Refers to a tied rank.

is, would researchers be comfortable being interviewed on television about the decisions they had made at work that day. For instance, would the research managers in the companies discussed in scenarios 3 and 4 heading this chapter believe their decisions would pass this test? Or, is the public being treated fairly by researchers conducting polls such as those in scenario 6?

Finally, the **professionalization** *of marketing research is imperative.* We end this chapter as we began it—discussing marketing research as a profession. There are several reasons why the practice of conducting marketing research can be considered a profession. For example, the existence of a code of ethics, a recognized body of knowledge, the use of the scientific method and the presumed objectivity of researchers—are all hallmarks of a profession. However, enough issues have surfaced in the preceding pages that might cause one to pause. In fact, a former president of the American Marketing Association, himself a marketing research practitioner, insightfully assessed the status of the marketing research profession and said strongly that: ". . . we must do everything in our power, both individually and collectively, to purge our ranks of persons involved in unethical, unscrupulous, and illegal behavior."[37]

We would like to advance three proposals to enhance professionalism in marketing research. First, we advocate the designation of *Certified Public Researchers* (CPRs), analogous to CPAs or CFAs, to audit the validity and accuracy of marketing research numbers used in public forums (e.g., in advertising claims, political polls reported in the media, or in legal/regulatory proceedings). This idea was proposed by a prominent member of the research community several years ago.[38] Two reasons were given why such verification is needed: (1) the public is being asked, more and more, to accept the accuracy of marketing research, and (2) there are a substantial number of managers (especially in the government and nonprofit sectors) who know little about the validity of marketing research but are using the results for important policy and decision making. Although the issue of certification is controversial, it is worth exploring.[39]

Second, the major marketing research professional organizations should work together in revising their codes to make them more useful for their members. It is our understanding that such a joint effort among the Advertising Research Foundation, American Marketing Association, Council of American Survey Research Organizations, Marketing Research Association, and Qualitative Research Consultants of America has begun. They hope to come out with baseline recommendations on a model code that are useful for all these associations. Another noteworthy event is the formation of the National Association for Ethical Research which hopes to establish an "honor code" for the profession. Potentially, an "honor roll" of exemplary practitioners could serve as an arbiter in problem situations that arise between researchers and clients or other researchers.[40]

There are a couple cautionary notes we want to voice concerning codes. Revisions to the code should follow the guidelines elaborated upon in Chapter 10. And enforcement is essential. Unless sanctions exist—even if they simply consist of publicizing questionable behavior—the efforts at enhancing professionalism in marketing research will be in vain. Another factor revolves around the realization that the research community is not a homogeneous group. There are many different types of researchers, from the junior corporate analyst to the high level consultant who only interacts with CEOs. Their ethical concerns regarding research are varied. Thus, professional associations should try to tailor not only the code, but also programs on ethics they might sponsor for their divergent constituencies.

Finally, education in marketing research should place a higher priority on professionalism. Both at the university level and within the vast continuing education empire, teachers of research methods need to stress the importance of a strong ethical posture so that researchers view themselves as professionals and not "hired guns." If those educated in research had the feeling they were truly professionals and embraced the concomitant responsibilities of professionalism, many of the problems discussed above would cease to exist.

Conclusion

This chapter captures some of the many and varied ethical issues facing practicing marketing researchers. Researchers have several obligations to respondents, clients, and the public. Likewise, clients also owe potential researchers a sense of fairness. Obviously, not all situations are covered here, but the research firm conscious of its ethical posture should establish appropriate ground rules and ethical standards for the firm. In the next chapter we turn our attention to ethical issues in marketing management. Here, the area of product management presents another set of ethical challenges.

Appendix 3A

Marketing Research Code of Ethics of the American Marketing Association

The American Marketing Association, in furtherance of its central objective of the advancement of science in marketing and in recognition of its obligation to the public, has established these principles of ethical practice of marketing research for the guidance of its members. In an increasingly complex society, marketing management is more and more dependent upon marketing information that is intelligently and systematically obtained. The consumer is the source of much of this information. Seeking the cooperation of the consumer in the development of information, marketing management must acknowledge its obligation to protect the public from misrepresentation and exploitation under the guise of research. Similarly, the research practitioner has an obligation to the discipline and to those who provide support for it—an obligation to adhere to basic and commonly accepted standards of scientific investigation as they apply to the domain of marketing research.

For Research Users, Practitioners, and Interviewers

1. No individual or organization will undertake any activity that is directly or indirectly represented to be marketing research, but that has as its real purpose the attempted sales of merchandise or services to some or all of the respondents interviewed in the course of the research.

2. If respondents have been led to believe, directly or indirectly, that they are participating in a marketing research survey and that their anonymity will be protected, their names shall not be made known to anyone outside the research organization or research department, or used for other than research purposes.

For Research Practitioners

1. There will be no intentional or deliberate misrepresentation of research methods or results. An adequate description of methods employed will be made available upon request to the sponsor of the research. Evidence that fieldwork has been completed according to specifications will, upon request, be made available to buyers of the research.

2. The identity of the survey sponsor and/or the ultimate client for whom a survey is being done will be held in confidence at all times, unless this identity is to be revealed as part of the research design. Research information shall be held in confidence by the research organization or department and not used for personal gain or made available to any outside party unless the client specifically authorizes such release.

3. A research organization shall not undertake marketing studies for competitive clients when such studies would jeopardize the confidential nature of client–agency relationships.

For Users of Marketing Research

1. A user of research shall not knowingly disseminate conclusions from a given research project or service that are inconsistent with or not warranted by the data.

2. To the extent that there is involved in a research project a unique design involving techniques, approaches, or concepts not commonly available to research practitioners, the prospective user of research shall not solicit such a design from one practitioner and deliver it to another for execution without the approval of the design originator.

For Field Interviewers

1. Research assignments and materials received, as well as information obtained from respondents, shall be held in confidence by the interviewer and revealed to no one except the research organization conducting the marketing study.

2. No information gained through a marketing research activity shall be used, directly or indirectly, for the personal gain or advantage of the interviewer.

3. Interviews shall be conducted in strict accordance with specifications and instructions received.

4. An interviewer shall not carry out two or more interviewing assignments simultaneously, unless authorized by all contractors or employers concerned.

Members of the American Marketing Association will be expected to conduct themselves in accordance with the provisions of this code in all of their marketing research activities.

Source: Reprinted with permission from the American Marketing Association, Chicago, IL 60606.

Endnotes

1. This vignette and the one that follows are adapted from Donald S. Tull and Del I. Hawkins, "Ethical Issues in Marketing Research." Chap. 23 *Marketing Research: Measurement and Method.* 5th ed. (New York: Macmillan, 1990).

2. A. Parasuraman, *Marketing Research* (Reading, MA: Addison–Wesley, 1986), 57.

3. William R. Dillon, Thomas J. Madden and Neil H. Firtle, *Marketing Research in a Marketing Environment,* 2nd ed. (Homewood, IL: Irwin, 1990), 41.

4. Charles Weinberg, "Ethical Dilemmas in Marketing Research." In *Marketing Challenges: Cases and Exercises,* 2nd ed., by C. H. Lovelock and C. B. Weinberg, (New York: McGraw Hill, 1988), 452.

5. Advertising Research Foundation, "Phony or Misleading Polls," ARF Position Paper, (September 1986).

6. Kenneth C. Schneider, "Ethics and Marketing Research." In *The Practice of Marketing Research*, by James E. Nelson, 591 (Boston, MA: Kent Publishing Company, 1982).

7. See note 1 above.

8. Steven J. Skinner, Alan J. Dubinsky and O. C. Ferrell, "Organizational Dimensions of Marketing Research Ethics," *Journal of Business Research* 16 (1988), 214–215.

9. Alice M. Tybout and Gerald Zaltman, "Ethics in Marketing Research: Their Practical Relevance," *Journal of Marketing Research* (November 1974), 357–368, and pp. 54–58 in the reference in note 1 above.

10. A. B. Blankenship, "Point of View: Consumerism and Consumer Research," *Journal of Advertising Research* (August 1971), 45.

11. See note 6 above.

12. Ishmael P. Akaah and Edward A. Riordan, "Judgments of Marketing Professionals about Ethical Issues in Marketing Research: A Replication and Extension," *Journal of Marketing Research* (February 1989), 112–120.

13. See note 1 above.

14. See note 6 above, p. 602.

15. See note 1 above.

16. Marvin Schwartz, "List Usage Ethics and Marketing Opportunity in Merge/Purge," *Direct Marketing* (August 1987), 52–59. See also Karl Zetmeir, "Privacy vs. Need to Know," *Direct Marketing* (April 1988), 40–41.

17. Jeffrey Rothfeder et al., "Is Nothing Private?," *Business Week* (September 4, 1989), 74–82.

18. Kirsten J. Means, "The Business of Ethics and the Ethics of Business," *AMS News* (January 1991), 16.

19. See note 6 above, p. 603.

20. See note 6 above, pp. 607–611 and Carl Mc Daniel and Roger Gates, *Contemporary Marketing Research* (St. Paul, MN: West Publishing Company, 1991), Chapter 20.

21. See note 1 above.

22. See note 6 above, p. 609.

23. Cleveland Horton, "Ethics at Issue," *Advertising Age* (December 21, 1987), 6.

24. See note 3 above, p. 43.

25. See note 1 above, pp. 726–727.

26. "Have It Your Way with Research," *Advertising Age* (April 4, 1983), 16.

27. Philip Maher, "Corporate Espionage: When Market Research Goes Too Far," *Business Marketing* (October 1984), 54.

28. Steven Flax, "How to Snoop on Your Competitors," *Fortune* (May 14, 1984), 29.

29. Michael E. Porter, *Competitive Strategy: Techniques for Analyzing Industries and Competitors* (New York: The Fee Press, 1980) and Michael E. Porter, *Competitive Advantage: Creating and Sustaining Superior Performance* (New York: The Free Press, 1985).

30. See note 28 above, p. 30.

31. "Keeping an Eye on Competition is Big Business," *The Arizona Republic* (November 3, 1985), E1, E12.

32. Brian Dumaine, "Corporate Spies Snoop to Conquer," *Fortune* (November 7, 1988), 68–76.

33. Craig Mellow, "The Best Source of Competitive Intelligence," *Sales & Marketing Management* (December 1989), 24–29.

34. Al Ossip, "Ethics—Everyday Choices in Marketing Research," *Journal of Advertising Research* (October–November 1985), RC10–RC12.

35. Thomas L. Greenbaum, "The Ethics of Focus Group Research." In *The Practical Handbook and Guide to Focus Group Research*, 143–149 (Lexington MA: Lexington Books, 1988).

36. Stephen B. Castleberry and Warren French, "The Ethical Framework Utilized by Individuals in the Advertising/Marketing Research Industry: A Moral Development Perspective," working paper, (January 1991).

37. William D. Neal, "The Profession of Marketing Research: A Strategic Assessment and a Prescription for Improvement," *Marketing Research* (September 1989), 21.

38. Alvin A. Achenbaum, "Can We Tolerate a Double Standard in Marketing Research?" *Journal of Advertising Research* (June–July 1985), RC3–RC7.

39. Howard Schlossberg, "Consensus Eludes Certification Issue," *Marketing News* (September 11, 1989), 1+.

40. Howard Schlossberg, "Founder Sees Ethics Organization as Potential Research Arbitrator," *Marketing News* (September 11, 1989), 25–26.

Chapter *4*

Product Management Ethics

The products and services that a firm produces are the reason for that organization's existence. Society grants corporations certain rights and privileges precisely because they operate to provide the many goods needed by society. The reward for producing and marketing products which serve consumer needs is profit. Obstacles to profit are shifting customer preferences, the competitive offerings of other firms, and an always dynamic business environment. For example, the market, the competitors, and the environmental trends that a firm such as Nissan must respond to as it produces automobiles are different from the ones General Electric deals with in producing medical or industrial equipment, or those Dominos reacts to as it cranks out pizza for the mass market. Common to all of these firms, however, are certain *ethical duties* that flow from the act of offering a product to users for purchase. Whenever a marketer places a product in the marketplace, there seems to be an implicit duty to make sure that the product is *safe*, the potential customer is provided with relevant product *information*, there are meaningful *product differences* among a single firm's offered product line, and, if something goes wrong after the product purchase, there is a mechanism for consumers to *redress* the situation.

Exactly when one of these fundamental duties is being shortchanged is subject to debate. The nature of such ethical responsibilities is the basic theme of this chapter. As we shall see, opinions about the morality of particular product management practices are not always uniform. Consider the following three product-related scenarios (see also Exhibit 4–1).

EXHIBIT 4–1   Light Dessert

The Yum-Yum Baking Company was considering launching a new line of packaged gourmet dessert products to be sold in supermarkets. Jeff Stanz, product manager, and Gene Simpson, vice president of marketing, were examining the staff research report on the new product line. The market research results projected an excellent consumer acceptance for the product line, which included strawberry French cheesecake, chocolate mousse, and classic German chocolate cake. The price would be premium. Distribution and advertising appeared to be in place and could be launched at short notice.

At issue was the research team's recommendation that the word "light" be used to describe each product in the new product dessert line. Thus, packaging would include titles such as *Light* Classic French Cheesecake and *Light* Classic Chocolate Mousse. The product manager had some reservations, because product specifications clearly suggested that the new line of classic dessert items, in fact, had more calories then Yum-Yum's comparable dessert items. For example, the proposed light classic cheesecake was significantly higher in calories than Yum-Yum's original cheesecake dessert.

In contrast, Simpson maintained that the recommendation of the venture team should be accepted, because each item in the proposed product line was lighter in the sense of having a lighter texture and color then comparable products in Yum-Yum's existing dessert line. As Simpson forcefully put it, "There are many meanings to the term *light* and in this case it refers to the fact that our new cheesecake is airier and fluffier then our regular cheesecake. The fact that it has *more* calories really doesn't matter. We are being truthful in one sense of the word. More importantly, we are strategically capitalizing on market research, which shows that the term *light* is a powerful word in attracting consumer attention."

Stanz contended that the reason light was such an important word was that consumers probably translated it to mean "a product that contained fewer calories." It was a very merchandisable term because most consumers assume that light made reference to health and nutrition rather than a product's color or texture. Simpson firmly concluded the discussion, "I'm pulling rank on this one Jeff, let's go with the term *light*."

Evaluate the above situation from an ethical standpoint.

Source: Adapted from Steve Schultze, "*Light* Cheesecake a Poor Choice for Dieters," *Milwaukee Journal* (September 6, 1989), C10.

Scenario 1

Curry, a British electronics retailer, manufactures and sells a *private brand* line of electronic products (e.g., televisions, VCRs, audio tape recorders) that it assembles from components made around the world. The brand name for these products is MATSUI. The motto for the product line is "Japanese technology made perfect." The product symbol is the rising sun—similar to that featured on the Japanese flag. Curry is not a Japanese company or subsidiary. The vast majority of components used in the MATSUI are *not* made in Japan. To add a further twist of irony to the entire endeavor, MATSUI is the name of a Japanese war criminal responsible for atrocities in China during the Second World War. Curry defends itself by saying that it never claimed that it was a Japanese company, that it has legal copyright for the brand name MATSUI, that the firm did not intend to mislead or offend anyone. Rather, the company managers "made the name up" because it was "a bit mystical and foreign sounding."[1] **Is the consumer being misled by this brand name scheme?**

Scenario 2

Bob Smith is product manager of the hypothetical Alpha Communications Corporation. Bob's unit is expected to increase its contribution to corporate profits by 12 percent each year. To do this, Bob figures he needs to launch two or three new products successfully. At present, Bob has three new products to bring before senior management. One of the three products is a customer service option that allows telephone users unlimited calls within a certain area during a particular time each day—5:00 P.M. to 7:00 P.M.—for a twenty dollar fee. The planned phone company campaign tells customers that they will be able to save at least twenty dollars on their phone bills each month if they sign up for the program. Upon closer examination of the market research data, however, Bob has determined there is little chance that most customers could realize the cost savings on this product as currently structured.[2] **Is it ethical for Alpha to launch a product that provides minimal advantages to the nondiscerning consumer?**

Scenario 3

Paul Klein is the president of a successful consumer electronic firm that specializes in the manufacturing of car telephones, compact disc/tape players for automobiles, and citizen's band radios for trucks. The company is cash rich and President Klein asked his vice president of marketing, Sue Simmons to suggest a product acquisition. Sue suggests acquiring the Acme Corporation, a small producer of radar detection equipment branded the "Cop Buster". The rationale contained in a written report is basically the following:

1. Radar detectors are very compatible with our existing lines.
2. Trends show that this product has been rapidly increasing its sales among young drivers.

In addition, Simmons points out that as women have become a more important part of the workforce, their purchases of radar detectors have been increasing dramatically. In summary, she recommends acquisition of the company along with an advertising campaign aimed toward young female drivers. President Klein responded, "as far as I can tell the only purpose of such a product is to circumvent the posted speed-limit laws. Aren't we advocating law breaking by adding such a product to our existing line?" **What do you think?**

As one reviews these scenarios, some of the ethical issues that emerge in the area of product management begin to crystallize. For example, what is the *degree of disclosure* that a product manager owes consumers who will be using the organization's branded product? To what extent should new products or services provide consumers with a *demonstrable advantage*? What responsibilities do product managers have to consider the *social ramifications* of the products they place on the market? While there are some aspects of the scenarios above which could be questioned on legal grounds, none of them are illegal *per se*. A major point of debate then is: do they represent unethical product practices? Do they cross the boundaries of proper and expected business protocol? This chapter provides guidance in grappling with such questions.

As this chapter unfolds, we discuss several major ethical questions inherent in product management. We cover a range of issues: products that are perceived to be in bad taste, products that are environmentally incompatible, and products that are challenged from the standpoint of their social acceptability.[3] We begin, however, with two areas that are quite regulated by existing law—product *safety* and product *counterfeiting*.

Product Safety

Many ethical issues flowing from product management pertain to the safety of products offered to the market. Safety would seem to be a fundamental ethical responsibility rooted in the adage that marketers should *never knowingly do harm*. The possible transgressions of this rule have many manifestations. For example, one of the longest running and most controversial issues is the area of toy safety and the extent to which toy manufacturers have put unsafe products into the marketplace. Each Christmas season, various consumer groups identify and publicize toys that are potentially dangerous to young children unless used with extreme care or under adult supervision. For example, a recent holiday season brought its usual array of unsafe products: those that easily break apart exposing sharp or jagged edges, others designed for young children that contained small pieces that could lead to chokings, and some which fired projectiles of various sizes and shapes. A general ethical principle, widely accepted in the industry, is that toy manufacturers have a special responsibility to their consumers, because children are a particularly vulnerable group. Despite the general acceptance of this principle, analysts of the toy industry are somewhat amazed that some unsafe toys reach the marketplace each year.[4] The Toy Manufacturers of America publish an annual fact book that articulates their positions on various ethical obligations concerning safety which their members should follow.

Another product category attracting great attention in recent years is all-terrain vehicles (ATV's). These are small motorized vehicles with wide tires that people ride "off road" for fun and recreation. The product is potentially dangerous because ATV's are regularly driven on rough terrain in areas with no enforceable operating rules. Many riders, especially youths, suffer injury or even death when ATV's crash or roll over. While sales of this product have rapidly increased, according to one recent report, 600 people have died in ATV accidents and 275,000 have been injured, many crippled for life. Many observers have remarked that this injury rate is unacceptable. At last report, several states had developed licensing requirements limiting use to those over sixteen years old. The Consumer Product Safety Commission is considering the promulgation of additional safety standards for ATV manufacturers.[5] The flip side of the issue is that if users are sufficiently warned about a product's potential hazards, the liberty principle (see Chapter 2) *might* suggest that no further regulatory steps should be taken.

A third general category of product safety concerns has to do with health claims for various products. A specific illustration is the product launch in the United States of *Good Start* infant formula by Carnation, a Nestlé subsidiary.[6] It initially was promoted as being "hypo-allergenic." In other words, the product was essentially positioned as a baby formula designed for babies allergic to milk—not an insignificant market segment. The difficulty with the product was that babies who are *extremely* allergic to milk may still have a reaction to the *Good Start* infant formula. Questions were raised as to whether (a) it was appropriate for Nestlé to promote the product as hypo-allergenic without recommending consultation with a physician, and (b) it should have been positioned to appeal to only mildly allergic babies. After considerable public pressure, Carnation did drop the "hypo-allergenic" designation from the label.

While safety issues such as those illustrated above easily come to mind under the category of product ethics, the product safety area is heavily regulated *by law.* As we shall see in other chapters devoted to marketing strategy topics, ethical responsibility is practiced on a plane of morality more demanding than legal requirements. That is, ethical duties go beyond legal responsibilities. However, the minimal obligation of marketers in the area of product safety is clearly specified in law. In the paragraphs below, we look at some of these areas of codified responsibility including warranties, product liability law, and some other federally-created assurances of product safety, including the Consumer Product Safety Commission (CPSC). We review these legal constraints because many of the charges about the unethical marketing of unsafe products are really criticisms of illegal activity.

Warranties

The first guarantee that a consumer has of product safety is the *warranty.*[7] There are two types of warranties. One is the written document that sometimes accompanies a product when it is purchased, called the *express* warranty. This document sets forth any specific obligations that the seller has concerning product performance. A second and more crucial warranty, is the *implied* one, so labeled because it need not be expressed or stated. Most important however, an implied warranty suggests that goods (or services) are "merchantable" (i.e., worthy of sale and fit for the ordinary purpose for which the goods are used). This, among other things, means that the product will perform safely. The net effect of the implied warranty is that there are certain minimum product performance expectations that the seller can never legally avoid. Thus, a warranty is an assurance given by the seller to the buyer. To the extent it is "expressed", the seller takes on additional obligations beyond those included in the implied warranty.

At times, express obligations are also utilized as *promotional warranties* such as the well-known "7 year/70,000 mile" guarantees on major repairs given by some automobile manufacturers or the Cross lifetime guarantee on its writing instruments. Such express warranties, which in this case extend coverage, are also sometimes provided *by retailers* who guarantee certain extra product performance levels (e.g., free repair and parts service for four years on a vaccuum cleaner). They are an attempt to attract buyers to a particular store or chain. The Magnuson-Moss Warranty Act of 1975, however, does not allow for a manufacturer to disclaim implied warranties by virtue of restrictions that are written into the express warranty. But this legislation does allow the seller to limit the express warranty to a specific time period. The key point, though, is that the fitness for intended purpose, including the fundamental safety of the product, can never be renounced.

Product Liability Law

The law of warranties suggests that a product's performance will be of a certain basic quality. However, additional protections are afforded to the consumer if a product does *not* perform as it was intended, and the consumer was injured or economically disadvantaged by this product failure. Such protection stems from the law of torts.[8] *Tort law* consists of principles developed as part of common law; it is fundamentally rooted in the *theory of negligence*. This theory holds that sellers of products are liable *if* the product is proven defective and has caused injury. Historically, the rules of negligence had established a standard of "ordinary care" or reasonableness. Marketers could be held liable if they failed to exercise a degree of care in product management that reasonably prudent sellers would have exercised in similar circumstances.

In 1963, the theory of *strict liability* was established and slowly adopted by many states.[9] This placed an even higher burden of responsibility upon the seller. The theory of strict liability established that firms can be held liable for injuries caused by the product if it was in defective condition and unreasonably dangerous. More importantly, the fact that the seller knew in advance that the product was dangerous did *not* have to be established. The rationale behind the theory of strict liability was that compensation should be provided to persons injured by defective products even if the injured parties could not establish a lack of ordinary care on the part of the seller (defined as any party in the channel of distribution including manufacturers, retailers, and wholesalers). (See Exhibit 4–2 for additional facts.)

The theory of strict liability ushered in an era of major customer litigation against manufacturers. Because the burden of proof upon the plaintiff was reduced, both court proceedings against manufacturers and the size of damage awards given to injured parties by various juries increased dramatically.[10] For example, in the period of 1974–1983 the number of cases filed at the federal level

---

EXHIBIT 4–2 Fast Facts About Product Liability

What are some of the major sources of product liability?

Liability can stem from *manufacturing defects*, from the *inadequate provision of warnings* or instructions, or from *design defects*—meaning that the product was manufactured correctly, but the design itself was inherently dangerous.

Is Congress doing anything about the high cost of product liability insurance in an era of strict liability?

A number of bills have been introduced in Congress that attempt (a) to limit the amount of damage that an organization would have to pay for a finding of liability, (b) reduce the time period during which a firm could be held as strictly liable, and (c) reduce the mechanism by which punitive damages were fixed in certain court cases.

Do the courts enact additional penalties for manufacturers when the violation of product safety standards is especially blatant?

Punitive damages are those damages that are assessed in addition to normal compensatory damages. The courts hold that punitive damages are appropriate when sufficient product safety testing was not conducted, when the organization failed to remedy an excessively dangerous condition that was known to exist, or when the company knowingly misled the public concerning the product's safety.

---

increased 600 percent. Adding to the frenzy of litigation were some spectacular cases wherein certain unsafe products did seem to cause substantial damage to consumers. For example, the Dalkon Shield intra-uterine contraceptive device (manufactured by A. H. Robins) caused infections in users that led to infertility and other complications; Firestone 500 brand tires (sold from 1973–1978) suffered from an extremely high incidence of ply separation, a defect which contributed to traffic accidents; and various super absorbent tampons were removed from the market because they have been linked to toxic shock syndrome.[11]

Many corporations responded by purchasing product liability insurance. After a number of large damage awards, the insurance premiums became so exorbitantly high in certain industries (e.g., the manufacturer of football helmets) that such protection was either unaffordable or it dramatically increased the cost of the product to consumers. Companies that wished to continue producing these products knowingly became part of a higher-risk economic endeavor. Business organizations were put on notice that if they marketed an unsafe product that causes consumer injury, the courts were likely to award damages and in certain cases invoke civil penalties (i.e., punitive damages) that could substantially impact the organization's financial position.[12]

Regulation by Federal Agencies

While tort law places possible civil penalties upon producers of unsafe goods and services, the federal government also regulates many products to insure their safety, quality, and performance. Such oversight is provided by various agencies with jurisdiction over certain product categories. Included among these are the Food and Drug Administration, the US Treasury Department, the US Department of Agriculture, and the Department of Transportation. The Consumer Product Safety Commission, which has an especially important role in this domain, is profiled in the following section. A brief sketch of the responsibilities falling to the other agencies is provided below.

- The United States Department of Agriculture (USDA) oversees agricultural products, including meat, poultry, eggs, fruits, and vegetables. The agency has the right to inspect manufacturing and processing facilities as well as take action against manufacturers and distributors when such products are judged to be adulterated. The USDA also has the right to establish a "grading system" for these regulated products, although the use of this system by sellers is not mandatory.
- The Food and Drug Administration (FDA) is responsible for overseeing drugs, medical devices, and cosmetics. The central responsibility of the FDA is to approve new drug applications and to certify the drugs as being "safe and effective" based on clinical tests. The length of this certification process and the requirements to establish such safety has been a source of controversy in recent years with pharmaceutical firms charging that the drawn out process stifles new product innovation. The FDA also oversees the safety of drugs, cosmetics, and non-prescription medical devices. If it finds these products create an unreasonable risk of harm to the consumer, the FDA has the ability to seize the products via a court order.
- The US Treasury Department has jurisdiction for alcohol, tobacco, and firearm products. These products raise social questions and some of the ethical aspects regarding such products will be treated later in this chapter.
- The Department of Transportation (DOT) is charged with the regulation of automobile safety in the United States. A DOT subsidiary, the National Highway Traffic and Safety Administration (NHTSA), conducts the much publicized "crash testing" program that results in guidelines for injury-reducing automobile design. For example, automobile bumpers must prevent certain levels of damage at pre-specified crash speeds.

The Consumer Product Safety Commission
The agency with the greatest authority to oversee product safety is the Consumer Product Safety Commission (CPSC).[13] This independent, regulatory commission was established by Congress in 1972 and charged to protect the public from unreasonable risks associated with consumer products. The commission also has a mandate to (a) develop product safety standards, (b) conduct research that investigates products that have led to consumer injury, illnesses, or death, and (c) to take steps that will assist consumers in making product safety evaluations. Other legislation which had been passed prior to 1972 was placed under the jurisdiction of the CPSC (examples of such legislation would be the Flammable

Fabrics Act and the Federal Hazardous Substance Act, which regulates products such as fireworks). Perhaps the single most important and controversial activity of the CPSC has been the promulgation of safety standards for various classes of products. Standards have been already written for power lawnmowers, bicycles, television antennas, and even match books. The commission also has the power to order manufacturers to disclose product testing information as well as the power to secure company files related to consumer injuries and/or complaints.

Through implied warranties, civil procedures available in product liability law, and the various federal oversights concerning product categories, we conclude that basic product safety is guaranteed by law in addition to being an ethical responsibility. Still, there are ethical questions regarding safety that must be asked. *How safe should a product be? How safe is safe enough?* For example, studies have shown that air bags save lives in automobile crash tests, but most consumers seem unwilling to incur the extra cost to voluntarily equip their new car with these safeguards. (Even after all automobiles had seat belts, it took legislation in most states requiring their usage to get even a majority of consumers to comply.) Despite their cost, should air bags be mandatory? Are automobile manufacturers who choose not to install them in all their models acting unethically? Thus far, attempts to answer such questions have used mostly utilitarian type analyses. Interestingly, beginning with their 1990 models, all Chrysler automobiles have driver air bags as standard equipment. Ford and Honda have announced plans to equip all their models with air bags as standard equipment before 1995. Most other manufacturers are quickly moving toward installing at least a driver's side air bag.

Product Counterfeiting

Product counterfeiting involves the unauthorized copying of patented products, inventions, and trademarks or the violation of registered copyrights. While it is often discussed as an unethical product practice, many forms of product counterfeiting are an outright violation of US law. Counterfeiting has become a major concern to American businesses as bogus products cost US organizations in excess of a billion dollars a year in lost sales. The US International Trade Commission estimates that $6–8 *billion* a year in domestic US exports are lost and in excess of 130,000 US jobs have been eliminated because of these foreign-made counterfeit products.[14] Essentially, what is involved in product counterfeiting is that other manufacturers produce look-alike branded products of well-known market leaders. The gamut of products that have been copied includes medical equipment, non-prescription drugs, shampoo, sunglasses, basketballs, liquor, and various pharmaceutical products. Recently, much has been written about some of the more sensational examples of product copying such as counterfeit Rolex watches (readily available in East Asian and Mexican markets), knock-off Levi jeans (especially popular in Eastern Europe), and numerous examples of illegally pirated video and audio tapes.

Product counterfeiting is unethical and (in the United States) illegal. Why? From a strategic standpoint, it represents an attempt of one firm to dubiously capitalize on the established goodwill that the originating company has generated for its own branded product via product quality and advertising. The key ethical issue is: when a counterfeit product copies design, packaging, or brand images to the degree that they violate patents and/or confuse the consumer, such knock-offs steal sales, market acceptance, and profits from the original product producers. Because of such practices, the brand name, known as a trademark, has been given specific legal protection. Brands are especially important to the firm, because they provide a shorthand device for customers to identify and recall the attributes of a particular product offering. Internationally recognized brand names, such as Pizza Hut, Coca Cola, Volkswagen, Sony, and Ivory soap, suggest a certain quality and dependability that the product counterfeiter wishes to exploit.

A *trademark*, according to the Lanham Act of 1946, is defined as any "word, name, symbol, device, or any combination thereof adapted and used by the manufacturer or merchant to identify his goods and distinguish them from those manufactured by others."[15] Trademarks (or brand names) can be registered in law and such action provides certain legal rights. The rights increase after the trademark has been used in commerce for five consecutive years—thereby preempting the practice of simply having organizations secure the rights to names that they will not use. The key clause of the Lanham Act, section 43(a), protects various brand and packaging identifications that have become so distinctive that the public identifies them with a single source. For example, McDonalds' golden arches would be protected under this clause. Because of wide-scale counterfeiting emanating from foreign markets, Congress passed the 1984 Trademark Counterfeiting Act, which provided steep penalties (up to a quarter of a million dollars and five years in prison) for those who knowingly traffic in counterfeit products.[16] It also allows plaintiffs to sue for triple the damages or an amount equal to the profits that the counterfeiter has made from the illegal product (whichever is greater).

As alluded to earlier, problems with counterfeiting stem especially from international producers competing with well advertised US, European, and Japanese brands. Many developing countries simply do not recognize the patent or copyright protections of developed countries. A 1985 Presidential Commission cited companies in Argentina, Brazil, Columbia, Mexico, and a number of East Asian firms as being particularly guilty of counterfeiting products.[17] Because of lax regulation in many countries, such as South Korea, some US brand names are unfairly imitated (see Exhibit 4–3).

While product counterfeiting is often thought of as an ethical issue, it obviously is a legal one as well. Current legal interpretations of the Lanham Act now assist manufacturers in establishing their investment in a particular brand name without necessarily having *to prove* that another organization intended to deceive the consumer. This makes it somewhat easier for original sellers to protect their trademark rights. In conclusion, trademark law is a complicated area. Marketing

EXHIBIT 4–3   How South Korean Brands Copy American Originals

Are these product packaging clones a violation of trademark protection or merely the clever use of *me too* marketing?

Source: Damon Darlin, "Where Trademarks Are up for Grabs," *The Wall Street Journal* (December 5, 1989), B1.

managers would be well advised to seek the counsel of a good patent attorney when attempting to establish their brand rights and to make sure that their investment in specific brand names are not violated by other sellers.[18]

The Ethics of Product Management

While the most serious violations such as product safety and outright product counterfeiting are at least partly covered by law, many other controversial areas of product development and management fall into the so-called "ethically gray" areas. In this section, we review some of the more prominent topics beginning with the issue of products which lack widespread social acceptability.

Socially Controversial Products

Many consumers question the social value of certain categories of products, especially cigarettes, alcoholic beverages, and firearms. For example, according to a *Wall Street Journal* consumer poll, the majority of consumers favor explicit health warnings on alcoholic beverages and the elimination of cigarette ads in newspapers and magazines.[19] The most strident critics of these products maintain that they should not legally be sold to the general public. Other less severe critics feel that the inherent nature of certain products calls for some restrictions concerning how they are marketed. The nature of commodities such as tobacco and alcohol seems to require special responsibilities on the part of the marketer in overseeing how they are sold in the marketplace.

Cigarettes

The (legal) product receiving the greatest amount of criticism concerning its social utility would surely be cigarettes. To a lesser extent, other tobacco products (e.g., chewing tobacco) have also fallen under this judgmental cloud. Cigarettes are somewhat different from other socially questionable products, because it appears that, based on the scientific evidence, cigarettes cause damage to their users' health *when they are used as intended*. This is not quite the same as for alcoholic beverages and firearms (for hunting and target shooting) where problems generally occur with abuse or misuse.

In a comprehensive analysis of the controversy over whether cigarettes should be banned, *Consumer Reports* magazine provides some provocative statistical information.[20] The story unfolds like this. On the one hand, tobacco companies spend more than a billion dollars a year on the advertising and promotion of their products in the United States. Since 1970, when cigarette advertising was banned from television, newspaper and magazine advertising has increased almost 200 percent from $64 million in 1970 to in excess of $200 million by the 1980s. In addition, huge amounts of money have been shifted to billboard advertising and sales promotions (including the *free* distribution of new brand samples). Moreover, commercial sponsorship of various sporting and entertainment events by tobacco companies has also greatly increased (e.g., the *Virginia Slims* women's professional tennis tour). On the other hand, the US Public Health Service puts cigarette-induced or related premature deaths in this country at 350,000 per year. This exceeds the total number of Americans who die annually in automobile accidents or by fire, murder, and suicide combined. Direct medical costs resulting from smoking-related illnesses are estimated at $22 billion a year, excluding problems caused by secondary smoke inhalation. Medical studies have shown that secondhand smoke can cause discomfort and perhaps adverse medical consequences to nonsmokers exposed to tobacco smoke.

Tobacco manufacturers contend that while smoking is correlated with certain health risks, it has not been *proven* beyond a doubt that cigarettes directly cause lung cancer or other health complications. The Tobacco Institute (the trade association and lobbyist group for the manufacturers) argues that cigarette advertising should not be banned, because it does not cause smoking any more than soap causes people to bathe or detergent advertising causes people to wash their clothes. They insist that tobacco promotion is sacrosanct, because it consists of information disseminated about a *legal* product.

Most interesting, the protection of commercial speech (i.e., advertising) via the First Amendment may not be as complete as the tobacco manufacturers insist.

In 1980, the Supreme Court (in the *Central Hudson* case) ruled that commercial speech can be restricted *when* it affects a substantial government interest and the intervention is not more restrictive than necessary. The tremendous health and medical costs to society that result from cigarette smoking appears to be a "substantial interest." Furthermore, a promotional ban on cigarettes probably causes fewer complications than completely outlawing the product. Contrary to the opinion of some, a complete advertising ban may be legally justifiable in the United States. Canada, Sweden, and New Zealand are countries that already have comprehensive promotional restrictions.[21]

A similar argument to restrict advertising can be made from an ethical perspective. Recalling our discussion in Chapter 2 of duty-based ethics—along with some of the duties that may be inherent in attempting to shape a virtuous organization—one could argue that restrictions on tobacco manufacturing and promotion are appropriate because of failure by tobacco producers to exercise their *duty to investigate* and their *duty to inform*.[22] Several major advertising agencies that have cigarette accounts allow employees who have philosophical objections to remove themselves from working on promotional campaigns for tobacco products.

Specifically, with regard to the *duty to investigate* one can argue that business organizations have a responsibility for the consequences and complications caused by their products. An examination of the outcomes of cigarette smoking should have led tobacco manufacturers to realize the damage that they are inflicting upon users and society by the continued production and promotion of the product. Various attempts by cigarette manufacturers to reduce the tar and nicotine of their cigarettes and to produce the smokeless cigarette (e.g., the ill-fated R. J. Reynolds' Premier cigarette) implies that tobacco manufacturers realize the hazards inherent in their product.[23] Similarly, the *duty to inform* evokes the obligation that business organizations make known the potential risks to product users. Tobacco manufacturers, of course, would argue that the warning labels on cigarette packages meet this obligation. However, in light of the mounting medical evidence about smoking, one could argue that society has the *duty to interdict* when a firm has failed to exercise its obligations. It is then that the social institution overseeing the subsidiary institution (i.e., the government overseeing business) should exercise its option to intervene.

Alcohol Products

Marketers of alcoholic beverages are not as vulnerable as tobacco manufacturers, because it is the *abuse* rather than the *use* of alcoholic beverages that seems to cause most problems. Alcohol-related illnesses and accidents caused by drunk drivers remain a major public concern, but these problems flow from the users' inability to control their alcohol consumption, possibly because of addiction. The general controversy, however, has not been lost on the marketers of alcoholic beverages. Bacardi Rum has advertised itself as the spirit that mixes with everything—except driving. Anheuser–Busch, the largest brewer in the United States, has had a long-running advertising campaign with the theme line "Know when to say when." Miller Brewing has launched a "think before you drink" advertising campaign. Both Anheuser–Busch and Miller now have nonalcoholic beers in their product portfolio. Social pressures to restrict alcoholic beverage advertising have also increased in recent years. For example, the current National Collegiate Athletic Association college football contract restricts the percentage of TV commercials for beer and wine that are shown during the telecasts of football games. Perhaps the most significant development has been the recent precedent-setting legislation requiring warning labels on alcoholic beverages.[24] These read:

> **Government Warning:** (1) According to the Surgeon General, women should not drink alcoholic beverages during pregnancy because of the risk of birth defects. (2) Consumption of alcoholic beverages impairs your ability to drive a car or operate machinery, and may cause health problems.

Because of the nature of alcoholic beverages as compared to tobacco products, it might be argued that alcoholic beverage marketers are meeting their responsibilities to investigate and inform. Perhaps they have done so reluctantly and only for economic reasons. For example, questions have been raised about the continued production of certain cheap fortified wines that primarily appeal to the street-person alcoholic and the underage drinker. Furthermore, a disproportionate amount of liquor advertising seems to be targeted at blacks, judging from magazine ads and city billboard placements.[25]

As the above two product categories illustrate, much discussion will continue about the inherent obligations of marketers who promote products that are viewed by a substantial segment of the public as having negative social consequences.

Environmentally Incompatible Products

An excellent illustration of negative social consequences has to do with products that, while perfectly useful, create some problem for the physical environment. Examples are (a) aerosol sprays which can potentially cause damage to the ozone layer, (b) packaging that is not biodegradable and causes long-term landfill problems, (c) various chemicals and detergents that are useful for processing or cleaning but that pollute land, air, and groundwater when improperly disposed, and (d) medical wastes, which sometimes have been dumped into oceans or lakes because the proper disposal of such material is difficult for the institutional user. Product packaging is an especially acute problem for marketers concerned with ethical considerations (see Exhibit 4–4).

The "disposable" lifestyle that many consumers have come to lead (disposable shavers, pens, cans, and even cameras) creates particularly severe waste-handling problems—a residue of our convenient, consumer society. The average American generates approximately 3.5 pounds of garbage a day of which 30 percent represents product packaging.[26] As some marketers have attempted to become more cost efficient and to design products better for handling and storage, they have often replaced environmentally compatible packaging with less

EXHIBIT 4–4   Product Packaging Questions Facing Marketing in
the 1990s

What responsibilities do marketers have to voluntarily provide nutritional labeling on packaged food items?

Should marketers consider special labeling to enhance visual acuity on products used regularly by senior citizens?

Is the packaging on certain potentially dangerous products (e.g., insect sprays, household cleaners,

disinfectants) so attractive as to disarm the consumer concerning their hazardous nature?

Is it ethical to intentionally mimic the color and graphics of the market leader's packaging when designing a competing product?

What responsibility do marketers have to enhance the disposibility of their product packaging?

Source: Adapted from R. J. Corey and P. F. Bone, "Ethical Packaging: Directions for the 1990s," *American Marketing Association Proceedings* (Chicago: American Marketing Association, 1990), 387.

environmentally sensitive versions. Some examples are the polystyrene egg cartons, which replaced the old-fashioned (and easily recyclable) cardboard predecessor, and plastic milk cartons, which superseded waxed cardboard or reuseable glass.

The fundamental issue here seems to be one of creating *externalities* (i.e., the cost of handling and disposing of product packaging) that are not paid for by the original producer or consumer. The stakeholder concept (discussed in Chapter 1) suggests that external costs should be foreseen and paid for by the manufacturer whenever possible. While consumer packaging does not create the front-page headlines associated with major oil spills, the environmental impact of product packaging and disposal promises to be a major social issue in the 1990s. For example, several states are considering a ban on disposable diapers in state landfills. And the Federal Trade Commission has asked for substantiation materials from several companies concerning the biodegradability claims regarding their products. Among the challenged products are First Brand Corporation's Glad wrap and Mobil Oil's Hefty trash bags.[27] Growing sensitivity to ecological concerns has prompted consumer groups to call upon US corporations to embrace the so-called Valdez principles (named after the 1989 Alaskan oil spill). The principles encompass the adoption of an ecological ethic that spans product design, use, and disposal. (A *summary* of these principles is provided in Exhibit 4–5.) Recently, organizations such as Wal-Mart, 3M and McDonalds have made the environmental compatibility of their operations the focus of advertising campaigns.

The practical difficulty of all of this is judging when product packaging is so environmentally incompatible as to require restraint by management. In the extreme, all product packages raise environmental questions, because it must be

---

EXHIBIT 4–5   A Summary of the Valdez Principles

Protection of the Biosphere. Signatories will try to eliminate pollutants that damage the air, water, or earth.

Sustainable Use of Natural Resources. Signatories pledge to use renewable resources, conserve non-renewable materials, and preserve biological diversity.

Reduction and Disposal of Waste. Signatories pledge to minimize use of and safely dispose of, hazardous wastes.

Wise Use of Energy. Signatories call for energy-efficient products and processes.

Risk Reduction. Signatories pledge to reduce environmental risks and prepare for accidents.

Inform the Public. Signatories pledge to disclose the environmental impact of products and services.

Compensation. Signatories pledge to restore damaged environments and compensate for injury.

Disclosure. Signatories pledge to disclose accidents and hazards and to protect employees who report them.

Environmental Directors and Managers. Signatory companies agree that at least one board member will be an environmental expert. A senior executive for environmental affairs will also be named.

Assessment and Annual Audit. Signatories pledge an annual environmental and public audit of worldwide operations.

Source: An amended summary as printed in Barnaby J. Feder, "Who Will Subscribe to the Valdez Principles?" *The New York Times* (September 10, 1989), F6.

disposed of or because it utilizes scarce resources. The issue then is to determine what level of incompatibility are we as a society willing to tolerate? Sometimes these judgments shift over time. For example, in Minneapolis there has been strong public support for a proposal that would ban the use of nonrecyclable plastics at food stores and restaurants.[28] Seattle has instituted a comprehensive (and some would argue costly) system to separate and recycle household garbage. As always, such judgments are difficult and most often require utilitarian trade-offs. It appears that issues involving *green marketing* and its ecological impact will be one of the major ethical concerns of the 1990s (see Exhibit 4–6).

Planned Obsolescence

The term *planned obsolescence* generally refers to a manufacturer building a limited life into a product so that the consumer needs to repurchase an item after a shorter period than might reasonably be the case (see Exhibitc 4–7 for a demarcation of the various types of product obsolescence). While this topic is often evoked as a possible ethical issue for consumer goods, stiff competition and technological advances have generally lessened the impact of this practice, because there is no

EXHIBIT 4–6   The Ethics of Green Marketing

The 1990s have been projected by many to be the decade of ecological concern. Various opinion polls have increasingly demonstrated that large segments of the US public have come to the realization that the physical environment must be protected and nurtured. As environmental sympathy has mounted, marketers have responded with a host of products that are actually or arguably "environmentally friendly." The hope of marketing strategists is that such products can create a sustainable competitive advantage for their product offerings. The movement by business in developing and promoting ecologically compatible products has been called *green marketing.*

The green marketing movement has yielded a host of so-called environmentally friendly products. Included here are items such as packaging made of recycled paper, cleaners and detergents that are presumably nonpolluting upon disposal, automobiles and small machinery that have been positioned as "energy efficient." On one level, the green marketing movement is a responsible reaction to increasing environmental concern. Unfortunately, many of the claims that are being made for environmentally friendly products are unsubstantiated, misleading, and in some cases, outright lies. For example, several major brands of trash bags have been promoted as being "photodegradable"—meaning that the product would break down in sunlight—although upon disposal, few of these bags would actually be subject to the physical conditions (i.e., sunlight, rain, and air) that would lead to such degradability. Similarly, various containers have been labeled "recyclable where facilities available." But investigations showed that such recycling centers were, in fact, only in place in a few geographic areas.

The heart of the issue then is that many of the product attributes promoted by green marketers such as "biodegradability" and "ozone friendliness" do not necessarily perform as promised. Competitors who do *not* make such environmental claims, but feel they may be losing sales because certain consumers are influenced by ecological appeals, have petitioned regulators to take action. At the time of this writing, the Federal Trade Commission had been asked to lead a consortium of government agencies in putting together guidelines that would specifically regulate the meaning of the various terms associated with environmentally friendly products. Various industries also plan to become involved in self-regulation via their National Advertising Division of the Better Business Bureau.

The ethical questions raised when manufacturers make environmental product claims without providing legal ecological benefit should be apparent. Specifically, such marketers may be unfairly attempting to exploit the environmental concerns of consumers in order to sell more of their product. Returning to the terminology of Chapter 2, duty-based ethical theories might suggest that marketers have an ethical responsibility not to make ecological claims unless they have made significant efforts to reduce external costs to the physical environment and can demonstrate this effort. Similarly, the virtue ethics approach might resurrect the concept of stewardship whereby product manufacturers ought to realize that they have a special responsibility to future generations to preserve and protect the physical environment where it might be affected by the products being produced.

For additional information see Randolph B. Smith, "Environmentalists, State Officers See Red as Firms Rush to Market *Green* Products," *The Wall Street Journal* (March 13, 1990), B1–2 and "The Green Marketing Revolution," *Advertising Age* (January 29, 1991).

EXHIBIT 4–7   Types of Product Obsolescence

Functional obsolescence occurs when technological breakthroughs render an existing product out-of-date. Microprocessors (computers on a chip), for example, caused the obsolescence of chip-laden circuit boards.

There are, however, three types of planned obsolescence: (1) postponed, (2) intentionally designed, and (3) fashion or style. *Postponed obsolescence* means holding back on adding product improvements until present inventories run out or demand falls off sharply. *Intentionally designed obsolescence* involves designing a product, or a critical part, to wear out within a given period of time. *Fashion or style obsolescence* is psychological.

A marketer may try to defend postponed obsolescence by saying a product improvement was withheld to provide more time to test it and to research potential customer demand and willingness to pay for it. Or marketers may argue that premature introduction would render some inventory worthless and that these losses would have to be offset by higher prices on the improved product. We speak of intentionally designed obsolescence when marketers of disposable products offer inexpensive products that have a very short life compared to more expensive and permanent versions. Fashion or style obsolescence may result from a marketer's effort to cater to market segments that demand "newness."

Some conservationists argue that marketers waste natural resources by devoting too much effort to developing new products when existing ones are satisfactory. Some ecologists complain that too many products are designed to be short-lived and that this creates a big solid waste-disposal problem as old models are discarded for new models.

Is planned obsolescence an ethical marketing practice?

Source: Reprinted by permission from William F. Schoell and Joseph P. Guiltinan, *Marketing, Contemporary Concepts and Practices*, 5th ed. (Boston: Allyn & Bacon, 1992), 331.

guarantee the consumer will again purchase the same brand from the original vendor. Such tactics may take place more often in the business-to-business sector. Product components would be the most likely candidate for such a practice. Again the availability of substitute items with a longer life and the competitive pressures to cut costs by increasing reliability mitigates against this practice, except in the case of single-source suppliers. Thus, the issue of building technical obsolescence into a product is no longer a major concern, as the threat of competition along with the realization that this is not a wise business practice has usually eliminated any possible economic gain from such efforts.

One continuing form of product obsolescence is sometimes referred to as *social (or fashion) product obsolescence.*[29] This practice entails the strategy where marketers create brands or styles of products that are usually promoted with substantial upscale advertising. The idea is to position the product as "high status" to a particular (often affluent) segment of consumers. Examples that come to mind here are designer jeans, Rolex watches and Gucci handbags. After a period of time, certain styles or models of these trendy brands are consciously replaced by new versions that in effect socially outdate their predecessor. The closets of many consumers are filled with devalued merchandise and effectively wasted material. There is probably an ethical *question* associated with this. At the same time, the *response* may be that such practices are not unethical, because they are directed to consumers' tastes and preferences.

The notion that people seek status and use the goods that they purchase to help them acquire it is an old idea. It was written about long ago by economists such as Thorstein Veblen who coined the term "conspicuous consumption." In the free-market economy, most persons see the creation of such status goods through advertising as an expression of consumer individuality and not subject to regulatory sanction. While one can question whether the society is better off because every ten years or so there is a shift from wide ties to thin or vice-versa in men's attire, pointing out exactly what damage occurs and to whom because of the existence of such fashion cycles is difficult. For example, jobs are supported and the economy is more dynamic in offering opportunities for new vendors. Therefore, fashion obsolescence appears to be controversial but not inherently unethical.

Products in Bad Taste

This topic is particularly tricky, as some marketers are regularly accused of crossing the ethical line by selling products which are in poor taste. Illustrations of products that have been publicly pilloried include semi-pornographic greeting cards, novelties such as plastic excrement, and certain violent toys designed for children. For example, consumers have been recently outraged by

- a toy company that during one Christmas season introduced a Building Blaster line that included a rocket ship, a bridge, and a communication tower that all were designed to collapse as if they had been detonated. Some were particularly concerned about the rocket ship, which looked a bit like a space shuttle. This called to mind the ill-fated *Challenger* explosion in 1986—a low point of the US space program—and thus the Building Blaster struck some consumers as a morbid product.[30]
- various X-rated computer software including one program called the Mac-Playmate. In the course of the game, a computer graphics female can be stripped and forced to engage in a variety of sexual acts utilizing devices chosen from the options menu including instruments such as handcuffs, shackles, spike-heels, and whips. The game even includes an escape command that will quickly project a spreadsheet on the screen if a supervisor enters the game player's office.[31]

The difficult ethical question, of course, is who determines what constitutes bad taste? It depends upon the audience involved. College students have a reputation for having a wide latitude of acceptance in terms of their open-mindedness—they are not easily offended. On the other hand, some religious fundamentalists are bothered by many things, including consumption of any alcohol, coffee, or even tea. Perhaps an ethical rule of thumb, consistent with duty-based ethics, would be that marketers should be extremely skeptical of any product which panders to people's base motivations or is directed at demeaning some group.

Part of the perceptual problem concerning certain products (e.g., feminine deodorant, condoms) is caused by the *spillover effect* of product promotion when the promotional message for a particular item reaches an unintended audience.[32] An ethical solution to problems involving what constitutes *bad taste* can come from management itself or society at large. In the *Building Blaster* example, the responsible toy company rapidly withdrew its product from storeshelves after certain large retailers requested such an action.

Products That Overpromise or Mislead

Another category of ethical issues has to do with products that promise more than they can deliver. In fact, some contend that this criticism could be leveled at most consumer products. The examples range from the ridiculous to the sublime. In the extreme, an apple drink branded *Sun Apple* contains absolutely no apple juice.[33] One could argue that the product is inherently misleading, as consumers would logically expect some apple content in an apple-flavored, apple-branded drink. However, the package does contain the statement, in relatively small print, "contains no juice." At the more debatable point on the scale, certain critics question fast-food menus because the product offerings contain high levels of fat, sugar, and sodium.[34] For example, observers point out that a quarter-pound hamburger, fries, and a shake will involve the consumer ingesting over 1,000 calories, fifteen teaspoons of fat, three teaspoons of sugar and 1,400 milligrams of sodium. This is the *maximum* amount of fat that an average person should consume in a day, and some physicians contend that the guideline is already too high. Are fast-food purveyors being unethical by not disclosing and publicizing such information? An encouraging development is the calorie information currently promoted by Hardees (see Exhibit 4–8) and the many steps taken by McDonald's and other fast food chains to develop healthier menu items (e.g., low-fat hamburgers).

As we will discuss in Chapter 6 on advertising, there are certainly legal thresholds that, when crossed, constitute outright product misrepresentation. However, the key ethical question involves those products that do not surpass the legal limit. Numerous promotions for weight-loss products and clinics fit this category. These ads often feature very attractive young men and women, implying that users of the featured products and equipment can easily shape their own physiques to such dimensions. One also wonders about the many so-called fertility institutes that prey upon childless couples by putting forward statistics about the percentages of pregnancies which their techniques have led to, neglecting to mention that a high proportion end in spontaneous miscarriages. Thus, these services have led to few live births—the critical matter.[35]

EXHIBIT 4-8   Nutrition Oriented Fast Food Information

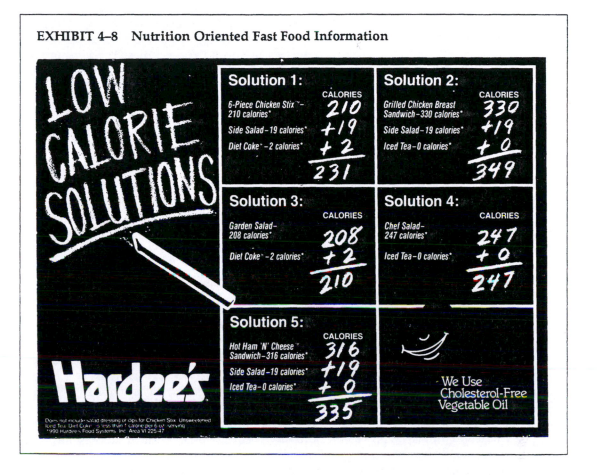

The key question becomes: when do products cross the ethical line and become inherently misleading? Certainly, when products are deceptive to a majority of consumers they cross the line. An example is *slack packaging*. Here manufacturers sell the product in a container that is only partially filled. The practice leads the typical consumer to conclude they are receiving more product than they actually do. Some cereal manufacturers have long been accused of using this technique (i.e., not filling the cereal box completely). To a certain degree this issue may simply be explained by the cereal "settling" after the package has been filled. General Mills has wrestled with the fill rate issue and has developed corporate policies to alleviate this problem. A more dubious variation of slack packaging would be coffee manufacturers who continue to sell their product in the standard one pound coffee tin but fill it with only twelve or thirteen ounces of ground coffee beans.[36] They contend that new roasting methods allow consumers to brew as many cups with thirteen ounces as they previously brewed with sixteen. Is this an acceptable ethical defense?

Still, the elusive question remains: how does one define "misleading"? If one consumer is deceived by a product claim, does that make it misleading? Or suppose many consumers are deceived by a product promise when put to the test, but the vast majority of product *users* (i.e., the likely target market), understands what is being promised. Now, is the product promise deceptive? These issues are truly the gray areas of marketing ethics. We try to provide guidance on these issues in the final two sections of the chapter.

How to Evaluate Ethics in Product Management

Intent is an important factor in judging ethical behavior. For example, in the situation where manufacturers sell products as new that are actually used, there is an obvious intent to deceive buyers. Contemporary illustrations of this practice have included the sale of grand pianos and expensive womens' apparel as new when they have actually been used.[37] Perhaps the most publicized example during the 1980s was the Chrysler Corporation, which acknowledged selling hundreds of cars as new that had been test-driven, often for several thousand miles, with their odometers disconnected. At first, Chrysler claimed that its top executives were merely "testing" the product. Later, then CEO Lee Iacocca appeared in a series of advertisements where he admitted a grave error in judgment on the part of the Chrysler Corporation. Warranties on these automobiles were extended and financial restitution was voluntarily made to buyers. Similarly, in the case of scenario 1 heading this chapter, it is important to judge what the intent of Curry Management was when they selected the brand name MATSUI.

Next, the *means* or method used to implement a particular marketing program must also be ethically analyzed. For example, FDA regulations require that food product labels disclose the addition of the popular flavor enhancer monosodium glutamate (MSG) to any product because some medical studies link the substance to various allergic reactions. However hydrolyzed vegetable protein (HVP), another natural flavoring, can contain MSG in concentrations up to 40 percent and is unregulated. As a result, certain food processors have circumvented a possible difficulty by using HVP as a flavoring *and* promoting their product as "containing no MSG."[38] In such cases, the methods selected to "comply" with the law raise ethical questions. The means is also a factor in the Alpha case (scenario 2) at the beginning of the chapter. It may very well be that most consumers are wise enough to determine whether such a telephone service is in their economic interest. But Alpha management should probably not use the "cost savings" claim as the hook to attract possible subscribers.

Third, *consequences* are also an important factor in judging when a product has been unethically managed. Consider the consumer shopping around for air service to a particular destination. Most of the time airline ads are a starting point for seeking out this product. The ads often offer seemingly cheap round trip fares but upon examination of the fine print—which sometimes necessitates phone calls to the air carrier to solicit additional information—many restrictions apply to the advertised rates making travel extremely difficult because of time, day, and seat limitations. Although technical disclosure is available, most consumers don't realize the restrictions until they actually engage in the purchase process. The outcome (or consequences) of the tactic suggests that often the product actually purchased (and its price) is different than the one initially desired. Thus, despite the technical disclosure and because of its consequences, this approach may be unethical. Scenario 3 at the beginning of this chapter represents another example. In this situation, it seems important to consider what the consequences of the wide-spread use of radar detectors would be for society.

Ideas for Ethical Action

How can marketing managers improve the level of ethical orientation of the product management process? First, *marketers should include a formal ethical analysis as part of their product development process.* Marketers have long subscribed to a specific analytical sequence as part of new product development. This usually begins with idea generation, followed by economic and business analysis, then product development/evaluation, test marketing, and finally, limited or perhaps national introduction.[39] As part of this process, a specific ethical product analysis should be conducted. Among the questions to be asked would be the following:

- Is the product safe when used as intended?
- Is the product safe when misused in a way that is foreseeable?
- Have any competitors' patents or copyrights been violated?
- Is the product compatible with the physical environment? (Products that pollute the environment or are inherently hazardous should undergo special scrutiny. The Valdez principles in Exhibit 4–5 could be of particular value.)
- Is the product environmentally compatible when disposed of? (Special consideration should be given to whether the product packaging can be recycled or whether, at minimum, it is biodegradable.)
- Do any organizational stakeholders object to the product?

One set of experts has come up with a decision formula that mathematically ranks the impact of new products upon key publics in terms of the benefit that the product provides to each key stakeholder group. Basically, they propose a weighted cost-benefit analysis be conducted.[40]

Second, *product managers should provide sufficient product instructions as well as appropriate warning labels for all products that they introduce and maintain in the marketplace.* As has been noted earlier, one of the fundamental duties of the marketer is the *duty to inform* the consumer. In the context of product management, this likely translates to a disclosure of full information about the product. Ultimately, this forthright approach benefits sellers by protecting them against some forms of product liability jeopardy. Exactly *what* information needs to be disclosed depends on the specific product category at hand. In many cases, the average consumer may properly assume the appropriate function of the product. For example, most consumers realize that a power lawnmower should not be used as a hedge trimmer. Nevertheless, the courts or society may hold the product's manufacturer to a higher standard. At least one consumer did believe that a power lawnmower could serve as a hedge trimmer. Thus, the amount of information disclosed should cover the product usage requirements of the majority of consumers (including, some would say, even the stupid and feeble-minded). Exhibit 4–9 presents an example of several warning labels that John Deere includes on its farm equipment. These warning labels seem especially well done because of their clear graphics in combination with the written warning.

The inadequate labels on packaged food products have received special attention recently because of some inflated health claims that have been made about what is essentially junk food.[41] For instance, granola cereals, which have a high sugar content and relatively low fiber, are an illustration of a relatively ordinary product masquerading as a health food. The Center for Science and Public Interest has presented specific ideas to the National Academy of Science which proposes changes in government required packaged food labeling. Their recommendations include

- a specific listing of all major ingredients, with sugar and other sweeteners consolidated in a single section.
- a summary of nutritional information, including specific calorie, fat, cholesterol, and sodium content.

EXHIBIT 4–9   Warning Labels Used on John Deere Farm Equipment

- government legislation to specify the allowable usage of the words "light" and "natural." For example, the FDA has an informal policy requiring that foods promoted as "light" contain one third less calories than regular product variations.[42]

Third, *when problems occur with any product that endangers consumer safety, the firm should be proactive in recalling the product from the market.* There have been too many sad chronicles of organizations dragging their feet in product recalls when product dangers have obviously been exhibited. The defensive reaction of Firestone regarding their 500 brand tire and Ford in the Pinto case are illustrations. On a more positive note, the response of Procter & Gamble in removing Rely tampons from the market when toxic shock syndrome became a reality provides an example of rapid product recall.[43] Similarly, an impressive 87 percent return rate for a product recall was accomplished by Black & Decker for their overheating Spacemakers Plus coffeemaker by engaging in a comprehensive multi-media campaign.[44] Organizations that are serious about proactive product recall need to develop effective mechanisms to reach dealers and consumers and provide proven "reverse channels of distribution". These guidelines should allow the organization to remove its product from distribution outlets quickly and get information out to its product users on a timely basis, should the need arise. Such product removal policies will generally require contingency funds that allow for the manufacturer to buy back all unused products (including promotional samples) and provide a subsidy to distributors to help them issue warnings to potential product users when a product danger exists.

Fourth, *just as the organization should have ethical standards for the development and introduction of new products so too should there be specific ethical policies that apply to the product elimination process.* Each year literally thousands of products disappear from the marketplace because their apparent usefulness or profitability has diminished. However, on occasion such product elimination causes severe hardship for the product user. Brand loyal consumers will miss a product that is withdrawn from the marketplace; current product users expect replacement parts and repair services to be available while they own the product. Ethical considerations that should come into play in the course of product elimination are the following:[45]

- Customers should be consulted with regard to their needs *prior* to the product elimination decision.
- Customers should be notified after the elimination decision has been made. There should be a reasonable period before the actual discontinuance of the product occurs.
- The company should have a replacement parts policy that insures that spare parts will be available to users of the product for a reasonable period of time.
- Replacement parts should be maintained by the organization for the expected usable life of the products that are presently in the marketplace.

Conclusion

In this chapter, a number of legal and ethical issues confronting product managers—including product safety, obsolescence, socially controversial and environmentally damaging products—have been reviewed. Realistically, there will always be some crooks (to use the terminology of Chapter 2) who will attempt to exploit certain products and customers unscrupulously to maximize their financial gain. But to those product managers concerned with maintaining a marketplace where competition among products is fair, we offer several ethical guidelines concerning new product development, product formation, product recall, and product elimination. As one writer noted,

> Products are our shared human creations through which we interconnect our ideas, efforts, resources, and technologies as well as express our life concepts, lifestyles, and life-qualities. Every product is a complex of aspirations, expectations, experiences, expressions, and ethics. As such, ethics cannot be turned off and on throughout the product management process. Ethics is present always, and it always pervades. . . . Ethical product management is grounded in confronting this challenge with quality consciousness, deep commitment, and constant vigilance. Ethical product management emerges through each caring, serving, and wise product-market realization. It involves a heroic struggle masked in practical tensions.[46]

These words capture the difficulties involved in ethical product management. We now turn our attention to two other strategic decisions of importance to marketing managers. In Chapter 5 we examine the distribution and pricing of products using the ethical precepts developed in this chapter and preceding ones.

Endnotes

1. Steve Lohr, *"Made in Japan* or Not? That is the Question," *The New York Times* (April 3, 1989), 1, 10.

2. *"Get the Ethics Pill:* A Prescription for Failure," *Ethikos* (September–October 1989), 5–7, 13.

3. For several papers on environmental issues in marketing, see Fall 1991 issue of *Journal of Public Policy & Marketing.*

4. "Danger is Lurking in Small Packages," *USA Today* (November 21, 1989), D4.

5. John R. Enshwiller, *"All-Terrain* Vehicles Spark Debate as User Deaths and Injuries Mount," *The Wall Street Journal* (February 11, 1987), 23 and "Court Agreement Fails to Reduce Number of Youths Killed on ATVs," *Milwaukee Journal,* (December 31, 1989), A17.

6. Alix M. Freedman, *"Bad Reaction:* Nestlé's Bid to Crash Baby-Formula Market in the U.S. Stirs a Row," *The Wall Street Journal* (February 16, 1989), A1, A6 and Alix M. Freedman, "Nestlé to Drop Claim on Label of its Formula," *The Wall Street Journal* (March 13, 1989), B5.

7. Some of this discussion is drawn from Jon G. Udell and Gene R. Laczniak, *Marketing In An Age of Change: An Introduction*, (New York: John Wiley and Sons, 1981), 509–517.

8. Some of the discussion in the following pages is based on the comprehensive coverage in Louis W. Stern and Thomas L. Eovaldi, *Legal Aspects of Marketing Strategy: Antitrust and Consumer Protection Issues* (Englewood Cliffs, NJ: Prentice–Hall, 1984).

9. Richard M. Jacobs, "Products Liability: A Technical and Ethical Challenge," *Quality Progress* (December 1988), 27–29.

10. Stephen Wermiel, "Courting Disaster: The Costs of Lawsuits, Growing Ever Larger, Disrupt the Economy," *The Wall Street Journal* (May 16, 1986), 1.

11. "Unsafe Products: The Great Debate over Blame and Punishment," *Business Week* (April 30, 1984), 96–104.

12. Fred W. Morgan, "The Evolution of Punitive Damages in Product Liability: Litigation for Unprincipled Marketing Behavior," *Journal of Public Policy & Marketing* 8 (1989), 279–293.

13. See note 8 above, p. 106–110.

14. Michael Harvey, "A New Way to Combat Product Counterfeiting," *Business Horizons* (July–August 1988), 19–28.

15. See note 8 above, p. 43.

16. Gary A. Taubes, "Getting Revenge on Imitations," *The New York Times*, (February 28, 1984).

17. Damon Daslin, "Where Trademarks Are up for Grabs," *The Wall Street Journal* (December 5, 1989), B1, B8.

18. For an excellent reference see John D. Oathout, *Trademarks: A Guide to the Selection, Administration, and Protection of Trademarks in Modern Business Practice* (New York: Charles Scribner's Sons, 1981).

19. "More Temperance in Marketing," *The Wall Street Journal* (November 14, 1989), B1.

20. "Ban Cigarette Advertising?: Advertising and Other Promotion Do Not Induce People to Smoke, Say Tobacco Companies. And, Anyway, the Constitution Protects an Advertiser's Rights to Free Speech. True?" *Consumer Reports* (September 1987), 565–569.

21. See note 20 above.

22. Frank B. Cross and Brenda J. Winslett, "*Export Death*: Ethical Issues and the International Trade in Hazardous Products," *American Business Law Journal* 25 (Fall 1987), 487–521.

23. Scott Ticer and Granna Jacobson, "Smoke, Smoke, Smoke That, Am . . . Gizmo?" *Business Week* (October 10, 1988), 145 and Peter Waldman and Betsy Morris, "RJR Nabisco Abandons *Smokeless* Cigarette," *The Wall Street Journal* (March 1989), B1, B10.

24. David Wessel, "Warning Labels on Alcohol: Just What Is Prominent?" *The Wall Street Journal* (May 4, 1989), B1 and J. C. Andrews, R. G. Netemeyer, and S. Durvasula, "Believability and Attitudes toward Alcohol Warning Label Information: The Role of Persuasive Communications Theory," *Journal of Public Policy & Marketing* (1990), 1–16.

25. Nancy Youman, "Minorities Are Also Targeted by Liquor and Beer," *Adweek's Marketing Week* (January 29, 1990), 28.

26. Patricia Leigh Brown, "An Environmental Rating for Product Packaging," *South Bend Tribune* (November 13, 1989), A7.

27. Jennifer Lawrence, "FTC Investigates Degradability Claims," *Advertising Age* (January 1, 1990), 2.

28. Russell Mitchell, "A Word of Advice, Benjamin: Stay Out of Plastics," *Business Week* (April 17, 1989), 23.

29. Roger Mason, "Ethics and the Supply of Status Goods," *Journal of Business Ethics* (December 1985), 457–464.

30. "Bravo to Challengers of Tacky Toy," *Milwaukee Journal* (December 23, 1989), A11.

31. Patt Morrison, "Sexy Computer Program Attracts, Repels," *Milwaukee Journal* (November 24, 1988), F2.

32. Steven H. Star, "Marketing and Its Discontents," *Harvard Business Review* (November–December 1989), 148–154.

33. Janet Guyon, "Apple Growers Protest New Drink That Lacks That Certain Something," *The Wall Street Journal* (August 24, 1981), 15.

34. Michael F. Jacobson, "Let People Know What They're Eating," *The New York Times* (January 12, 1986), F2.

35. "The Pinocchio Awards: With Skepticism Afoot and Activism in Full Gear, The New Rallying Cry is *Marketer, Heal Thyself,*" *Adweek's Marketing Week* (October 23, 1989), 36–50.

36. See note 35 above.

37. John Bussey, "Pretested or Used? Some Products Bought as New May Have a History," *The Wall Street Journal* (July 27, 1987), 17.

38. Bruce Ingersoll, "Hidden MSG in Food Comes Under Attack," *The Wall Street Journal* (January 30, 1990), B1–B6.

39. See note 7 above, Chapter 10 and Patrick E. Murphy and Ben M. Enis, *Marketing,* (Glenview, IL: Scott, Foresman and Company, 1985), Chapter 10.

40. Gregory D. Upah and Richard E. Wokutch, "Assessing Social Impacts of New Products: An Attempt to Operationalize the Macromarketing Concept," *Journal of Public Policy & Marketing* 4 (1985), 166–178.

41. Ronnie Liebman, "Nouveau Junk Food: Consumers Swallow the Back-to-Nature Bunk," *Business and Society Review* (Fall 1984), 47–51.

42. Nanci Helsmich, "Proposals to Improve Product Information," *USA Today* (December 6, 1989), D4.

43. Elizabeth Gatewood and Archie B. Carroll, "The Anatomy of Corporate Social Response: The Rely, Firestone 500, and Pinto Cases," *Business Horizons* (September–October 1981), 9–16.

44. N. Craig Smith, "Black & Decker Corporation: Spacemaker Plus Coffee Maker" (A&B), Harvard Business School Case, N1–590–100 (1990).

45. Geroge J. Avlonitis, "Ethics and Product Elimination," *Management Decisions* 21 (1983), 37–45.

46. Michael P. Mokwa, "Ethical Consciousness and the Competence of Product Management," in *Philosophical and Radical Thought in Marketing,* eds. A. F. Firat, N. Dholakia, and R. Bagozzi, 71 (Lexington, MA: Lexington Books, 1987).

Chapter 5

<hr>

Ethical Issues in Distribution, Retailing and Pricing

Scenario 1

Mike Pinter, the purchasing agent at State University, just learned that one of his major suppliers of computer paper decided to discontinue the product. Kim Wells, the salesrep for another computer paper distributor, called on Mike at the time he learned of the product discontinuance. She said, "We really want more of your business, Mike. We have an attractive price and a good quality product. By the way, I am not using my four luxury box tickets to Saturday's Bulls and Celtics game, would you like them?" Mike replied that he would give her a call within twenty-four hours. **Is there an ethical issue here?**

Scenario 2

The Wholesome Snack Food Company, a regional manufacturer, developed a new chip product that contained only half the salt of competing brands, yet retained the desired taste. Consumer taste tests in two Midwestern cities yielded very favorable results with consumers preferring the new Wholesome product two to one over the market leader. Joe Frederick, the marketing manager, went to meet with the buyer from Roberts Supermarkets. He described the new chip product and its favorable test results and asked the buyer to consider placing it in the Roberts stores. The buyer replied, "We are now charging a fee of $1,000 per store for any new product. For our twelve stores, that comes to $12,000." Joe gulped and realized that would exceed the entire marketing budget he had planned for the product. He told the buyer he would have to check with Wholesome management about the fee. **Does there appear to be a problem with this practice?**

Scenario 3

The Coat Store has a shipment of winter coats that the company buyer purchased in large quantity; they have not sold well. Mark Lynch, the manager, tried unsuccessfully to sell the coats at $89.95. He decided to put the coats on sale at the approximate cost of $59.95. The coat was still not moving. A new price tag was then made that listed the original price as $129.95 with a slash over it and a sale price of $59.95. The coats quickly sold out at this price.[1] **Was Mark's action proper?**

This chapter examines a range of ethical concerns facing distribution and pricing managers. Exhibit 5–1 summarizes several legal guidelines that set the ground rules for distribution decisions. For example, certain practices, such as tying the sale of one product to the purchase of another or exclusive dealing arrangements, are explicitly covered by law.[2] The law is the ethical floor; some practices labeled as unethical are, in fact, illegal. In the pages below, we discuss distribution, retailing, and pricing issues that meet legal guidelines, but have some questionable (ethical) aspect to them.

First, we discuss ethics in managing the channel of distribution—beginning with the supplier and moving to the final consumer. Among the areas to be analyzed are several overarching ethical concerns, purchasing ethics, wholesaling ethics and ethical issues stemming from retailing and franchising. Then we turn our attention to pricing both within the business-to-business sector as well as in the channel of distribution. The areas of ethical analysis here are price setting, discounting and price advertising. Finally, we conclude with several ideas for ethical action.

Channel of Distribution Issues

A distribution channel often refers to the route taken by finished goods as they move from manufacturer to end consumer. Our conception of a distribution channel is a bit broader in that we see channels as beginning with the supplier of materials and ending with the customer. Thus, our interpretation of a typical channel is depicted as follows:

Supplier $\longrightarrow$ Manufacturer $\longrightarrow$ Wholesaler $\longrightarrow$ Retailer/Dealer $\longrightarrow$ Customer

In order to meet customer needs, the varying organizational goals of the channel members must be compatible. Each of these channel linkages (e.g., manufacturer with wholesaler) can create ethical problems for either party. For instance, dealers or retailers want to offer a variety of products to satisfy their consumers, while wholesalers may want to push primarily one manufacturer's brand in order to gain the largest quantity discount. Thus, the inherent nature of conflict in the channel of distribution is a major factor contributing to potential ethical problems.

EXHIBIT 5–1   Legal Issues Affecting Distribution Decisions

Mergers. Vertical and horizontal integration is particularly significant in channel management. A merger is one means of achieving such integration. Mergers are not illegal per se; they are subject to the Clayton Act (Section 7) and its Celler-Kefauver amendment provisions relating to the "probably injurious effect upon competition" or "tendency to create a monopoly."

Dealer Selection. In general, manufacturers have the right to select the middlemen with whom they will deal. This right was enunciated in the Colgate case and was formalized in Section 2(a) of the Robinson-Patman Act. The Colgate doctrine has been modified to cover cases where refusals-to-deal could be interpreted as restraining trade or fixing prices.

Exclusive Dealing. Agreements by middlemen that they will not handle the products of a manufacturer's competitor are not illegal per se. They are, however, subject to the provisions of the Clayton Act

(Section 3) and the Federal Trade Commission Act (Section 5), i.e., the arrangement must not substantially lessen competition or tend to create a monopoly, and both parties must enter voluntarily into the agreement.

Exclusive Territories. Agreements between manufacturers and middlemen giving a middleman the exclusive right to sell the manufacturer's product within a defined territory are not illegal per se. The key to legality appears to be a bilateral vertical agreement between the manufacturer and each individual middleman. Horizontal market divisions are prohibited by the Sherman Act.

Tying Arrangements. A tying arrangement allows middlemen to buy one product only if they buy others. This activity is illegal under Section 3 of the Clayton Act, provided that there is evidence of injury to competition resulting from the arrangement.

Source: Adapted from Patrick E. Murphy and Ben M. Enis, *Marketing* (Glenview, IL: Scott Foresman, 1985), 344. See also Michael Levy and Barton A. Weitz, "Legal, Ethical-Social Issues in Retailing." Chap. 4 in *Retailing Management* (Homewood, IL: Richard D. Irwin, 1992). Reprinted by permission of HarperCollins Publishers.

Overarching Ethical Concerns

Before examining the ethical concerns *within* the channel of distribution, we address several issues that pervade the entire channel. The first is the *power/control* issue. Simply put, this means that the organization within the channel with the greatest power is the channel leader (sometimes called the "channel captain"). With this leadership comes the potential for ethical abuse. Reports of large manufacturers or retailers taking advantage of small, dependent suppliers are legion. Whether this power leads to coercion within the channel can be viewed as an ethical issue. Firms such as Du Pont, General Motors, and IBM appear to have inherent ethical responsibilities to the other members in the channel based purely on their size and market power. In other words, they have special ethical obligations precisely because they *are* powerful.

Exhibit 5–2 summarizes the *power-responsibility equilibrium* and it represents one duty-based ethical approach that might be applied to the channels area. Basically, this perspective holds that power and responsibility must be approximately equal for any business institution to be effective in society. A corollary statement defines the "iron law of responsibility," which stipulates that, in the long run, those who do not use power in a way that society considers responsible will lose it.[3] In a channels context, this seems to imply that economically strong organizations, whether manufacturers or retailers, must use their power beneficially and prudentially, or they may lose it through government regulation or societal sanctions.

During the 1980s the growth of high-volume chain retailers in discount stores (e.g., K mart, Wal-Mart, Target), supermarkets (e.g., Kroger, Safeway, Albertsons) and drugstores (e.g., Walgreens, Eckerd, Thrifty) shifted the power balance toward retailers. A number of new ethical issues have emerged, including slotting allowances (as in scenario 2 at the beginning of this chapter) and forward buying (to be examined later in this chapter). Both suppliers and smaller retailers acknowledge that some abuses of power exist. The common sentiment is that retailers exercise great control over the market for products on their shelves. Thus, retailers must now shoulder more of the ethical responsibility for what happens in the channel.

A second overarching concern within channel relationships is *gift-giving/bribery*. A long-standing business custom is to entertain clients or give gifts to business associates. The major ethical question is: when does a gift end and a bribe

---

EXHIBIT 5–2   The Power-Responsibility Equilibrium

Power–Responsibility Balance	*Direction of Change*
$\dfrac{\text{Power}}{\text{Responsibility}} > 1$	1. Lose power 2. Increase responsible behavior 3. Combination thereof
$\dfrac{\text{Power}}{\text{Responsibility}} < 1$	1. Seek more power 2. Lose some responsibility 3. Combination thereof

The power-responsibility–equilibrium states that whenever power and responsibility are substantially out of balance with each other, long-term forces will be generated to bring them closer into balance. If power is greater than responsiblity as in the top of the diagram, the organization may lose power or increase its responsibility or a combination of both. If responsibility is greater than power, the firm is likely to seek power or lose some responsibility or both.

Source: K. Davis, W. C. Frederick, and R. L. Blomstrom, *Business and Society*, 2nd ed. (New York: Mc-Graw–Hill, 1980), 33–34. Reprinted with permission of McGraw–Hill.

begin? Some retail buyers and purchasing agents are offered expensive gifts or vacation trips as inducements to do business with a certain supplier. It is a responsibility of channel members to sort out the appropriateness of such practices. (For a more complete discussion, see the Gifts and Entertainment section of Chapter 7 and Exhibit 8–3 on international supplier relationships).

A third issue is *price setting and price advertising.* Channel members, whether they be manufacturers, retailers, or wholesalers, must make a determination about prices. The setting of prices at artificially high levels may be legal, but it may not be ethical. For example, insulation manufacturers and contractors precipitously inflated their prices in the 1970s when the demand for their products increased because of the energy shortage. Various channel members may be "squeezed" by other more powerful members to give price concessions. For instance, one technique involves taking unauthorized invoice deductions, such as a 2 percent discount for early payment, even when the deadline is passed. Or "retailers often deduct from a supplier invoice amounts far in excess of the typical 10 percent allowance that retailers receive to advertise suppliers' products."[4]

The *advertising of prices* has long been of concern to consumers and social critics. Of course, laws exist to curb "bait-and-switch" tactics and other forms of blatant deceptive pricing. For example, the Federal Trade Commission (FTC) has rules governing availability of advertised specials. As discussed later in this chapter, the use of small-print qualifiers in advertisements for financial institutions and airlines has been much criticized, as has the difficult to prove retail pricing claim of "guaranteed lowest price."

A fourth area of concern is *competition.* The intensity of competition within the channel of distribution recently has become particularly acute. Competition both at the same level within the channel (wholesaler versus wholesaler) and at different levels (manufacturer versus retailer) raises ethical issues. Why? The market for most products in the United States is mature and, thus, gains must come at the expense of competitors rather than from growing markets. Although consolidation has occurred at the retail level and some of the largest consumer packaged goods firms have merged (e.g., Philip Morris bought General Foods and then acquired Kraft), most observers view the competitive situation as more cutthroat. Some managers use competitive pressures as a rationalization for unethical conduct. For example, if one competitor engages in lavish entertaining to woo clients, then others do too. This trend toward more intense competition shows no sign of abating, and ethical concerns will continue to be an outgrowth of this situation.

Ethics in Purchasing

Manufacturers, nonprofit organizations like hospitals, and services firms all deal with suppliers. The point of contact for suppliers is usually the purchasing department. Most large organizations have a separate purchasing unit staffed by professional buyers. Ethical issues sometimes arise when the individuals in the purchasing department view their personal goals as more important than the organizational ones. On the other hand, ethical problems in purchasing can also occur when the department is forced to implement corporate policies that may lead to discriminatory practices (e.g., reciprocity with suppliers who are friends or relatives of key executives). In addition, ethical situations can happen when power imbalances in the buyer–seller relationship are abused to advance organizational goals. To guard against problems occurring in the purchaser–supplier interface, three possible avenues exist—develop corporate policies, stress moral values, or promulgate professional standards.

Purchasing Policies

Many companies have formal written policies, but only a minority have policies that are explicitly designed for the purchasing department. One recent report indicated that although buyers showed an increased willingness to accept gifts supplied by vendors, top management is issuing fewer policy statements today concerning ethical standards than it did a decade ago.[5] Exhibit 5–3 provides statistical information on this topic and tells how employees learn about a firm's ethical standards. The frequency of corporate policies regarding gift-giving and receiving are also shown in the exhibit. To return to scenario 1, accepting tickets to one sporting event would be an acceptable practice in many of these companies. However, purchasing agents who continually accept tickets, lavish trips, or other major perks may be acting in an unethical manner, even if there is not a written corporate statement on the practice. (See Exhibit 5–4 on Raytheon's purchasing policies for common sense guidance on gift giving and receiving.)

Moral Principles and Purchasing

A second approach to enhancing ethics in purchasing calls for a return to moral principles (such as those discussed in Chapter 2). This is an alternative to increasingly complex corporate policies or government regulation. Typically, legalistic approaches lead to a "letter of the law" mentality rather than relying on the spirit of fair and honest business practices. Emphasizing the value of an ongoing partnership between purchaser and supplier often proves effective. This can be contrasted with the federal government's procurement process, which stresses an arm's length relationship between the supplier and purchaser. An example of one type of thinking that is not mechanically rule-bound is

> If a bid comes in after closing, is it ethical to accept it if it is a lower bid or a better bid? If a supplier has time, money, and resources invested in making his product the best choice for your firm, it's morally wrong to pick another, less qualified, bidder based on an arbitrary deadline for bids.[6]

Professional Standards

A third possibility, and the one advocated by the National Association of Purchasing Management (NAPM), is to increase the professionalism of both buyers and suppliers. NAPM views enhanced professional conduct as a major safeguard to unethical behavior. Part of the NAPM effort involves revising the ethical stan-

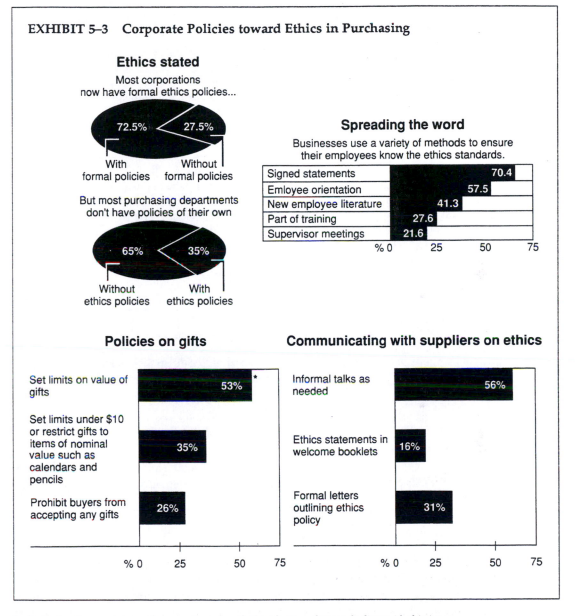

EXHIBIT 5–3   Corporate Policies toward Ethics in Purchasing

Ethics stated

Most corporations
now have formal ethics policies...

72.5%   27.5%

With   Without
formal policies   formal policies

But most purchasing departments
don't have policies of their own

65%   35%

Without   With
ethics policies ethics policies

Spreading the word

Businesses use a variety of methods to ensure
their employees know the ethics standards.

Signed statements	70.4
Emloyee orientation	57.5
New employee literature	41.3
Part of training	27.6
Supervisor meetings	21.6

% 0   25   50   75

Policies on gifts

Set limits on value of
gifts   53% *

Set limits under $10
or restrict gifts to
items of nominal   35%
value such as
calendars and
pencils

Prohibit buyers from   26%
accepting any gifts

% 0   25   50   75

Communicating with suppliers on ethics

Informal talks as   56%
needed

Ethics statements in   16%
welcome booklets

Formal letters
outlining ethics   31%
policy

% 0   25   50   75

1. Indicates the percentage of corporate codes of ethics having clauses dealing with this issue.
Source: Survey results reported in Peter Bradley, "Purchasing Ethics? The Rest of Business Should Be So Strict,"
Purchasing (May 4, 1989), 24–25.

EXHIBIT 5–4   Raytheon Purchasing Policies

Suppose a supplier sitting beside your desk offers you one of his company's pencils. Do you have to turn it down? Of course not. You won't be influenced in your decisions by a pencil.

Then where do you draw the line? Right here:

You must refuse anything—gifts, service, or consideration—other than an advertising novelty such as a paper-weight, key chain, or coffee cup. Even then, if it has an apparent value of ten dollars or more, it is not acceptable. The best rule to follow is, "When in doubt, send it back." What about luncheons with suppliers? Maybe. If there's a legitimate business purpose for that get-together. But don't make it a habit. And use company facilities whenever possible. We don't encourage outside business lunches. Go only when you think it is necessary.

Do you have to fight the supplier for the check? No. But take turns paying for luncheons, particularly when you're on home ground.

What about dinners and other forms of evening or weekend entertainment? These are almost always prohibited. There might be a special situation where you think you should make an exception. If so, ask your manager for approval in advance.

Source: Raytheon Company, "You're Involved," (1989).

dards of their profession. The preamble to their code incorporates some of the basic moral principles noted earlier. The code begins:

LOYALTY TO YOUR COMPANY
JUSTICE TO THOSE WITH WHOM YOU DEAL
FAITH IN YOUR PROFESSION

From a rather generic ten-point "Principles and Standards of Purchasing Practice," the NAPM has developed a new set of ethical standards that are being reviewed by its affiliates. (See Appendix 5A for the association's recently revised code.)

Ethics in Channel Management

In the distribution of consumer goods, especially packaged products, several developments have changed the balance of power between manufacturers and retailers. With the widespread implementation of supermarket scanner systems, retailers now have the data to know exactly which manufacturer's brands are contributing most to the retailer's profit margins. Two of the most interesting retail buying practices having ethical implications are forward buying and slotting allowances.

Forward Buying
This practice pertains to purchasing products "on deal" for future needs during the end of a deal period while the prices are still low. Forward buying necessitates

adequate warehousing facilities on the retailer's part. The savings can be passed on to the customer, taken as profits or subsidize other costs. An ethical question occurs because "a large proportion of deal dollars are considered as . . . profits."[7] In other words, only a small percentage actually ends up as savings to the final consumer. Many retailers would maintain that retaining their savings as profits is not an ethical issue. Rather, they are simply engaging in a "good business practice" which may change depending on competitive pressures.

Slotting Allowances

One of the most pervasive channel activities in recent years is the imposition of slotting allowances on manufacturers. This practice involves distributors or retailers requiring additional compensation (in the form of money or free goods) to take on a new item in their warehouse or store. The tactic originated in Europe and Canada, then moved into the Northeast in the early 1980s. Slotting fees now have become a major expenditure for firms. One estimate holds that 55 percent of all promotional expenditures (consumer and trade) go for this purpose, and 70 percent of all slotting fees contribute directly to the retailer's bottom line and not to lowering the cost of goods sold.[8]

The justification for slotting fees is that new products have proliferated—over 10,000 items are introduced annually with a doubling of new products in supermarkets during the last decade—to the point where the retailer must be compensated for storing, handling, shelving, and eventually removing these products. Retailers now require manufacturers to cover these major expenses. For example, *Business Week* reported that it is common for a manufacturer to pay $100 per store to gain entry to a supermarket chain; some are even charging a $2,000 "failure fee" for products they must pull from the shelves.[9] The analogy that is often used in discussing slotting fees is that the supermarket shelves are valuable "real estate" and the retailer should be able to make money "renting" shelf space to manufacturers.

Although retailers consider these slotting fees as forms of insurance or incentives, they have received much criticism. Some of the more outspoken critics call them "ransom," "extortion allowances," or even "institutional bribery." From a legal standpoint, the fees are of concern because they are usually charged to less well known brands and may represent a type of price discrimination. The FTC is reported to be investigating the antitrust implications of these fees.[10]

Is it possible for a manufacturer to avoid paying slotting fees? The answer is "sometimes yes." Three corporate examples illustrate the point. Miles, Inc. introduced Alka-Seltzer Plus Night-Time cold remedies in the late 1980s without paying slotting fees. They provided the retailer with much needed information on the likely profitability of the product. Miles viewed their relationship with retailers as a partnership rather than a power game.[11] In 1989, Campbell Soup Company reversed its earlier position on slotting and voluntarily launched a "failure fee" guaranteeing that each new item would achieve certain sales after six months or Campbell would pay the retailer a specified amount.[12] Campbell is now shouldering some of the new product risk with the retailer. A national manufacturer of pet supplies refuses to pay slotting fees that they deem excessive (e.g., $25,000 to one Eastern retailer) and will only pay in free goods, not dollars.

Several ethical problems about this practice have surfaced. First, the slotting fees commonly are negotiated privately and orally. This approach makes one suspect that the retailer has something to hide and may be treating various manufacturers quite differently. Second, slotting allowances may be stifling innovation. Often, the smaller manufacturers are first to introduce new product categories. One observer of the supermarket trade remarked: "If we had had slotting allowances a few years ago, we might not have had granola, herbal tea, or yogurt."[13] A question that comes to mind is: are new innovative products being kept from the market by major supermarket chains? Third, certain supermarket buyers are reportedly charging hundreds of dollars as presentation fees for a new item. This evokes the ethical question of free access to product information. Slotting fees continue to remain a concern because some supermarkets are demanding fees for every stage of a product's life (e. g., annual renewal fees) and because the practice is spreading to drug chains and computer retailing.[14]

To help resolve this issue (and add to scenario 2 heading this chapter), a virtue ethics position might state that manufacturers and retailers should be open and forthright in their dealings and should share the burden of new product introductions. Then, only justifiable costs could be passed along via slotting fees. A utilitarian (cost–benefit) approach might argue that the retailer appropriately gains from slotting fees because these charges are justifiable in terms of costs. To the extent that the monies from slotting lead to higher profitability, retailers have a greater flexibility to provide innovative services to their customers.

Ethics in Wholesaling

Wholesalers are relatively invisible institutions in the channel of distribution. Their lack of consumer contact, location in generally out of the way places, and various specialized functions (e.g., drop shippers or rack jobbers) all make wholesaling activities somewhat mysterious. Just as manufacturers have recently been squeezed by retailers, wholesalers have long had to cope with pressures from other channel members. One ethical question does arise in parallel channels where manufacturers use wholesalers (and independent reps) for the low volume/high risk segments of the market and compete with them for the choicer parts of the business. The other ethical issues pervading wholesaling are generally similar to those discussed above and elsewhere. For instance, ethical questions pertaining to purchasing, personal selling, gift-giving, and entertainment (see also Chapter 7) are among the most central.

Ethics in Franchising

The growth of franchises is one of the major contemporary developments within the US distribution system. About one-third of all retail sales in the United States now flows through franchise systems.[15] Examples include Mazda dealerships,

Pepsi and Miller distributorships, ComputerLand stores, Holiday Inn motels, Budget Rent-a-Car agencies, and Pizza Hut restaurants, as well as most other fast-food outlets. Franchises are essentially legal agreements between the franchisor and franchisees regarding the use of brand names, product lines, suppliers, locations of outlets, and advertising strategies. Many of the serious potential problems that might occur between the contracting parties are covered in law by the franchise agreement. Still, ethical issues do arise to the extent that (a) areas of mutual interest and potential conflict are not included in the contract, (b) contractual terms are open to differing interpretations, and (c) compliance with contractual terms is either not enforced or indeterminable through normal reporting or other control mechanisms.

One inherent ethical concern relates to the power-control issue introduced earlier in the chapter. The franchisor is usually a large national or international organization and the franchisee is commonly an individual or small group of people. The power-responsibility equilibrium (see Exhibit 5–2) applies to this relationship. It appears that since franchisors have most of the power, they must also shoulder more responsibility. The unequal footing of franchisees relative to franchisors is demonstrated by the following comment in *Business Week*:

> Franchising has always attracted mom-and-pop operators because it offers a relatively cheap way to own a business. And franchisees have always been at the mercy of franchisors, whose decisions about new products, marketing, and capital spending can determine whether the franchisee's lifesavings go up in smoke.[16]

This article went on to say that a major fast-food franchisor had been charged with engaging in efforts to delay bonuses and incentives and had slowed down bill paying.[17] As a result of these developments, franchisees are employing a variety of techniques to shift the balance of power more in their favor. We now turn to a couple recent examples that illustrate the ethical issues that may surface in the franchisor–franchisee relationship. A further instance is discussed in Exhibit 5–5.

The automobile manufacturer–dealer franchise relationship is under particular scrutiny. A manufacturer may occasionally offer incentives to its dealers and their salespeople to engage in questionable behavior. For example, one European car manufacturer received negative press coverage (and inquiries by state and federal regulators) when the company instituted a major rebate program on discontinued models but then offered salespeople bonuses to sell some of their new models. This was perceived by many as a bait-and-switch tactic and the company quickly had to make major changes in the program.[18]

Ford found it necessary to warn its dealers about tinkering with the company's consumer satisfaction instrument. Some dealers were trying to inflate their "satisfaction scores" and circumvent the evaluation process. This happened when some dealers tampered with the forms; others completed the surveys on the customer's behalf and mailed them to Ford. Additional tactics used were giving

EXHIBIT 5-5   Problems with Benetton and Its US Licensees

Benetton, the Italian clothing manufacturer and retailer, has built an empire of 4,500 stores around the world since 1965. From 1983 to 1988, the number of stores in the United States grew from 250 to over 750. (See table for exact numbers.) The Benetton stores in the United States are technically licensees, because they are individually owned and do not pay royalties as typical franchisees do.

A number of the store owners have complained about too many stores located too close together, difficulty in securing ordered merchandise, receiving products they did not order, and the company's refusal to take back the unordered merchandise. For example, one Benetton franchisee's story was discussed in *The Wall Street Journal*. The franchisee complained that even though her store was located in the deep South, most of her first shipment consisted of heavy wool sweaters. The company also sent damaged merchandise to her and shipped over $80,000 worth of clothing she had not ordered. As a result of these and other factors, some Benetton stores prospered while others floundered. Many of the store owners believe that "Benetton didn't care anything about them."

Benetton has carefully structured their arrangement with store owners so that it does not come under US franchising laws. This has caused problems for some licensees, because they do not see financial disclosure statements prior to signing on with the company. Benetton does set strict marketing guidelines from store fixtures to even requiring some shops to display mail order catalogs for which they do not get a commission.

Corporate spokespersons deny that major problems exist in the United States and insist that its US operations are in good shape. Executives contend that some stores do need more hands-on guidance. The firm has hired a merchandising manager to design clothing displays that store owners can adopt. The business press, however, indicates that a feeling of mistrust exists between the store owners and the company.

Do you think that Benetton is meeting its ethical responsibilities to its store owners? Why or why not?

A Lot of Benettons

	US Stores[1]
1983	250
1984	307
1985	393
1986	564
1987	731
1988[2]	758

Source: Benetton
1. Includes Canada and Caribbean
2. Estimate

Source: Teri Agins, "Benetton is Accused of Dubious Tactics by Some Store Owners," *The Wall Street Journal* (October 24, 1988), A1, A4. (Reprinted by permission of *The Wall Street Journal*, © 1988 Dow Jones & Company, Inc. All rights reserved worldwide.) See also Amy Dunkin et al., "Why Some Benetton Shopkeepers are Losing their Shirts," *Business Week* (March 14, 1988), 78–79.

gifts to customers who sent the survey to the dealership instead of the company, giving rewards to customers who rated the dealer favorably, coaching customers on how to fill out the survey, and even tossing out negative ones.[19] One question that could be asked about these events is did the manufacturer place too much emphasis on this one instrument, if it caused dealers to adopt such extreme measures?

Fantastic Sam's Family Haircutters (a chain of 1,400 hairstyling salons) and General Mills entered into a joint promotion where coupons were placed on Cheerios boxes giving a free haircut for children and two dollars off an adult haircut. No money changed hands between these parties and the promotion amounted to free advertising for Fantastic Sam's. The franchisor headquarters promised General Mills a 95 percent compliance by the franchisees (the salons). However, the offer was not honored by some franchisees and General Mills received many calls and letters indicating refusal or restrictions set on the coupon redemption. General Mills surveyed the franchisees and found that 25 percent were accepting the coupons with restrictions and 25 percent were not accepting them at all. Although several marketing reasons were advanced for the coupon offer's failure (it was too enticing—the premium's value is worth more than the box of cereal and the coupon's eighteen-month life was too long), most dealt with the franchisor–franchisee relationship. Specifically, the promotion's cost came from the franchisee's cash register instead of the national headquarters. Also, the franchisor did not have the necessary control over its franchisees to fulfill its promise of 95 percent participation, and franchisees did not fully support the promotion from the beginning, because they had not been involved in the decision-making process.[20]

Ethics in Retailing

Many potentially troublesome issues also exist in the retail sector. The retailer not only interacts with consumers on a daily basis, but also interfaces with manufacturers and other middlemen within the channel. We find ethical problems arising in retail buying, the product assortment, retail pricing, sales personnel, and retail advertising.

Retail Buying

Retailers often employ professional buyers to secure their merchandise. Buyer activities are similar to that of purchasing agents and the issues related to ethics in purchasing apply as well to retail buying. The extensive amount of travel that is involved in securing products means that retail buyers often do much of their work off-site. The use of expense accounts, their negotiation practices, and ongoing relationships with key suppliers can sometimes lead to ethical problems.

One particular problem that has arisen in recent years is the bribery of retail buyers. *The Wall Street Journal* characterized it as pervasive. Two reasons were given for the growth of this practice. First, the absolute size of many retail accounts has grown due to organizational mergers. One buyer can account for millions of dollars of sales. Therefore, the patronage of this person can be vital to the existence of the selling firm. Second, the rise of imported merchandise to the United States now accounts for over 30 percent of several key categories including clothing. Kickbacks and graft are more of a way of life in certain foreign countries, and some manufacturers continue to use these practices to entice buyers from US-based companies.[21]

Explanations of why retail buyers are susceptible to bribes may be as simple as having employees who are disgruntled or just plain greedy. The problem for the retailer is that the dishonest buyer often does not negotiate favorable discounts (such as advertising allowances) that are provided to other more scrupulous and honest buyers. This is not to suggest that unethical practices are rampant. One observer notes that for every publicized case of illegal activity, there are many retail buyers who walk away from bribes that are offered.[22] A mechanism to deal with the problem is for the employer to place limits on the amount of gifts that buyers may receive. For example, Wal-Mart doesn't even allow its buyers to accept a free lunch. The Certified Grocers—Midwest "sends letters to vendors each year stating that any Christmas fruit basket, flowers, or similar holiday gift worth more than twenty-five dollars will be returned. It suggests vendors make contributions to their favorite charities instead."[23]

Product Assortment

An ethical issue can arise from the products that the retailer chooses to carry. The quality of the products that are sold represents one potential problem. For example, sometimes retailers acquire lower quality merchandise to be utilized for so-called clearance sales. One retailer cunningly brought in truckloads of special merchandise for a going-out-of-business sale that lasted for at least six weeks. Consistency of merchandise quality is essential for any retailer's success. The use of price lines (e.g. Sears's good, better and best line of paint) should represent meaningful differences in product quality and not be intended to confuse the consumer. Adherence to the precept means that the retailer subscribes to the principle of meaningful consumer choice. Customer service, return policies, and merchandise value are also areas where the "total product" offered by a retailer has ethical implications. For example, Dayton Hudson clearly states its position on these matters in its policy statement (see the Serving Society and Operating The Business sections from Dayton Hudson's corporate principles in Appendix 5B).

Retailers also have responsibilities to monitor the safety of products they sell. They have a duty to warn consumers whenever they know of a dangerous product and to cooperate in product recalls. The retailers of products such as firearms, alcoholic beverages, farm pesticides, and prescription drugs must be especially aware of product safety requirements.[24] (See Chapter 4 for more details on these issues.) Furthermore, some retailers refuse to sell beer and cheap wine and certain theaters restrict themselves to family movies.

Retail Pricing

The dubious practices of bait-and-switch, lowballing, and resale price maintenance are all covered by legal statutes. We will examine the subject of ethics in pricing shortly. One immediate concern, however, is the overall pricing posture taken by the retailer. A number of retailers, most notably Sears, have moved toward a concept called "everyday low prices." Here prices are marked lower than the regular price, but a bit higher than during sale periods. A reason for this change is that the word "sale" has lost its meaning and many consumers are fed up with constantly changing sale prices that make it difficult to recognize a "fair deal." Some retailers even "mark up" goods so they can then put them on sale and maintain their profit margins (see scenario 3 above). Continuous specials and price promotions, even during peak selling seasons like Christmas, jade consumers and confuse retailers. One report indicated that certain retailers viewed ethics as playing a part in moving to the "everyday low price" concept.

> By lowering all prices, some merchants are even claiming a higher moral ground. Workbench, for instance, reduced its prices about 15 percent last summer and decided to run only two annual sales instead of six, each of which had lasted a month or more. The New York furniture chain trumpeted the change by handing out "No Bull" buttons and flyers decrying "the phony pricing policies" of competitors that inflate *regular* prices so they can artificially reduce *sale* prices.[25]

Retail Salespeople

Selling in a retail environment raises a number of potential ethically charged issues. (For a more complete discussion of ethics in selling, see Chapter 7). First, retail salespeople often face ethical dilemmas where they are torn between short-term pressures from management, such as achieving an ambitious sales quota, and long-term goals of achieving customer trust. For example, should retail sales clerks inform one of their best customers who is planning to make a purchase today that the item is going on sale next week? Second, the variety of tasks retail salespeople perform (e.g., from ringing up the sale to handling customer complaints) can cause a number of ethical problems (e.g., under what conditions should a salesperson refuse to exchange a customer's merchandise?). Third, retail salespeople generally receive little sales training on how to handle ethical issues. Few retailers provide the necessary guidance to deal with these three areas.[26]

Exhibit 5–6 shows a list of various situations that have been identified as posing ethical problems. These range from deliberately overcharging a customer to yielding to pressures from other salespeople. In order to give the proper guidance to retail salespeople, management was advised to take several actions including (a) establishing policies that are both specific, yet flexible, (b) holding periodic sessions where salespeople and management can openly discuss ethically troublesome issues, (c) maintaining a high ethical posture (i.e., lead by example).[27] Although aggressive retail salespeople were originally included in these points above, we believe that not every activity found distasteful is a breach of ethics. Thus, pushy, but not dishonest, selling is generally ethical.

Another ethical issue regarding retail salespeople is the use of *push money* (also known as PMs or spiffs) as an incentive to promote a particular product. Spiffs can take the form of a shoe company offering a free pair of shoes to a store

EXHIBIT 5–6   Ethical Temptations Experienced by Retail Salespeople

Customer-Related Situations

Charge full price for a sale item without the customer's knowledge.

Give incorrect change to customers on purpose.[1]

Don't tell the complete truth to a customer about the characteristics of a product.

Whether to deal with a customer suspected of damaging the product in the store and then wanting a markdown.

Peer-Related Situations

Pressure from fellow employees not to report employee theft.[1]

Pressure from a friend to give him/her your employee discount.[1]

The temptation to take sales away from a fellow salesperson.

Work-Related Situations

Cheat on the time card.[1]

Allowing the inexperienced salesperson to receive an unfair workload.

1. Typically covered by company policies.
Source: Adapted from Alan J. Dubinsky and Michael Levy, "Ethics in Retailing: Perceptions of Retail Salespeople," *Journal of the Academy of Marketing Science* (Winter 1985), 6–8.

salesperson with the highest monthly sales or a beer distributor offering local restaurant servers a $0.25 inducement for every bottle sold. The use of push money is usually a legitimate and potentially worthwhile sales promotion, because it gives the product an extra push at the point of sale. However, it can be misused if the vendor provides the incentive without the approval of store management. Also the same incentive should be offered to all salespeople, and it should not involve "unfair" or "predatory" behavior.[28]

Retail Advertising

Few topics generate as much immediate reaction from the public than advertising by retailers. Almost everyone at some point has had an experience of seeing a retailer's ad that promises an extraordinary low price or a hard to find item, only to find that the advertised product is not available or comes at a much higher cost. In fact, the Better Business Bureau developed an extensive Code of Advertising outlining their position on such practices as advertising by factory outlets (should only be used when merchandise is actually manufactured by the advertiser or in factories owned by the advertiser), use of the word *sale* (should be a significant reduction from the bona fide former price and be available for a designated time period), and superlative claims (objective claims should relate to tangible qualities that can be measured against accepted standards).[29]

Responsibility to Stakeholders

Since retailers are such visible institutions in society, their responsibilities to employees, customers, suppliers, shareholders, and the local community are closely scrutinized. The wave of mergers and consolidations within the retailing community in the late 1980s shifted some of these responsibilities from local, to national, and sometimes international ownership (e.g., British American Tobacco (BAT) purchased several US-based retailers). We believe that retailers concerned about their ethical posture should continue to evaluate their performance with various stakeholders (recall our discussion of stakeholders in Chapter 1). One retailer that has an exemplary record in dealing with its stakeholders is Dayton Hudson, which contributes 5 percent of its taxable income to community giving. (See the section entitled Serving Society in Appendix 5B.)

Status of Ethics in Retailing

Late 1980s store managers were found to be more ethical and consumer-oriented than their counterparts in the late 1970s. These results held for retail managers in discount, specialty, and department stores.[30] Furthermore, interviews with selected supermarket executives indicated that the ethical climate in their industry is generally good, although some felt that expectations on different practices vary by region or individual company.[31]

There is an inherent perceptual problem between the retailer's view of its ethical position and the consumer's view. Other than the most ethical retailers (e.g., Nordstrom), few stores would likely perceive as their ethical responsibility to include calling a consumer who received a rain check for an inexpensive item. Consumers, on the other hand, hold retailers to a very high ethical standard. They often expect complete disclosure of information about prices and availability of merchandise, including notification of when a rain check item is available. Retailers need to be aware of this implicit "ethics gap" and fully inform consumers of their policies, so that misunderstanding and disappointment are kept to a minimum.

The overriding problem is that *caveat emptor* (let the buyer beware) often shortchanges ethics in retail settings. There can be abuses with the products themselves, pricing, selling, and information sharing. Many consumers are ill-equipped and indisposed to engage in pre-sale tests of truth, usefulness, and fair pricing. Post-purchase remedies and legal sanctions may not be sufficient in many cases. Therefore, retailers must continue to strive toward closing this ethics gap in all marketing activities.[32]

Pricing Issues

One of the most difficult marketing topics to examine from an ethical viewpoint is price. A contributing factor to this difficulty is that pricing decisions are still looked upon as more art than science. Thus, price setting is not the deterministic process with accepted procedures that economics textbooks would lead the reader to believe. The major limitations for pricing are set by cost considerations, corporate objectives, and existing law (see Exhibit 5–7). For example, attempting to price discriminate among similar classes of buyers or to fix prices in an industry are explicitly covered by these laws. Still, pricing remains a difficult area from an ethical perspective because of the sensitivity and concern for monetary matters by corporations and consumers alike. One writer observed, "Perhaps no other area of managerial activity is more difficult to depict accurately, assess fairly, and prescribe realistically in terms of *morality* (emphasis added) than the domain of price."[33]

A number of situations illustrate the troublesome nature of ethics and pricing. Among the most predominant occurrences (left column) and their resulting ethical problems (right column) are the following:

Pricing Situation	*Ethical Concern*
(1) the market is at overcapacity[34]	firms may dump products on the market at cost or below, undermining competitors and, for environmentally sensitive products, encouraging wasteful consumption
(2) the market is characterized as an oligopoly	firms prefer to compete on nonprice dimensions and this may lead to higher prices and illusory differentiation
(3) products are undifferentiated	firms may price high to signal quality
(4) pricing is on an individual job basis	different customers may be charged differing prices for similar work
(5) profit is the sole evaluative criteria for company performance	firms may ignore social costs such as pollution
(6) top management is perceived not to be concerned about pricing ethics	firms may place pressure on middle managers to price gouge
(7) employees have regular and frequent opportunities to meet with competitors	firms may be tempted to engage in informal price fixing
(8) ethical rules and compliance procedures are lax or do not exist	firms and their employees may "short" the buyer

EXHIBIT 5–7   Legal Issues Affecting Pricing Decisions

Predatory Pricing. In times past, a firm might sell its products for less than their cost for a period of time, in hopes of driving a competitor out of business. Such practices are regulated at the national level by antitrust legislation (Sherman and Clayton Acts), and several states have unfair trade practices acts.

Horizontal Price Fixing (Collusion). Agreements among direct competitors to charge an identical price are generally held to be illegal per se under the Sherman and Clayton Acts. However, agreements under the supervision of government agencies are legal. Collusion on prices is difficult to prove because identical or very similar prices may also result from legal tactics such as (a) extremely competitive markets where prices are generally equalized (e.g., gasoline and beer), or (b) the industry following a price leader and engaging in parallel pricing.

Price Discrimination. Selling a product of like grade and quality to different consumers for different prices is illegal under the Robinson-Patman Act "where the effect of such discrimination may be to substantially lessen competition or may tend to create a monopoly in any line of commerce." Price discrimination litigation under the Robinson-Patman Act is perhaps the most complex and time consuming (and criticized) of all marketing litigation. The Robinson-Patman Act provides for bona fide efforts to meet competition and cost differences (e.g., quantity discounts), and it covers promotional allowances.

Price Deception. Posted prices for some products, particularly consumer goods, sometimes bear little relationship to the actual price of the product. Bait-and-switch tactics (advertising a product for a low price to get consumers into the store and then pressuring them to buy a higher priced model), "buy one, get one free" promises and "going out of business sales" are examples. Laws, such as the Automobile Information Disclosure Act, Truth in Lending Act, and unit pricing statutes have been enacted to combat deceptive advertising. The Federal Trade Commission also has issued "Guides Against Deceptive Pricing."

Markup Pricing. There are state laws that set the minimum amount that any product must be marked up. For example, some grocery products must carry a 6 percent markup. Therefore, supermarket chains may not sell these products for less than 6 percent above their cost. These statutes are sometimes controversial because retailers do not always follow them, and they tend to take away efficiency advantages of chain stores and other mass merchandisers.

Vertical Price Fixing (Resale Price Maintenance). "Fair-trade laws" used to allow the manufacturer to control prices at all levels in the channel of distribution. Currently, this type of price fixing is not allowed. The Consumer Goods Pricing Act of 1975 repealed earlier statutes in this area. Despite the absence of these laws, some manufacturers exert substantial control over pricing their products. They argue that this is justified to maintain a quality image. The future of resale price maintenance is uncertain.

Source: Adapted from Patrick E. Murphy and Ben M. Enis, *Marketing* (Glenview, IL: Scott Foresman, 1985), 415. Reprinted by permission of HarperCollins Publishers.

The notion of price is also closely tied to utilitarian thinking about ethics. Buyers enter into an exchange with the seller when they perceive the benefits from the product to exceed the costs (defined here as price). Sellers, of course, are interested in making a profit from this exchange. In fact, price is the only revenue generator of the marketing mix variables. A reasonable profit enables a firm to continue to market products for the benefit of society. Thus, the good of society is being satisfied by a firm's achieving a reasonable profit.[35] However, the logical extension of this argument is often what gets business firms in trouble. Much can be justified in the name of profit. Such ills as deceptive advertising, pollution, product defects, and ignoring the poor and minority groups sometimes result from the overemphasis of the profit motive and its utilitarian rationale.

We advocate considering two other philosophical views toward price. One is the idea of *proportionate reason.* Here the price set by a firm should be either equal to or proportional to the benefit received.[36] Greater benefits, for example in terms of the lifesaving services of some surgeons, then would dictate higher prices. Ethical questions arising from this approach are

> Does the perceived benefit of a product morally justify charging a higher price, especially when the action also has some negative side effects (e.g., charging very high prices for electronic games and toys aimed at youngsters who experience peer pressure to buy these games even though they [or their parents] often have limited means)?

> Is it wrong to charge a price that yields extraordinary profit to the firm even if the market is willing to pay the price (e.g., women's perfume or designer watches)?[37]

The second philosophical perspective for dealing with price has to do with the *principle of fairness.* This perspective implies that manufacturers should be fair in their pricing to channel intermediaries and customers, wholesalers should be fair to retailers, and retailers should be fair to end consumers. Pricing fairness may also be a buyer phenomenon when large retailers squeeze suppliers, who have no choice but to go along, to make late payments, take unearned discounts, or insist on extraordinary services. This common sense approach is intuitively appealing, but difficult to implement effectively because it is often hard to define fairness in a highly competitive environment. However, consumers seem to have a reasonably well-developed sense for what they perceive to be "fair" prices (see Exhibit 5–8).

Ethics in Price Setting

Setting a price for a product is often not an easy decision to make. Marketers rely on several bases from which to set prices: costs, competitors, customers, and the government. One central ethical question revolves around the issue of price gouging (i.e., taking advantage of those who must have your product and are willing to pay an inordinately high price for it). It is commonly accepted that price

---

EXHIBIT 5–8   Perceived Fairness in Pricing

A survey of consumers revealed that people do have an inherent sense for what they think to be fair pricing by marketers. Although the situations posed are somewhat simplistic, they do show that firms need to think about justifying price increases and that base prices do mean something to the buyer. Below is a subset of the questions and the percentage of respondents who felt the pricing was acceptable or unfair.

Question 1. A hardware store has been selling snow shovels for fifteen dollars. The morning after a large snowstorm, the store raises the price to twenty dollars. Please rate this action as: Completely Fair, Acceptable, Unfair, or Very Unfair. (The two favorable and the two unfavorable categories are grouped together.)
(N=107) Acceptable 18% Unfair 82%

Question 5A. A shortage has developed for a popular model of automobile, and customers must now wait two months for delivery. A dealer has been selling these cars at list price. Now the dealer prices this model at $200 above list price.
(N=130) Acceptable 29% Unfair 71%

Question 5B. . . . A dealer has been selling these cars at a discount of $200 below list price. Now the dealer sells this model only at list price.
(N=123) Acceptable 58% Unfair 42%

Question 7. Suppose that, due to a transportation mixup, there is a local shortage of lettuce and the wholesale price has increased. A local grocer has bought the usual quantity of lettuce at a price that is thirty cents per head higher than normal. The grocer raises the price of lettuce to customers by thirty cents per head.
(N=101) Acceptable 79% Unfair 21%

Question 10. A grocery store has several months supply of peanut butter in stock, which it has on the shelves and in the storeroom. The owner hears that the wholesale price of peanut butter has increased and immediately raises the price on the current stock of peanut butter.
(N=147) Acceptable 21% Unfair 79%

Question 12. A severe shortage of Red Delicious apples has developed in a community and none of the grocery stores or produce markets have any of this type of apple on their shelves. Other varieties of apples are plentiful in all of the stores. One grocer receives a single shipment of Red Delicious apples at the regular wholesale cost and raises the retail price of these apples by 25 percent over the regular price.
(N=102) Acceptable 37% Unfair 63%

Question 13. A grocery store chain has stores in many communities. Most of them face competition from other groceries. In one community the chain has no competition. Although its costs and volume of sales are the same there as elsewhere, the chain sets prices that average 5 percent higher than those in other communities.
(N=101) Acceptable 24% Unfair 76%

Source: Daniel Kahneman, Jack L. Knetsch and Richard Thaler, "Fairness as a Constraint on Profit Seeking: Entitlements in the Market," *American Economic Review* (September 1986), 728–741. Reprinted by permission of the authors and the American Economics Association.

gouging is unethical. However, exactly what constitutes price gouging is less clear. Most observers believe that prestige pricing (sometimes disparagingly called "snob appeal" pricing) like that used for Cross pens and BMW automobiles is acceptable. One business ethicist stated that he does not think "there should be a limit on the price of a non-necessity" and that an unrestricted price ceiling in a competitive environment "is the best mechanism for arriving at fair prices in the long run."[38] Exhibit 5–9 discusses a contemporary "charge all that traffic will bear" approach to pricing (for the drug AZT) that has generated substantial controversy. We now turn our attention to ethical issues related to price setting for industrial products, as well as consumer goods and services.

Industrial Products

The ethical issues associated with the pricing of industrial goods revolve around the competitive nature of the market and the type of buying relationship. Areas where industrial firms have run afoul of the law are in *price fixing* and *competitive bidding*.[39] Legal restrictions now exist to help insure that price fixing does not occur and that bidding is fair. However, in some industries, such as defense contracting and construction, bid rigging and other price-related scandals still seem to be pervasive. It appears that an intense competitive environment may cause industrial firms to lower their standards in order to meet the prices of competitors.

In business-to-business pricing of products, the ethical responsibility of each party increases as firms move more toward a long-term relationship.[40] Cooperation, not competition, with suppliers seems to be the watchword during this era of growing international operations. In this environment, price negotiation becomes more cooperative. The traditional hard negotiation associated with pricing industrial products is now giving way to a more forthright system where information on costs is shared. For example, A. O. Smith, the Milwaukee-based manufacturer of automobile frames, set up a research and development office in Detroit to work more closely with the car makers. Thus, we see an environment developing where ethical problems involved in pricing within the industrial sector are perhaps diminishing.

Consumer Goods

On the surface, ethical issues seem more predominant in the pricing of consumer goods, because the prices are the subject of much everyday discussion. Words like "deceptive," "unfair" and "misleading" are sometimes associated with prices for consumer goods. Much of the advertising conducted, especially by retailers, deals with price. Therefore, the sheer magnitude of price information causes ethical concerns to surface. For example, one questionable practice prevalent in the mid-1980s dealt with the retail pricing of mattresses. The president of Serta explains, "Retailers would ask us to set high suggested retail prices, so they could claim their retail prices were 50 percent off list. Now we only set wholesale prices."[41]

EXHIBIT 5–9   The AZT Pricing Decision

In 1986 Burroughs Wellcome Company introduced the first major breakthrough against acquired immune deficiency syndrome (AIDS). It was the life-prolonging drug AZT. The product has turned out to be very successful for the company and, largely because of AZT's success, Wellcome's profits have doubled in the three years ending in 1988. The Food and Drug Administration plans to expand the authorization for the drug's usage to those who are infected with the AIDS virus, but not yet showing signs of serious illness. The estimate of the size of this market is hundreds of thousands rather than the tens of thousands who are currently sick with AIDS.

The controversy over the drug centers on its price. It costs about $8,000 for a year's supply for each patient (lowered from $10,000 in late 1987). Critics in the gay, medical, and legal communities contend that Wellcome executives are "corporate extortionists." Some believe that the company has already made too much money at the expense of the sick. The price is so far out of the reach of indigent and moderate-income people that the federal government had to step in with subsidies of millions of dollars.

Burroughs Wellcome defends its pricing practices by stating that its profit margins (in the 50–70 percent range) are in line with those companies introducing new drugs. They contend these high returns are necessary to finance research and recoup the millions of dollars invested in developing the drug. They initially gave the drug free-of-charge to as many as 5,000 AIDS patients and spent $80 million on a new plant.

Additional criticism revolves around the actual development of the drug. *The Wall Street Journal* stated, "But Wellcome's moral position is undercut by its relatively minor role in the creation of AZT." Researchers at the Michigan Cancer Foundation, from West Germany, and at the National Cancer Institute are credited with the major discoveries which led to AZT. Nevertheless, Wellcome performed toxicology, pharmacology, and animal studies before AZT was given to the first human volunteer. It also financed the big clinical trial and bankrolled the give-away to the patients in the initial experiment.

Wellcome is under pressure to cut its price. The government is attempting to institute a "reasonable price" clause where an unduly high price could trigger a government order for a company to open its books. Any company found in violation could be sued for breach of contract. Congress is also studying AZT and one Congressman wrote the company contending that the original price rationale (achieving a decent return on investment during a short product life) no longer exists as the drug has been on the market for three years and the market is growing for the product.

Do you think the price for AZT is too high? Why? What should Burroughs Wellcome executives do?

Source: Condensed from Marilyn Chase, "Burroughs Wellcome Reaps Profits, Outrage from Its AIDS Drug," *The Wall Street Journal* (September 15, 1989), A1, A4. (Reprinted by permission of *The Wall Street Journal*, © 1989 Dow Jones & Company, Inc. All rights reserved worldwide.) See also Brian O'Reilly, "The Inside Story of the AIDS Drug," *Fortune* (November 5, 1990), 112–129.

Services

The service sector of the economy represents one of the major growth areas of the future. Since services are often labor-intensive, they are more variable and perishable than most tangible products. Thus, pricing becomes a more difficult task, because costs are harder to accurately measure. From the consumer's perspective, the risk is viewed as higher. One commentator contends that the power–responsibility equation (see Exhibit 5–2) holds for services firms too. She said:

> When risk perception runs high among customers, the provider is left with a special responsibility—far different from that in goods manufacturing—of maintaining the personal relationship by establishing trust, emotional comfort, and confidence in the encounter. One way to do this (and there are several) is to present strong and unassailably consistent ethical behavior.[42]

Unfortunately, not all services firms have followed this advice. One specific instance deals with the pricing practices of the financial services industry. Sometimes, in promoting various services, the minimum balance requirements and service charges are not spelled out. Only the most favorable interest rate is promoted. Many consumers do not know what "daily interest" means, or how often interest is compounded, or what service charges are associated with what specific balance amounts. One firm, the Bowery Savings Bank of New York City, tried to counteract this trend by promising to disclose its rate of return in "dollars and cents" and not just in percentage terms.[43]

Ethics of Nonprice Price Increases

One practice—called downsizing—often associated with pricing ethics is reducing the quality or quantity of a product without reducing the price. The confectionary industry is one of the best known practitioners of this "nonprice, price increase" by shrinking the candy bar but not the price. Similarly, certain diaper manufacturers reduced the number of diapers per package, but kept the price the same. Marketers of baseball cards have sometimes reduced the number of cards per package or eliminated the bubble gum while keeping the price the same.

Manufacturers defend these practices for several reasons. First, nonprice price increases are often a convenient way to respond to cost increases when price structures are not flexible, e.g., products sold in vending machines. Second, the practice sometimes brings the product packaging and content amount more in line with competition. Third, modern technology allows companies to reduce the weight of the package or contents while maintaining its yield of finished product.

Critics counter these arguments with statements such as: "It doesn't change the fact that the consumer is getting less product," and "I would characterize it as a way to increase margins at the expense of the consumer."[44] In fact, this issue has received more attention recently with several state attorneys general claiming these practices are deceptive. New York is proposing a law that would require a notice be put on the "principal display panel" of a downsized product for six months.

Ethics in Price Discounting

The 1980s were called the "decade of the discount." Beginning with the inflationary early eighties, rebates were offered by manufacturers on almost any product imaginable, from socks to toasters to automobiles. The retail sector saw the growth of warehouse food stores, discount shopping malls, and superstores that offered name brand appliances at substantial price savings. From such developments, an ethical problem in the retail sector has arisen. Some discount stores have billed themselves as *outlet stores* (where they offer only one manufacturer's product at presumably lower than retail prices). Consumers sometimes find that these stores do *not* really offer significant price breaks.

In general, this trend toward price discounting has made consumers not only more price conscious, but also more susceptible to discount price appeals. Scenario 3 heading this chapter presents a questionable price discounting scheme. We believe that the practice of creating false price tags is unethical (and possibly illegal). It not only undermines the accepted notion of a "customary price" level, but also misleads consumers and does not properly discharge the marketer's duties to stakeholders (i.e, customers and general public). In the same vein, a major chain of fitness centers promoted a 50 percent discount on dues but failed to disclose an initiation fee of up to $1,100. The New York state attorney general cited the firm for unfair sales tactics and false advertising.[45] Most of the time, price discounts are conveyed to consumers via advertising. Below, we examine this topic.

Price Advertising

Some advertising relies heavily on price appeals. For instance, in newspaper advertising most classified ads (e.g., automotive), food ads, and ads for many undifferentiated services (e.g., lawn care) use primarily price-oriented messages. As mentioned earlier, price advertising for services often utilizes large and bold print to indicate a low price. Typical are the ads for airlines, auto rentals, and many financial services. However, the small print at the bottom of the ad usually places many restrictions on the advertised price. Much of this type of advertising can be misleading (if not outright deceptive) and raises ethical questions. For example, the Better Business Bureau of New York found that fourteen of the twenty-nine surveyed rental-car companies and airlines did not fully disclose all the restrictions in their ads despite the fine print.[46]

One outgrowth of the price discounting trend is the extensive advertising of "lowest-price" claims. Retailers more frequently contend that they will not be undersold and "guarantee" that they will offer the consumer the lowest price. These assertions mean that the retailer must monitor all of its competitors' prices, or they imply that the consumer is a full-time price-comparison investigator.[47] Both of these implied actions are not very realistic. The pervasiveness of the we-won't-be-undersold philosophy is illustrated by the fact that some of the nation's top retailers (Hechts, Penneys, Sears, and Wards) have been reprimanded by the Better Business Bureau or by state/local consumer protection offices for using such practices.[48]

To counteract this trend, which has led to negative publicity of retail pricing in general, the Council of Better Business Bureaus and twenty-one of its national members created a task force to draft a code of comparative price advertising. This code outlines specific acceptable practices in a range of price advertising areas. This initiative was applauded by *Advertising Age*, which made this comment in an editorial:

> Here is an example that proves again that major advertisers can come together to deal with a situation that threatens their credibility. The code should enable them to compete vigorously on price, and still play fair with the consumer and competition.[49]

Ideas for Ethical Action

We propose several ideas that both distribution and pricing managers might utilize in their firm to encourage ethical behavior.

First, *a firm should develop explicit guidelines to cover the purchasing function within the organization.* Rather than rely on codes and guidance provided by trade and professional organizations, such as the National Association of Purchasing Management, we advocate that companies (even small ones) consider developing explicit guidelines geared toward their industry. Exhibit 5–10 depicts an excellent twelve-point process that a company can use for this purpose. Committing the organization's policies to writing and setting specific value limits on gifts seem to be good ways for a company to implement such procedures. Furthermore, setting penalties for violations is another essential part of this policy-setting process, because if enforcement does not happen, the guidelines can quickly be viewed as platitudes that are never taken seriously.

Second, *retailers should set up mechanisms for discussing ethical issues within their companies that are most relevant to their business.* Retailers who are interested in a more concerted effort toward integrating ethics into the organization need to decide how to best evoke ethical questions. Some use short phrases that convey to employees the company philosophy. For example, Olive Garden (a Pillsbury restaurant chain) places four words on the revolving door to the kitchen that serve as a constant reminder for the waiters and waitresses. They are *honesty* (noteworthy because it appears first on the list), *action, detail,* and *urgency.*

EXHIBIT 5–10   An Ethics Proposal for Purchasing Managers

A prominent marketing executive and past president of the Council of Sales Promotion Agencies suggested the following points should be followed in purchasing situations. He indicated these steps should occur.

1. Establish a definitive policy that prevents greed from overpowering common sense.
2. Commit the policy to writing and make it part of your company's standard operating procedure.
3. Set monetary maximums for gifts accepted by employees and for gifts given to clients/vendors.
4. Set value limits for major entertainment occasions (e.g., holiday parties for clients).
5. Limit the number of people in your organization who have purchasing authority.
6. Get to know your employees with purchasing authority. If you identify life-style characteristics that

are not commensurate with salary, check into it.
7. Establish a system of checks and balances. For example, require purchase orders involving large amounts of money to be countersigned by someone else of authority in the organization.
8. Hold meetings with major vendors once a year under the guise of working toward a better relationship.
9. Check purchase orders periodically to identify patterns that may signal a conflict of interest.
10. Make it firmly understood that your organization will not do business with anyone who expects a kickback or who offers something more than excellent work.
11. Enforce penalties for violations of the policies you establish when the need arises.
12. Set an example for acceptable conduct at the very top of your organization.

Source: Interview with Vincent Sottosanti, President of Comart Associates, July 31, 1991.

This is a good beginning, but retailers can go further. For example, Ralphs, the California-based supermarket chain, requires its managers to sign the company code of ethics every year. (See Appendix 5C for Ralphs ten-point Philosophy and Commitment statement.) The company also holds an annual seminar for its marketing staff to teach them about ethics and remind them of pertinent and emerging legal requirements. The discussion of ethics is clearly evoked using this approach. Other possibilities include ethical discussions at sales and management meetings. The format of such gatherings is discussed in Chapter 10.

Third, *companies should consider developing a pricing* Bill of Rights *for their consumers and suppliers.* Since pricing is a difficult area and one about which customers are cynical, firms may want to consider a pricing Bill of Rights. (Recall Exhibit 2–5 on Chrysler's car buyer's bill of rights.) One such declaration is shown in Exhibit 5–11. It represents the type of thinking that is needed by firms

---

EXHIBIT 5–11   A Consumer's Bill of Rights for Pricing

A consumer is entitled to receive fair value for the money spent to purchase a product or service. He or she has the right to expect that the price was realistically and analytically arrived at by the firm and was calculated to give the firm a reasonable profit (defined earlier in this chapter). The price should be fully disclosed by being stated in advertisements for the product or service, posted at the point of sale, and placed on the product (although the use of UPCs confounds this requirement). The price on the product should be the price at which the seller is willing to enter into an ex-change. It should not be artificially high, so that it causes the buyer to believe he or she has received a bargain when the price is lowered in negotiation to its intended level. When the product is changed in quality or quantity, the customer is entitled to receive a proportional change in price. Price changes should be promptly announced and completely implemented. Questions concerning price should be honestly answered. Customers are always entitled to fair and equal pricing treatment in the marketplace.

Source: William J. Kehoe, "Ethics, Price Fixing, and the Management of Price Strategy." In *Marketing Ethics*, by G. R. Laczniak and P. E. Murphy, 81 (Lexington, MA: Lexington Books, 1985). Reprinted by permission.

who want to be more forthcoming regarding their pricing decisions. We advocate such a statement for both consumer and channel pricing decisions. If all marketing personnel were to agree with this philosophical statement, we would anticipate that many ethical problems in pricing could be solved. The often used "satisfaction guaranteed or your money back" is a thumbnail version of the approach we envision. However, the firm should consider going further and being more explicit. For example, Montgomery Wards's lowest price policy allows consumers who find a lower price within thirty days of purchase to have the difference rebated.

Conclusion

Distribution, retailing, and pricing decisions contain many ethically-charged aspects that marketing managers must face. The relationships between supplier and purchaser, manufacturer and retailer, franchisor and franchisee, and retailer and consumer all raise ethical questions. Similarly, the pricing strategies employed by all these firms raise the specter of potential ethical abuse. In this chapter, we offer directions for firms seeking guidance on how to better handle ethical questions. In the next chapter, we move to a discussion of marketing's most criticized function—advertising. We examine advertising's role in society and various mechanisms for generating a more ethical approach to this emotionally-charged area.

Appendix 5A

NAPM Code

Principles and Standards
of Purchasing Practice

LOYALTY TO YOUR COMPANY
JUSTICE TO THOSE WITH WHOM YOU DEAL
FAITH IN YOUR PROFESSION

From these principles are derived
the NAPM standards of purchasing practice.

1. Avoid the intent and appearance of unethical or compromising practice in relationships, actions, and communications.

2. Demonstrate loyalty to the employer by diligently following the lawful instructions of the employer, using reasonable care and only authority granted.

3. Refrain from any private business or professional activity that would create a conflict between personal interests and the interests of the employer.

4. Refrain from soliciting or accepting money, loans, credits, or prejudicial discounts, and the acceptance of gifts, entertainment, favors, or services from present or potential suppliers which might influence, or appear to influence purchasing decisions.

5. Handle information on a confidential or proprietary nature to employers and/or suppliers with due care and proper consideration of ethical and legal ramifications and governmental regulations.

6. Promote positive supplier relationships through courtesy and impartiality in all phases of the purchasing cycle.

7. Refrain from reciprocal agreements which restrain competition.

8. Know and obey the letter and spirit of laws governing the purchasing function and remain alert to the legal ramifications of purchasing decisions.

9. Encourage that all segments of society have the opportunity to participate by demonstrating support for small, disadvantaged and minority-owned businesses.

10. Discourage purchasing's involvement in employer sponsored programs of personal purchases which are not business related.

11. Enhance the proficiency and stature of the purchasing profession by acquiring and maintaining current technical knowledge and the highest standards of ethical behavior.

Adopted 5/90   5M

Source: Reprinted with permission from the National Association of Purchasing Management, Inc.

**Dayton Hudson
Corporate Principles**

Operating The Business

We set <u>high standards</u> for any store that's in our "family" of companies.

Good housekeeping. Service that meets customer expectations. Clearly signed and well-organized with clearly presented trends.

We believe in having a clearly stated <u>return policy</u> throughout the corporation. No hassles. No arguments.

We aim for <u>premier locations</u>. Our long-range success depends as much on a sound real estate strategy as it does on a sound merchandise strategy.

Retailing is a very <u>competitive business.</u> We're committed to reducing any expense that doesn't contribute -- one way or another -- to serving our customers.

We aim to be a <u>leader</u> in adopting proven systems and equipment. But, as a rule, we don't intend to invest large sums in pioneering new technology.

We are an honest-dealing business. No deceptions. No short-cuts. No gray areas. Being honest is not only right, it's good business.

Serving Society

We believe the <u>business of business</u> is serving society, not just making money. Profit is the means and measure of our service, but not an end in itself.

Our ultimate success depends on serving <u>four major publics</u>, and none at the expense of the other: customers, employees, shareholders and communities.

We strive to serve our <u>communities</u> because we know that a community's health ultimately affects our "bottom line," just as surely as our merchandising and management practices do.

Corporate <u>public involvement</u> is a fully integrated, fully committed, fully professional part of our strategy and operations.

- We annually budget an amount equal to <u>five percent</u> of our federally taxable income for community giving. We focus our giving in arts and social action programs.

- We maintain open lines of communication between <u>business and government</u> to achieve mutual respect and credibility.

- We encourage our people -- throughout our organization -- to give their <u>time, talent and expertise.</u>

At Dayton Hudson, we believe that our personal and financial involvement in community giving, community development and government affairs all <u>help us manage</u> our business better.

Community involvement helps us <u>manage change.</u>

Source: Dayton Hudson Corporation, *Management Perspectives*, Executive Summary, (1989), 3, 8.

Appendix 5C

Ralphs Credo

Philosophy & Commitment

1. Customers Are Number One.

The success of Ralphs depends on satisfying the needs of customers. Treat them with respect and courtesy.

2. We Recognize Dedicated, Loyal Members.

We are committed to Ralphs continuing success. We work hard to achieve Company objectives and encourage and reward contribution.

3. We Are Ethical And Honest In Our Dealings With Others.

We maintain the highest standards of ethics and honesty in fulfilling our job responsibilities, and in our dealings with each other, customers and suppliers.

4. We "Grow Our Own."

We value our members and are alert for opportunities to help them increase their effectiveness. We take time to coach, train and develop our people as individuals and as contributing members of our organization.

5. We Listen With Respect To Each Other's Ideas To Reach Better Decisions.

We seek input on concerns and needs from the people who have a stake in the decisions. We work hard to achieve agreement and mutual commitment. If a decision must be changed, it is done through appropriate channels.

6. We Look For Better Ways Of Doing Things.

We're always looking to improve what we do and how we do it. New ideas and alternatives are explored and tested so that the organization remains adaptive to changing environments. In doing so, we seek to provide a working environment for all members which is not only clean, safe and attractive, but free of fear. We encourage all supervisors to maintain open channels of communication with their subordinates.

7. We Make Decisions.

People are expected to make decisions appropriate to their responsibilities. We get satisfaction from successful decisions; those decisions which don't work out well are accepted as learning experiences.

8. Our Actions Reflect A Strong Sense Of Social Responsibility.

We make our expertise and resources available to the communities we serve. We contribute in many ways to a wide variety of charitable and philanthropic causes. We support Affirmative Action and equal opportunity for all.

9. The Tougher The Challenge, The Better We Are.

When there's a crisis, everyone willingly accepts responsibility and contributes as much as possible to solve the problem. Diverse groups submerge their own needs and join together as one when dealing with a crisis.

10. Ralphs Is In For The Long Term.

We have a responsibility to ourselves, our customers and our suppliers to seek long-term growth, profits and a good return from every investment. Our planning reflects these goals.

Endnotes

1. Adapted from John B. Gifford and Donald G. Norris, "Ethical Attitudes of Retail Store Managers: A Longitudinal Analysis," *Journal of Retailing* (Fall 1987), 302.

2. See Louis W. Stern and Thomas L. Eovaldi, *Legal Aspects of Marketing Strategy* (Englewood Cliffs, NJ: Prentice–Hall, 1984), Chapters 5 and 6 and Thomas T. Nagle, *The Strategy and Tactics of Pricing* (Englewood Cliffs, NJ: Prentice–Hall, 1987), Chapter 13.

3. Keith Davis and William C. Frederick, *Business and Society: Management, Public Policy, Ethics,* 5th ed. (New York: McGraw–Hill, 1984), 34.

4. William F. Schoell and Joseph P. Guiltinan, *Marketing,* 3rd ed. (Boston, MA: Allyn & Bacon, 1988), 414.

5. Laura B. Forker and Robert L. Janson, "Ethical Practices in Purchasing," *Journal of Purchasing and Materials Management* (Winter 1990), 19–26.

6. Louis DeRose quoted in Hugh G. Willett, "Getting Back to Basic Ethics," *Purchasing: Electronic Buyers' News* (October 23, 1989), 43–45.

7. Willard R. Bishop, Jr., "Trade Buying Squeezes Marketers," *Marketing Communications* (May 1988), 52. See also Rebecca Fannin, "Bring a Bag of Money," *Marketing & Media Decisions* (June 1987), 38–45.

8. Judann Dagnoli and Laurie Freeman, "Marketers Seek Slotting-Fee Truce," *Advertising Age* (February 22, 1988), 12.

9. Lois Therrien, "Want Shelf Space at Supermarket? Ante Up," *Business Week*, (August 7, 1989), 60–61. See also Richard Gibson, "Supermarkets Demand Food Firms' Payment Just to Get on the Shelf," *The Wall Street Journal*, (November 1, 1988), A1+.

10. Laurie Freeman and Judann Dagnoli, "FTC Centers Its Sights on Slotting Allowances," *Advertising Age* (July 4, 1988), 1, 35.

11. Scott Hume, "Miles Combats *Slotting* Beast with Information," *Advertising Age* (February 22, 1988), 12, 68.

12. See note 9 above.

13. See note 9 above.

14. Christine Donahue, "Conflict in the Aisles," *Adweek's Marketing Week*, (September 4, 1989), 20–21; David Kiley, "Drug Chains Bleed Suppliers and Offer Little in Return," *Adweek's Marketing Week*, (September 4, 1989), 24–25; Alan Radding, "Egghead Loads up on Software Slotting," *Advertising Age*, (July 24, 1989), 70.

15. Louis W. Stern, Adel I. El-Ansary and James R. Brown, *Management in Marketing Channels*, (Englewood Cliffs, NJ: Prentice–Hall, 1989), 282.

16. Gail DeGeorge, "Fed-Up Franchisees: They're Mad as Hell and . . ." *Business Week*, (November 13, 1989), 83. See also Michael J. McCarthy, "When Franchisees Become Rebellious," *The Wall Street Journal* (September 13, 1989), B1.

17. See note 16 above.

18. Bradley A. Stertz, "Audi Rebate Plan on 5000 Has the Look of Bait and Switch," *The Wall Street Journal* (June 21, 1988), Section 2, 41.

19. "Ford Cracks Down on Dealer CSI Abuse," *Wards Auto World* (June 1988), 24 and John T. McCarrier, "Ethics in Research Also Affects Consumers," *Marketing News* (August 29, 1988), 4.

20. Bill Stack, "Cheery Coupon Deal Turns Hairy for Fantastic Sam's," *Marketing News* (October 9, 1989), 6, 9, 14.

21. Hank Gilman, "Bribery of Retail Buyers Is Called Pervasive," *The Wall Street Journal* (April 1, 1985), 6.

22. See note 21 above.

23. Steve Weinstein, "Changing Values in Changing Times for Business," *Progressive Grocer* (June 1989), 36.

24. J. Barry Mason and Morris L. Mayer, *Modern Retailing*, 4th ed. (Plano, TX: Business Publications, 1987).

25. Francine Schwadel, "The *Sale* Is Fading as a Retailing Tactic," *The Wall Street Journal*, (March 1, 1989), B1.

26. Michael Levy and Alan J. Dubinsky, "Identifying and Addressing Retail Salespeople's Ethical Problems: A Method and Application," *Journal of Retailing* (Spring 1983), 46–66.

27. Alan J. Dubinsky and Michael Levy, "Ethics in Retailing: Perceptions of Retail Salespeople," *Jounal of the Academy of Marketing Science*, (Winter 1985), 1–16.

28. Michael Levy and Barton A. Weitz, "Legal, Ethical-Social Issues in Retailing." In *Retailing Management* (Homewood, IL: Richard D. Irwin, 1992).

29. Council of Better Business Bureaus, *Code of Advertising* (1985).

30. John B. Gifford and Donald G. Norris, "Ethical Attitudes of Retail Store Managers: A Longitudinal Analysis," *Journal of Retailing* (Fall 1987), 307.

31. See note 23 above.

32. This point was suggested by Professor Thomas Klein of the University of Toledo.

33. Clarence C. Walton, *Ethos and the Executive* (Englewood Cliffs, NJ: Prentice–Hall, 1969), 209.

34. William J. Kehoe, "Ethics, Price Fixing, and the Management of Price Strategy." In *Marketing Ethics*, G. R. Laczniak and P. E. Murphy, 71–83 (Lexington, MA: Lexington Books, 1985).

35. Norman E. Bowie, and Ronald F. Duska, *Business Ethics,* 2nd ed. (Englewood Cliffs, NJ: Prentice–Hall, 1990), 25–27.

36. Oliver F. Williams, C.S.C., "Business Ethics: A Trojan Horse?" *California Management Review* (Summer 1982), 14–24.

37. See note 34 above.

38. Henry Altman, "Who's Gored by Gouging?" *Nation's Business* (June 1987), 6.

39. See note 2 above.

40. Gregory T. Gundlach and Patrick E. Murphy, "Ethical and Legal Foundations of Exchange." In *1990 AMA Winter Educators' Conference Proceedings*, eds. David Lichtenthal et al., 188 (Chicago: American Marketing Association, 1990).

41. Celia K. Lehrman, "Bedtime Stories," *Adweek's Marketing Week,* (October 23, 1989), 45.

42. Nancy L. Hansen, "Ethics: Critical Factor in Service Strategy." In *Designing a Winning Service Strategy*, M. J. Bitner and L. A. Crosby, eds. (Chicago: American Marketing Association, 1989), 69–72.

43. Monica Langley, "Bank Ads Trumpet Interest Rates but Keep the Real Yield Hidden," *The Wall Steet Journal* (February 10, 1986), 17.

44. Professors Joseph Hotchkiss of Cornell University and Stephen Greyser of Harvard Business School quoted in John B. Hinge, "Critics Call Cuts in Package Size Deceptive Move," *The Wall Street Journal* (February 5, 1991), B6 and David E. Kalish, "Consumers Rap Shrinking Food Packages," *South Bend Tribune* (January 6, 1991), E5.

45. David Kiley, "It's Time to Shape Up," *Adweek's Marketing Week* (October 23, 1989), 38.

46. Jeff Wise, "On a Wing and a Prayer," *Adweek's Marketing Week* (October 23, 1989), 45.

47. Stephen J. Sajko, "Misleading Advertising Claims Could Cause Uncle Sam to Step in," *South Bend Tribune* (October 30, 1989), A9.

48. Robert Johnson and John Koten, "Sears Has Everything, Including Messy Fight over Ads in New York," *The Wall Street Journal* (June 28, 1988), 1+.

49. "Retail Code Worth the Price," *Advertising Age* (September 25, 1989).

Chapter *6*

Ethical Concerns in Advertising

Scenario 1

The Country Cereal Company plans to introduce a new bran cereal with oat bran and other ingredients that reduce cholesterol. Management is contemplating an advertising campaign with a strong health appeal that guarantees the product will lower the consumer's cholesterol level. In addition, one manager suggested making the back of the cereal box look like an insurance policy with the message being that this cereal is "insurance" against high levels of cholesterol. One of the newest, and least senior, marketing managers, Bob Francis, wonders if this is overselling the new brand. **Should he raise this issue with his manager?**

Scenario 2

A women's shoe company is evaluating possible ad campaigns. One that has increased sales 70 percent in two test markets contains a heavy dose of sex appeal. For instance, one ad features a scantily clad woman killing a spider with her shoe. Another shows a couple embracing in the back seat of an automobile. In both instances, the shoe plays a secondary role to the sex appeal (see Penaljo ads in back of chapter). Sue Jones, the company's vice president of marketing, questions whether this approach is ethically proper, but the "test market" scores are the highest she has ever seen. **Should she go ahead with this campaign?**

Scenario 3

James Patrick, a product manager for a US manufacturer of children's computer games, plans to introduce several new products with a major ad campaign. He wants to convey "excitement," but is not comfortable with such value-laden words as bombard, stab, defend, and shoot. These words are used in the current campaign by a Japanese competitor which, interestingly, has the *largest* market share. He wonders how the firm can arouse kids' interest without conveying violent themes. **What should he do?**

As the above vignettes illustrate, advertising is an emotional and value-laden topic. Business managers defend advertising as playing a central role in furthering their marketing mission, as well as being a form of free speech. Social critics, on the other hand, contend that advertising often manipulates consumers and may in fact create frivolous consumer needs. Some of advertising's staunchest supporters, who see it as the fuel that powers the capitalistic engine, use their economic defense to justify almost any type of advertising, including the sex role stereotyping of women, exaggerated hype, and unduly persuasive messages aimed at children. The critics are often equally strident in that they would like to see strictly informative advertising such as classified ads in newpapers. Probably advertising should be evaluated from a perspective that falls between these two extremes. We elaborate on each of these positions later.

The Power and Complexity of Advertising

Advertising is a significant economic force in society. Over $130 billion ($30 billion for TV alone) was spent on it in 1992. Since *by definition* advertising is communication by an identified sponsor about its products (goods, services, or ideas) meant to inform or persuade consumers using a mass-media vehicle, it is often inherently biased (one-sided), somewhat intrusive, and advocative. These characteristics lead some observers to state that advertising swirls about the eye of an ethical storm.

The subject of advertising ethics is particularly complex because three major sets of actors are involved in most advertising decisions. First, the *agency,* including its copywriters, account executives, and management, develops the creative campaign for any product. Second, the *company* marketing executives, such as the brand management team and high level marketing personnel, work with the agency in devising the campaign, and ultimately must approve it. Third, the *media and their salesreps,* standards department, media managers, and station or network top executives all make decisions whether to carry the ad, based on the appropriateness of its message. With all of these individuals and institutions involved, one would think that the ethical posture of advertising would be rather high. However, it is possible that the complexity of these relationships and the shared responsibility they represent may work against a concerted ethical evaluation of much advertising.

We believe that management, whether from the agency, the client firm, or the media, has the responsibility to maintain the ethical dimensions of ad campaigns. Such ethical concerns range from the spokesperson used (e.g., use of well-known actors Art Linkletter and Ed McMahon to plug seemingly low-cost life insurance aimed at the elderly) to the message itself (e.g., rental-car companies' and airlines' use of large print price appeal headlines with small print disclaimers), the media utilized (e.g., visual pollution caused by billboards), and the suitability of the particular ad for its intended audience. (See Exhibit 6–1 for a discussion of the ethical implications of an ad campaign for toys.)

In the following pages, we address five major topics: (1) the role of advertising in society, including the respective positions of critics and supporters of advertising, (2) how advertisers implicitly or explicitly use moral philosophy, (3) several important ethical questions facing advertising managers, (4) recent positive developments and future challenges that relate to ethical standards in advertising, and (5) specific ideas for ethical action that might help upgrade the ethical sensitivity in the advertising world.

Advertising and Society

Advertising's role in society is controversial. The aforementioned positions of both critics and supporters of advertising can be summarized as "a dialogue that never happens."[1] It has been a long running debate. Exhibits 6–2 and 6–3 depict representative quotations that delineate these positions. In this section we discuss these quotes and other perspectives that amplify both ends of the advertising ethics spectrum. In addition, we examine the existing regulation of advertising by industry and government in the context of societal concerns.

The Views of Advertising's Critics

Consumer Critics

Almost every public-opinion poll in past years that asks samples of consumers about their reaction to the ethics of advertising has found very negative results. For example, in a 1978 study conducted for *Advertising Age*, 43 percent of the respondents said that advertising is an occupation with "the lowest ethical standards."[2] In Gallup polls conducted in both 1977 and 1983, advertising practitioners fell *near the bottom* in terms of honesty and ethical standards. In both polls they ranked only ahead of another maligned *marketing* occupation—automobile salespeople.

Additional surveys examined the advertising message and its content, rather than the occupation itself. Although in one poll 88 percent of the public indicated that advertising is essential and 57 percent believed that advertising results in better products, consumers have regularly raised several reservations about it. One study found that almost 60 percent of the people perceive that "most advertising insults the intelligence of the average consumer." A Harris poll showed 80 percent feeling that "the claims for most products advertised on TV are exaggerated" and just over half stating that most or all TV advertising is "seriously misleading." Finally, a Yankelovich study in the 1980s reported that the vast

EXHIBIT 6–1   Toy Wars

Tom Daner, president of Daner Associates ad agency, was caught in a dilemma. His firm had recently taken on a new client, Crako Industry and its newest product—a battery-operated toy helicopter. It was modeled on the military helicopter used in Rambo movies, and Crako wanted to create a "mean and tough" image for the product, so it could compete with the successful GI Joe line of toys. Crako managers felt that the company's future might depend on the success of this new toy.

Tom was unwilling to have his company develop television ads that would increase what he already felt was too much violence in television aimed at children. He suggested that instead of promoting the Crako helicopter through violence, it should be presented in some other manner. When Tom presented the Crako account to his executive committee, he found that they did not share his misgivings. The other committee members felt that Daner should give Crako exactly the kind of ad it wanted; one with a heavy content of violence. The creative department, in fact, quickly produced a copy-script that called for videos showing the helicopter "flying out of the sky with machine-guns blazing" at a jungle scene below.

After viewing the copy, Tom Daner refused to accept it. They should produce an ad, he insisted, that would meet their client's needs but that would also not glorify violence and war, but should somehow support cooperation and family values. Disappointed and frustrated, the creative department went back to work. Their second proposal showed the toy helicopter flying through the family room of a home as a little boy plays with it. Then, the scene shifts to show the boy on a rock rising from the family room floor and the helicopter swooping down and picking up the boy, as though rescu-

ing him from the rock where he had been stranded. Although the creative department felt this was too tame, Tom liked this version and it was filmed.

Tom met with Crako executives to view the pilot ad, but the client turned down the ad and instructed Daner to make the next version "tougher and meaner." Tom was disappointed and reluctantly told the creative department to design an ad like they originally wanted. They quickly designed an elaborate jungle village set, and the new ad proposal called for the helicopter to be shown blowing up in the village.

Once again, Tom was not happy with the results. He met with the creative department and said, "The basic issue here is violence. Do we really want to present toys as instruments for beating up people? This ad is going to promote aggression and violence. It will glorify dominance and do it with kids who are impressionable. Do we really want to do this?" The creative department responded that they were merely giving their client what he wanted. Moreover, they said, every other advertising firm in the business was breaking the limits against violence set by the networks.

Tom made one last attempt. Why not market the helicopter as an adventure and fantasy toy? He suggested filming the ad with the same jungle backdrop, while instead of showing the helicopter shooting at the burning village, showing it flying in to rescue the people from the village. He proposed to create an ad that showed excitement, adventure, and fantasy, but no aggression. He said later, "I was trying to figure out a new way of approaching this kind of advertising. We have to follow the market or we will go out of business trying to moralize to the market. But why not try a new approach? Why not promote

EXHIBIT 6–1   *Continued*

toys as instruments that expand the child's imagination in a way that is positive, and that promotes cooperative values instead of violence and aggression?"

A new film version of the ad was made, now showing the helicopter flying in over the jungle set. In this ad quick shots and heightened background music give the impression of excitement and danger. The helicopter flies dramatically through the jungle and over a river and a bridge to rescue a boy from a flaming village. As lights flash and shoot hap-

hazardly through the scene, the helicopter rises and escapes into the sky. The final ad was clearly exciting and intense. And it promoted the saving of a life instead of violence against life.

Should Tom Daner risk the Crako account by submitting only the rescue mission ad? Or should he let Crako executives also see the ad that showed the helicopter shooting up the village, knowing that they would probably prefer that version if they saw it?

Source: Condensed from Manuel Velasquez, "Toy Wars." In *Business Ethics*, 3rd ed., by M. Velasquez, 312–316 (Englewood Cliffs, NJ: Prentice–Hall, 1992). Reprinted with permission.

majority of the American population was concerned with truth, distortion, and exaggeration present in advertising.

Some of the percentages in these polls seem suspiciously high. However, the conclusion that must be drawn is that advertising has a credibility problem and quite likely an ethical problem with the general public.

Social and Academic Critics

Many other critics of advertising and of its ethical posture have surfaced over the years. Most likely from the day of the first primitive form of advertising, there was criticism. The views of several outspoken and influential (from the standpoint of academic reputation) individuals are shown in Exhibit 6–2. These comments span many of the decades of the twentieth century and concentrate on the social role and character of advertising. The words "values" and "morals" are used often in these commentaries. These writers seem to suggest that advertising has undermined the social and moral fabric in the United States—a charge the marketing community must take seriously even if it believes the critics to be overly harsh in their evaluations.

The Views of Advertising's Supporters

The Advertising Community's Response

Well-known ad agency spokespeople, representing the advertising community, have responded to these criticisms by defending the inherent freedom of speech (i.e., the right to advertise). In the 1980s, CEOs of major ad agencies authored books delineating the economic, social, and moral benefits of advertising.[3] The

EXHIBIT 6–2   The Views of Advertising's Critics[1]

Early Critics

Advertising Appeals to Base Motives. "On the moral side, it is thoroughly false and harmful. It breeds vulgarity, hypnotizes the imagination and the will, fosters covetousness, envy, hatred, and underhand competition."[2]

Advertising Is Influential, but Not Socially Responsible. "...though it [advertising] wields an immense social influence, comparable to the influence of religion and learning, it has no social goals and no social responsibility for what it does with its influence, so long as it refrains from palpable violations of truth and decency. It is this lack of institutional responsibility, this lack of inherent social purpose to balance social power, which I would argue, is a basic cause for concern about the role of advertising."[3]

Recent Critics

Advertising Molds Children. "...I don't think the advertisers have any real idea of their power not only to reflect but to mold society.... And if you reflect us incorrectly, as I believe you are doing, you are raising a generation of children with cockeyed values as to what men and women, and life and family really are. You may be training them as consumers, but you are certainly not educating them as people."[4]

Advertising Creates Insatiable Desires. "Advertising and its related arts thus help develop the kind of man the goals of the industrial system require—one that reliably spends his income and works reliably, because he is always in need of more.... In the absence of the massive and artful persuasion that accompanies the management of demand, increasing abundance might well have reduced the interest of people in acquiring more goods.... The consequence—a lower and less reliable propensity to consume—would have been awkward for the industrial system."[5]

Advertising Affects Morals. "...advertising begins to play a more subtle role in changing habits than merely stimulating wants.... Though at first the changes were primarily in manners, dress, taste, and food habits, sooner or later they began to affect more basic patterns: the structure of authority in the family, the role of children and young adults as independent consumers in the society, the pattern of morals and the different meanings of achievement in the society."[6]

Advertising Is Subversive. "If I were asked to name the deadliest subversive force within capitalism, the single greatest source of its waning morality—I would without hesitation name advertising. How else should one identify a force that debases language, drains thought, and undoes dignity?"[7]

1. These quotations are taken from Richard Pollay, "The Distorted Mirror: Reflections on the Unintended Consequences of Advertising," *Journal of Marketing* (April 1986), 18–36.
2. John Danier Logan, "Social Evolution and Advertising," *Canadian Magazine* 28 (1907), 333.
3. David M. Potter, *People of Plenty* (Chicago: University of Chicago Press, 1954), 177.
4. Marya Mannes, *But Will It Sell?* (New York: Lippincott, 1964), 32.
5. John Kenneth Galbraith, *The New Industrial State* (Boston: Houghton Mifflin, 1967), 219.
6. Daniel Bell, *The Cultural Contradictions of Capitalism* (New York: Basic Books, 1976).
7. Robert Heilbroner, "Demand on the Supply Side," *New York Review of Books* 38 (June 11, 1981), 40.

EXHIBIT 6–3   The Views of Advertising's Business Supporters

Advertising is Misunderstood. "The government regulators, and the consumer advocates dedicated to influencing them, do not understand what advertising is and how it is perceived by the consumers. And their overwhelming fear that one is always trying to deceive the other leads them to demand from advertising the kind of product information that characterizes *Consumer Reports.* They expect advertising to be journalism, and they evaluate it by journalistic standards. Since it is not, advertising, like the ugly duckling, is found wanting."[1]

Advertising Enhances Freedom of Choice. "The drive for material goods which characterizes most Western societies may be less admirable than a different kind of reward and motivation set of goals. The fact is that the system works, and that it does both motivate and reward people. If it appears to critics that the motivations are inferior, and the rewards are vulgar, it must be remem-

bered that at least the people have their own choice of what those rewards will be, and observation tells us that they spend their money quite differently. It is essentially a democratic system, and the freedom of individual choice makes it valuable to the people who do the choosing."[2]

Advertising Yields the Greatest Good. "But I believe advertising's net effect is good. It helps promote the greatest good for the greatest number. I believe it helps to satisfy the needs and desires of human beings. I believe that it does make possible many more of the good things of life, not only for the affluent but also for those who can least afford them. If you believe that, as I do, then I don't think you can stand by and let advertising be destroyed. We need a cooperative effort among believers ... a cooperative effort and a personal contribution toward educating people about the real truth of the value of advertising."[3]

---

1. John O'Toole, "What Advertising Is—and Isn't," *Across the Board* (April 1982), 42.
2. John Crichton, "Morals and Ethics in Advertising." In *Ethics, Morality and the Media: Reflections on American Culture*, ed. Lee Thayer, 113 (New York: Hastings House, 1980).
3. Vincent T. Wasilewski, "Advertising: Does It Have a Future?" In *Ethics, Morality and the Media: Reflections on American Culture*, ed. Lee Thayer, 205 (New York: Hastings House, 1980).

quotations shown in Exhibit 6–3 summarize their views and those of presidents of the National Association of Broadcasters and the American Association of Advertising Agencies (AAAA).

Marketing Academics' Response
Marketing academics also have come forcefully into the debate on the social role of advertising. They contend that, for better or worse, advertising is a mirror of the current character of US society. This metaphor has advertising as a "looking glass" reflecting the values and morals of a society and not as a molder of societal standards.[4] The following statement captures this view: ". . . advertising does not have the power to dominate other forces (i.e., family, church, literature, etc.) that

contribute to the values of society, which have evolved over centuries . . ."[5] The academic defenders of advertising downplay its institutional influence on society, but they argue that it contributes economically by providing useful information for potential customers, supporting the mass media in the United States, employing many people directly and indirectly, and generally fueling the engine of our capitalistic economy.

The Views of Advertising's Regulators

The job of refereeing the raging debate between the critics and supporters falls on the shoulders of industry self-regulators and several governmental agencies. Each are examined briefly here to provide a demarcation of the ethical "floor" above which all advertisers should operate.

Advertising Self-Regulation

The media and advertising industries attempt to control the actions of their members, often to avoid what may be harsher government regulation.[6] The National Advertising Division (NAD) of the Better Business Bureau was established in 1971 for this purpose. It investigates over 180 cases annually and resolves about 98 percent of the disputes. For example, the NAD has chastized Ford and Chevrolet for their truck ads and told them to clean up their claims. In about half of the cases the firm is exonerated and in half the company changes the ad or discontinues it. Since most of the ads have finished running before the NAD makes a ruling, the issues are often moot.

In the 2 percent of cases that are not resolved in one of the above ways, the National Advertising Review Board (NARB) becomes the court of appeals. The NARB consists of fifty members from the advertising profession (agency and client) and general public. If the case is still not resolved, it is referred to the government for further action. While the NAD and NARB attempt to resolve disputes, neither has any real power except to threaten that the case will be sent to the Federal Trade Commission (FTC). In spite of this, these groups have been effective, for the most part, in controlling outright deception and misleading advertising. At the local level, the Better Business Bureau refers cases to local authorities.

Government Regulation

A number of government agencies are charged with the regulation of advertising (see Exhibit 6–4). The most prominent of these is the Federal Trade Commission. The agency has gone through periods of high activity and relative inactivity regarding regulation of false and deceptive advertising. For example, the late 1970s were characterized by an activist FTC while the 1980s saw the agency pursue few deceptive advertisers. The FTC's power to require advertising substantiation along with the industry self-regulatory initiatives provide the advertising community with legal, but not ethical, guidance on what is acceptable practice.

EXHIBIT 6–4   Governmental Regulation of Advertising

Federal Trade Commission (FTC)

The Federal Trade Commission, established in 1914, is the major federal regulator of advertising. The Bureau of Consumer Protection (BCP) received its mandate with the passage of the Wheeler–Lea Amendment to the Federal Trade Commission Act in 1938. The BCP regulates national marketing and advertising. During its history the agency has gone through cycles of active and passive attitudes toward the regulation of advertisers. The range of remedies the FTC can use are consent order, cease and desist order, ad substantiation, affirmative disclosure, and corrective advertising.[1]

Food & Drug Administration (FDA)

The FDA regulates pharmaceutical advertising, i.e. ads directed at medical practitioners for drugs and products that may be sold only by prescription. The FDA requires that certain content must be included in every advertisement, such as warnings, and side effects, though it does not necessarily state how prominently that information must be displayed.

Federal Communications Commission (FCC)

The FCC possesses great potential for influencing advertising content, even though they do not have any power over advertisers, advertising agencies, print media, or broadcast networks. The FCC grants operating licenses to all TV and radio stations, and reviews them periodically for possible violations of their standards.

State Regulation

Most states have passed "little FTC" Acts that allow them to bring cases against local or state-wide ad campaigns that they feel are deceptive or unfair. During the deregulatory 1980s when little advertising was challenged, the state attorneys general stepped in to become a more significant force in the regulation of deceptive advertising. The states of New York, Texas, and Illinois were particularly aggressive during this time of FTC inactivity. In the early 1990s it appears that the FTC will look more closely at the claims made by national advertisers and, once again, will scrutinize the content of advertising.

For further information on the FTC, see Patrick E. Murphy and William L. Wilkie, eds. *Marketing and Advertising Regulation* (Notre Dame, IN: University of Notre Dame Press, 1990).

How Advertisers Use Moral Philosophy

The dominant perspective used by most managers to evaluate advertising ethics is utilitarian (recall our discussion in Chapter 2). This means the benefits of promoting products in our consumption-oriented society justify the social costs of advertising and most of the persuasive techniques used by advertisers. Many business executives defend advertising on the grounds that it communicates with the mass market and therefore contributes to the well being, if not happiness, of large numbers of consumers. For example, advertising Mercury automobiles not only informs consumers about the features of the cars (e.g., some models have anti-lock brakes) but also stimulates demand for this brand and thereby lowers the cost of Mercurys for everyone.

Interestingly, the critics of advertising also sometimes use consequences as the benchmark from which to evaluate the field of advertising. Many of the quotes in Exhibit 6–2 at least indirectly make reference to the type of society that results from the influence of advertising. The consequentialist critique of advertising is articulately captured by the following:

> Advertising's unintended consequences are seen by many as a pollution of our psychological and social ecology, which raises moral alarm and tempts a defensive reaction from those of us whose expertise and sense of personal worth is drawn from our knowledge of, and at least implicit assistance in, the processes of persuasion.[7]

From a strictly utilitarian standpoint, advertising is sometimes used to rationalize the viability of the entire market system which is assumed to be self-corrective. As one defender of advertising puts it, "if they don't like the advertising we do, they won't buy the product, and we'll be punished at the cash register." However, since it is inherently difficult to determine a specific advertisement's effect, there are serious problems in predicting the consequences of advertising in general.[8] In fact, some well-known "insulting" advertising campaigns (e.g., Wisk's "Ring Around the Collar" and Cascade dishwashing detergent's "Spotless Glasses") had positive consequences in terms of recognition and profits for the product.

The other category of philosophical theories used to evaluate ethics in advertising is duty-based. Such analysis would begin with an implication of Kant's moral imperative: "advertising should never treat its audience or spokespersons as mere means." Persuasive advertising, which attempts to change attitudes and values in order that a product solve a heretofore unrecognized problem, may assault individual dignity. Furthermore, blatant sex appeal advertising would probably not meet this imperative of *never* using women (or men) as means to an end. Conversely, information directed at assisting choice, solving real needs and consumer problems, irrespective of its commercial motivation, serves consumer goals and is, therefore, of positive ethical value according to this view.

Advertising is also analyzed as duty-based when references are made by defenders of advertising to the Golden Rule and Kant's so-called *absolute* duties. That is, advertisers subscribe to moral principles that are negatively stated, e.g., do *not* lie to customers or clients, do *not* steal competitors' ideas and do *not* cheat the media. However, other advertising practitioners would be less likely to follow the so-called *meritorious* duties, which are positive in tone, e.g., always tell the whole truth to client and customers; come to the aid of a failing supplier, and routinely inform the media of an upcoming change in a promotional campaign. Exercising such positive meritorious duties would be more in line with the virtue ethics theory also examined in Chapter 2.

The *principle of fairness* is an embodiment of a meritorious duty, and implies that advertisers take fairness into consideration in their day to day dealings with customers and clients. In a 1987 survey of advertising executives, an open-ended question was asked about the most difficult ethical problem confronting advertisers in their daily work.[9] Exhibit 6–5 shows the results. "Fairness" to clients, suppliers, vendors and media, employees and agency management, and, other agencies made up four of the six major categories of responses. It seems curious that fairness to customers did not make the list.

The conclusion we draw is that ethics in advertising, in proper perspective, has its underpinnings in several moral philosophies. Therefore, advertising, media, and product managers probably should consider using multiple philosophical perspectives in evaluating the impact of their advertising. We return to this point later in the chapter.

Ethical Questions Facing Advertising

A number of ethical questions have been asked about advertising. In this section, we examine four of the most frequent and ethically charged queries.

EXHIBIT 6–5   Ethical Problems of Advertising Agency Executives[1]

Problem	Responses	
	No.	%
Treating clients fairly.	80	28
Creating honest, nonmisleading, socially desirable advertisements.	66	24
Representing clients whose products/services are unhealthy, unneeded, useless, or unethical.	34	12
Treating suppliers, vendors, and media fairly.	25	9
Treating employees and management of agency fairly.	15	5
Treating other agencies fairly.	7	2
Other.	11	4
None.	43	15
Overall	281	99[2]

[1]These problems were extrapolated from responses to the following open-ended question: "In all professions (e.g., law, medicine, education, accounting, advertising, etc.), managers are exposed to at least some situations that pose a moral or ethical problem. Would you please briefly describe the aspect of advertising that poses the *most difficult* ethical or moral problem confronting you in your daily work?" Two judges independently evaluated the issues, resulting in a 96 percent interjudge reliability.
[2]Does not add up to 100 percent because of rounding.
Source: Shelby D. Hunt and Lawrence B. Chonko, "Ethical Problems of Advertising Agency Executives," *Journal of Advertising* 16, 1987, 4:19.

How Persuasive Should Advertising Be?

One of the most persistent areas of debate about advertising is its persuasive content. One useful way of looking at this area is in terms of a continuum.

Complete truth			Total lie
Probably ethical	*Possibly unethical*		*Illegal*
Information	Persuasion	Embellishment	Deception

This continuum implies that as one moves from left to right the potential for an ethical problem increases. That is, strictly informative advertising is likely to be less ethically suspect than advertising that relies more heavily on persuasion. And in turn, *embellishment* (to make something appear better than it is) or *puffery* (exaggerating a claim) is probably more likely to present ethical problems. For example, embellishment is commonly used by marketers of men's and women's toiletries, suggesting that one just has to use the product to be more attractive to someone of the opposite sex.

Puffery is sometimes defended by advertisers who say that everyone else does it or that consumers can decide for themselves if a product is the "best." Since puffery is a claim based on opinion and thus cannot be substantiated, it cannot be considered deceptive under the law. For example, a computer diskette manufacturer made the following claim: "Somebody has to be better than everybody else." This claim cannot be proven true or false. Most "puffs" are harmless exaggeration such as "this auto's engine purrs like a kitten" or "this golf putter will make your stroke as smooth as a baby's skin." But, the potential exists for unethical (and even arguably illegal) puffs in advertising.[10]

The solid vertical line in the continuum in front of the word "deception"— misrepresenting the facts—indicates that it is not only unethical, but also illegal. (Recall our discussion of the Federal Trade Commission and advertising self-regulation earlier in the chapter.) The special case of *subliminal advertising* is briefly reviewed in Exhibit 6–6.[11]

This debate concerning the ethics of persuasive versus informative advertising has long raged. One advertising executive argued that *all* advertising is persuasive because its intention is to sell products. And some philosophers view all persuasive advertising as unethical, because it reduces the consumer's autonomy. In a series of articles appearing in the *Journal of Business Ethics*, philosophers and marketing academics debated the merits of persuasive advertising.[12] The analysis was often overdrawn, but the sense of that group seemed to be that any informative or persuasive advertising for unsafe or unhealthy products (e.g., cigarettes and handguns) was unethical. Obviously, not everyone holds this view.

EXHIBIT 6–6   What Is Subliminal Advertising?

"During a six-week period in 1956, a New Jersey movie theater was reported to have flashed the subliminal messages "Hungry? Eat Popcorn" and "Drink Coca-Cola" during the popular movie *Picnic*. Over 45,000 people attended the theater during this period and apparently were influenced by the subliminal ads. Compared with previous sales records, the sales of popcorn increased 58 percent and the sales of Coca-Cola increased 18 percent during this time. When this story hit the press, a popular uproar arose. Angry charges of "sinister plots," "breaking and entering people's minds," and the like were freely raised. . . .

Subliminal advertising occurs below a person's conscious threshold level. There are two types: "visual stimuli presented so briefly that we cannot consciously detect them, and sound messages that are presented very rapidly and at such a low volume that we cannot detect them. . . .

"The 1950s furor really concerned possible abuse of subliminal stimulation for *persuasive purposes*. Brainwashing was feared, in which consumers would be manipulated by forces that they could not consciously perceive or even know about. This raises the question, "how effective is subliminal stimulation in the area of persuasion?" Note that this question introduces a further step in the process—not only must the subliminal stimulus be perceived, but a consumer's behavior must also be affected.

"The evidence on this question is mixed. Most studies indicate such "hidden persuasion" is unlikely to occur. The original results claimed in the movie theater, for example, have been strongly criticized. There were no scientific controls in the theater test, and the results could have been due entirely to other factors, such as consumer reaction to the movie's scenes of eating and drinking, the summer weather, or the types of customers. It is notable that the theater results have not been repeated (replicated) in later studies (and there is some question as to whether the study was even actually performed). Also, a more controlled study on TV ads in Indianapolis was conducted shortly thereafter and showed no evidence of even the slightest effects in persuading the mass audience. Within marketing, one study did report significant effects, but other studies have provided no significant effects of subliminal ads.

"On balance, then, the evidence seems to suggest that subliminal advertising will not be very effective in persuading consumers to buy. Many leaders in the advertising community, moreover, view this as an unethical technique and would likely support legislation to ban it if it were found to be effective."

What is your view on the ethics of subliminal advertising?

Source: William L. Wilkie, *Consumer Behavior*, 2nd ed. (New York: John Wiley, 1990), 246–248. Copyright © 1990, John Wiley & Sons, Inc. Reprinted by permission.

For example, the advertising community staunchly defends its right to advertise all legal products.

One noted economist argued that persuasive advertising, even though it may strongly influence the consumer, is morally acceptable. He believes that being persuasive is an *indirect* form of informative advertising. Advertising is seen as helpful to the consumer on two levels: first, the consumer can judge from the fact that a product is advertised that it is successful, because otherwise it would not pay the company to advertise unsuccessful products; and second, even if consumers misunderstand the content of the ad and buy the product, they are not necessarily irrational.[13] Not surprisingly, this view was taken to task by a philosopher who contended that heavy persuasive advertising is not necessarily a sign of quality, and that Madison Avenue attempts to sell anything, regardless of its nature or quality.[14]

One might contend that persuasive advertising is acceptable if it does not coerce the consumer into making decisions. That is, consumers should make decisions based on their own desires and not those created by the use of persuasive appeals. Certain puffery or embellishment is problematic, especially if it is aimed at a market that may not fully understand the implications of the message, such as children or immigrants. We will return to this point later.

What Role Should Advocacy and Conflict Play in Agency–Client Relations?

Advocacy in Advertising

Advocacy (supporting a cause or position) is central to advertising. The institution of advertising is one of an advocate. It serves as a vehicle for marketers, whether they be companies, political candidates, or religious or cultural organizations. A primary purpose of advertising has always been to advocate a point of view or a behavior change on the part of the consumer (see ad for Handgun Control, Inc. at end of chapter). In trying to achieve this, advertising makes use of drama, words, symbols, music, pictures, and demonstrations to make its point. It asks for attention, absorption, conviction, and action from its audience.[15]

This advocacy role for advertising leads to at least some of the issues already discussed. Although opinion polls seem to indicate that consumers do not necessarily appreciate advertising's advocacy position, they are realistic enough to understand that the purpose of ads is to sell products. Still, they are justifiably skeptical of much advertising. Most consumers accept the advocacy role *as given* and believe that the intrusion and inconvenience may be balanced by the fact that advertising subsidizes the mass media. Without advertising, the newspaper, television, and radio industries would be radically different from what exists today.

Advocacy is also related to advertising in another way. The advertising agency is an *advocate* for the company whose products it is representing. This is a contractual, and usually an intermediate term, arrangement. Clients switch advertising agencies, but do not often do so, because it is costly in terms of consistency of advertising campaigns, and it requires establishing new working relationships.

Possible Advocacy Roles

One useful distinction for evaluating the ethical responsibility of an advertising or public-relations agency is to differentiate between the technician role and the advisor approach. The *technician* can be viewed as giving advice only on the message content, appropriate audiences and media. This approach would place the agency in what could be considered almost an employee role with a loyalty obligation to the client organization. The *advisor* perceives that the duty to the client is outweighed by the important obligation to act on behalf of a larger constituency. Thus, advisors would be remiss if they failed to point out discrepancies within company decisions that might adversely affect customers. The advisor role in advertising agency ethics involves taking on more of a stakeholder perspective.[16] For example, executives at Leo Burnett or Hill & Knowlton who handle a fast-food account may take it as their responsibility as advisors to question the client's managers about the fat and sodium content of certain heavily advertised menu items.

Two ethical principles useful for examining the advocacy role of advertising agencies are the *veracity* and the *hierarchy* principles.[17] The veracity principle states that an advocate should always be truthful. Not only should the agency that follows this principle not lie or distort, it should also avoid using manipulation in making arguments. Possibly, one could interpret this to mean the ad agency then should not use strong social acceptance or ageist appeals if the intention is to manipulate consumers. Second, the hierarchy principle entails the agency deciding that its primary role is a broad advisory one that takes into consideration various stakeholders.

How Agencies Should Treat Their Clients

The advisor role is likely more ethically justifiable and would probably ensure a cooperative, rather than subservient, position for the agency, *if* the agency has the leverage to make it work. Advocacy is a fact of life in advertising. To heighten the ethical sensitivity of advertising, the advocacy role must be tempered by some of the techniques suggested above. The "anything goes" philosophy in the name of advocacy would seem outdated; agencies, their clients, and the media should recognize the higher obligations inherent in being an effective advocate in the long run.

Client–Agency Conflicts

The overriding ethical dictum is that agencies should not work for companies selling products which compete with existing clients. During the decade of the 1980s many changes in the advertising agency and client businesses occurred. With large companies continuing to diversify and agencies merging and buying out competitors, the opportunity for potential conflict of interest increased. This tends to happen when firms acquire other businesses (RJR bought Nabisco) and expand, or are acquired by international firms (Japanese banks acquire US counterparts). In these instances, existing client–agency relationships are often jeopardized. The two central questions in this continuing struggle seem to be

Are clients becoming unreasonable by telling their agencies more and more product categories are "off limits"?

Are agencies too militant in demanding a softening of traditional conflict policy from their clients as their own interests spread?[18]

Most client managers and agency executives report that they have experienced conflict problems firsthand. Although there is no universal solution to this problem, the clients use words such as "trust" and "loyalty" as virtues that they are looking for in their agencies. They want to be able to share confidential information and enter into a partnership arrangement with the ad agency. Both sides want the potential conflict rules spelled out, so that they understand what is expected.[19] One way to deal with these areas of conflict ethically was described by the trade publication, *Advertising Age.*

An agency is attracted to a new possibility that it knows could cause trouble with a current client. In these cases, it seems that advertisers almost without exception want agencies to be candid, honest, and forthright in notifying them and explaining the circumstances. The client would then set the rules and give the agency its choice. In a few apparently enlightened situations, the agency got an okay to go ahead and *pitch* a competitor. If the agency lost, the client would let bygones be bygones. But in most cases, the implied insult of pursuing a more attractive competitor either destroys or weakens the relationship.[20]

What Ethical Responsibility Do Advertisers Have to Their Audience?

This question would likely elicit a range of answers from *some* responsibility to an *extreme* amount, depending on whether the respondent was an advertising person or a consumer advocate. Since advertising is by nature directed at the mass market using the mass media, the utilitarian argument (which essentially states that the majority of consumers benefit from advertising) is a strong and intuitively appealing one. The educated adult consumer seems equipped to deal with most advertising. However, several significant groups appear to require special attention—children, the elderly, and the "market illiterate."

Advertising Honestly to Children

Many public and consumer interest groups (such as the Action for Children's Television) have noted advertising's unique responsibility toward children. For younger children (less than eight years old) it is a question of understanding the difference between advertising and program content. The use of cartoon characters as product spokespersons is generally discouraged. Still, there is a strong relationship between toy companies and many cartoon shows. For example, GI Joe, Ghostbusters, and Teenage Mutant Ninja Turtles are both a line of toys *and* a cartoon program. Some critics argue that these shows are actually thirty minute commercials. These "program length commercials" (PLCs) have come under attack by those who believe that these shows manipulate impressionable children. Ethical questions that might be asked about PLCs are

Should media managers allow such shows to be programmed?

Should ads that feature the main character(s) of the PLC be run during the actual show?

In addition, other observers contend that some ads aimed at children are simply too violent. (See the two ads for *Konami* video games at the end of this chapter.)

A number of suggestions have been offered by government, business, and other groups to restrict or improve advertising aimed at children. Probably, the best known is the ill-fated attempt by the FTC in the late 1970s. The FTC recommended a comprehensive series of changes including proposals to (a) ban all TV advertising on programs directed to young (under 8) children, (b) ban TV advertising for sugared food products directed at older (8–12) children, and (c) require all other TV advertising for sugared food products seen by significant proportions of older children to be balanced by health message paid for by advertisers.[21]

Many were skeptical of the FTC's proposed action (later withdrawn) and labeled the agency the "National Nanny" for intruding on parental responsibility. Although former President Reagan vetoed a bill that would have restricted the number of commercial minutes on shows directed toward children, President Bush let such a bill become law without his signature. This law imposes a limit of ten minutes and thirty seconds of television commercials per hour of children's programming on weekends and twelve minutes per hour on weekdays.[22] Since governmental policies are only a partial answer in this area, advertisers' ethical obligations remain very important.

The following public position, taken by the advertising industry regarding self-regulation, leaves some observers skeptical regarding their genuine interest in ethics.

The AAAA's position is that advertising self-regulation provides adequate safeguards against advertising abuses; that advertising does not harm children and that, therefore, there is no need to protect them from it; and that if a program has "too many" commercials, children will stop watching it. In sum, market forces will serve the interest of children by naturally regulating what is broadcast to them.[23]

Despite this disclaimer by the AAAA, industry has been actively involved in the self-regulation of advertising to children. The Children's Advertising Review Unit, established in the early 1970s by the Better Business Bureau, monitors advertising directed to children under age twelve and seeks modification or discontinuance of ads it finds to be inaccurate or unfair.[24] (See Appendix 6A for some of their detailed guidelines on the advertising of teleprograms (audio-taped telephone programs available through [900/976 numbers] to children.)

The marketing of potentially unsafe products to children and adolescents also has been questioned from a moral standpoint. One philosopher noted that the moral propriety of marketing dangerous products becomes even more questionable when the ads are aimed at children, since the likelihood that children will misuse the product or misunderstand its proper function is far greater than for adults. He gave the example of advertising guns in Boy Scout magazines which circulate to boys as young as age twelve. The practice was characterized as "of particularly dubious moral propriety."[25] A similar targeting strategy was noted by *Advertising Age* with the headline "RJR Aims New Ads at Young Smokers." Advertising and sales promotion of beer directed toward college students is another instance of possibly unhealthy products pitched toward a youth market.

Ethical Advertising to Other Groups

The elderly are another vulnerable and growing market segment. Until recently, they were relatively ignored and often stereotyped by advertisers. Now, they are not only living longer, but more of them are affluent and engage in active lifestyles. This has made the elderly particularly good targets for advertisements on hair-care products, denture creams, financial services, and travel packages to name but a few product categories. Some elderly see the television as a companion, and get much of their news and product information from this source. This raises special ethical issues about TV advertising directed to elderly markets. Advertisers need to consider their ethical responsibilities to this emerging market in terms of disclosure of information, accurate pricing information, and product design. Exhibit 6–7 also shows that high percentages of elderly can potentially be misled by advertising.

Another audience that advertisers need to understand more fully are those labeled as *market illiterates*. The demographics of this group are characterized as follows: low income, low education, and naive in understanding the ways of the marketplace. The burgeoning number of immigrants to the United States, including undocumented residents, probably means that the number in this segment has grown substantially in the last decade. In their purchasing habits they are generally more national brand loyal, more likely to buy home remedy health care products (possibly because they can't afford or prefer not to see a physician), and not as nutrition conscious.[26]

The responsibility for market illiterates is not primarily with advertisers any more than it is primarily a government, education, or health care community issue. However, market illiteracy is a significant long-term ethical problem if these individuals are being misled by advertising or if the ads contribute to other social problems. (See Exhibit 6–8 for a discussion of the issues surrounding athletic shoe advertising.) The ad community needs to offer avenues for these consumers to become more market literate. For example, the Giant supermarket chain in the Washington, DC and Baltimore areas has engaged in extensive consumer education aimed at all consumers, but especially at those in less privi-

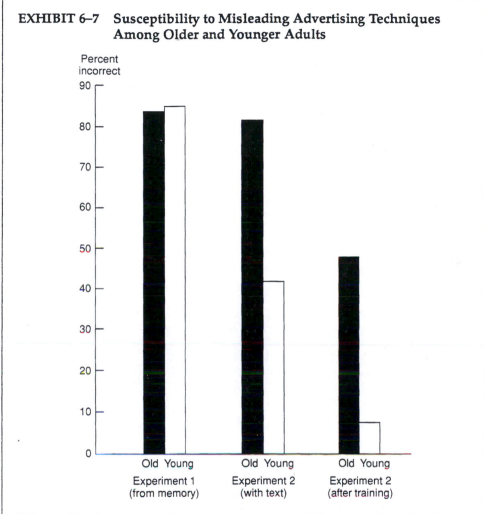

EXHIBIT 6–7   Susceptibility to Misleading Advertising Techniques Among Older and Younger Adults

This small-scale series of three experiments reported the reaction of young adults (thirty-six and thirty-eight college students) and older adults (twenty and twenty-one individuals with a mean age of seventy-six) to several ads for fictitious products. In Experiment 1 the respondents were asked to respond from memory to three questions about the claims made in one-paragraph ads for fourteen different products. In Experiment 2, the respondents were allowed to review the ads before answering the series of questions, while in Experiment 3, respondents received a seventy-five minute, three-phase training program on false and misleading advertising before they were exposed to the ads and answered the questions. **What conclusions do you draw from this study?**

Source: Gary J. Gaeth and Timothy B. Heath, "The Cognitive Processing of Misleading Advertising in Young and Old Adults: Assessment and Training," *Journal of Consumer Research* (June 1987), Figure D on 49, 43–54. Reprinted by permission of the University of Chicago Press.

EXHIBIT 6–8   The Controversy over Sneaker Advertising

In 1990, an article appeared in *Sports Illustrated*, entitled "Senseless," that chronicled the outbreak of violence in many cities that led to injury and even death over sneakers and other athletic apparel. Some of these products were linked to drug dealers and associated with certain gangs. The author made a strong case for the partial responsibility of the athletic shoe and apparel industry for this sad state of affairs. The following are some provocative selections from the article.

"In a country that has long been hung up on style over substance, flash over depth, the athletic shoe and sportswear industries (a projected $5.5 billion in domestic sales of name-brand shoes in 1990; more than $2 billion in sweatpants, sweatshirts, and warmup suits) suddenly have come to represent the pinnacle of consumer exploitation. In recent months the industries, which include heavyweights like Nike and Reebok, as well as smaller players Adidas, Asics, British Knights, Converse, Elesse, Etonic, Fila, L. A. Gear, New Balance, Pony, Puma, Starter, and numerous other makers of sport shoes, caps, and jackets, have been accused of creating a fantasy-fueled market for luxury items in the economically blasted inner cities and willingly tapping into the flow of drug and gang money. This has led to the frightening outbreak of crimes among poor black kids trying to make their mark by "busting fresh," or dressing at the height of fashion.

"But of course, these assailants aren't simply taking clothes from their victims. They're taking status. Something is very wrong in a society that has created an underclass that is slipping into economic and moral oblivion, an underclass in which pieces of rubber and plastic held together by shoelaces are sometimes worth more than a human life. The shoe companies have played a direct role in this. With their million-dollar advertising campaigns, superstar spokesmen, and over-designed, high-priced products aimed at impressionable young people, they are creating status from thin air to feed those who are starving for self-esteem. . . .

"Advertising fans this whole process by presenting the images that appeal to the kids, and the shoe companies capitalize on the situation, because it exists. Are the companies abdicating responsibility by doing this? That's a hard one to speak to. This is, after all, a free market. . . .

"But what about social responsibility? One particularly important issue is the high price of the shoes—many companies have models retailing for considerably more than $100, with Reebok Pump leading the parade at $170. There is also the specific targeting of young black males as buyers, through the use of seductive, macho-loaded sales pitches presented by black stars."

Are the advertising appeals for athletic shoes described in this magazine excerpt unethical?

Source: Rick Telander, "Senseless," *Sports Illustrated* (May 14, 1990), 38–44. Reprinted by permission.

leged areas. The difference principle, introduced in Chapter 2, suggests that marketers have a special obligation to these individuals.

The three audiences examined here are special cases for advertisers, but they are not the only ones. There are also responsibilities inherent in marketing to blacks, women, and the handicapped. For example, in scenario 2 heading the chapter, the executive should consider whether the sex appeal message is stereotyping women as unthinking consumers. The use of sex appeals may be justified with a utilitarian analysis, because sales often increase using this approach. For example, the Penaljo ads depicted at the end of this chapter appeal to rather primitive motivations.

It seems that advertising agencies and their clients have a special obligation, given their considerable influence, to look out for the needs of special groups. For example, toy and cereal firms should examine closely how they are socializing children's consumption patterns. In other words, they should ask themselves what values are fostered by their advertising. Health care firms should better understand the needs and information processing capabilities of elderly consumers before targeting them in their advertising. Fast-food and snack-food marketers should consider upgrading their product messages when they are aimed at the market illiterates.

What Role Do the Media Play in Advertising Ethics?

At the most basic level, advertising revenues contribute greatly to the structure and income of newspapers, magazines, radio, and television. Therefore, the media need advertisers. And thus the relationship among advertisers, agencies, and media can become ethically strained in many ways.

Ethics and the Media

The different categories of media are print, broadcast, and direct. Newspapers and magazines make up the first group. From an ethical standpoint, newspapers tend to specialize in informative advertising—classified ads, ads in food sections, and notices of sales by department stores and other retailers. Therefore, most newspaper advertising content is not questioned on ethical grounds, although sometimes "small print" restrictions on advertised specials raise ethical questions. One type of newpaper ad that may prove troublesome is the so-called "advertorial," which is intentionally made to look like a news story. Although these ads must be clearly labeled "advertisement," the small print may be missed by some readers, especially the elderly. One possibility would be that publishers consider using a larger typeface for such ads than legally required.

Magazines (with the exception of the newsweeklies) are often targeted to specialized audiences that have a greater interest in a specific subject, such as skiing or architecture. Thus, magazine advertisers can use more sophisticated, customized messages in appealing to their target market. Since the persuasive content of magazine advertising is higher than newspapers, ethical questions about status-oriented messages are more common. However, neither newspapers nor magazines have a captive audience for their ads. The reader is free to skim or ignore the ad. Consequently, magazine advertisements are not viewed as highly intrusive. Still, certain print ads raise ethical questions as several of the sample ads in this chapter make clear. (See Exhibit 6–9 for recent AMA print advertising guidelines.)

Advertising in the broadcast media, on the other hand, is perceived as very intrusive. Our favorite sporting event or news program is too often interrupted by commercials, many times at a perceived higher audio pitch than the regular programming. The local car dealer ad distracts from our preferred music during our ride home from the office with claims of the lowest financing or sticker prices. From this intrusive and often emotional position, then, broadcast media advertising is regularly questioned on ethical grounds.

Since the commercial message is much more fleeting in broadcast media, the advertiser usually relies on persuasive and emotional appeals rather than upon the primarily informative posture of the print media. Therefore, people are generally more suspect about the messages conveyed by television and radio. The advertiser defends this type of promotion, because consumers want to be "entertained" especially when they watch television. Also, TV is a "low involvement" medium (i.e., viewers are not actively attempting to gain informational messages

---

EXHIBIT 6–9   American Marketing Association Advertising Documentation Policy

The Ethics Committee of the American Marketing Association (AMA) heard a dispute over two software suppliers' superiority claims. The issue revolved around third-party claims that were used by one of the advertisers. Although the committee did not find a per se violation of the AMA code (recall Exhibit 1–7), the association decided to issue new guidelines to guard against this problem in the future. The policy went into effect on April 1, 1991 and stipulates:

All advertisements placed in AMA publications that make a specific claim based upon a third-party source (expert opinion, survey, etc.) shall contain documentation of the source within the advertisement. Such advertising will be accepted for placement only when accompanied by a signed release from the quoted source as to the accuracy and appropriateness of the representations.

In commenting on this new policy, AMA president Jeffrey Heilbrunn commented, "We feel it's a very high road, not typically done in the media. We are setting a new standard for the industry . . . to ensure the integrity of the advertising."

Source: Howard Schlossberg, "AMA Ethics Committee Orders Advertisers to Document Claims," *Marketing News* (March 4, 1991), 5, 34.

from this medium), and therefore advertisers feel they must enchant, startle, trick, or cajole the consumer into watching the commercial.[27] For these reasons and others, television and radio advertising bears a larger burden of criticism from an ethical standpoint.

As for the direct media, *billboards* necessarily carry little information and unless they give deceptive information, they are less often questioned ethically (although liquor and tobacco companies are great users of billboards). However, billboard advertising *of any kind* raises the issue of how outdoor advertising detracts from the natural beauty of the outdoors, i.e., the question of "aesthetic pollution."

Direct mail (sometimes called direct marketing) is a burgeoning business in the United States. It can be targeted exclusively to the consumer's home and personalized with the use of computer technology. Since much of direct mail advertising goes directly into the wastebasket, marketers have become more creative in making their message appear more "official." Some envelopes are made to look as if they come from the government (e.g., same size and color as the ones containing a tax refund) and other direct mail appeals state that the recipient has won something. These techniques are manipulative, if not deceptive.

Tactics like those described above make the list of unethical practices presented in Exhibit 6–10, but several other approaches were felt to be even more dubious, such as outright misrepresentation and misleading claims. The Direct Marketing Foundation has an extensive code of conduct to help discourage such practices, but the industry still has received criticism for the intrusive and deceptive nature of some direct mail messages.

Ethics and Sponsor–Agency Relations
Another area of ethical concern regarding the media has to do with the advertiser and its agency. For example, the decision of the media manager not to run a particular ad because it is controversial is a difficult one. Some media managers like to avoid advocacy-type advertising, such as Mobil's politically motivated ads, because of the media's requirement to give equal access to competing viewpoints. The question that must be asked is: what principles are used to justify censorship decisions by the media?

Another related ethical concern centers around the media's objective of getting more advertising time or space when it conflicts with the needs of advertisers to effectively reach their markets. What should an ad space manager do, if they know that the demographics of the customer's market most closely fit the readership of another magazine or even another type of media like radio? For instance, should they decline the business and/or send the potential customer to a "friendly" competitor? Furthermore, should the media manager resist the tendency of agencies to recommend excessive advertising to their clients (since they are paid on a commission basis)? We offer guidance for answering these questions later in the chapter.

EXHIBIT 6–10   A Listing of Unethical Practices in Direct Marketing

Most Unethical Practices	*Number of Mentions by Respondents*
Misrepresentation of product, misleading advertising claims, or selling products that do not work.	39
Pirating, theft, or unauthorized multiple use of lists.	33
No intention of fulfilling orders.	24
Billing "customers" who did not place orders, or sending magazine subscriptions to people who have previously received a free, sample issue.	12
Offers that look like important bills, checks, etc.	10
Photographs touched up in order to make merchandise look more appealing.	8
Taking orders for products one does not have or that do not yet exist (i.e., "dry testing").	8
Use of negative options in the hope that customers will forget to send back the card.	7
Using deception to build lists (e.g., phone research, offering free or cheap items).	5
Making it difficult to get money back from a "moneyback" guarantee.	4
Nonfulfillment of information requests.	4
Use of illegal names (people who asked to be removed from list).	4
Use of fraudulent addresses or simply post office boxes.	3
Use of endorsers who do not know that they are being used.	2
Promotion of "free" items which are not free in the long run.	2
Telemarketers posing as researchers in order to sell products.	2
List not updated or cleaned.	2
Noncompliance with FTC rules.	2
Other unethical practices, each mentioned only once.	21

Source: Gordon Storholm and Hershey Friedman, "Perceived Common Myths and Unethical Practices among Direct Marketing Professionals," *Journal of Business Ethics* 8 (1989), 975–979. Reprinted by permission of Kluwer Academic Publishers.

The Advertising–Media Conflict

Broader concerns between the media and advertisers present even more difficult problems. Social critics, such as Ralph Nader, contend that the media have been "captured" by advertising and as a result, editorial content may be suppressed if it is counter to the interests of advertisers. There is little recent evidence to support this position, but the perception remains that the advertising and editorial sides of media may not be independent. Several specific questions relate to this issue.

Should the media attempt to accommodate more advertisers, either by adding more advertising pages or reducing the length of commercials so that more ads may be run?

Should media create new marketing entities (home buying services, network news breaks) largely for the purpose of selling more advertising?

Should content or programming be arranged largely for the benefit of the advertiser?

Should publishing or broadcasting ventures be undertaken only because of market-dominated criteria?

Should publication of a newspaper or magazine be stopped entirely due to weakened advertising without questioning the readers as to whether they would be willing to pay more to keep it in circulation?[28]

Media executives need to follow certain principles in order to make such ethical judgments. More specific guidance will be offered in the next and concluding section. Undoubtedly, there are additional ethical questions that can be raised about advertising such as *what* products should be advertised and *how* messages should be constructed to be most ethical. Other more specialized works treat these issues, and the reader is encouraged to consult such sources.[29]

Positive Developments and Future Challenges for Ethics in Advertising

Several developments have occurred that may signal a more ethical posture by the advertising community. At the same time, there are areas of emerging concern for advertisers in the 1990s. We begin first with the good news.

Positive Developments

There are at least five significant favorable trends regarding ethical issues in advertising. First, it seems that some advertisers have made genuine efforts to promote more positive images (see the AT&T ad at the end of this chapter). For instance, they have reduced sex stereotyping and appeals. Women are now depicted more frequently in professional and business roles. As *Business Week* pointed out, "Sex Still Sells—But So Does Sensitivity."[30] The magazine indicated that women show up in far more professional roles in today's ads. Advertisers not only want to avoid exploitation of women, but actually want to target them as consumers. For example, Lotus management nixed a marketing brochure featuring a busty woman in a revealing T-shirt, and Ford broke with tradition by hiring actors who reflect their average customers rather than utilizing beauty queens at a recent auto show. No doubt more can be done in this area, but substantial progress seems to have been achieved despite some examples which continue to generate controversy.[31]

Other groups are portrayed more favorably by advertisers. For instance, the elderly are used as spokespersons for many consumer products (e.g., Wilfred Brimley for Quaker Oats), and blacks and other minorities appear in a variety of ads. Also, more handicapped (including the hearing-impaired) are depicted in ads by Apple, Citibank, Colgate–Palmolive, McDonalds, Nike, and General Motors.[32]

Second, the increasing specialization of the mass media via cable television and specialized magazines means that some of the abuses of the mass market advertising are less likely to happen due to the more defined audiences for these media. One well-publicized marketing development of the 1980s is the splintering of the mass market. Thus, messages intended for one market are less likely to offend those to whom they are not targeted. A cautionary note should be sounded here to indicate that some cable stations do not have standards in place to counteract potentially unethical advertising. For instance, the three networks have elaborate guidelines and strict standards for advertising to children, while some independents and cable companies have looser or no controls.[33]

Third, companies have begun shifting more money from advertising into sales promotion techniques such as coupons and rebates or pricing discounts for retailers. Why? The advertising industry is increasingly criticized for ineffective communication.[34] Therefore, it would seem that the advertising community may be more receptive to changing its creative and *ethical* stance, if it feels that consumers are more likely to be influenced by advertising in their buying decision. Fourth, advertisers are becoming more responsive to consumer complaints regarding the program content of the shows they sponsor. This may lead advertisers and their agencies to take a closer look at the quality and type of TV and radio programming they want to support.

Finally, advertising self-regulation and government regulation is alive and well throughout the world. One study that evaluated advertising self-regulation in twelve countries indicated that its purpose is "more moral/ethical than disciplinary."[35] In the United States, the FTC and state consumer protection offices have become more active in the regulation of advertising. The FTC brought thirty consumer protection cases in 1990, which more than doubled the 1987 total. Firms in the brewing, food, tobacco, automobile (see Exhibit 6–11 on Volvo), and airline industries were prosecuted for their ad claims in 1990.[36]

Future Challenges

Two areas seem to represent particular ethical challenges to advertisers in the 1990s. The first is "infomercials." These half hour or longer shows follow several formats—talk show, news, or entertainment. They carry innocuous titles like "Consumer Challenge" and sometimes feature celebrities like George Hamilton and Fran Tarkinton as spokespersons. Infomercials are a growth business with $300 million spent on TV air time in 1990, and gross sales are projected to rise from the current $450 million to $1.2 billion in 1992.[37]

EXHIBIT 6–11 A Case Study in Questionable Advertising

Volvo, the well-known Swedish auto manufacturer, was involved in one of the most embarrassing events in advertising history during 1990. The ad in question featured Bear Foot, a four-wheeled drive truck driving over a line of cars in a car crushing contest. Only the Volvo withstood the test. Was this too good to be true? You bet. The Volvo was reinforced with steel and wood to withstand the pressure, and the other cars were doctored to collapse even more easily under Bear Foot.

The company claimed to have no knowledge of this misrepresentation, and the ad agency placed the blame on the production company that shot the ad. Volvo did take out ads apologizing for the episode after the Texas Attorney General filed suit. Volvo was fined $315,000 by the state of Texas. Also, the ad agency resigned the account, presumably to avoid being fired.

Another Volvo ad analyzed by *The Wall Street Journal* showed a truck on top of a Volvo sedan, but the ads did not show the jacks under the car to prevent the tires from blowing out. The company claims that the only thing being illustrated was the strength of Volvo's roof and frame, not that their tires and suspensions could support such loads.

The larger cost to Volvo from these ads may be damage to what has been a longstanding reputation for safety and credibility.

What do you think about Volvo's reputation? Has the firm's image been tarnished?

Source: Statistics from Stuart Elliot, "Volvo Says It's Crushed over Misleading Ads," *USA Today* (November 6, 1990), B1. See also Barry Meier, "New Volvo Ad Calls Old One Phony," *New York Times* (November 6, 1990), D1, D7 and David Kiley, "Candid Camera: Volvo and the Art of Deception," *Adweek's Marketing Week* (November 12, 1990), 4–5.

The ethical (and legal) issue is whether consumers are being misled into thinking that these infomercials are legitimate shows. Furthermore, those most likely to buy into such appeals and to be financially injured are the market illiterates. Evidence suggests that TV stations have inadequate safeguards in place to deal with infomercials.[38] The broadcast industry is proposing self-regulation in terms of clear disclosures at the beginning and end of the program, and the FTC has brought a few cases against such advertisers. This appears to be an industry where ethical duties need to be spelled out more clearly.

A second growth area for the 1990s is green marketing (see Exhibit 4–6). The health claims of the 1980s are being replaced by environmentally oriented messages. Marketers have begun using epithets such as "biodegradable," "recyclable" and "environmentally friendly" on many packages and promoting the environmental compatibility of their products in their advertising. One of the most suspect campaigns featured aseptic packaging and used the tag line "Drink boxes are as easy to recycle as this page."[39] State and federal agencies like the FTC are prosecuting the most egregious violations. We believe that many marketers want to cooperate toward a cleaner natural environment and a reduction of packaging as part of the solid waste stream. However, a much more responsible approach must be taken by marketers and advertisers in not "walking so close to the line" in terms of promoting the unjustified environmenal benefits of their products.

Ideas for Ethical Action

Four specific suggestions are offered for improving the ethical posture of advertising. First, *all businesses involved in advertising and public relations should develop specific ethical principles of operation.* Advertisers, advertising and public-relations agencies, and the media should spell out the principles by which they operate. One reason for the strong criticism of advertising appears to be its "anything goes" attitude. For example, companies that advertise should make clear their posture regarding the type of advertising content that fits the company's image, and the type of media and programs they will and will not support. In examining many codes of conduct over the last several years, we found that almost none spell out the company's ethical perspective on advertising, even though millions of dollars are spent on promotion. For example, several large corporations spend over $1 million per day on advertising.

Similarly, agency executives should delineate the principles by which they operate. Agencies must be prepared to *walk away* from certain potential clients because of ethical concerns, but a rationale needs to be developed and articulated for substantiating this position. The public-relations industry has focused on ethics education, strong sanctions against violators, and professionalism to enhance its ethical posture.[40] At the same time, television media have reduced the number of employees in their standards departments due to cost cutting. It seems even more imperative, then, that the principles to which the media subscribe in their relationship with advertisers be clearly delineated. One agency's principles of operation are shown in Exhibit 6–12.

Second, *the advertising community should push for revised association codes.* As shown in Exhibit 6–5, most of the ethical problems perceived by ad executives themselves relate to fairness in dealing with the various stakeholders in formulating advertising campaigns. An analysis of the codes of four major advertising industry associations (see Appendices 6B and 6C for the codes of the American Advertising Federation and the American Association of Advertising Agencies) reveal that these codes deal almost exclusively with the content of advertising and not fairness in business dealings.[41] The industry also needs to think more explicitly about fairness to the consumer. The results in Exhibit 6–5 are disconcerting in that it does not appear that agency executives consciously perceive fairness to consumers as an important ethical issue. The leadership of these associations should consider revision of their codes to overcome this deficiency. In a recent survey of advertising practitioners, it was found that two-thirds of the industry respondents believed that a code of conduct was "an excellent idea" for the industry. However, only 19 percent were aware of the existing association codes.[42]

Third, *the idea of an ethical ombudsman for advertising should be considered.* This individual would probably be employed by one or more of the advertising associations mentioned above, monitor advertising, and sit in on all deliberations of boards such as the National Advertising Review Board. The ethical ombudsman would represent the consumer in the advertising transaction and would intro-

---

EXHIBIT 6–12   One Advertising Agency's Credo

FRANK C. NAHSER, INC./ADVERTISING

10 S. Riverside Plaza, Chicago, IL 60606 (312) 845-5000

Our purpose is to create and implement outstanding ideas to help our clients' businesses grow, benefit the user, and contribute to the well-being of society.

To provide this vital service, our experience has led us to believe in the importance of certain values — the characteristics of deeply committed people working in a supportive community.

Statement of Organizational Values:
GROWTH
FAIRNESS
RESPONSIBILITY
RESPECT

Statement of Personal Values:
ATTITUDE
INTEGRITY
HARD WORK
TALENT

November 21, 1980. (Updated June 6, 1989, on the occasion of our 50th Anniversary.)

---

duce the sometimes missing dimension of fairness. The establishment of an ethical ombudsman program would help to implement both of the above ideas for ethical action. The benefits from such a program are several. First, this action would assure that ethical issues would be raised that are not currently addressed. Also, the ombudsman should heighten the consciousness of ad practitioners, which would result in a greater sensitivity to ethical issues. In addition, the ongoing presence of the ethical ombudsman would assure that the corporate culture includes ethical thinking. The industry would essentially be saying to advertising employees, "We take ethics seriously."[43]

Fourth, *ethical questions about advertisements and advertising strategies need to be more frequently asked.* A final and related proposal is for advertisers and agencies to develop an ethical questions checklist for mutual consideration. Exhibit 6–13 contains a series of questions about the impact of advertising on stakeholders and deals with the fairness issues outlined above. We contend that the process of asking the questions would highlight the importance of ethics in advertising. A raised awareness toward the issues is more important than specific answers. This type of evaluation would also allow the advertiser to insure that the agency follows the ethical principles set down by the company. The exercise could also protect the ad agency, in that the agency would know what was expected of it. The resulting campaign would communicate the sentiment of the client, thereby reducing the possibility of having to develop expensive, alternative campaigns because of ethical deficiencies. Questions could be developed for the media as well. (See the advertising section of Appendix 10B for additional questions.)

EXHIBIT 6–13   Advertising Ethics Checklist

In judging whether a certain ad or advertising strategy is ethical, a large number of factors must be considered. The following questions cover many of these points and may serve as a preliminary checklist:

General
- What does the advertiser intend to accomplish?
- Are the effects of this advertising potentially detrimental to the individual and to society as a whole?
- Are these effects accidental, or do they result almost necessarily from the techniques used?

On Technique
- Does the ad provide information, or does it appeal only to status and emotions?
- If the latter is true, does the ad attempt to bypass the individual's judgment?

On Content
- Is the information in the ad truthful?

- Are relevant (material) facts omitted?

On Psychological Effects
- Does the ad seriously disturb the existing psychological position of the person without sufficient reason?
- Does the ad appeal to purely materialistic, sexual, or selfish values?

On the Advertised Product
- Does the ad lead to the misallocation of individual resources relative to the person's basic needs?
- Does it encourage an abusive use of any particular product?

On Social Consumption
- Does the ad and the product advertised lead to a waste of natural resources?

Final Judgment
- When the intent and techniques are not troublesome in and of themselves, and where the harmful effects are not necessary, are there other effects that outweigh the harmful effects?

Adapted from Thomas J. Garrett, S. J. *An Introduction to Some Ethical Problems of Modern Advertising* (Rome: Gregorian University Press, 1961), 180. Reprinted by permission.

Conclusion

Advertising is an important institution in our society. It contributes much information value to consumers and contributes to economic efficiency. But we believe the ethical standards of the industry can be raised. Many persons perceive ethical problems in advertising and, therefore, benefits would accrue from a greater concern for ethics. Some major questions facing advertising, as well as specific proposals for reform are set forth for marketing and advertising executives to consider in enhancing the ethical posture of their advertising programs. We now move to an examination of another major promotional technique used by marketers—personal selling—and the ethical questions that arise from it.

BBB Children's Advertising Review Unit Advertising Policies

Guidelines for the Advertising of 900/976 Teleprograms to Children

The Children's Advertising Review Unit (CARU) of the Council of Better Business Bureaus offers the following guidelines for consideration and use by marketers and teleprogram providers engaged in the advertising of 900/976 services directed to children. These advertising guidelines are intended to provide minimum and voluntary self-regulatory standards for the protection of children and their families. The development and dissemination of these guidelines by CARU does not represent its endorsement or approval of the marketing of these services to children.

1 Under no circumstances should youngsters who are too young to dial the telephone themselves be instructed or encouraged to hold the telephone receiver near their television set for "automatic" tone dialing by a signal transmitted over the TV.

2 Young children are still developing strategies for understanding the concept of time. Their ability to recognize measurable differences in time is limited, as is their understanding of the incremental structure of telephone charges. One method available to address this problem is an announced unit or ceiling charge – of a reasonable and appropriate amount for a product marketed to children – for each teleprogram advertised. This fee would be in place and constant, regardless of the length of the recording or the amount of minutes the child "held on." This information would allow youngsters to know the cost of the full teleprogram prior to placing the call.

3 In light of children's still developing ability to interpret abstract information, each juvenile teleprogram commercial should contain a written "super" and clearly stated "voice-over," in language that young children understand and presented at a moderate rate of speed, outlining exactly what the product is and what the cost will be. The language should be distinct and conspicuous. For example: "This call will cost $2.00 for a 2-minute recorded story." And, instead of "ask your parent's permission," the audio language could be simplified to state: ask, "Your mom or dad must say it's okay before you call."

4 Words like "now" and "only" should not be used in an advertisement directed toward youngsters to create a sense of urgency or exclusivity for the child audience. In the same spirit, wording such as "children can call" should be utilized, rather than the imperative "call now."

5 Advertisements for teleprograms should inform the child caller that he/she will hear a story "about" or recorded by a particular subject or character, not "speak to" or interact with the Easter Bunny, Tooth Fairy, their favorite rock star or any other mythical or real character if the child will not actually be able to do so.

6 Visuals in advertisements for teleprograms should not include cartoon characters, celebrities or other individuals whose voices are heard on these programs, actually holding a telephone, standing in a telephone booth or talking on a telephone. Regardless of audio disclaimers, scenes such as these imply to the young caller that he or she will actually be able to speak with the character featured in the teleprogram.

7 In creating a truthful, accurate and realistic sense of the product to be purchased, advertisements should not utilize production techniques that may misrepresent or overpromise the entertainment value of the teleprogram to the child audience. Currently, for example, some of the advertising is more elaborately produced than the teleprogram, a practice that could lead to an unrealistic expectation of the product by youngsters.

8 Commercials for teleprograms for children should include a warning to dial carefully. In addition, where the technology is available to do so, assigned numbers for telemarketing programs designed for children should be separated from exchanges that carry adult entertainment. Separation by exchange or numerical distance will assist in reducing the potential risk of children's exposure to adult programs.

9 Special care should be exercised in the use of premiums and other direct marketing promotions, especially with toy products, within a teleprogram advertisement for children. If a premium is to be offered during a program, that fact, as well as its separate charge, if any, should be disclosed within the commercial. The use of premiums may, potentially, cause confusion as to what product is being marketed—the premium or the teleprogram. The young consumer may infer that the premium will come as a direct result of placing the phone call without the need for any additional puchases or procedures. In addition, the use or presentation of conditions associated with the term "free" should be in compliance with the BBB Code and CARU Self-Regulatory Guidelines.

10 The teleprogram itself must be the entire length that is advertised in the commercial. Any additional commercial or promotional messages, references to the availability of related merchandise or film and TV programs should be identified as advertising and be placed separately after, or "bumpered" appropriately from, the completed advertised teleprogram.

11 Teleprograms for children should consist of totally self-contained story lines or completed audio products. These programs should contain no "cliff hangers" or references to other books, or products for sale, or additional telephone programs needed to achieve story endings. In addition, there should be no undue pressure placed on children—including requests to dial an additional 900/976 number to vote—embedded within a program for youngsters.

Source: Reprinted with permission of the Council of Better Business Bureaus, Inc.

American Advertising Federation Principles

THE ADVERTISING PRINCIPLES
OF AMERICAN BUSINESS*

TRUTH

Advertising shall tell the truth, and shall reveal significant facts, the omission of which would mislead the public.

SUBSTANTIATION

Advertising claims shall be substantiated by evidence in possession of the advertiser and advertising agency, prior to making such claims.

COMPARISONS

Advertising shall refrain from making false, misleading, or unsubstantiated statements or claims about a competitor or his products or services.

BAIT ADVERTISING

Advertising shall not offer products or services for sale unless such offer constitutes a bona fide effort to sell the advertised products or services and is not a device to switch consumers to other goods or services, usually higher priced.

GUARANTEES AND WARRANTIES

Advertising of guarantees and warranties shall be explicit, with sufficient information to apprise consumers of their principal terms and limitations or, when space or time restrictions preclude such disclosures, the advertisement should clearly reveal where the full text of the guarantee or warranty can be examined before purchase.

PRICE CLAIMS

Advertising shall avoid price claims which are false or misleading, or savings claims which do not offer provable savings.

TESTIMONIALS

Advertising containing testimonials shall be limited to those of competent witnesses who are reflecting a real and honest opinion or experience.

TASTE AND DECENCY

Advertising shall be free of statements, illustrations or implications which are offensive to good taste or public decency.

*Adopted by the American Advertising Federation Board of Directors, March 2, 1984, San Antonio, Texas.

American Association of Advertising Agencies Policies

Standards of Practice of the American Association of Advertising Agencies

FIRST ADOPTED OCTOBER 16, 1924—MOST RECENTLY REVISED SEPTEMBER 18, 1990

We hold that a responsibility of advertising agencies is to be a constructive force in business.

We hold that, to discharge this responsibility, advertising agencies must recognize an obligation, not only to their clients, but to the public, the media they employ, and to each other. As a business, the advertising agency must operate within the framework of competition. It is recognized that keen and vigorous competition, honestly conducted, is necessary to the growth and the health of American business. However, unethical competitive practices in the advertising agency business lead to financial waste, dilution of service, diversion of manpower, loss of prestige, and tend to weaken public confidence both in advertisements and in the institution of advertising.

We hold that the advertising agency should compete on merit and not by attempts at discrediting or disparaging a competitor agency, or its work, directly or by inference, or by circulating harmful rumors about another agency, or by making unwarranted claims of particular skill in judging or prejudging advertising copy.

To these ends, the American Association of Advertising Agencies has adopted the following *Creative Code* as being in the best interests of the public, the advertisers, the media, and the agencies themselves. The A.A.A.A. believes the Code's provisions serve as a guide to the kind of agency conduct that experience has shown to be wise, foresighted, and constructive. In accepting membership, an agency agrees to follow it.

Creative Code

We, the members of the American Association of Advertising Agencies, in addition to supporting and obeying the laws and legal regulations pertaining to advertising, undertake to extend and broaden the application of high ethical standards. Specifically, we will not knowingly create advertising that contains:

a. False or misleading statements or exaggerations, visual or verbal

b. Testimonials that do not reflect the real opinion of the individual(s) involved

c. Price claims that are misleading

d. Claims insufficiently supported or that distort the true meaning or practicable application of statements made by professional or scientific authority

e. Statements, suggestions, or pictures offensive to public decency or minority segments of the population.

We recognize that there are areas that are subject to honestly different interpretations and judgment. Nevertheless, we agree not to recommend to an advertiser, and to discourage the use of, advertising that is in poor or questionable taste or that is deliberately irritating through aural or visual content or presentation.

Comparative advertising shall be governed by the same standards of truthfulness, claim substantiation, tastefulness, etc., as apply to other types of advertising.

These Standards of Practice of the American Association of Advertising Agencies come from the belief that sound and ethical practice is good business. Confidence and respect are indispensable to success in a business embracing the many intangibles of agency service and involving relationships so dependent upon good faith.

Clear and willful violations of these Standards of Practice may be referred to the Board of Directors of the American Association of Advertising Agencies for appropriate action, including possible annulment of membership as provided by Article IV, Section 5, of the Constitution and By-Laws.

Endnotes

1. Raymond A. Bauer and Stephen A. Greyser, "The Dialogue That Never Happens," *Harvard Business Review* (November–December 1967), 2–4.

2. These statistics and those that follow are taken from John O'Toole, "What Advertising Is—and Isn't," *Across the Board* (April 1982), 32, 34.

3. David Ogilvy, *Ogilvy on Advertising* (New York: Crown Publishers, 1983) and John O'Toole, *The Trouble with Advertising* (New York: Chelsea, 1981).

4. For a discussion of these points see Morris Holbrook, "Mirror, Mirror, on the Wall, What's Unfair in the Reflections on Advertising," *Journal of Marketing* (July 1987), 95–103, and Geoffrey P. Lantos, "Advertising: Looking Glass or Molder of the Masses?" *Journal of Public Policy & Marketing* 6 (1987), 104–128.

5. David A. Aaker and John G. Myers, *Advertising Management* (Englewood Cliffs, NJ: Prentice–Hall, 1975), 548.

6. Michael L. Rothschild, *Advertising* (Lexington, MA: D.C. Heath and Co., 1987), 204.

7. Richard W. Pollay, "The Distorted Mirror: Reflections on the Unintended Consequences of Advertising," *Journal of Marketing* (April 1986), 19.

8. Clifford G. Christians, Kim B. Rotzoll, and Mark Fackler, *Media Ethics: Cases and Moral Reasoning*, 3rd ed., (New York: Longman, 1991), 161–174. For an egoistic view of advertising see Jerry Kirkpatrick, "A Philosophic Defense of Advertising," *Journal of Advertising* 15 (1986), 2: 42–48.

9. Shelby D. Hunt and Lawrence B. Chonko, "Ethical Problems of Advertising Agency Executives," *Journal of Advertising* 16 (1987), 4: 16–24.

10. Jef I. Richards, "A *'New and Improved'* View of Puffery," *Journal of Public Policy & Marketing* 9 (1990), 73–84.

11. For a discussion of a moral analysis of deception and subliminal advertising see Thomas L. Carson, Richard E. Wokutch, and James E. Cox, Jr., "An Ethical Analysis of Deception in Advertising," *Journal of Business Ethics* 4 (1985), 93–104 and J. E. Gratz, "The Ethics of Subliminal Communication," *Journal of Business Ethics* 3 (1984), 181–184.

12. Robert Arrington, "Advertising and Behavior Control," *Journal of Business Ethics* 1 (1982), 3–12; Paul C. Santilli, "The Informative and Persuasive Functions of Advertising," *Journal of Business Ethics* 2 (1983), 27–33; H. Emamalizadeh, "The Informative and Persuasive Functions of Advertising: A Moral Appraisal—A Comment," *Journal of Business Ethics* 4 (1985), 151–153; Kam-Hon Lee, "The Informative and Persuasive Functions of Advertising: A Moral Appraisal—A Further Comment," *Journal of Business Ethics* 6 (1987), 55–57.

13. Philip Nelson, "Advertising and Ethics." In *Ethics, Free Enterprise and Public Policy*, Richard De George and Joseph Pichler, eds. 187–198 (New York: Oxford University Press, 1978).

14. Roger Crisp, "Persuasive Advertising, Autonomy, and the Creation of Desire," *Journal of Business Ethics* 6 (1987), 413–418.

15. John Crichton, "Morals and Ethics in Advertising." In *Ethics, Morality and the Media*, by Lee Thayer, 110 (New York: Hastings House, 1980).

16. Thomas H. Bivins, "Applying Ethical Theory to Public Relations," *Journal of Business Ethics* 6 (1987), 195–200.

17. Robert Audi, "The Ethics of Advocacy," working paper, Department of Philosophy, University of Nebraska–Lincoln, (March 1989).

18. Herbert Zeltner, "Client–Agency Conflicts," *Advertising Age* (March 5, 1984), M64–M68.

19. "Clients Want Agency to Be *Partner*," *Advertising Age*, (April 6, 1987), 3+.

20. See note 18 above, p. M68.

21. Federal Trade Commission, *FTC Staff Report on Television Advertising to Children* (Washington, DC: Federal Trade Commission, (1978). For a brief discussion of the report see W. Wilkie, *Consumer Behavior*, 2nd ed. (New York: John Wiley, 1990), 285–288.

22. Barbara Gamarekian, "Ads Aimed at Children Restricted," The *New York Times* (October 18, 1990), C1, C5.

23. Patty Siebert, "A.A.A.A. Files Kid-Vid Comments with FCC," *The 4A's Washington Newsletter* (January 1988), 2.

24. Gary M. Armstrong and Merrie Brucks, "Dealing with Children's Advertising: Public Policy Issues and Alternatives," *Journal of Public Policy & Marketing* 7 (1988), 98–113.

25. Burton M. Leiser, "The Ethics of Advertising." In *Ethics, Free Enterprise and Public Policy*, eds. R. De George and J. Pichler, 173–186 (New York: Oxford University Press, 1978).

26. Clifford G. Christians, Kim B. Rotzoll, and Mark Fackler, *Media Ethics:* Cases and Moral Reasoning, 3rd ed. (New York: Longman, 1991), 161–174.

27. Herbert Krugman, "The Impact of TV Advertising: Learning Without Involvement," *Public Opinion Quarterly* 29 (Fall 1965), 349–356.

28. See note 8 above.

29. Edmund B. Lambeth, *Committed Journalism: An Ethic for the Profession* (Bloomington, IN: Indiana University Press, 1986).

30. Zachary Chiller, Mark Landler, and Julia Flynn, "Sex Still Sells—But So Does Sensitivity," *Business Week* (March 18, 1991), 100.

31. A survey by Linda Lazier-Smith reported that the number of women portrayed as sex objects or in traditional roles within ads in four magazines declined only from 75 percent to 72 percent from 1983 to 1989.

32. Skip Wollenberg, "Advertisers Discovering Disabled," *South Bend Tribune*, (October 30, 1989), C6 and Joanne Lipman, "Deaf Consumers Aren't Ignored Anymore," *The Wall Street Journal*, (February 28, 1990), B5.

33. Joanne Lipman, "Double Standard for Kids' TV Ads: Non-Network Stations' Lax Rules Lure Toy Makers—and Rile Critics," *The Wall Street Journal*, (June 10, 1988), 21.

34. Raj Sethuraman and Gerald Tellis, "An Analysis of the Tradeoff Between Advertising and Price Discounting," *Journal of Marketing Research* (May 1991), 160–174.

35. J. J. Boddewyn, *Advertising Self-Regulation and Outside Participation: A Multinational Comparison* (New York: Quorum Books, 1988).

36. Howard Schlossberg, "The Simple Truth: Ads Will Have to be Truthful," *Marketing News* (December 24, 1990), 6; J. Lipman, "FTC Is Cracking Down on Misleading Ads," *The Wall Street Journal* (February 4, 1991), B5; and Jane Bryant Quinn, "The FTC Cop Is on the Beat Again, Eager to Root out Deception, Fraud," *Chicago Tribune*, (February 25, 1991), Section 4, 5.

37. Nancy Ryan, "*Infomercials* Get Guidelines," *Chicago Tribune* (March 4, 1991) Section 4, 3. See also J. Lipman, "*Infomercial* Industry Takes Steps to Clean Up Its Late-Night Act," *The Wall Street Journal* (March 4, 1991).

38. Patrick R. Parsons and Herbert J. Rotfeld, "Infomercials and Television Station Clearance Practices," *Journal of Public Policy & Marketing* 9 (1990), 62–72.

39. Rinker Buck, "As Easy to Recycle as Baloney," *Adweek's Marketing Week* (December 3, 1990), 18. See also David Stipp, "Lunch-Box Staple Runs Afoul of Activists," *The Wall Street Journal* (March 14, 1991), B1, B4. See also Mark Landler, Sachary Schiller, and Tim Smart, "Suddenly, Green Marketers Are Seeing Red Flags," *Business Week* (February 25, 1991), 74, 76.

178

40. Cornelius B. Pratt, "Public Relations: The Empirical Research on Practitioner Ethics," *Journal of Business Ethics* (March 1991), 229–236.

41. Priscilla LaBarbera, "Analyzing and Advancing the State of Art of Advertising Self-Regulation," *Journal of Advertising* 9 (Summer 1980), 27–38.

42. Bonnie B. Reece and Stephen A. Greyser, "Executives' Attitudes Toward Advertising Regulation: A Survey." In *Marketing and Advertising Regulations: The Federal Trade Commission in the 1990s*, P. Murphy and W. Wilkie, eds. 255–262 (Notre Dame, IN: University of Notre Dame Press, 1990).

43. Kim Rotzoll and James Haefner, *Advertising in Contemporary Society*, 2nd ed. (Cincinnati, OH: Southwestern, 1990), 171–173.

Positive Role Portrayal Advertising

When Grace was just a kid,
AT&T was just the phone company.

Today AT&T has spawned a whole
new generation of computer and
communications technologies.

AT&T Healthcare Solutions

Thanks to AT&T's physician information
network, a busy doctor like Grace
can have immediate access to
everything from lab results
to ultrasound images.
Giving her more time
to do what she
always wanted to
do. Take care
of people.
    And
that's just
one of
the ways
AT&T can
help you get
things done in
today's world. And
tomorrow's.

© 1990 AT&T

The way things get done.

AT&T
The right choice.

Source: © 1990 AT&T. Reprinted by permission.

Anti-Violence-Oriented-Advertising

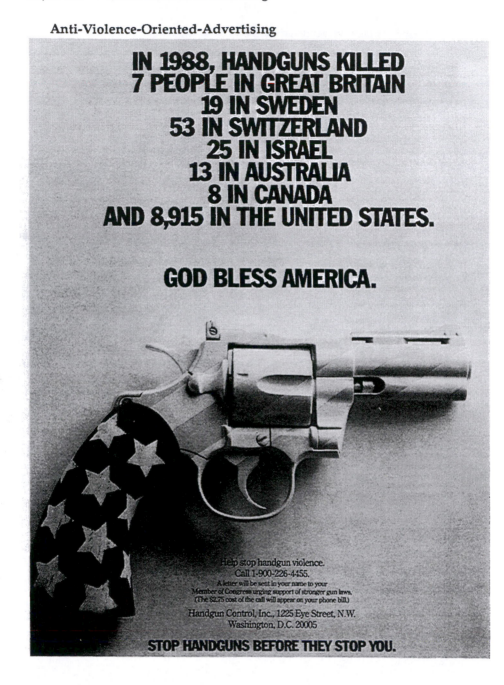

IN 1988, HANDGUNS KILLED
7 PEOPLE IN GREAT BRITAIN
19 IN SWEDEN
53 IN SWITZERLAND
25 IN ISRAEL
13 IN AUSTRALIA
8 IN CANADA
AND 8,915 IN THE UNITED STATES.

GOD BLESS AMERICA.

Help stop handgun violence.
Call 1-900-226-4455.
A letter will be sent in your name to your
Member of Congress urging support of stronger gun laws.
(The $2.75 cost of the call will appear on your phone bill.)
Handgun Control, Inc., 1225 Eye Street, N.W.
Washington, D.C. 20005

STOP HANDGUNS BEFORE THEY STOP YOU.

Source: Reprinted by permission of Handgun Control, Inc.

Sex Appeal Advertising

PENALJO & LUXURY

Leather and value. Sizes and fit. Comfortable and supple. Penaljo shoes and women. **PENALJO** *The fine art of comfort*

Sex Appeal Advertising

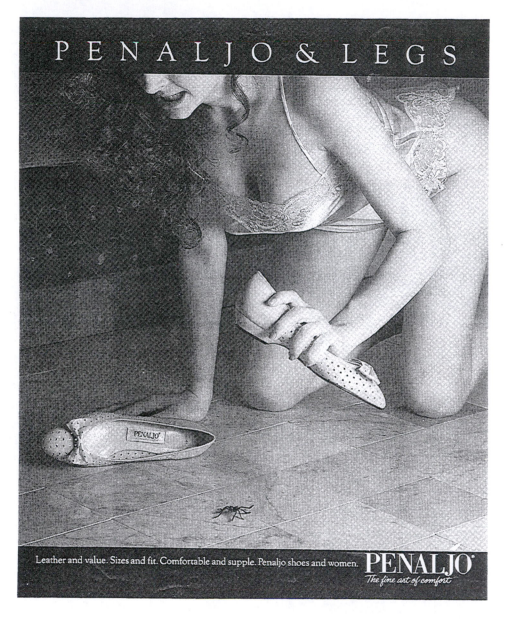

Aggression-Oriented Childrens' Advertising

As seen in Marvel Comics

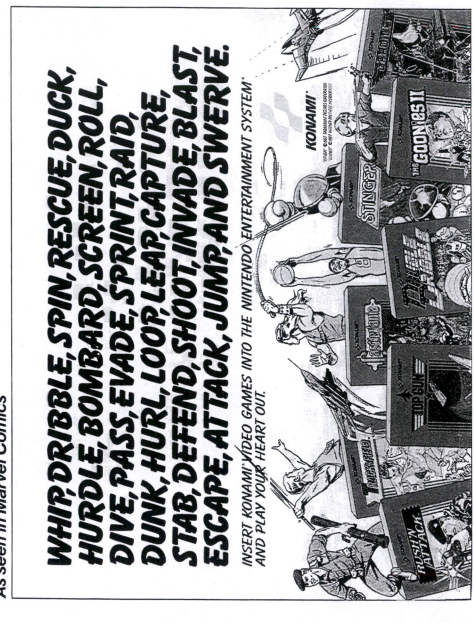

$$Chapter \quad 7$$

Personal Selling Ethics

Personal selling accounts for over eight million jobs in the United States. For every position in advertising, there are over thirty jobs in personal selling. The vast majority of organizations employ some salespeople. And while highly reliable estimates of industry expenditures for sales management and personal selling are not available, it is generally recognized that financial outlays for these activities exceed the amount spent on advertising, product development, or any other major component of marketing. Moreover, sales is the typical entry-level position for students who are trained in marketing. Selling, which involves direct contact with the buyer and requires extensive product knowledge, provides the necessary experience for advancement into marketing management and other high-level organizational positions. The express purpose of most personal selling is to convince the customer that the salesperson's product or service represents the *best* solution to the customer's need. Thus, it is little wonder that, because of its financial magnitude and persuasive aspects, personal selling is an area of marketing that generates many ethical questions.[1]

Consumer Irritation With Sales Efforts and Salespeople

To say that salespeople don't exactly enjoy a positive image among American consumers is an understatement. In a recent national opinion poll conducted by *The Wall Street Journal*, salespeople and their activities dominated the list of situations that most annoyed the American consumer (see Exhibit 7-1). In terms of *sales efforts*, computerized selling messages, getting a sales call during dinner,

---

EXHIBIT 7–1   Consumer Irritations with the Selling Process

Americans' Pet Peeves

Things that bother Americans the most as consumers:

Waiting in line while other windows or registers are closed	36%
Solicitations using prerecorded messages	31
Being quoted one price, then learning real price is higher	21
Getting a sales call during dinner	21
Learning that sale items aren't in stock	20
Dealing with complicated health insurance forms	18
"Urgent" mail that is only trying to sell something	17

Americans' biggest complaints about service:

Staying home for delivery or salespeople who fail to show	40%
Poorly informed salespeople	37
Sales clerks who are on the phone while waiting on you	25
Sales clerks who say, "It's not my department"	25
Salespeople who talk down to you	21
Sales clerks who can't describe how a product works	16

Note: Totals don't add to 100 percent because each respondent was allowed up to three responses.
Source: D. Wessel, "Sure Ways to Annoy Consumers," *The Wall Street Journal* (November 6, 1989), B1.

and junk mail are irritating to a substantial percentage of consumers. In terms of the *sales service*, sales clerks who are poorly informed, condescending, or engaged in other activities while waiting on the consumer, bothered high percentages of buyers. The common denominator among all of these complaints is that American consumers seem to feel that salespeople too regularly waste customers' time.[2]

While consumers are often irritated with salespeople, things are just as difficult on the other side of the sales exchange. Salesmen and women often feel strong pressure to succeed, because their performance and selling success are linked to organizational rewards and advancement. For example, upon attainment of the annual quota, a salesrep may receive a $5,000 bonus. Being close, but not at, this goal could influence year-end selling tactics. In normal selling situations, temptations occur that arguably may hurt the customer, but would benefit the salesperson. Consider the issues involved in the following scenarios.[3]

Scenario 1

Paul Fisk, a young computer salesperson, faced the following dilemma. A newly installed computer system continually malfunctioned. The customer demanded that the system be replaced with a new, not used, model. Unbeknownst to the customer, management would only replace the computer in need of repair with a used model that looked new. Paul was uncertain whether he should inform his customer about management's intentions and thus, risk losing the sale as well as attendant commission, or defer to management's judgment and possibly salvage the installation. **What should Paul do?**

Scenario 2

A health and beauty aids sales representative, named Angela Jeffers, confronted the following dilemma. On the last day of the fiscal year, she was below quota. When calling on a particular customer, Angela had an important decision to make. She could oversell the customer and achieve her quota; such action, however, could lead to long-term customer dissatisfaction if the buyer were unable to move the overstocked merchandise. Most likely though the extra product could be sold without difficulty. Alternatively, she could sell the customer only the quantity that was needed, thus failing to obtain quota (and not earning the bonus) but maintaining customer satisfaction. **What do you recommend that Angela do?**

Scenario 3

Jim Cotton, a real estate agent, faced a potential conflict. He was trying to sell a particular house to a client who had at last decided to make an offer. The offer was well below the list price of the house and the agent felt very confident that the current owner of the home would decline the offer. In hopes of getting the buyer to make a more acceptable offer, Jim was thinking about telling his customer that the seller was currently considering a higher offer from another potential buyer. In reality, no such offer existed. **Should Jim go ahead with his plan?**

These scenarios raise important questions about personal selling ethics.

> To what degree does a sales representative owe disclosure to a customer?

> Is it appropriate to oversell a customer for the purposes of attaining a quota? Is this practice acceptable if the sales representative knows that overstocking the customer will not likely create a long-term problem for the buying organization?

> Is it acceptable for salespeople to lie or misrepresent the seller in order to increase the probability of a sale if the salesrep believes that misrepresentation will not hurt the potential buyer?

In the balance of this chapter, we explore the ethical underpinnings of such questions. We also review some of the major laws governing personal selling, as well as the gray areas of sales that most likely raise ethical questions. We conclude the chapter with several suggestions for modifications in the organizational selling process. Our suggested approach has the potential to improve sales ethics.

Why Personal Selling Presents Particularly Difficult Ethical Questions[4]

Because sales representatives attempt to balance the interests of the seller who they represent and the buyer who they try to serve, ethical conflicts and choices are inherent in the personal selling process. Salespeople face many of the same general ethical issues that other marketing managers must deal with. Yet, they often do not have the organizational support structure afforded to other employees of the firm. Because of the dynamic and autonomous nature of the selling situation (i.e., the negotiation process), salesreps often must make instant choices about what to do when faced with a particular situation. For example, in scenario 2, Angela, the health products salesrep, cannot interrupt the selling process in order to make a phone call and ask her supervisor if it is okay that she overstocks one of her accounts "just enough to make quota." Most salespeople simply do not have the luxury of being able to sit back and leisurely contemplate the ethical propriety of their actions. In other words, salesreps often operate in relative isolation. Similarly, their results are often "evaluated" by sales managers who look at sales call reports that have been submitted from the sales territory. Such "paper-driven evaluation" can contribute to the perceived distance between management and the sales team. This autonomous aspect of certain types of selling necessitates forthright actions if ethics are to play a positive role.

The nature of pressures on the sales force may take many forms. For example, the heavy travel schedules associated with most selling positions may lead to the temptation to inflate expense account reports. Long periods away from the home office, sometimes in a foreign country, create special problems. While on assignment, salesreps become conditioned to utilizing company resources as if they were their own. Or the provision of a gift—perhaps even a *very large* gift—may seem like a small sum to give to an organizational buyer after a salesrep has spent months (possibly even years) on an account that could result in a commission worth thousands of dollars or more.

Because many theories of effective selling recommend rewarding superior *sales performance*, the behavior that occurs in securing sales may be counterproductive to organizational ethics and culture. In other words, companies that give lip service to ethical selling may in fact counteract that by only financially rewarding sales achievement. Many salesreps have faced the temptation to sell unneeded product because their compensation was heavily based upon commission, or overpromise the performance characteristics of the product line when competitive pressures suggest that the sale might be lost. Below, certain difficult areas of the personal selling process are discussed, because they seem especially likely to raise legal and ethical questions (see Exhibit 7–2).

EXHIBIT 7–2 Legal and Ethical Reminders for Salespeople

→ Use factual data rather than general statements of praise for the product during the sales presentation. Avoid misrepresentation.

→ Thoroughly educate customers, before the sale, on the product's specifications, capabilities, and limitations.

→ Do not overstep authority, as the salesperson's actions can be binding to the selling firm.

→ Avoid discussing these topics with competitors: prices, profit margins, discounts, terms of sale, bids or intent to bid, sales territories or markets to be served, rejection or termination of customers.

→ Do not use one product as bait for selling another product.

→ Do not try to force the customer to buy only from your organization.

→ Offer the same price and support to all buyers who purchase under the same set of circumstances.

→ Do not tamper with a competitor's product.

→ Do not disparage a competitor's product without specific evidence for your statements.

→ Avoid promises that will be difficult or impossible to honor.

Source: T. N. Ingram and R. W. LaForge, *Sales Management* (Chicago: Dryden Press, 1989), 393. © 1989 by The Dryden Press, a division of Holt, Rinehart and Winston, Inc. Reprinted by permission.

Sales and the Law

The first principle an organization needs to follow is that sales representatives ought to follow the law. As noted previously, the law is the lowest common denominator of ethical behavior. Ideally, ethical conduct exists at a level well above that required by the law. There seem to be many situations where sales representatives are accused of being unethical. More accurately though, what the accusers mean is that certain salespeople are engaging in *illegal* behavior.

Consider the following legal strictures that attempt to constrain dubious selling efforts.[5]

Federal Regulation

The Clayton Act (1914) and the Robinson–Patman Act (1936) are federal laws that restrict the price reductions and promotional concessions that can be promised by salespeople. For example, the Robinson–Patman Act states that selling firms cannot *indiscriminately* grant price concessions even when important customers demand larger discounts in order to retain their business. Such discounts are not legally allowed. The selling firm must grant equivalent discounts to all buyers. The seller can only grant unusual discounts or allowances if they are made available to all other customers or if there is a compelling cost differential to justify the discounting practice. The Clayton Act prohibits tie-in sales where the customer of a particular line of merchandise is required to buy other unwanted products in order to secure the primary purchase. In addition, various other unfair selling practices are illegal under the Federal Trade Commission Act (1914) and the Wheeler–Lea Amendment (1938). While the FTC Act does not define the nature of unfair competition, a large body of case law has evolved over the years. The following sales practices would clearly be legally dubious: making false, deceptive, or disparaging statements about competitors or their products; having a buyer provide *kickbacks* in order to secure a critical supply or component; presenting rebuilt or secondhand products as new; engaging in *industrial espionage* in order to learn competitive trade secrets; or making false or *misleading claims* about services that accompany the purchase of a product.

The Uniform Commercial Code (UCC)

In addition to federal law, the UCC, which regulates business contracts, has been modified in various ways by most states. The UCC spells out the various rules of contract law that apply to selling. It is true that the laws governing selling vary somewhat from state to state. However, most state regulations include provisions concerning the *implied* warranty with regard to products that are sold and the maximum allowable percent of interest when a sale is financed. Salespeople are also subject to legal sanction if they do not understand the difference between *puffery* (i.e., statements of subjective opinion concerning a product or service) and statements of *fact* concerning product performance characteristics.

Cooling Off Laws

Most states have laws that protect buyers from unscrupulous door-to-door salespeople and telemarketing sales representatives. The idea here is that some consumers may be subject to undue pressure from such selling sources. As a result, customers normally have three days to inform the seller that they have changed their mind. Therefore, they may void the contract, return any merchandise, and obtain a full refund in situations where the committed purchase is for an amount greater than twenty-five dollars.

Green River Ordinances

These are local ordinances which require non-residents who are selling goods or services to people in the locality to register with city authorities. In this instance, credentials of salespeople are checked by the local authorities, thereby eliminating some of the so-called "fly-by-night" con-artists and scam operators. (Incidentally, the name of these regulations comes from Green River, Wyoming where the first such legal measure was instituted.)

Judging from the above discussion, one can see that there is a great deal of selling activity which is already controlled by existing *law.* In the terminology introduced in Chapter 2, sales representatives who engage in practices violating existing legislation would be classified as crooks, because they are probably knowingly breaking the law. There are other practices in sales, however, which are *not* illegal but certainly are subject to debate concerning their appropriateness. It is to these that we now turn our attention.

The Gray Areas of Selling

There are several categories of personal selling behavior that fall into a "shade of gray." These areas include the sales representatives' use of company assets, dealings with customers, relationships with competitors, and the potential conflicts of interest inherent in the selling process.[6]

Company Assets

The nature of personal selling often requires that the sales representative use company resources in order to interact with the buyer. This lends itself to such things as the padding of expense accounts, the use of company-supplied automobiles for personal business, and the utilization of other company equipment or materials (e.g., photocopiers and telephones) for personal advantage, all of which raise ethical questions. Abuses of this kind can result in substantial organizational costs. It is estimated that the average cost of a *single* business-to-business sales call is approximately $230.[7] Companies rightly hold that they do not wish to add bogus expenses to these already considerable costs. Some salesreps feel that they have the right to inflate expense accounts because of various business-related expenses that may not normally be reimbursed (e.g., certain gratuities). Also, certain salesmen and women believe that using the company automobile (without a required co-payment) is acceptable because separating business and personal travel is often difficult. There are no simple answers concerning *when* use of company assets becomes unethical. However, it is important for organizations to have detailed guidelines appropriate to their situation.

Relationship with Customers

This category includes a wide variety of business practices that might be considered questionable. Among the potentially dubious personal selling tactics would be (a) overstocking a customer because the salesrep wishes to win a sales contest or meet a quota, (b) overselling a customer in the sense of providing a more expensive or complex product than is needed, (c) overpromising a delivery, hoping that the order will not be cancelled when the unattainable delivery terms are not met, and (d) failing to keep confidences (i.e., passing on information about competitors that a salesperson might have picked up through a buyer–seller interaction). Other areas that come to mind in this general category are *lying to customers* about product performance characteristics or *paying bribes* in order to secure an account. However, again, these latter items fall under the general heading of illegal activity. While organizations should take steps to make clear that the above practices are not allowed (see the Xerox policies in Appendix 7A), they are not strictly ethical concerns, since the law passes a judgment concerning the prohibition of most of this behavior.

While having a policy dealing with each of the possibly unethical issues listed above does not *guarantee* ethical behavior by the sales force, at least the company makes its position clear concerning the appropriateness of certain practices. (See Exhibit 7–3 for a burgeoning area of sales that is also raising ethical problems.) One study of sales managers and representatives found that the majority of those surveyed desired *additional* company guidance concerning what constitutes appropriate action.[8] The areas where salesreps most often felt that greater policy clarity was needed had to do with allowing the buyer's personality to affect terms of price, delivery, and other aspects of the sale; charging a less competitive price when the selling company was the sole source of supply; and providing "purchase volume incentive bonuses" for larger buyers. The point here is that even when an organization has an articulated statement of selling ethics, it may be worthwhile to periodically ascertain from the salesforce (either through a meeting, formal survey, or a focus group) the areas where further guidance is needed.

Relationship with Competitors[9]

While salesreps may not interact directly with competitors, certainly the presence of competitors is always felt as other vendors make their alternative proposals to the buyer. When attempting to secure a sale, it is often necessary for salesreps to make product comparisons. In general, outright disparagement of competitive offerings should be avoided. Whenever possible, any product comparison should be based on objective, accurate, scientific information. The salesrep should try to appeal to the prospective buyer using a certifiable product track record when claiming superiority for one's product or product line. Within this realm there are two other practices that are almost always unethical. First, there is *product tampering* with the competitors' offering—a practice that usually occurs in retail stores or at trade shows. Such "dirty tricks" fall under the domain of unfair competition and may be subject to legal sanction. A second practice that definitely falls in the dubious category has to do with *spying on competitors*. Certainly, it is tempting for salespeople to use whatever means they can to obtain valuable competitive information. Clearly, an astute sales representative will fearlessly probe the buyer concerning any information that can be secured regarding the competitors' price offerings or new product attributes. However, obtaining such information by subterfuge (e.g., taking competitive information from a buyer's desk) is unquestionably unethical. Recall our discussion of competitive intelligence gathering in Chapter 3 where specific guidelines were offered.

EXHIBIT 7–3   Telemarketing: Some Emerging Ethical Concerns

The fastest growing method of soliciting sales in recent years has been via telephone selling. In 1986 the Direct Marketing Association reported that approximately 46 percent of all money spent on direct marketing could be attributed to telemarketing efforts. These techniques involve the so-called *telephone-out*—the active solicitation of a customer through the telephone call—and *telephone-in*—whereby customers are provided with a number (often a toll-free 800 number) that they can use to place an order or to make a product inquiry. A combination of these techniques—referred to as *telemarketing*—has been the subject of explosive growth because of the high costs of individual interpersonal contact in the selling process, as well as the efficiencies that are brought to the selling process because of the electronic capabilities of the telephone.

With computer assisted hardware and software, as well as a touch tone telephone at the receiver's end, buyers are able to secure merchandise and respond to a specific set of questions that are computer-generated, thereby eliminating the need for human telephone representatives. Moreover, telephone area codes and prefixes allow marketers to reach certain target markets with uncanny accuracy.

The growth of mail order merchandisers, such as L. L. Bean and Lands' End (for casual clothing and outdoor equipment), are testimony to the effectiveness of (telephone-in) telemarketing. Widespread use of (telephone-out) telemarketing is evident for charitable fund solicitations, political polling, and of course, the ever present magazine subscription sales.

A particularly interesting manifestation of telephone-in telemarketing has been the use of 900 numbers, which allow people to place calls usually at a charge of fifty cents (or more) for the first minute and thirty-five cents a minute thereafter (although rates are rapidly increasing). Such numbers have been used to give people up-to-date access to sports scores, political results, the financial markets, and specialized conversation networks featuring themes such as romance or intimate confessions of young girls or serving certain groups, such as singles over thirty-five.

The boom of telemarketing raises many ethical questions with which marketers have yet to effectively grapple. Among such questions would be the following:

To what extent are at-home telephone solicitations intrusive?

When telephone numbers are randomly dialed within an area code or prefix, to what extent do such calls represent an invasion of privacy when they reach an unlisted number?

To what degree are computer-generated sales inquiries or telephone surveys considered to be "annoying" by the receivers of such calls?

Why do so many of the services offered by 900 telephone numbers add to the poor image of marketing as "pitching" trashy services?

Source: Adapted from W. P. Dommermuth, *Promotion*, 2nd ed. (Boston: PWS–KENT Publishing Company, 1989), 328–330. © by PWS–KENT Publishing Company, a division of Wadsworth, Inc. Reprinted by permission.

Relationships with Fellow-Workers and Supervisors[10]

Salesreps certainly have implied ethical responsibilities to their co-workers, be they peers or members of the sales management group. For example, salespeople work not only alone but also as part of a team. However, individual rewards usually provide stronger motivation than group rewards. In some instances, sales representatives may try to take business away from colleagues. This occurs when they sell to customers in another (maybe an adjacent) territory. The issue gets especially muddy when one considers buying firms with multiple locations. Because of this, and the individualistic reward system, salespeople may engage in unethical practice, because the compensation system promotes selfishness and fails to reward teamwork adequately. Similarly, given the isolation of salesreps, they usually can exercise great latitude in how they report their activities to their supervisors. For example, they may claim they made ten calls on Friday when they actually made five morning calls and took the afternoon off. Or they can say they made ten calls but omit that they made five via telephone merely "checking in" rather than canvassing the account.

Conflicts of Interest

Another common area of sales concern stems from conflicts of interest. These problems are partly inherent in the selling process, as salespersons are intermediaries between the companies they represent and the buyers they serve. Some sellers, such as travel agents and stockbrokers, are faced with conflicting allegiances, because their compensation may come from someone other than the client with whom they are working. A typical example is real estate sales. Individuals looking for a house coordinate with a real estate agent and will often place some confidence in that individual's judgment. Yet, they must know full well that the commission is paid *by the seller* of the house and therefore, the seller is the agent's first loyalty. In summary, the duties of *honesty* and *fairness* are perhaps the key virtues for salesreps to adhere to in their relationships with customers, co-workers, and their employer.

Gifts and Entertainment: Areas That Are Not Unethical Per Se

Gifts and entertainment are two areas often subject to detailed scrutiny in the realm of personal selling, yet they have their proper role in the selling process. The majority of salespeople feel that giving certain gifts, like coffee mugs, as well as the provision of lunches, and some forms of entertainment, are a perfectly normal part of the sales process and do not necessarily raise an ethical question.[11]

Gifts

The giving of small gifts by sales representatives to customers is a time-honored American tradition, especially prevalent at holiday time. In business-to-business selling, salespeople and purchasing agents often develop a close working relationship. Thus, gifts become a mechanism to express appreciation for past and, perhaps, future business. The ethical question regarding gift-giving, of course, is: *When* does a gift become a bribe? Most buying organizations probably do not object to some of their purchasing representatives receiving a gift-wrapped bottle of wine at Christmas time. However, at what point does the value of a given gift cross the ethical line? For example, a company branded pen and pencil set as a gift may be considered acceptable; a pair of center ice tickets for a National Hockey League game might be considered a bit more debatable; a color television set for the purchasing agent's den is extremely questionable; and the provision of sexual favors by call girls, arranged and paid for by the seller, is deemed undeniably unethical.

The difficulty, again, is establishing exactly where the ethical line should be drawn. The Internal Revenue Service places a *twenty-five dollar annual limit* on the amount that may be deducted for business gifts to any one individual. Some organizations, such as General Dynamics, do not allow their sales representatives or employees to give or receive a gift of *any* value. From the standpoint of helping shape the sales representative's judgment, it is best that firms have an explicit written policy concerning gift-giving and receiving. Exactly what goes into this policy depends upon the corporate culture and the tradition of the industry and corporation (see Chapter 10 for illustrations). However, time-tested guidelines would suggest that (a) inordinately expensive gifts be avoided, (b) gifts should never be given *before* a particular buyer does business with an organization, (c) one should probably avoid giving gifts to the buyer's spouse or significant other, and (d) an explicit dollar limit should be placed on all gifts to be given.[12]

Entertainment

Most of the discussion pertaining to gift-giving also applies to entertainment. Virtually all salespeople will agree that taking a customer to lunch is reasonable, and often an *expected* way of conducting business. Again, the fundamental issue resides in determining *when* entertaining is construed as an attempt to influence a buyer to purchase a product for reasons other than its inherent merits. In one survey of buying organizations, the majority of respondents strongly agreed that the provision of business lunches and small advertising specialties (for example, pens or drinking glasses) were appropriate forms of entertainment and sales promotion, and other items, such as "an evening on the town" for buyers and their friends were rated as inappropriate.[13] Again, it is probably best if an organization has an explicit, written policy concerning the types of entertainment that sales representatives can provide. Exactly *what* is appropriate depends upon the situation, although as noted previously, some practices are never acceptable. In the case of negotiations for multi-million dollar contracts (e.g., an airline buying several planes), it is not uncommon for top executives from the buying organization to be flown to the seller's headquarters for product demonstrations and briefings. At least one study has found a positive correlation between the provision of entertainment to buyers and a subsequent first purchase of the seller's product.[14] Clearly, entertainment is a means to an end, meant to obligate the buyer in some way. Entertainment is intended to smooth the pathway for subsequent sales. Exhibit 7–4 provides a listing of the twelve most common entertainment activities used by salesreps.[15]

When Are Salesreps Most Pressured to Compromise Their Ethics?

The answer to this question depends upon many of the factors that were examined in Chapter 2. Certainly, salesreps will be more likely to cross the ethical line when they are given the *opportunity* to engage in unethical behavior. Similarly, when they realize that the likelihood of being caught is low, or when their behavior will likely lead to a substantial personal or financial reward, the probability of acting improperly increases. One can also speculate that the larger the extent to which a given sales representative has developed an ethical sensitivity (i.e., they are higher in their level of moral development), the smaller the likelihood of their engaging in unethical selling practices. These are elements that come into play for *all* marketers. However, there may be certain issues that

---

EXHIBIT 7–4   The Twelve Most Prevalent Entertainment Activities Ranked According to Their Frequency of Use by Sales Representatives

1. Taking a client to lunch.
2. Taking a client to dinner.
3. Taking a client to breakfast.
4. Giving a client free product samples for personal use.
5. Playing golf with a client and paying the client's way.
6. Paying a clients' travel expenses to visit a product demonstration.
7. Giving a client a work-related gift (e.g., desk pen set).
8. Buying a client alcoholic beverages at a cocktail lounge.
9. Playing tennis with a client and paying the client's way.
10. Inviting a client to your home for entertainment purposes.
11. Taking a client to a sporting event.
12. Playing handball [racquetball] with a client and paying the client's way.

Source: Robert E. Hite and Joseph A. Bellizzi, "Salespeople's Use of Entertainment and Gifts," *Industrial Marketing Management* 16 (1987), 281. © 1987 by Elsevier Science Publishing Company, Inc. Reprinted by permission.

directly impact the ethics of sales representatives because of their selling tasks. We speculate, for example, that sales representatives will be pressured to act unethically *when*

- competition is intense.
- economic times are difficult.
- compensation is based primarily upon commission.
- questionable dealings are a common industry practice (e.g., providing kick-backs or elaborate entertainment).
- corporate sales training is abbreviated.
- they have limited selling experience.

Interestingly, most of these propositions have not been systematically studied. However, one limited research project found a minimal relationship between industrial sales representatives' reported ethical discomfort and a variety of factors including time in their position, the compensation mechanism by which they were remunerated, the intensity of the competition in their target market and their level of education.[16] In another study conducted by the Wharton School of Business, 443 industrial salespeople reacted to situations similar to those posed in this chapter. Twelve percent of the salespeople were labeled "sinners" because of their disposition to endorse unethical actions, 38 percent were considered "saints" because of their tendency to consistently resist the unethical option, while the rest fell somewhere in between. Competitive markets seemed to make unethical choices more likely while experience and close supervision were factors associated with more ethical actions.[17] In short, management should be sensitive to the hypothesized organizational factors that may tempt salesreps into violating ethical norms.

Sales Management Ethics

This chapter would not be complete without some discussion of the special ethical responsibilities that fall on the sales manager. Many of the ethical issues with which the sales manager must grapple are the same difficult areas found within the domain of most administrators. For example, the issue of employing, promoting, and firing personnel, and the inherent obligation *in justice* that all managers conduct such affairs evenhandedly are concerns of all supervisors. (See Exhibit 7–5 for a short case that deals with the hiring process for new salesreps.) Further, many of the issues related to mainstream sales management fall under the jurisdiction of the law. For example, legislation such as the Equal Employment Opportunity Act forbids discrimination against employees *on any basis* except performance-related criteria. Similarly, in the area of salary administration, the just and prompt reimbursement of sales force expenses, as well as the accurate payment of salary, commissions, and bonuses are ethical (and legal) responsibilities implicit in honest compensation management. However, there are at least

---

EXHIBIT 7–5   The Sales "Aggressiveness" Test

A company heavily involved in industrial sales is recruiting students at a university campus. The president of the company has written a memo to the chief recruiter suggesting that the students that have been hired in the recent past have not been aggressive enough in their sales efforts and have not worked long enough hours to satisfy the desires of certain members of top management. As a result, the president has suggested using the following scenario during the job interview. He writes:

> Students we interview should be told that they are on a raft with their spouse and small child. The raft overturns in some heavy white water, and they can save only one person. If they choose to save themselves, the other two family members will perish. If they choose to save a particular family member that effort will be successful, but they will be swept away by the current and not saved.

The president went on to write that there is probably no answer to this dilemma. However, the organization should *not* want to invite anyone for a *second* interview who does not suggest saving themselves. Why? "Because our company is interested in cultivating people who look after their *own* interest before that of their family or others."

The director of student recruiting expressed some concern and cautiously asked why the organization would want to use such an unconventional method. The president answered, "Read my lips, son. We want to hire salesreps who put themselves ahead of their family, who put their egoistic self-interest ahead of everything else. We want go-getters. That way we can use cash incentives and advancement as effective motivational technique to maximize our sales. Money talks to a sales force composed of such individuals."

Is it unethical to use such a scenario as a job interview technique?

---

three areas that are somewhat unique to sales management and which call upon the sales manager to exercise a high degree of ethical propriety.[18] These are the administration of sales territories, the setting of sales quotas, and various competitive considerations.

The Administration of Sales Territories

Obviously, the selling territory assigned to the salesrep goes far towards determining the potential sales level and (possibly) compensation levels that the salesrep can attain. Thus, the assignment and administration of territories must be undertaken by the sales manager with special care. Sometimes it is necessary to reassign territories because of selling efficiencies. Loss of income to the individual salesrep or increased degrees of selling responsibility must be taken into consideration in such shifting of assignments. Also, certain accounts become important enough over time that they become designated national accounts. That is, there are customers who become so important that they are handled exclusively by top management or headquarters personnel. In such situations, the sales manager seems to have an ethical responsibility to provide early notification to the salesrep who will lose future national (sometimes called "house") accounts. It also seems incumbent upon management to consider providing that salesrep with some sort of financial reward, additional new accounts, or expanded territory to make up for the loss of the key customer.

The Setting of Sales Quotas

Often a large proportion of compensation in the area of personal selling is determined by commissions and bonuses. Attainment of sales quotas by the sales force will determine the level of financial remuneration that they receive. If sales quotas are not perceived as fair by salesreps, pressures for unethical behavior can increase. If the sales force regularly falls short of established quotas, there will be a decline in the morale of the reps. While a review of the various methods used to establish sales quotas is beyond the scope of this book, clearly, such decisions should be made with the degree of equity that allows for the realistic assessment of the quotas.[19] All members of the sales force should have a fair chance to attain their quotas and receive a just wage given the constraints of the territories they serve.

Competitive Considerations

The written, promotional material that is developed by headquarters to accompany the product becomes an important sales aid for members of the selling team. Sales managers have a special responsibility to avoid alienating buyers via product misrepresentation or providing the sales force with material that can carelessly be used to disparage competitors. Since the sales manager is typically responsible for overseeing sales materials as well as the sales force, the responsibility to see that this information passes ethical muster falls on the sales manager. Exhibit 7–6 delineates some specific steps that organizations can take to avoid alienating buyers through the materials their sales representatives use in the selling process.

Ideas for Ethical Action

The following suggestions are offered to help sales managers establish a more nurturing ethical climate in which their salesreps might operate.[20]

First, *develop, circulate and promote a detailed and explicit sales ethics policy statement.* Topics covered in this statement should address the major questions that arise in the course of the seller–buyer interaction. Issues discussed previously, such as gift-giving, bribery, entertainment, and conflict of interest, should be treated in as much detail as the organization's selling experience allows. The Xerox policy statement included in Appendix 7A as well the Direct Selling Education Foundation code in Exhibit 7–7 provide illustrations of the level of detail

---

EXHIBIT 7–6   A Checklist to Avoid Alienating Buyers

✓ Review all promotional material and sales correspondence before distribution to minimize the possibility that defamatory material is inadvertently distributed by the sales force.

✓ Tell salespeople not to repeat unconfirmed trade gossip, particularly about the financial condition of a competitor.

✓ Tell salespeople to avoid statements that may be interpreted as damaging to the reputation of a business or individual.

✓ Ensure that salespeople avoid making unfair or inaccurate comparisons about a competitor's product. Mere "puffing" or claiming superiority over a competitor's product is not disparagement as long as the comparison attempts to enhance the quality of your product without being unfairly critical of the competitor's.

✓ Avoid sending customers written comparisons of competing products. One way to make comparisons is to include scientific facts or statistical evidence documented or prepared by an independent research firm supporting factual claims.

Source: R. E. Anderson, J. F. Hair, Jr., and A. J. Bush, *Professional Sales Management* (New York: McGraw–Hill, 1988), 569–570. Reprinted by permission of McGraw–Hill, Inc.

to which such statements can go. It is also imperative that such policy statements address any special issues that may come up in the sales force's handling of the product. For example, sellers of farm herbicides may have special obligations concerning safety disclosures. Pharmaceutical salesreps may have extraordinary responsibilities with regard to highlighting a new drug's potential side effects to busy physicians. The selling organization must also make clear that policy statements on ethics will be enforced. When this occurs, it should be done visibly and vigorously. Sales managers must take special care to reprimand ethical violations evenhandedly. One national poll of sales managers indicated that sanctions are more likely to be meted out when the unethical action caused negative outcomes for the selling organization, or when the salesrep involved was a poor performer to begin with.[21]

Second, *sales quotas should always be realistically set by management.* Pressure to attain management established sales quotas, even though possibly unrealistic, will create an environment whereby the salesrep is likely to become the rationalizer (discussed in Chapter 2). In such situations, the exaggeration of product characteristics, overselling a client, bribery, or kickbacks may occur as the seller seeks a mechanism to achieve the needed sale and move toward quota. The implication here is that sales managers have a particular responsibility to closely monitor sales force behavior. This takes many traditional forms, including occasionally accompanying salesreps on calls, and carefully auditing the *sales call reports* that most organizations routinely require. Individuals who have historically submitted questionable expense vouchers or accumulated extraordinary

---

EXHIBIT 7–7   Ethical Standards Salespersons Should Follow

"As you work, keep in mind the following guidelines for ethical sales and make sure you are following them.

- Offers should be clear, so consumers understand exactly what they are buying and how much they will have to pay.
- The order form should clearly describe the goods and quantity purchased, the price and terms of payment, and any additional charges.
- Receipts and contracts should show the name of the sales representative and his or her address or the name, address and telephone number of the firm whose product is sold.
- All salespersons should promptly identify themselves to a prospective customer and should truthfully indicate the purpose of their approach to the consumer, identifying the company or product brands represented.
- A salesperson should obey all applicable federal, state and local laws.

- A salesperson should explain the terms and conditions for returning a product or cancelling an order.
- Salespersons should not create confusion in the mind of the consumer, abuse the trust of the consumer, nor exploit the lack of experience or knowledge of the consumer.
- Salespersons should respect the privacy of consumers by making every effort to make calls at times that best suit the customer's convenience and wishes.
- It is a consumer's right to end a sales call and salespersons should respect that right.
- All references to testimonials and endorsements should be truthful, currently applicable and authorized by the person or organization quoted.
- Product comparisons should be fair and based on substantiated facts.
- A salesperson should not disparage other products or firms."

Source: Direct Selling Education Foundation, Washington, DC, 1989. Reprinted by permission.

---

sales only during contest periods are candidates for special monitoring on the part of management. Prudential scrutiny may help purge members of the sales force that might later cause embarrassment or even legal action against the organization because of unethical actions.

Third, *sales managers should encourage sales representatives to ask for help when they face an ethically troublesome sale.* As noted previously, sales representatives operate with a great deal more independence than other line employees. However, this independence may foster a climate that creates a moral vacuum. The organization should designate someone who can be approached when salesreps are troubled by ethical concerns. The idea of a "sales chaplain" has been suggested as a mechanism for providing the guidance that sales persons might need in the ethical realm.[22] This chaplain could be a retired sales executive or perhaps someone trained in ethics and familiar with the workings of the organization. His or her role would be to provide ethical guidance and counsel on issues that less experienced salesreps may not have previously encountered.

Fourth, *if ethical problems persist in the selling environment, management should take proactive measures.* If there appears to be a persistent problem of unethical sales behavior in an industry—for instance, a climate of kickbacks or payoffs—top management should consider meeting with competition to hammer out an industry-wide code of sales ethics which will level the competitive playing field. Collusion to *improve* the ethical climate of the industry does not violate federal antitrust law. The defense industry, one certainly deserving of censure for past unethical selling practices, has attempted to develop such an industry-wide code.

Ethical abuse may stem from many factors, such as continuing unethical sales practices by competitors or improper requests by buyers. If salesreps become aware of continuing abuses and their immediate supervisor provides no help, there should be a mechanism by which they can "blow the whistle." The whistle blowing mechanism allows the employee to have someone in the organization who they can approach concerning moral conduct when their immediate line manager seems unwilling or unable to resolve the situation that has been repeatedly reported.[23] The sales chaplain mentioned earlier (or some other ethical ombudsman) may be the individual who is designated by the organization as the one to approach in such difficult instances. Importantly, protection from retribution against the employee who has bypassed the chain of command should be built into the whistle blower mechanism. McDonnell Douglas Corp., a firm that has had its share of ethical and legal scrapes with the government in the past, has now developed a corporate ombudsman position that includes the protection of whistle blowers as part of its mandate (see Exhibit 7–8).

EXHIBIT 7–8   McDonnell Douglas Corporation (MDC) Hotline

"If you suspect a violation of MDC's Code of Ethics or Standards of Business Conduct, it is your obligation to report your suspicions to one or more of the following:

- your supervisor; or,
- your department or function head; or,
- another function with applicable expertise, such as the Fiscal Division or Security Department; or,
- your component Ombudsman or alternate point of contact:

Name

Telephone No.   Address
or,
- the Corporate Ombudsman.

Information concerning possible violation of federal procurement laws or other improper actions relating to or affecting MDC's business with the U.S. Government must be promptly referred to the Law Department."

Source: McDonnell Douglas Corp., Reprinted by permission.

A Simple Framework to Evaluate Sales Ethics

In addition to the above organizational measures, the following guidelines might be useful to the individual sales representative who is facing an ethical dilemma. There are limitations to any procedural approach, but we are often asked what general mechanisms can be utilized by salespersons facing ethical dilemmas. In this regard we recommend the *proportionality framework*.[24] While some experts have called for a normative approach that is much more comprehensive, this approach was designed with the decision-maker in mind. Thus, we endorse it as a starting point for the action-oriented and pragmatic salesrep. The following points capture the highlights of this approach.[25]

1. Actions that have ethical ramifications can be dissected into at least three components: (a) the intent behind the action, (b) the action itself (the means), and (c) the outcomes which flow from that action. In considering the ethical propriety of an action, one must consider all three components. Thus, scrutiny only of what the salesrep *does* (the action) is too limited. One must also look at the intent that preceded that action and the subsequent outcomes.

2. If the action is to result in a substantial negative outcome (i.e., a so-called major outcome), then the action is almost always unethical. For example, if an organization is engaged in bid-rigging (the means) with the outcome of driving competition from the marketplace, the action is unethical (a significant negative outcome), even though the by-product may be the provision of some product to customers at a currently lower price (a good outcome). Similarly, even if a salesrep has made full disclosure (an appropriate means), it would probably be unethical to sell a buyer a product that had attributes that the buyer simply did not need (a negative outcome).

3. If there are unintended side effects (outcomes) to an action taken by a salesrep and these side effects cause a *major* negative outcome, the action is almost always unethical. Suppose the salesrep of a pharmaceutical house has been providing experimental drugs to a research institute to be used in animal research. In the course of the sales process, the salesrep learns that the drugs are to be used on human subjects. In such an instance, it may be unethical for the salesrep to go ahead with the transaction, because the side effects of the sale could produce significant negative consequences for other individuals (the unsuspecting human subjects). Major negative side effects, even if unintended, must be avoided.

4. Almost any action can have unintended side effects. A salesrep may take an action that has unintended side effects assuming that the foreseen consequences of that side effect are *minor*. For example, in making a sale to a buying organization, a salesrep may learn that the culmination of the sale will result in a competing salesperson losing a sales contest that involved an overseas trip. Obviously, it would still be ethical for the salesrep to complete the transaction even though there would be a negative consequence for his or her counterpart. Minor negative side effects, if unintended, can be tolerated.

Clearly, the above framework is still highly judgmental. For example, what constitutes a *major* negative outcome versus a *minor* negative outcome? If a salesrep believes that there may be side effects, does this mean that these side effects were intended? For example, in the situation posed within point number four above, suppose the salesperson realizes that his making a large sale will cause another seller, desperately hoping for the contract, to file for bankruptcy. Does this mean that the salesrep at focus has caused a major negative outcome? Certainly not, as many other factors would have contributed to the insolvency. Still, the model provides only limited guidance. In addition, the framework depends on the individual representative's ability to recognize the inherent lack of propriety in certain actions as well as the likelihood of negative outcomes. That is, the workability of this mechanism depends on the salesperson's moral sensitivity and sophistication. And the model is meant to be applied to *actions* of a questionable nature. For example, if the actions taken by a salesrep are honest, well-intentioned, and totally professional, there is little to be gained in calculating possible side effects and unintended outcomes. These limitations aside however, the approach sketched in the above sequence of steps does come to grips with the primary ethical components of decisions that salesreps must make in the field.

Conclusion

In this chapter, we describe the major factors that might cause ethical difficulties for members of the sales force. We review the laws regulating personal selling and constraining the actions of salesreps. In addition, we discuss some of the major areas of ethical conflict that occur in many selling situations. We also propose mechanisms with which the organization might experiment in order to provide the sales force with guidance in these situations. In the final analysis, however, the necessity of making ethical judgments cannot be eliminated from the marketplace. Many of the organizational approaches discussed elsewhere in the book can overcome some of the ambiguity that salesreps must deal with when facing an ethical question. However, the persuasive nature of the selling process itself often includes, as part of its residue, tough ethical cases that are difficult to confidently resolve. We now turn our attention to the special ethical problems that arise when companies operate in international markets.

Appendix 7A

The Ethics of Selling for Xerox[1]

A customer buys from Xerox for two reasons. S/he wants the product. S/he trusts the sales representative.

These two factors mesh like two gear wheels. Neither is going very far without the other. Together, they move.

Our technology may be superb, the reputation of our products may be unmatched. A purchaser buys from the salesperson s/he trusts.

Don't sell ethics short. Xerox doesn't. We lay claim to idealism in our company and make no apologies for that. But we also recognize the simple economic fact that our success rests heavily on your relationship with each of your customers, the service you provide, and the confidence each customer has in it and in you.

Because your performance in this respect is so important, because it can be critical in our competitive business environment, Xerox has developed a specific code of ethical selling practice for sales representatives. We ask you to understand it! We insist you adhere to it: your work will be measured against it.

The first five points in the list below involve the fundamental integrity of the entire corporation in the eyes of the public. You are responsible for meeting established revenue, net-addition and expense objectives, but in doing that, you are also the custodian of the company's reputation. You are indeed Xerox to your customers, to your own immediate competitors. And you are Xerox in a legal sense. Your obligations are precise and not negotiable.

The last three points are essentially internal. They are no less compelling, no less significant than the first five.

Xerox management has its own clear responsibilities—obligations to you under this code. It must keep informed; and encourage a free flow of communication from sales representatives and sales managers. Management must determine quickly and fairly the validity of any seeming infractions. It must act promptly and decisively when deviations from the code occur. Xerox management is obligated to you to make the code work and help you make it work.

The Xerox Selling Code

1. The only sales proposal you present to a customer is the proposal that best meets the customer's real needs: what it takes to do his job effectively without wasted capacity, equipment, or products. Anything else hurts Xerox in the long run—in the short run, too, for that matter.

---

[1] This statement was promulgated in the 1960s. A more detailed code was published in 1988, entitled "Business Conduct Guidelines." Reprinted by permission of Xerox Corporation.

2. You make sure that the customer understands exactly what s/he is contracting for, what the contractual obligations are to Xerox. You make equally sure that s/he understands just as clearly what Xerox contracts to do.
3. You never knowingly misrepresent any Xerox product or service or price. You exercise initiative and responsibility to avoid doing so unknowingly.
4. You never knowingly misrepresent any competitive product or service or price. You exercise initiative and responsibility to avoid doing so unknowingly.
5. You make no disparaging statements, directly or by any kind of inference or innuendo, about competitors and their products and services—even if you believe them to be true.
6. You conduct your activities so that they do not impinge in any way on the personal or business interests and integrity of your Xerox associates.

    • You do not knowingly engage in any practice that provides personal gain at the expense of others.
    • Territory and accounts are so managed as to permit territory transition and account changes without affecting other sales people adversely.

7. You recognize your responsibility to understand this code and to operate within it without exception.
8. You recognize the importance of bringing any problems you experience in implementing the code, internally or externally, to the attention of your management.

The Criterion

The fact that you work for Xerox gives you high visibility. It makes you the guardian of a prestige and a reputation that is always on the line. People tend to expect more of you because you are Xerox.

Endnotes

1. The statistics in this paragraph are drawn from R. F. Lusch and V. N. Lusch, *Principles of Marketing* (Boston: Kent Publishing, 1987), Chapter 15 and J. G. Udell and G. R. Laczniak, *Marketing in an Age of Change* (New York: John Wiley & Sons, 1981), Chapter 16.

2. D. Wessel, "Sure Ways to Annoy Consumers," *The Wall Street Journal* (November 6, 1989), B1.

3. These scenarios are taken from Alan J. Dubinsky, "Studying Salespeople's Ethical Problems: An Approach for Designing Company Policies." In *Marketing Ethics*, eds. G. R. Laczniak and P. E. Murphy, 41 (Lexington, MA: Lexington Books, 1985).

4. This section is loosely adapted from Clarke L. Caywood and Gene R. Laczniak, "Ethics and Personal Selling: *Death of a Salesman* as an Ethical Primer," *Journal of Personal Selling and Sales Management* (August 1986), 81–89.

5. The following discussion is drawn from W. J. Stanton and R. H. Buskirk, *Management of the Sales Force*, 6th ed. (Homewood, IL: Richard D. Irwin, 1983), Chapter 23 and B. R. Anderson, *Professional Selling*, 3rd ed. (Englewood Cliffs, NJ: Prentice–Hall, 1987), Chapter 18.

6. Anderson (see note 5 above.)

7. *Sales & Marketing Management* (June 22, 1992), 8.

8. A. J. Dubinsky, E. N. Berkowicz, and W. Rudelius, "Ethical Problems in Field Sales Personnel," *MSU Topics* (Summer 1980), 11–16.

9. R. E. Anderson, J. F. Hair, Jr., and A. J. Bush, *Professional Sales Management* (New York: McGraw–Hill, 1988), 423, 552.

10. The authors thank Joseph A. Bellizzi of Arizona State University for suggesting the examples in this section.

11. Robert E. Hite and Joseph A. Bellizzi, "Salespeople's Use of Entertainment and Gifts," *Industrial Marketing Management* 16 (1987), 279–285.

12. See Stanton and Buskirk in note 5 above.

13. W. Dempsey, F. A. Bushman, and R. E. Plank, "Personal Inducements of Industrial Buyers," *Industrial Marketing Management* 9 (1980), 281–289.

14. G. M. Zinkhan and L. A. Vachris, "The Impact of Selling Aids on New Prospects," *Industrial Marketing Management* 13 (1984), 187–193.

15. See Stanton and Buskirk in note 5 above.

16. Alan J. Dubinsky and Thomas N. Ingram, "Correlates of Salespeople's Ethical Conflict: An Exploratory Investigation," *Journal of Business Ethics* 3 (1984), 343–353.

17. Reported in: T. D. Schellhardt, "Rivalries, Law Policies Take a Toll in Ethics," *The Wall Street Journal* (March 22, 1990), B1.

18. See note 9 above.

19. For a solid discussion of how to set sales quotas, see Gilbert A. Churchill, Jr., Neil M. Ford, and Orville C. Walker, *Sales Force Management*, 2nd ed. (Homewood, IL: Richard D. Irwin, 1985), 215–227.

20. Partially adapted from "It's Time to Repeal the Right to Do Wrong," *Sales & Marketing Management* (October 11, 1976), 42.

21. Joseph A. Bellizzi and Robert E. Hite, "Supervising Unethical Salesforce Behavior," *Journal of Marketing* (April 1989), 36–47.

22. See note 4 above.

23. For further information on this topic, see Douglas J. Dalrymple, *Sales Management*, 3rd ed. (New York: John Wiley & Sons, 1988), Chapter 13.

24. Thomas Garrett, *Business Ethics* (Englewood Cliffs, NJ: Prentice–Hall, 1966).

25. The following steps are taken from Caywood and Laczniak. (See note 4 above.)

Chapter 8

International Marketing Ethics[1]

Harvard marketing professor Theodore Levitt in his controversial article "The Globalization of Markets"[2] envisions the world as one large market segment. Levitt perceives improved technology as the primary force driving the world toward a converging commonality which has resulted in the emergence of global and standardized consumer markets of a previously unimagined scale. Whether one completely agrees with Levitt or not, the dawning of many global marketing *opportunities* has been a final stage in the evolutionary process. The process began with the exporting of US products, and then moved to the expansion of production facilities to points in the world where the greatest cost efficiencies and profit could be obtained. But with the growth of international manufacturing and then marketing come a host of ethical problems associated with the internationalization of economic activities. Ethical issues resulting from expanded international marketing include the following:

- The selling of inferior or unsafe products in less developed or less regulated markets. For example, chemical and pharmaceutical products banned as unsafe in a developed country are sometimes exported to markets abroad where such controls do not exist.[3]
- The extent to which large corporations systematically exploit less developed countries through their marketing methods. The sale of certain items (such as infant formula) without the provision of accurate or sufficient instructions for the buyer to properly utilize the product is an example.[4]
- The degree to which political intervention or influence is necessary to protect organizational assets from host country interference. Typical of this is the

threat of nationalization after substantial marketing investment has been made in a particular country. Refusal of entry to a key market is often another encountered obstacle. For example, suppose a US-based bicycle manufacturer can provisionally gain access to a large Asian market (and the potential sales that it represents). Should the firm pay a substantial bribe in order to receive permission to enter the market?

- Diplomatic skirmishes focusing on the trade-offs between free trade tariffs and quotas protecting domestic industries from internationally marketed products. Automobile quotas on Japanese cars, which exist in the United States, Europe, and Australia, are an illustration of this issue.

This list can easily be expanded, but it represents typical ethical issues that are endemic to international marketing operations.

A debate exists about the extent to which markets have become truly globalized and world economies fully integrated.[5] However, most students of management will concede that for the most part the "global economic village" is a reality. For an organization of any size or scope, the term international management is redundant, because a manager cannot be successful without being internationally capable.

Motivations for Expanded Global Marketing

There are five motivations that underlie most global marketing strategies. These are (a) obtaining improved economies of scale, (b) accessing lower labor cost or materials, (c) responding to national investment incentives, (d) dodging trade barriers via direct investment, and (e) achieving access to strategically important markets.[6] Each of these areas has ethical implications. For example, if a computer manufacturer switches its production of components to Korea or Malaysia and closes existing plants in the United States as a result, what ethical responsibility does the organization have to its current employees in the United States? Similarly, if a company expands its production or distribution in a certain country (e.g., Mexico) because of incentives such as free land or buildings, low taxes, reduced interest loans, or publicly provided energy and transportation, does that firm owe special or extraordinary obligations to that host community for providing these incentives? When an organization headquartered in a developed country moves to a lesser developed country, such as Brazil, primarily for its low labor costs or logistical efficiencies, what responsibility (if any) does that organization have to provide high-level wages and fringe benefits to the employees of this new facility? Put another way, is an organization justified in providing employees, each in a different country but doing the same work, with different wages and benefit packages? As the foregoing questions and examples should make clear, the advent of global manufacturing and marketing has multiplied the issues that marketing executives must deal with.

Causes of Ethical Problems in International Marketing

While a domestic US organization can practice at least some consistency by using US federal law as a baseline of appropriate behavior and by adhering to a general value structure rooted in the Judeo-Christian heritage, no such consistency appears to be available to the firm operating in many international markets. In this sense, multinational organizations face more complex ethical problems than do purely domestic corporations. There are two factors that are particularly critical in a global context. These are cultural relativism and economic development issues.

Cultural Relativism

By cultural relativism we mean acceptance by the corporation of the customary morality of the host country. This basically translates to "when in Rome, do as the Romans do." The fundamental idea is that there are few universal standards or rules of ethical behavior that are applicable to all business decisions in all cultures. Rather, there is a wide spectrum of standards, which is patently evident in multinational settings that cut across cultures, whether they are Christian, Moslem, Hindu, or Buddhist. Even when two countries share an important cultural denominator—for example, the Philippines and the United States have Christianity as a common-base religion—economic development and socio-cultural values may greatly limit the similarity between nations and the basic attitudes held by their people (see Exhibit 8–1). As a result, bribery and grease payments may be accepted as customary in the Philippines, while they are forbidden in the United States. It appears that the greater the cultural boundaries that are to be transcended, the more striking the philosophical differences that will confront the business decision-maker.[7] Because of the wholesale acceptance of cultural relativism by many firms, a number of organizations have been criticized for engaging in practices in foreign (i.e., international) markets that are illegal in their home country. The most widely debated instance of this kind involves the question of the payment of bribes.

Bribery as a Sales Tool
The controversy surrounding the Foreign Corrupt Practices Act (FCPA) of 1977, which applies to US-based organizations, illustrates the problems of cultural relativism quite well. This law prohibits any unreported payments to foreign officials in order to obtain contracts for overseas business. For each violation—that is, the payment of a bribe—the culpable US organization is subject to a $1 million fine. In addition, the manager responsible for this payment is subject to a $10,000 fine per violation and a maximum of five years in prison.[8] The law does distinguish between so-called "grease payments", which are small sums of money given to minor officials to expedite the purchase process (i.e., to get them

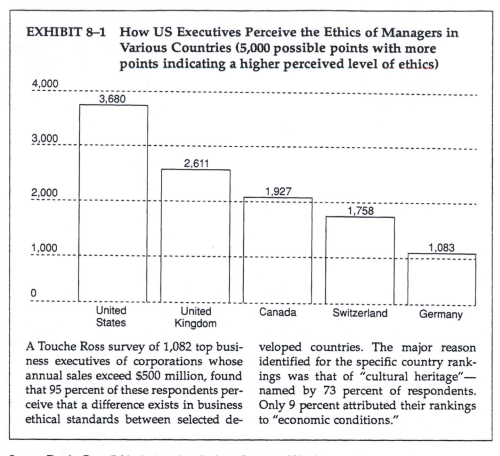

EXHIBIT 8–1   How US Executives Perceive the Ethics of Managers in Various Countries (5,000 possible points with more points indicating a higher perceived level of ethics)

A Touche Ross survey of 1,082 top business executives of corporations whose annual sales exceed $500 million, found that 95 percent of these respondents perceive that a difference exists in business ethical standards between selected developed countries. The major reason identified for the specific country rankings was that of "cultural heritage"—named by 73 percent of respondents. Only 9 percent attributed their rankings to "economic conditions."

Source: Touche Ross, *Ethics in American Business* (January 1989), 6.

to do their job), and bribery, which involves large amounts of money to get officials to take an action that they would not normally take (i.e., to get them to provide special favors) (see Exhibit 8–2). Many organizations not operating in the United States will contend that such payments are standard operating procedure in certain countries. That is, all grease payments and many bribes should be viewed as "customary" from an economic standpoint and should simply be considered as a cost of doing business (see Exhibit 8–3).

Because of widespread criticism of the FCPA, especially the notion that it places US firms at an economic disadvantage to other transnational marketers, the act was amended in 1988. The result was that permissible payments were more broadly and clearly defined. They include payments "for a routine government action, such as processing papers, stamping visas, and scheduling inspections."[9] Such payments, and others related to smoothing the bureaucratic process, are now seen as perfectly legal.

EXHIBIT 8–2   Bribes vs. Grease Payments

Definitions	*Applications*
Grease Payments	
Relatively small sums of money given for the purpose of getting someone to	Money given to minor officials (clerks, attendants, customs inspectors) for the purpose of expediting. This form of payment helps get goods or services through red-tape or administrative bureaucracies.
• do what they are supposed to be doing.	
• do what they are supposed to be doing faster or sooner.	
• do what they are supposed to be doing better than they would otherwise.	
Bribes	
Relatively large amounts of money given for the purpose of influencing someone to make a decision or take an action that he/she otherwise might not take. If the person considered the merits of the situation only, he/she might take some other action.	Money given, often to high-ranking officials. Purpose is often to get these persons to purchase or influence the purchase of goods or services from the bribing firm. May also be used to avoid taxes, forestall unfavorable government intervention, secure favorable treatment, etc.

Source: Archie B. Carroll, *Business & Society: Ethics and Stakeholder Management* (Cincinnati, OH: South-Western Publishing Company, 1989), 151. © 1989 by South-Western Publishing Company. All rights reserved. Reprinted by permission.

Why do so many businesses persist in making questionable payments in order to secure business? The case *for* bribery involves the contention that it is (a) an accepted practice in many countries, (b) a form of compensation *via* commission to intermediaries involved in the purchasing process, and (c) necessary in order to secure business in that particular market and therefore to compete effectively in the long term. The arguments *against* bribery are basically that it (a) is inherently wrong, (b) fosters corrupt governments and business practices, and (c) deceives stockholders concerning expenses that are being put forward as legitimate costs of doing business.[10]

To underscore the sense of controversy about the FCPA, one of the authors had an interesting experience in an MBA-level marketing strategy course in Australia. The class enrollment included students representing six countries, none of whom were from the United States and none of whom were from countries that had laws prohibiting the payment of bribes in order to secure overseas business. The MBA students (all of whom had experience as *practicing* managers)

**EXHIBIT 8–3   Gift-Giving, Grease Payments and Bribery—
Around the World**

Japan. In Japan there is no legal limit to what can be given. "Getting" is part of a social ritual. Everything in Japan is looked at in a social context rather than a legal context; therefore, shame is equivalent to guilt. One must not "overdo" their giving or they will be socially shamed. Japan has a bi-annual gift-giving season.

Kenya. In Kenya, money buys efficiency. Officials are low paid individuals but they make up for that via "taxes." The expectation is that grease payments subsidize the salaries of civil servants. There are a lot of "personal bribes" paid for such things as licenses, tickets, and work permits. The people of Kenya realize the true value of "pay and the job gets done."

Hong Kong. In Hong Kong, middlemen are very common. They help to get one businessperson in contact with another, *but* a fee must be paid for that service. Favors are not always repaid with cash, often they are accumulated for use at a later time. Large-scale bribes are prosecuted in Hong Kong. The Independent Commission Against Corruption (ICAC) has been formed to help stop large-scale bribery.

China. China threatens the punishment of "social disgrace" as an outcome for accepting bribes. Importantly, along with social disgrace, comes long prison terms and possibly death. But, bribes are still common. A shift is occurring, as there was a 54% increase in court cases concerning bribery in 1987. This is due to the fact that China feels that "black markets" and "profiteering" are threatening the success of economic reform.

Korea. Gift-giving is part of the Korean business ethic although lavish gift-giving is reserved for "special occasions" such as weddings or funerals. Gift-giving has become the norm and those who choose not to follow the custom are socially ostracized. Korea has regulatory statutes similar to the U.S.; however, their tax laws allow a 10% deduction of corporate taxes due in order to account for situations which do not lend themselves to documentation.

Philippines. In the Philippines, corruption became a way of life with Mr. Marcos as President. The Aquino government created the Presidential Commission on Clean Government (PCCG). However, day-to-day payments still occur such as gratuities to get through customs. Relatively lavish entertainment is also part of the culture.

Argentina. Argentina has a complicated maze of government agencies and it is costly to get through this labyrinth in a timely fashion. Small bribes and gratuities are the norm. Bribery and "commissions" hit a high during 1976–1983 and are estimated to involve hundreds of millions of dollars.

Brazil. There is a problem of corruption in Brazil that is closely identified with political patronage. Local justice works best when purchased. Billions of dollars in dubious payments were recently disclosed, yet the system of jurisprudence in Brazil initiated few prosecutions.

United Kingdom. In the United Kingdom, civil servants are not allowed to accept gifts of any kind. Ways around the law are many. As in many cultures, including the United States, "everyone has a price." Thus, the buyer with enough money and enough friends may acquire most things that are desired.

Source: S. Shariff and Cristina Lees, "A Fine Line Divides Customs and Crimes," *Journal of Commerce* (November 2, 1988), 1A ff. Reprinted by permission.

unanimously thought that the existing US legislation was rather naive and placed a needless economic constraint upon US organizations.

How then should companies deal with such issues of cultural relativism? Two observations seem pertinent. One is that problems of cultural relativism will be greater in some countries than others. And, as we will suggest, in international markets the relativist position has been gaining popularity. Second, there is common ground. That is, there are universal principles, such as honesty, devotion to product safety, etc., that can be strived for despite the wide diversity of settings in which multinational organizations operate. These issues are elaborated on later in the chapter.

The Sale of Unsafe Products

Other than bribery, probably the most pervasive ethical problem stemming from international marketing has to do with the sale of unsafe or otherwise questionable products by US companies in foreign markets. The most sensational current example has to do with the marketing of cigarettes by American tobacco manufacturers to overseas markets, especially Asian countries, a presumed growth area for cigarette manufacturers in the 1990s. As health concerns about cigarettes are not as great in these markets as in the United States, hard-sell tactics are often used. In Taiwan, for example, female models pass out promotional packs of cigarettes outside movie houses and nightclubs. Moreover, teenagers and females are often the obvious target of cigarette advertising in these countries.[11]

The tobacco lobby has been pushing hard at the Office of Trade in the US Department of Commerce to get the federal government to aggressively pursue the goal of fully opening up *foreign* markets to American tobacco.[12] Exports of US-made cigarettes currently earn about $2.5 billion in annual revenue. In the period 1986–87, tobacco exports to the Asian region rose by 76 percent. Since health concerns have become stronger in developed countries, such as the United States, Canada, and the United Kingdom, tobacco marketers have moved their promotional budgets to areas of the world where such concerns are not as paramount. Ironically, American cigarettes are one of the few US products that is rapidly expanding its market share in Japan. US tobacco manufacturers have also been among the first companies to sign distribution agreements in the deregulated Eastern European markets.

Similar actions have been taken by pharmaceutical manufacturers. One such controversy involved Upjohn Corporation, marketing the drug Depo-Provera in Malaysia for use in a government coordinated birth-control program.[13] The US Food and Drug Administration (FDA) had refused to license the drug in the United States because it had been shown to cause menstrual difficulties and had been linked with heart cancer in animals. Bangladesh and other Third World countries have become dumping grounds for chemicals and pesticides that can no longer be sold in other markets.[14] Clearly, the shifting of these products from one market (where they are more difficult to sell or not allowed at all) to another market where their sale is unregulated, raises ethical questions—especially in light of the potential negative health and safety effects that such products *might* have.

Ethics and Economic Development

With regard to the point that ethical problems are greater in some countries than others, prevailing opinion (supported by some empirical research) is that in many less developed countries, pressures on organizations to succeed are often more fierce than in a developed country setting.[15] Under such intense, survivalist conditions, bribery, extortion, nepotism, and fraud may be considered necessary and essential modes of behavior in order to assure continued organizational viability. Such behavior is consistent with psychologist Abraham Maslow's famous *hierarchy of needs*, which suggests that the satisfaction of primary needs, such as economic survival and safety, precedes the satisfaction of "higher order" needs, which are secondary.

Satisfying *primary needs* (in the context of economic development) means taking actions that will lead to the financial improvement and stability of an organization. The rationale here is that in many poor countries major economic progress or social change cannot occur until a solid financial and business infrastructure is in place. To insure initial financial success, sometimes unethical steps will be taken (e.g., bribes paid for government protection or some damage done to the environment) in order to maximize the probability of generating a stable stream of profits. Once a level of financial security has been attained, the firm feels relatively more free to turn its attention to *secondary* requirements, such as its need to be perceived as "a good corporate citizen" and conduct business ethically.

As some countries have made substantial economic gains, they have suppressed corruption, and many of their local organizations increasingly practice significant charitable and/or socially oriented activities. For example, South Korea seems to have clamped down on corruption as its economic lot has improved. Under depressed economic conditions and when faced with intense competition, organizations are tempted to apply lower standards of ethical behavior. In some markets, marketers may even be pressured by the *host* government to operate in an unethical fashion. For instance, some countries, eager for hard currency, have invited alcohol and tobacco manufacturers into their home markets despite the health and lifestyle issues associated with these products.

The Quest for Common Ground

It is the *relativist* position that seems to predominate in most organizations. A frequently quoted international code of conduct is the one developed by Citi-Corp, and it is representative of this approach. It states:

> *We must never lose sight of the fact that we are guests in foreign countries. We must conduct ourselves accordingly. We recognize the right of governments to pass local legislation and our obligation to conform. Under these circumstances, we also recognize that we can survive only if we are successful in demonstrating to the local*

authorities that our presence is beneficial. We believe that every country must find its own way politically and economically. Sometimes we believe that local policies are wise; sometimes we do not. However, irrespective of our views, we try to function as best we can under prevailing conditions. We have also felt free to discuss with local governments matters directly affecting our interests, but we recognize that they have final regulatory authority.[16]

Recognizing this general perspective, just because a particular culture or community says something is "right," that does not necessarily mean it is "ethically proper." In fact, similarities in the human condition across various situations seem to enable mankind to formulate general principles of action that can be applied to similar future situations. Despite the diversity of international cultures, empirical evidence indicates that different societies around the world share basic needs and hold common values. The famous anthropologist Clyde Kluckhohn concludes, "Psychology, psychiatry, sociology, and anthropology, in different ways and on somewhat different evidence, converge in attesting to similar human needs and psychic mechanisms."[17]

The list of commonalities about the human condition is indeed long: the satisfaction of biological needs, the importance of work, food, shelter, propensity for securing safety, and the enjoyment of friendship. In addition, almost all cultures aspire to several common values. These have to do with feelings of good will, the importance of sexual expression, and the development of some rules of justice or fair dealing. Some may argue that when one gets specific about the nature of these common areas of human concern—for example sexual practices—there will always be exceptions to the rule. Aristotle long ago recognized that uniformity of human behavior across *all* human conditions is unattainable. However, principles must be developed for the majority of human beings that guarantee the fulfillment of their needs and interests *under most* conditions. Thus, the evidence of some aberrant behavior does not eliminate the possibility that common principles which govern human and marketing behavior can be developed.

An interesting example of a compilation that lists the fundamental requirements of the human condition is the United Nations Universal Declaration of Human Rights, adopted by the General Assembly in 1948. Included in this document are thirty specific articles that articulate common human rights. Particularly notable in the context of business and marketing is Article 23, which reads as follows:

1. Everyone has the right to work, to free choice of employment, to just and favorable conditions of work, and to protection against unemployment.
2. Everyone, without discrimination, has the right to equal pay for equal work.
3. Everyone who works has the right to just and favorable remuneration insuring for himself and his family an existence worthy of human dignity, and supplemented, if necessary, by other means of social protection.
4. Everyone has the right to form and to join trade unions for the protection of his interests.

World-Wide Codes of Ethics

In order to capitalize on manifest commonality, a number of corporations have written worldwide codes of ethics. They expect these rules to be followed in *all* areas of operation and across *all* markets. Examples of firms that have such worldwide codes are IBM, Caterpillar, S. C. Johnson, and Rexnord.

Core Values and Ethics Codes

One way of looking at codes of ethics is that they essentially embody the core values inherent in a particular organization. *Core values* are beliefs that are part of the organizational structure that are so fundamental that they will not be compromised. An example of such a core value might be, "Our organization will never market a product unless we are highly confident that that product is safe." Such core values, because they are fundamental to the corporate culture, will be uniform throughout the organization in whatever market the organization operates. In contrast to core values, there are *peripheral values*, which may be adjusted according to the local custom of culture. An example of a peripheral value or attitude would be that in certain cultures managers are permitted to leave the office to attend to personal business at some point during the business day. A key distinction between core and peripheral values is that the organization draws its strength and identity from its core values. And when value conflicts occur, core values help shape what action a particular organization will select. Core values should *not* normally be ethnocentric. *Ethnocentrism* has to do with the tendency to evaluate all other cultures by the standards of one's own culture.

In general, marketers should attempt to maximize diversity and tolerance in their international marketing operations. That is, they should strive to develop a *geocentric* world view. However, when pressure is brought to bear on an organization by a host community or a local culture that is in conflict with the core value of the organization, firms should consider the suspension of marketing activities. Thus, the goal of an international code of ethics is to give expression to what the actual core values of an organization are. Codes are prescriptive and normative in the sense that they attempt to capture what an organization should do about certain issues regardless of the market in which they are operating. (See Exhibit 8–4 for the Japanese translation of Johnson & Johnson's Credo.)

The Sullivan Principles

It is interesting to note that the actions taken by a number of organizations in the marketing sphere conform to a normative ethic that attempts to articulate core values. Several companies have taken steps, for example, to insure that a large percentage of the profits earned in foreign markets continue to be invested in those host countries. Other firms have been especially careful to insure that operations in foreign countries are eventually staffed—including top manage-

EXHIBIT 8–4 Japanese Language Johnson & Johnson Credo

Reprinted by permission of Johnson & Johnson.

ment levels—by foreign nationals from the host country.[18] Several multinational organizations have been models of how an organization should treat its workers. The policies that some of these companies have adopted, such as the *Sullivan principles* for South African operations, have often exceeded the quality of employer–employee relationships of domestic firms. Some further elaboration of the Sullivan principles is in order.

The Sullivan principles were formulated in 1977 by Reverend Leon Sullivan, a black director of General Motors, who drew up seven principles of policy for American corporations operating in South Africa. These principles are shown in Exhibit 8–5. They were a reaction to the apartheid government of South Africa. Their foundation was that if companies continued to operate there, they should conduct their affairs in a manner that treats all races equally. Well over one hundred American companies operating in South Africa became signatories to the code. The principles themselves represent a provocative example of how organizations can create statements of policy to guide their management and marketing decisions.[19]

Constructing International Codes of Ethics

Exactly what statements international codes should include depends upon the corporate culture of the originating organization and the core values of that firm. For example, given the growing importance of the "ecological ethic" in the 1990s, a number of mineral resource firms have taken the position that they will not petition for mining rights in Antarctica. (This particular view may also soon be

---

EXHIBIT 8–5   The Sullivan Principles

Principle 1 • Nonsegregation of the Races of All Eating, Comfort, Locker Room, and Work Facilities

Principle 2 • Equal and Fair Employment Practices for All Employees

Principle 3 • Equal Pay for All Employees Doing Equal or Comparable Work for the Same Period of Time

Principle 4 • Initiation and Development of Training Programs That Will Prepare Blacks, Coloureds, and Asians in Substantial Numbers for Supervisory, Administrative, Clerical, and Technical Jobs

Principle 5 • Increasing the Number of Blacks, Coloureds, and Asians in Management and Supervisory Positions

Principle 6 • Improving the Quality of Employees' Lives Outside the Work Environment in Such Areas as Housing, Transportation, Schooling, Recreation, and Health Facilities

Principle 7 • Work to Eliminate Laws and Customs Which Impede Social and Political Justice

Source: Herbert B. Taylor, "The Sullivan Principles," *Management Notes* 3 (Fall 1986). Reprinted by permission of the Arthur D. Little Management Education Institute.

enshrined in an international accord, which would give this perspective added force).

Whatever issues are part of such codes, these worldwide codes of ethics should be assembled keeping the following points in mind. First, the core values, which were determined to be central to the organization's culture, should be expressed in the code. For example, if "equal opportunity for women" is determined to be a central belief in a particular company with multinational operations, then that position should be part of its international code.

Second, core values should be examined with an eye towards eliminating those which are parochial, ethnocentric, or idiosyncratic. The essence of having a worldwide code of ethics is to articulate principles that the firm is prepared to support *wherever* it operates. It is possible to espouse values that are not widely accepted in all countries (or markets), but then the firm must be willing to withdraw from that market if its values are challenged to the detriment of the organization. For example, a hypothetical example of a core value that could economically harm operations in certain markets would be the view that to the greatest extent possible there should be "affirmative action" policies to promote women to top ranks in management.

Third, the firm developing a worldwide code of ethics should attempt to integrate the *stakeholder* perspective to the greatest degree possible. (See Chapter 1 for a more detailed explanation of the stakeholder concept.) Basically, the idea is that the core values embraced by a marketing organization should be those that inherently balance the interests of the various publics that are influenced by the firm. For example, the organization which states that it will never dispose of products declared unsafe in one market by selling them in another (unrestricted) market, takes a prudential position in protecting its *customers* but also may be acting in the best long-term interests of *stockholders*. Numerous case histories have shown that the dumping of questionable products (some of which are eventually declared safe) often results in substantial negative publicity and causes reduced sales and lessened goodwill when this short-term strategy to reduce inventory write-offs becomes public.

Strategic Planning and International Marketing Ethics

The concept of strategic planning serves as a double-edged sword enhancing or inhibiting ethics depending upon how the planning process is conducted. At its lowest common denominator, strategic planning has to do with the long-range process of selecting the *products* an organization will sell along with the *markets* it will cultivate; the process also includes the decisions that determine the allocation of resources to individual products and markets. Significantly, most major US-based companies have developed plans to expand the international market for their products due to a leveling of demand in the United States. Given the understanding that many managers have of the strategic planning process, the resulting strategies are sometimes incompatible with ethically enlightened marketing in an international context. Consider the following assumptions, which many marketing managers accept almost as second nature.

- The *end goal* of the strategic planning process is the development of differential advantage and profitability.
- The *means* to this goal is the efficient utilization of economic resources (i.e., labor, technology, financial capital, etc.), which are generally viewed as interchangeable.
- The total process should be as *value neutral* as possible. It is generally not for the individual manager to second guess the objectives postulated by top management.

If one accepts this view of the strategic management process then (among other things) people are simply equal to other forms of capital, profitability is normally weighted more heavily than the social and ethical outcomes of business decisions, and stockholders are often given higher accord than other organizational *stakeholders*. Taking this viewpoint a step further, it is easy to see why certain organizations operating in an international setting find it possible to justify acts such as:

- Bribing government officials to lower tariff rates. (Why? Because it expands market options.)
- Unloading products that are unsuited to a particular market or judged unsafe in their own market, to market segments where they might be sold. (Why? Because it reduces inventory and improves distribution efficiency.)
- Paying the lowest possible wages and benefits in a given labor pool in an effort to squeeze out maximum economic advantage. (Why? Because it is an apparently efficient use of resources.)

Incorporating the Stakeholder Concept in International Markets

Do all managers buy into this set of assumptions and justifications concerning strategic planning? Of course not, and that brings us to the other side of the issue. Increasingly, progressive organizations have accepted the *stakeholder concept*. That is, they believe a firm's decisions must take into consideration all the stakeholders of that firm, including customers, employees, the host community, relevant government agencies, and so forth. This is especially important in an international market, because multinational corporations are often the subject of particular scrutiny or suspicion by the host government and local residents. If a corporation is interested in a continuing presence in a particular market, a long-term perspective ought to be taken (see Exhibit 8–6). The premise behind the stakeholder concept is precisely that it is the *long-term* economic and social benefits to the organization that should be maximized rather than short-term profit. (The case situation presented in Exhibit 8–7 raises such issues.) Some organizations have adopted an even more enlightened position and have accepted the tenet that

---

EXHIBIT 8–6   How Clerics See the Responsibility of Multinational Corporations

The US Catholic bishops in a pastoral letter on the economy implied an affirmative action ethic regarding less developed countries and urged special efforts and responsibilities to such countries that were less well off. The bishops wrote, "We call for a US international economic policy designed to empower people everywhere and give them a sense of their own worth, to help them improve the quality of their lives, and to assure that the benefits of economic growth are shared equitably among them." The Catholic bishops—as well as other groups that endorse such *general* principles—readily admitted that there may be legitimate disagreements as to how particular policy options that embody the overall principles can be applied. However, the bishops pulled no punches in suggesting that persons have a fundamental social responsibility. That is, the economic order should be structured to guarantee the minimum conditions of human dignity in the economic sphere for all persons. Some business executives reacting to these words felt they possibly smacked of "world socialism."

Source: Adapted from T. R. Martin and G. R. Laczniak, "The Bishop's Letter: Implications for US Management," *Business* (April–June 1987), 46–51. Reprinted by permission.

people are more important than other forms of capital. In other words, when an economic or marketing decision is made that has implications for employees or customers, those outcomes are given a higher weight than options that simply impact money, machines, or new technology.

Ethically speaking, the *techniques* used in strategic planning can be proactively used to assess the economic *and ethical* implications of the various product and market choices. As these techniques (e.g., forecasting models and planning matrices) tend to be forward looking and consequence oriented, they readily lend themselves to examining the ethical impacts of marketing decisions as well as their economic potentials. When a marketing organization is at a decision point, a marketing manager can use such consequence-oriented thinking to ask questions such as:

- What will the reaction of the host country's population be to such a decision?
- Does the advertising and promotional campaign associated with this item respect the culture of the host community? Does the product itself enhance the dignity of the host community?
- Can the action contemplated be put in the context of a "partnership in progress" between the organization and the host community or is it simply "a window of opportunity" that merely serves the economic advantage of the firm?

These questions may seem abstract but, in fact, marketing in an international context regularly generates such questions with ethical implications.

EXHIBIT 8–7   The Alpine Mineral Water Case

Basil, SA, a Swiss-based company, is one of the world's largest producers of bottled mineral water. In the past year, it shipped 850 million bottles of its flagship brand, Alpine, to forty countries in Europe and worldwide. Basil, SA's expenditures on advertising and promotion have been substantial enough to develop a strong brand following in the marketplace. The product has been promoted with a global advertising campaign using the theme "you can search the whole world over, but you will never find a purer bottle of water."

Recently during routine testing, chemists at the company's central production plant discovered traces of benzene in the bottled water. It was estimated that this problem affected the last two months of production and most of this output had already been distributed worldwide. Benzene is a toxic substance. The trace amounts found in the water would most likely not cause serious health effects according to public health consultants who had been quickly brought in to assess the situation. Some stomach discomfort could be expected among a few consumers. Plant managers pinpointed the contamination to a breakdown in the maintenance of the bottling system's filtration devices. Steps were taken to immediately rectify this situation.

After deliberating for most of the day, management came up with the following plan to rectify the situation.

1. Action would be taken to assure the production problems were corrected immediately and the benzene problem would not further occur.
2. Basil, SA, would quietly begin to recall about 100 million bottles of product mostly from Europe and North America. (Management noted that there had not yet been any complaint concerning benzene in Alpine water. Left unchecked, eventually consumer protection agencies in Europe and the United States would detect the problem.)
3. Management stated that the public reason for the recall should be concern over the shelf life of certain shipments of Alpine that had been mistakenly sent forward. Quality control experts estimated that as much as 80 percent of the contaminated product could be retrieved in this way from European and North American markets.

One of the Basil managers asked what the approach would be in other markets where Alpine was distributed. The managing director replied as follows: "We will let the product work its way through the system in other markets. Many of the Second and Third World countries will never be able to detect any problems. Some of the other markets, such as New Zealand and Iceland, are too small and geographically removed to worry about. Chances are we can weather this storm before anyone knows there has been a problem." **What is your reaction to the managerial and ethical solution that Basil management is utilizing to handle the problem with Alpine bottled water?**

Source: Information gathered for this case is fictional but constitutes an amalgamation of events that occurred in various bottled beverage industries during 1985–90.

Ideas for Ethical Action

What can corporations do to improve ethics when operating in an international context? First, *marketing organizations should develop clear codes of conduct that specify their objectives, duties, and obligations in the international markets in which they operate.* To the greatest extent possible, such codes should be company-wide, regardless of the area of operation. As noted earlier, the formulation or refinement of a code of ethics provides an opportunity for the organization to establish what its core values are.

Marketers have incurred some of their harshest criticism by operating with divergent sets of rules in different countries, thereby giving the impression that the differences were motivated exclusively by economic considerations. Thus, there normally should *not* be two or more sets of ethics, one for the United States and others for countries abroad—at least insofar as core values are involved. In addition, any code of ethics should take into account the legitimate interests of the host governments and populations. The codes developed can then perhaps serve as a policy guide for the propriety of a contemplated action. Caterpillar Corporation, as noted previously, specifically designed its code of ethics for *worldwide* operations. The company first published its *Code of Worldwide Business Conduct* in 1974 and it has been revised regularly since then. The code was distributed to its 1,300 managers around the world, and they are expected to adhere to it. Appendix 8A at the end of the chapter reprints a portion of the Caterpillar code. A basic principle of this code (which has served as a model to other organizations) states, "We support laws of all countries which prohibit restraint of trade, unfair practices, or abuse of economic power. And we avoid such practices in areas of the world where laws do not prohibit them."[20] It can be argued that ethical responsibilities are greatest in nations where the legal and regulatory environments are the least developed. If corporations are driven exclusively by local custom, they may be ignoring the areas that are most in need of universal standards (for example, environmental protection).

In addition to general principles, Caterpillar's code includes detailed guidelines that deal with payments of all kinds that may be "required" in various markets. Where unavoidable, the code states that they must be limited to customary amounts and made only to facilitate correct performance of public officials' duties. This portion of the code provides an explication of the Foreign Corrupt Practices Act to which, according to law, the company must adhere. Caterpillar even goes so far as to urge its dealers worldwide to adopt written codes similar to its own. The rationale for this is that for both dealers and Caterpillar, much more may be lost than gained by unethical practices.

A second recommendation for discouraging ethically questionable strategies is for *the international marketing organization to always provide high-quality, safe, and culturally appropriate products.* This is a core value that can be operationalized as a standard, worldwide operating procedure. This dictum applies equally well when dealing with less developed countries. Corporations should not assume that developing countries want, nor would be satisfied with, "cheap" products (i.e., substandard by home country requirements). While a policy that strives to provide high-quality goods may sometimes go unnoticed by the average citizen of the host country, it will go far in avoiding the negative attention received by firms that market unsafe, substandard, or culturally inappropriate products. For example, Australian meat packers were subject to well-deserved censure, as well as economic backlash, when "beef" shipments to the Middle East were found to contain pork, and those destined for Japan contained kangaroo meat.

Third, *ethics should be treated as a significant factor in the formulation of international marketing strategy by multinational corporations.* In other words, beyond the establishment of a code of ethics, specific goals should also be set and checked by management as part of the control process. When corporations with international operations point out the benefits of their economic activity in various reports and publications, they should strive to identify situations where they have been ethically sensitive to host governments and local consumers. Strides in this direction have already been made by some corporations (see Exhibit 8–8). For example, Dow Corning sends members of its Business Conduct Committee to the company's foreign operations on a regular basis; the committee members ask questions concerning troublesome areas of operation, including those having ethical implications.[21] Castle and Cooke Corporation has invited a panel of academics to study its Philippine plantations and to audit these operations for

---

EXHIBIT 8–8   On What Multinational Corporate Responsibility Really Is

Kenneth Mason, former CEO of Quaker Oats, writes:

"It is useful to begin by identifying what corporate responsibility is not. Giving generously to the Crusade of Mercy is not an act of corporate responsibility, nor is providing financial support to one's local hospital, museum, or symphony orchestra, nor sending a shipload of food to help the hungry in Third World countries. These are acts of corporate philanthropy. Similarly, refusing to grease the palm of foreign government officials, not accepting kickbacks from suppliers, insisting on strict safety rules in plant operations, demanding truthfulness in its advertising, and guaranteeing equal opportunity for all its employees are examples of corporations obeying the law, and are not corporate responsibility.

The definition of corporate responsibility I would like to suggest is this: corporations which control the use of socially important assets have the responsibility to use those assets in a way which makes social sense."

Source: Kenneth Mason, "The Multinational Corporation: The Central Institution of Our Age." In *Corporations and the Common Good*, R. B. Dickie and L. S. Rouner, eds. 81 (Notre Dame, IN, University of Notre Dame Press, 1986).

socially responsible behavior.[22] The results of this evaluation serve as feedback for future corporate action. Control Data has published a detailed report on its social performance in international markets. While many organizations make similar efforts, Control Data has subsequently attempted to generate some ethical guidelines, such as not to sell powerful computers to countries that are human-rights violators.[23]

At its core, this perspective implies that not only should a company study the characteristics of consumers in various markets, but also should be familiar with the ethical norms of the cultures involved. An approach that might help corporate executives develop culturally appropriate responses would be the regular use of group discussions between headquarter staff and management teams of nationals from the various international market areas. The goal of such meetings should be the clarification and exchange of values to reach a consensus on how to deal with the problems confronting the corporations. Pillsbury Corporation has used a variation of this approach. Caterpillar invites in its worldwide dealers once every two years for such sessions.

If ethics is to become a significant factor in the formulation of international marketing strategy, top management should consciously and systematically determine and develop the ethical profile it wishes to cultivate throughout the world. In doing this, long-term consideration should predominate over short-term concerns. Corporate strategy will thereby be affected by the type of ethical profile the corporation chooses to project. The fact that the company states the principles to which it abides may earn it a measure of respect, even approval. In any event, companies must increasingly consider the ethical impact of their strategies or face marketplace consequences that may be costly and damaging in both the short and the long term.

Fourth, *when unbridgeable gaps appear between the ethical values of the host country and those of the multinational corporation, the firm should consider voluntarily suspending activities in that market.* US corporations have not hesitated to leave markets when their managerial autonomy is challenged. For example, International Paper temporarily pulled out of Venezuela when the government there threatened to control how corporate resources would be used.[24] Additional examples of such situations include the withdrawal of various companies from South Africa in response to apartheid policies, and the (temporary) suspension of activities during the 1970s by IBM and Coca-Cola in India because of that country's position concerning the extent of national ownership and control of firms operating in the Indian subcontinent.

Organizations ought to be ready to proceed with a similar disengagement when core ethical values are threatened. Since many developing countries look to multinational corporations for leadership, due in no small part to the resources and expertise they command, a high moral posture may influence the competitive environment. For those companies that chose to stay the course, Thomas A. Murphy, former chairman and CEO of General Motors Corporation, made this point this way: "While we may not agree with the underlying philosophy of laws and institutions in certain countries where we conduct business, we nevertheless recognize that we have an opportunity, by our example and by our good business practice, to work within the existing framework and to act as a positive force of progressive change."[25]

Fifth, *in order to encourage the consideration of ethical issues by multinational corporations, the regular development of "ethical impact statements" should be conducted.* Periodic reviews of ethical impact, which may be part of more broadly conceived audits (see final chapter), should attempt to measure the external influence of planned or ongoing marketing activities on the social and cultural welfare of the people concerned. This is the so-called "externalities effect." Companies should make greater efforts to define, and if possible, quantify the ethical impact of their activities beyond the financial health of the organization. Business academics are making progress in creating frameworks and techniques that can be used to systematically monitor a firm's ethical concerns.[26] A broad social audit might examine the impact of a corporate decision on the employment and incomes of local workers. An ethical impact statement would also examine the moral values involved in arriving at that corporate decision in the first place.

Some European marketers are already engaged in social audits that attempt to identify the benefits (and costs) of particular operations for the local economy. Dunlop, Unilever, and ICI have prepared cost–benefit analyses of their subsidiaries in Malaysia, Nigeria, Zambia, and India.[27] The inclusion of ethics-specific considerations, in the sense used here, is rare however. In other words, seldom do organizations attempt to quantify and report on the *economic* implications of decisions made on the basis of *ethical* concern. (See Exhibit 8–9 for a list of possible questions to be used in an international ethics audit.)

The United Nations has called for formal agreements between multinationals and host countries that clearly define the corporation's responsibilities, specifies penalties for infringements, and requires complete financial disclosure concerning operations. While most corporations would resist additional mandates for financial disclosure requirements, a voluntary social audit and ethical impact statement will prepare a corporation for a time in the future when such disclosures might become mandatory.

Conclusion

It is increasingly clear that it is in their own interest that international marketers consider themselves as agents of change in terms of the economic and social development of countries where they do business.[28] Willingly or unwillingly, their impact in foreign countries is often substantial and long-lasting. These influences on local cultures, institutions, religions, and ways of life must therefore be carefully assessed. Companies should conduct periodic ethical impact audits to measure such effects. Ethical considerations must become a necessary and vital element in the strategic planning. Failing this, questions raised about international marketing behavior could result in regulations set by either the host governments or international bodies, such as the Organization for Economic Cooperation and Development (OECD) or the United Nations, with regional or

---

**EXHIBIT 8–9   A Set of Questions with Ethical Implications for
International Marketers**

Product

Is the product damaging to the people or the environment of the target market country?

Will the product enhance the lives of people in the target market country?

Promotion

Will the promotion be viewed as a bribe or a payoff by the home country or by the foreign market?

Will the promotion mislead or confuse the people in the target foreign market?

Distribution

Is a bribe or a payoff required to enter the foreign market?

What is the likelihood that an agent within the foreign market could force extortion payments for access to the market?

Price

Will the price charged in the foreign market be viewed as dumping by foreign competitors or governments?

Is the price charged in the foreign market competitively fair given current operating costs?

Source: David J. Fritzsche, "Ethical Issues in Multinational Marketing." In *Marketing Ethics: Guidelines for Managers*, eds. G. R. Laczniak and P. E. Murphy, 95 (Lexington, MA; D. C. Heath & Company Books, 1985). Reprinted by permission.

worldwide influence. Thus, it appears in the best interests of international marketers to set a single ethical posture for all worldwide operations, to set it at as high a level as possible, to implement it consistently, and to conscientiously communicate it to all its employees across the globe.

Appendix 8A

Caterpillar's Code of Worldwide Business Conduct and Operating Principles[1]

Business Purpose
The overall purpose of Caterpillar is to enhance the long-term interests of those who own the business—the shareholders.

This in no way diminishes the strong and legitimate claims of employees, dealers, customers, suppliers, governments, and others whose interests touch upon our own—nor, indeed, of the public at large. Nor is this to assert that profit

[1]Reprinted by permission of Caterpillar, Inc.

should be maximized in any short-term framework of months, or even years, at the expense of other valid considerations.

Rather, it is to say we attempt to take a long-range view of things. We believe we can best serve the interests of shareholders and the long-term profitability of the enterprise by fair, honest, and intelligent actions with respect to all our constituencies.

With this in mind, our business aims are as follows:

1. Generate real growth in sales and profits, remain financially strong, and maximize long-term return on common stock equity.
2. Be competitive—and measure our performance against the realities of the marketplace.
3. Provide customers a total value—in terms of product quality, product support, and price—that will maximize profit on their investment, as compared with competitive alternatives.
4. Follow product and sourcing strategies that utilize the best combination of Caterpillar's and suppliers' strengths and resources . . . and that are consistent with users' needs and world economic, political, and social conditions.
5. Work with suppliers, and those who sell our products, in upgrading their capabilities—to the end that each is the best available when judged by appropriate criteria.
6. Treat employees fairly, and seek their involvement in improving their own work methods and results, and those of the enterprise as a whole.
7. Remember that management is an acquired skill, not an intuitive art—and work continuously at improving the practice of management by objectives and judgment by results.
8. Consider cost reduction and quality as matters for annual improvement.
9. Enhance our reputation for quality by pursuing excellence in all we do—in the belief that such is not only the best way to operate this business, but also a key to personal satisfaction and happiness.
10. Improve our pursuit of goals, principles, and philosophies contained in this document.

Business Ethics

The law is the floor. Ethical business conduct should normally exist at a level well above the minimum required by law.

One of a company's most valuable assets is a reputation for integrity. If that be tarnished, customers, investors, suppliers, employees, and those who sell our products will seek affiliation with other, more attractive companies. We intend to hold to a single high standard of integrity everywhere.

We will keep our word. We won't promise more than we can reasonably expect to deliver; nor will we make commitments we don't intend to keep.

The goal of corporate communication is the truth—well and persuasively told. In our advertising and other public communications, we will avoid not only untruths, but also exaggeration and overstatement. Caterpillar employees shall not accept costly entertainment or gifts (excepting momentos and novelties of nominal value) from dealers, suppliers, and others with whom we do business. And we won't tolerate circumstances that produce, or reasonably appear to produce, conflict between personal interests of an employee and interests of the company.

We seek long-lasting relationships—based on integrity—with all whose activities touch upon our own.

The ethical performance of the enterprise is the sum of the ethics of the men and women who work here. Thus, we are all expected to adhere to high standards of personal integrity. For example, perjury or any other illegal act ostensibly taken to "protect" the company is wrong. A sale made because of deception is wrong. A production quota achieved through questionable means or figures is wrong. The end doesn't justify the means.

Involvement of People

People have intrinsic worth and dignity. We believe any system or institution that subtracts from that worth and dignity is wrong.

Our business experience shows that employees want to work, to contribute, to be a factor in improving things. Few people really wish to leave the job feeling they haven't made a contribution, or been challenged in some way.

If business errs, we believe it's often on the side of not fully utilizing the human energies, skills, and loyalties that are available—for the intelligent asking—from its own employees.

Toward that end, we aim to involve employees in improving their own work methods and results, and those of the enterprise as a whole. We intend that participative styles be the cornerstone of our management philosophy. We wish to manage in such a fashion that employees will come to identify in a personal way with the company's economic health.

Human Relationships

We aspire to a high standard of excellence in human relationships. Specifically, we intend:

1. To select and place employees on the basis of qualifications for the work to be performed—without discriminantion in terms of race, religion, national origin, color, sex, age, or handicap unrelated to the task at hand.
2. To place people only on jobs which are truly productive and necessary for achievement of approved organizational objectives.
3. To show each employee the purposes of his or her job and work unit, and insist that work be done efficiently and well.
4. To ask that people give their best efforts, including their ideas and suggestions for innovation and improvement.
5. To maintain uniform, reasonable standards of work, and offer people opportunities to make the best use of their abilities.

6. To encourage self-development, and assist employees in improving and broadening their job skills.

7. To protect people's health and lives. This includes maintaining a clean, safe work environment as free as practicable from health hazards.

8. To provide employees with timely information concerning company operations and results, as well as other work-related matters in which they logically have an interest.

9. To compensate people fairly, according to their contributions to the company, within the framework of national and local practices.

10. To develop human relationships that inspire respect for, and confidence and trust in, the company.

11. Where employees elect in favor of—or are required by law to have some form of—union representation, Caterpillar will endeavor to build a company–union relationship based upon mutual respect and trust.

12. To seek to provide stable, secure employment consistent with the long-term success of Caterpillar.

13. To refrain from hiring persons closely related to members of the board of directors, administrative officers, and department heads. When other employees' relatives are hired, this must be solely the result of their qualifications for jobs to be filled. No employee is to be placed in the direct line of authority of relatives. Nepotism—or the appearance of nepotism—is neither fair to employees, nor in the long-term interests of the business.

14. To place operating decisions at the lowest level in the organization at which they can be competently resolved.

15. To develop a climate that encourages good people to want to work for Caterpillar, and support the achievement of company objectives.

16. To give special effort to working directly with each other in a helpful, friendly way—seeking to avoid bureaucracy and other hazards common to large organizations—and remembering that the Golden Rule is as applicable to human relationships in the workplace at it is in the community and home.

Ownership and Investment

In the case of business investment in any country, the principle of mutual benefit to investors and country should prevail.

We affirm that Caterpillar investment must be compatible with social and economic priorities of host countries, and with local customs, tradition, and sovereignty. We intend to conduct our business in a way that will earn acceptance and respect for Caterpillar, and allay concerns—by host country governments and others—about multinational corporations.

In turn, we are entitled to ask that such countries give consideration to our need for stability, business success, and growth; that all enterprises receive equal treatment whether owned by national or foreign investors; and that countries honor their agreements, including those relating to rights and properties of citizens of other nations.

We recognize the desire of certain countries to favor joint ventures and other forms of local sharing in ownership of a business enterprise.

However, good arguments exist for full ownership of operations by the parent company: the high degree of control necessary to maintain product uniformity and protect patents and trademarks ... and the fact that a single facility's profitability may not be as important (or as attractive to local investors) as its long-term significance to the integrated, corporate whole.

Since arguments exist on both sides of the issue, we believe there should be freedom and flexibility—for negotiating whatever investment arrangements and corporate forms best suit the long-term interests of the host country and the investing business, in each case.

Sharing of Technology

We view technology transfer in a broad context. Such transfer can involve information about product and manufacturing innovations, accounting and data processing know-how, purchasing and marketing expertise—in short, all the technical and managerial knowledge needed for efficient functioning of an enterprise.

Caterpillar shares technology with employees worldwide, while observing national restrictions on transfer of such information. We also share technology with a worldwide network of suppliers and dealers. We seek the highest level of technology—regardless of origin—applicable to our manufacturing processes, products, and business generally.

Where appropriate, employees are encouraged to participate in professional and trade societies. We encourage equitable relationships with inventors, consultants, universities, and research and development laboratories having technical capabilities compatible with our needs.

One of the principal threats to future relationships among nations involves the widening gap between living standards in industrial and developing countries. Intelligent transfer of technology is a major means by which developing countries can be helped to do what they must ultimately do—help themselves.

However, technology transfer is dependent not only on the ability of people in one nation to offer it, but also on the ability of people in other nations to utilize it—and their willingness to recognize that technology is valuable property. It requires time, effort, and money to create. An owner of such property is entitled to be fairly compensated for sharing it.

We recommend that countries create an environment of law and practice that permits maximum use of transferred technology. Toward this goal, we support effective investment and industrial property laws, reasonable licensing regulations, unrestricted and efficient movement of data, and other measures which truly encourage transfer of technology. This goal is advanced when owners' legitimate interests are protected, and owners are permitted reasonable returns on their shared technology.

Under appropriate conditions, we enter into licensing arrangements to manufacture products locally. Such arrangements vary, depending upon products involved, scope of technical assistance required, and applicable laws and regulations. Caterpillar's products and operating methods lend themselves to licensing agreements that contemplate a continuing flow of technology. From our experience, this also produces the most benefit for host countries. Therefore, we aim at arrangements that provide continuing compensation reflecting the value of benefits generated.

Currency Transactions

The main purpose of money is to facilitate trade. Any company involved in international trade is, therefore, obliged to deal in several of the world's currencies, and to exchange currencies on the basis of their relative values.

Our policy is to conduct such currency transactions only to the extent they may be necessary to operate the business and protect our interests.

We buy and sell currencies in amounts large enough to cover requirements for the business, and to protect our financial positions in those currencies whose relative values may change in foreign exchange markets. We manage currencies the way we manage materials inventories—attempting to have on hand the right amounts of the various kinds of specifications used in the business. We don't buy unneeded materials or currencies for the purpose of holding them for speculative resale.

Differing Business Practices

Understandably, there are differences in business practices and economic philosophies from country to country. Some of these differences are a matter of pluralism—there isn't necessarily "one best way." Other differences, however, may require changes in proven, well accepted, fair business procedures. Such differences may be a source of continuing dispute. And they may inhibit rather than promote fair competition.

Examples of the latter include varying views regarding competitive practices, boycotts, information disclosure, international mergers, accounting procedures, tax systems, intercompany pricing, national content requirements, product labeling, repatriation of profit, export financing, credit insurance, and industrial property and trademark protection laws. In such areas, we favor more nearly uniform practices among countries. Where necessary, we favor multilateral action aimed at harmonizing differences of this nature.

Observance of Local Laws

A basic requirement levied against any business enterprise is that it know and obey the law. This is rightfully required by those who govern; and it is well understood by business managers.

However, a corporation operating on a global scale will inevitably encounter laws which vary widely from country to country. They may even conflict with each other.

And laws in some countries may encourage or require business practices which—based on experience elsewhere in the world—we believe to be wasteful or unfair. Under such conditions it scarcely seems sufficient for a business manager merely to say: we obey the law, whatever it may be!

We are guided by the belief that the law is not an end but a means to an end—the end presumably being order, justice, and not infrequently, strengthening of the governmental unit involved. If it is to achieve these ends in changing times and circumstances, law itself cannot be insusceptible to change or free of criticism. The law can benefit from both.

Therefore, in a world characterized by a multiplicity of divergent laws at international, national, state, and local levels, Caterpillar's intentions fall in two parts: (1) to obey the law, and (2) to offer, where appropriate, constructive ideas for change in the law.

Relationships with Public Officials
In dealing with public officials, as with private business associates. Caterpillar will utilize only ethical commercial practices. We won't seek to influence sales of our products (or other events impacting on the company) by payments of bribes, kickbacks, or other questionable inducements.

Caterpillar employees will take care to avoid involving the company in any such activities engaged in by others. We won't advise or assist any purchaser of Caterpillar products, including dealers, in making or arranging such payments. We will discourage dealers from engaging in such practices.

Payments of any size to induce public officials to fail to perform their duties—or to perform them in an incorrect manner—are prohibited. Company employees are also required to make good faith efforts to avoid payment of gratuities or "tips" to certain public officials, even where such practices are customary. Where these payments are as a practical matter unavoidable, they must be limited to customary amounts; and they may be made only to facilitate correct performance of the officials' duties.

International Information Flow
Free flow of information among nations is vital to Caterpillar. We transmit a large, growing volume of business data between countries: machine and parts orders, financial and inventory information, engineering, and other data. Restrictions on the flow of such information—and on equipment used to send and receive it—can harm the effectiveness and competitiveness of a company like Caterpillar.

Governments, understandably, want to ensure that national security and privacy of individual citizens aren't jeopardized when information is sent abroad. But even well-meant government regulations of data transmission can quickly become serious obstacles to international business. If deemed absolutely necessary, such regulation should be undertaken carefully . . . and with an opportunity for input by business firms affected.

The Organization for Economic Cooperation and Development, (OECD) an international associate of industrialized democracies, has developed a set of guidelines that strike a balance between privacy protection and the need to maintain the free international flow of information. Caterpillar supports these OECD guidelines.

Free Enterprise, Worldwide

We believe the pursuit of business excellence and profit—in a climate of fair, free competition—is the best means yet found for efficient development and distribution of goods and services. Further, international exchange of goods and services promotes human understanding, and thus harmony and peace.

These aren't unproven theories. The enormous rise in post–World War II gross national product and living standards in countries participating significantly in international commerce has demonstrated the benefits to such countries. And it has also shown their ability to mutually develop and live by common rules—among them the gradual dismantling of trade barriers.

Among the most significant factors in a fair, reliable world trading system are the relative values of currencies. Nations should seek to minimize factors which artificially or unfairly affect those relationships.

As a company that manufactures and distributes on a global scale, Caterpillar recognizes the world is an admixture of differing races, religions, cultures, customs, political philosophies, languages, economic resources, and geography. We respect these differences. Human pluralism can be a strength, not a weakness; no nation has a monopoly on wisdom.

It isn't our aim to attempt to remake the world in the image of any one country. Rather, we hope to help improve the quality of life, wherever we do business, by serving as a means of transmission and application of knowledge that has been found useful elsewhere. We intend to learn and benefit from human diversity.

We ask all governments to permit us to compete on equal terms with competitors. This goes beyond the influence a country can exert on our competitiveness *within* its national boundaries. It also applies to the substantial way a government can control or impact on our business in *other* lands—through domestic taxes and regulations affecting the price of products to be exported, and through "host country" laws affecting our sales and operations outside that country.

Reporting Code Compliance

Each officer, plant or subsidiary manager, and department head shall prepare a memorandum by the close of each year: (1) affirming a full knowledge and understanding of this Code; and (2) reporting any events or activities which might cause an impartial observer to conclude that the Code hasn't been fully followed. These reports should be sent directly to the company's General Counsel; Peoria, Illinois.

Endnotes

1. Portions of this chapter are adapted from Gene R. Laczniak and Jacob Naor, "Global Ethics: Wrestling with the Corporation Conscience," *Business* (July–September 1985), 3–9.

2. Theodore Levitt, "The Globalization of Markets," *Harvard Business Review* (May–June 1983), 92–103.

3. Michael deCourcy Hinds, "Products Unsafe at Home Are Still Unloaded Abroad," *The New York Times* (August 22, 1982), B6.

4. James E. Post, "Assessing the Nestlé Boycott," *California Management Review* (Winter 1985), 113–131.

5. See for example Jagdish Sheth, "Global Markets or Global Competition?" and Philip Kotler, "Global Standardization—Courting Danger," *Journal of Consumer Marketing* (Spring 1986), 9–16.

6. Adapted from David Aaker, *Strategic Market Management* (New York: John Wiley & Sons, 1988), 283–297.

7. Helmut Becker and David J. Fritzsche, "A Comparison of the Ethical Behavior of American, French, and German Managers," *Columbia World Journal of Business* (Winter 1987), 87–95.

8. Jack G. Kaikati and Wayne A. Label, "American Bribery Legislation: An Obstacle to International Marketing," *Journal of Marketing* (Fall 1980), 38–43.

9. US Department of Commerce, "The New Trade Act: Tools for Exporters," *Business America* (October 24, 1988), 2–6.

10. Archie B. Carroll, *Business & Society: Ethics and Stakeholder Management* (Cincinnati, OH: Southwestern Publishing Company, 1989), 149–150.

11. "Fuming Over a Hazardous Export," *Time* (October 2, 1989), 82.

12. "Trade Liberalization's Dark Shadow," *The Economist* (March 26, 1988), 70–71.

13. David J. Fritzsche and Helmut Becker, "Linking Management Behavior to Ethical Philosophy—An Empirical Investigation," *Academy of Management Journal* (March 1984), 166–174.

14. "Watchdogs Abroad: Consumer Protection is Undeveloped in the Third World," *The Wall Street Journal* (April 8, 1980), 1, 23.

15. See note 2 above.

16. Jacob Naor, "A New Approach to Multinational Social Responsibility," *Journal of Business Ethics* 1 (1982), 219–225.

17. Clyde Kluckhorn, "Ethical Relativity: *Sic et Non*," *Journal of Philosophy* 52 (1955), 673.

18. Stephen J. Korbin, "Are Multinationals Better after the Yankees Go Home?" *The Wall Street Journal* (May 8, 1989), A15.

19. George F. Steiner and John F. Steiner, *Business, Government and Society*, 4th ed. (New York: Random House, 1985), 616–623.

20. Watson Dunn, M. F. Cahill, and J. J. Boddewyn, *How Fifteen Multinational Corporations Manage Public Affairs* (Chicago: Crain Books, 1979).

21. Patrick E. Murphy, "Creating Ethical Corporate Structures," *Sloan Management Review* (Winter 1989), 81–86.

22. Leonard Marks, Jr., "Multinational Corporations and Third World Poverty," *Review of Social Economy* 40 (December 1982), 438–453.

23. Timothy Smith, "The Ethical Responsibilities of Multinational Companies." In *Corporations and Their Critics*, 77–86, eds. T. Bradshaw and D. Vogel, (New York: McGraw Hill 1980).

24. Art Pine, "Debt Ridden Nations Impose Many Barriers on Foreign Investors," *The Wall Street Journal* (January 21, 1985), 1.

25. Thomas A. Murphy, "Two Vital Issues: Business Ethics and National Planning," *University of Michigan Business Review* (October–December 1976), 1–6.

26. Robert H. Miles, *Managing the Corporate Social Environment* (Englewood Cliffs, NJ: Prentice–Hall, 1987).

27. *World Business Weekly,* December 22, 1982, 1.

28. For a comprehensive treatment of ethical problems in international business operations, we recommend Thomas Donaldson, *The Ethics of International Business* (New York: Oxford University Press, 1989).

Chapter *9*

The Ethics of
Social, Professional, and
Political Marketing

Scenario 1

A local community hospital experienced a declining patient load for the third consecutive year. The administrator, Sandra O'Brian, indicated to the executive committee that she thought an advertising campaign should be undertaken. "The hospital is an essential local resource and the community would be in trouble if it weren't here," she said. "I just read in *Hospital News* about a hospital in a similar situation. That hospital used a strong fear appeal campaign focusing on possible medical problems that could affect area residents. The locals, now worried, began using the hospital again. One ad asked parents if their child were injured in an accident, and there were no local hospital, would they want their child to be transported an hour away to the nearest hospital for treatment. **Should we try a similar campaign?**"

Scenario 2

Jim Smith and Tim Thompson were talking over lunch during another out-of-town audit trip for a major accounting firm. They were tired of the travel and explored the idea of setting up their own practice back in Bradford (their home town of 800,000 people). Smith remarked, "We would need substantial promotion to get clients quickly. What about formulating an advertising campaign and providing "rebates" for our first clients? We could offer free tickets to the local race track for those hiring us to do tax or estate work. Maybe we could also put a coupon in the local newspaper ad." **Are these proper marketing activities for professionals?**

Scenario 3

Randy Rome was a thirty-two-year-old state senator in a western city of 300,000 inhabitants. He won his party's primary and opposed a seven-term Congressman for office. Since Randy's state record did not have many "big and flashy" accomplishments, he wondered how he would do against the incumbent. He did know that his opponent had a drinking problem and was reputedly a womanizer. "Maybe, I should make my opponent's personal life the focus of my campaign," he thought. **Is it appropriate for Rome to launch such a campaign if there is substance to the rumors about the incumbent?**

The 1980s brought ethical questions, like those raised in the above scenarios, to the forefront of American consciousness. The 1990s are bringing more. Ethical issues touch almost all social, professional, governmental, and nonprofit sectors of society. Some of the abuses have been clear-cut. Ethical scandals of recent years have included favoritism in contractor selection at the US Department of Housing and Urban Development (HUD), politicians engaging in negative advertising aimed at their opponents' integrity rather than the issues, elite colleges' price fixing their tuition levels, hospitals' deceptive advertising, and the dubious marketing practices of television evangelists. Whether these occurrences are due primarily to an erosion of the moral fabric of society, a relaxed view of regulation by government, more aggressive reporting by the media, or some other factor is uncertain. However, the subject of ethics is one that receives almost daily discussion in the mass media. *Time* magazine recently instituted an ethics section as a regular feature. Social and nonprofit marketers, although they toil in a vineyard where many good works are done, cannot consider themselves immune from ethical controversy.

The chapter covers three emerging areas in marketing where ethical problems occur. We call them emerging issues because these topics fall under the "broadened" concept of marketing that includes many types of marketing happening in the growing social service and nonprofit sector.[1]

Social marketing deals with the use of marketing by social agencies and nonprofit organizations. For example, the American Cancer Society and Montana State University adopt marketing techniques, such as segmentation, product positioning, innovative services distribution, and other methods, to more effectively meet their organizations' missions. Also, *marketing by professionals* has grown over the years due to landmark legal cases that allow for advertising by professional practitioners. Still, the view of many professionals (e.g., physicians and attorneys) has been that marketing demeans their occupation. Our third topic of discussion, *political marketing*, has been around for some time, but it has become much more sophisticated in recent years. The trend toward "packaging and selling" candidates and the extensive use of so-called negative advertising evokes a number of critical ethical questions.

Light can be shed on some of these ethical issues by understanding the concept of *market exchange*. Ethics is closely linked to marketing because exchange, the central concept of marketing (e.g., money for services, votes for a political candidate's representation in government), is based on "fairness." Three conditions for a *fair* exchange must be satisfied.[2] First, the transaction must be entered into freely by both parties. A coerced exchange, for instance, is unfair. Second, the marketer and consumer both realistically expect to benefit from the exchange. For example, the hypertensive consumer hopes to benefit in terms of improved health from dietary changes advocated by the American Heart Association, which fulfills part of its mission by promoting these changes. Third, both marketer and consumer must have access to appropriate information concerning the exchange to have a fair transaction. For instance, the primary problem with marketing certain types of contraceptives in underdeveloped countries is that many consumers do not have appropriate knowledge concerning the correct use of the product.

We turn our attention in this chapter first to social marketing, then to marketing by professionals, and finally to political marketing. We examine several general ethical issues pervading each of these three areas and make suggestions for improving their ethical posture. Each section concludes with several ideas for ethical action.

Social Marketing[3]

Social marketers should be held to a high ethical standard. Because they are usually promoting the "social good" (e.g., using seat belts, acquiring further education, smoking cessation, donating to charity, etc.), it is imperative that organizations engaged in such marketing walk the ethical line. If potential consumers feel that they are coerced or not given complete information, the fallout in terms of both goal attainment and public scrutiny can be great. Another very compelling reason why social and nonprofit marketers should meet high ethical standards is because potentially more *harm* to consumers and society can result from unethical social marketing than from unethical commercial marketing. For example, the consumer who elects to have cosmetic surgery partly because of a psychological advertising appeal by a hospital is at a greater disadvantage than a consumer who buys a particular brand of chewing gum because of an advertising campaign. Therefore, ethics should be "top of mind" for all social marketers.

Types of Social Marketing

Marketing expert Philip Kotler classifies the marketing of social causes into three groups: (a) beneficial social marketing, which assists certain segments of society in achieving an improved quality of life; (b) protest social marketing, which attempts to shift societal priorities and resources in new directions; and (c) revolutionary social marketing, which proposes a fundamental change in the existing social system.[4] (See Exhibit 9–1.) As one moves from *beneficial* social marketing (e.g., "don't drink and drive campaigns") to *protest* social marketing (e.g., campaigning to protect animal rights) and on to *revolutionary* social marketing (e.g., advocating the right to euthanasia), the potential for ethical abuse increases substantially.[5] The possible political and personal harm accelerates as one moves across these three social marketing types because the proposed outcomes become more socially debatable with each category.

Social marketing is a double-edged sword. It has major beneficial elements, but also contains the potential to cause significant ethical controversies.[6] There seems to be a connection between *applying* marketing techniques to social ideas and the perceived ethical sensitivity of the public to the ideas themselves. For example, individuals who view legalized gambling as unethical also will say that

---

EXHIBIT 9–1   Ethical Issues in Social Marketing

Type of Social Marketing Program	*Examples*	*Potential for Ethical Abuse*	*Possible Ethical Questions*
Beneficial	Preventive health care program United Way	Low	Is the information about the soliciting organization clear? Are fear appeals appropriate in promotion?
Protest	Ban tuna fishing (to save dolphins) Campaign for improved TV programming	Moderate	Should attempts be made to present an objective argument? Should certain individuals or organizations be singled out as targets?
Revolutionary	Support First Amendment rights (including the right to promote pornography) Euthanasia	High	Are the mass media appropriate vehicles? Should individual program developers be required to identify themselves?

Source: Adapted from Patrick E. Murphy, Gene R. Laczniak, and Robert F. Lusch, "Ethical Guidelines for Business and Social Marketing," *Journal of the Academy of Marketing Science* 6 (Summer 1978), 199.

its *marketing* is unethical as well. Perhaps these strong feelings occur because the products promoted by social marketers (e.g., health care, education, political issues) "affect the human condition more profoundly" than consumer products do.[7] (See Exhibit 9–2.)

Ethical Problems Facing Social Marketers

Exhibit 9–3 shows five generic ethical problems facing all marketers. Associated with each one are questions that social marketers should ask themselves. Because marketing is the business function with the most public contact, the potential for ethical abuse is great. Social marketers need to be especially aware of these problems because of the sensitive nature of many social marketing issues. We realize there are few easy answers to these questions; some are nearly unanswerable. However, it is important that they be asked. Just the process of raising these questions may sensitize social marketers to ethical concerns and diminish the probability that they will violate moral norms. We now turn our attention to these generic problems.

Marketing Is Unfair

This observation stems from the concern that some marketers engage in overt lying, nondisclosure of relevant information, collusion, extreme embellishment, or the perpetuation of planned product obsolescence. If marketing and promotion are viewed as a continuum from absolute truth to a complete lie, many marketing activities fall in the middle range labeled as persuasion and embellishment. (For a more complete discussion of this point, see Chapter 6.) Some consumer marketing campaigns have been characterized as unfair due to high pressure selling or less than full disclosure of information.

Social marketers must be concerned with the questions relating to unfairness shown in Exhibit 9–3. They must decide how much information to disclose to consumers. Social ideas such as getting vasectomies, using condoms, and eating high-fiber diets all have potential risks associated with their promotion that social marketers need to consider. Sometimes, only the beneficial effects of such products are disclosed; this may not be enough.

Another common ethical question deals with fear. Fear appeals (i.e., heightening the levels of consumer anxiety) are sometimes used by marketers. Certain social marketers have also raised consumers' fears in their desire to bring about behavioral change.[8] The marketing of cholesterol testing, long-term health care insurance, and seat belt usage can include generating high levels of anxiety on the part of the target audience. Exhibit 9–4 discusses some of the problems associated with the pervasive marketing by the health care system. Fear appeals are not unethical *per se*. The question is how much anxiety is reasonable? For example, we believe that the fear appeal campaign suggested in scenario 1 is probably

EXHIBIT 9–2   The Ethics of College Admissions Marketing

Money magazine ran an in-depth article on college admissions and the questionable tactics used to "sell" schools to prospective students. Some of the most critical comments were leveled at college marketing activities. Among the most relevant passages from that article are the following:

> All colleges are selling themselves more aggressively to more students than ever before. Marketing budgets increased 64% between 1980 and 1986; the typical institution now spends an average of about $1,700 to bring in each new student. Academics hire marketing consultants, consort with public-relations advisers and grill prospective students in focus groups; colleges no longer change their curricula, they "reposition" themselves; admissions offices don't just admit freshmen, they "manage enrollment."

> Even worse, most admissions departments spend the bulk of their energies not in trying to identify students who could benefit from studying there but rather in deploying commercial marketing techniques to lure new applicants ... The colleges lead students on, making them think they'll be accepted ... then in April they start boasting to their alumni about how many kids they turned down.

> The heart of college marketing is junk mail. To attract a freshman class of 500, a college might send out 22,000 brochures to a list of student names collected from the standardized testing services such as the College Board and the American College Testing Service. Practically any C student can expect at least 50 pieces of collegiate junk to show up in his mailbox beginning in the spring of his junior year. A top student, an athlete or a member of an ethnic minority may get 500.

> Most of a college's marketing campaign—the viewbooks, the videos, the recruiting junkets—simply provides more trivialities to choose from. It is not so much that colleges seduce kids into picking the wrong colleges, but rather that they encourage them to make the choice for the wrong reasons.

> But the real cost of the marketing war is more subtle, and potentially much steeper. ... Dorms, fancy lab equipment, fitness facilities, grounds-keeping, subsidized rock concerts are all part of the battle to stay attractive to the widest possible number of 17-year-olds. And no college dares to stop escalating the competition. ... this spiral adds two percentage points to the inflation in college prices.

> What is probably the saddest irony in the whole mess, though, is that education has its own Gresham's law: as marketing drives up the price of higher education, it tends to drive down its quality. Good marketing and good teaching are incompatible: the one requires that you find out what the customer wants and provide it, the other that you demand things of the student that he may prefer not to do. "The more the college thinks of its students as customers, the more it will be tempted simply to give them what they want," says Williams College economics professor Michael MacPherson. The danger is that in battling with each other to give students what they want, the colleges are losing sight of their more important task: to give students what they need.

Source: Eric Schurenberg, "The Agony of College Admissions," *Money* (May 1989), 142–150. © copyright 1989 The Time Inc. Magazine Company. Reprinted by special permission.

EXHIBIT 9–3   Generic Ethical Problems for Marketers

Problem	*Social Marketing Questions*
Marketing is unfair	How much disclosure is enough?
	How much fear is reasonable?
	Are appropriate selling tactics being used?
Marketing is manipulative	Is the idea/cause worthy?
	Will successful marketing of the primary idea produce for an unworthy secondary cause?
Marketing is wasteful	Should scarce resources be used to promote offerings that are intrinsically valuable?
	How much should be spent on reluctant consumers?
	Would causes be better off by not raising the ante?
Marketing plays favorites	Do benefits of segmenting outweigh the costs?
	When has enough been done for a less-advantaged group?
	Who speaks for the mass market?
Marketing is intrusive	Is the cause being promoted in "good taste"?
	What information is appropriate and reasonable to seek from people?
	How can confidentiality of research results be maintained?

unethical, because it likely violates the first and third conditions of a fair exchange (i.e., such promotions may be coercive and misleading).

An additional question refers to the appropriateness of certain selling tactics. The use of persuasion is often necessary to raise the consciousness of consumers to social problems such as the need for blood-pressure screening or breast self-examination. However, there are some selling tactics that may be less appropriate to use in the nonprofit sector than the commercial sector. Possibly in this category is the use of fundraising approaches such as the so-called "door-in-the-face" where a request for an inordinately large donation [e.g., $1,000] is made in hopes of receiving a smaller one [e.g., $100]. When the consumer responds negatively to the first appeal, the solicitor quickly requests a much smaller donation.

Marketing Is Manipulative
Some critics view the issue of inappropriately manipulating consumer wants to be marketing's greatest sin. Many of the ills of our consumer culture are blamed

---

EXHIBIT 9–4   One Physician's View on Health Industry Marketing

According to Dr. Joseph Wassersug, a retired internist, we are being bombarded with information about our well-being that plays on our apprehensions and fears. He believes that the medical profession is "creating demands and huckstering claims that were, only so recently, not only unethical but unthinkable."

He cites the current fear of high cholesterol. Wassersug feels that the health industry has exaggerated its theoretical dangers and builds fears that "sell more fiber foods, more unsaturated spreads, some fish-oil capsules, a multitude of costly medicines, and the need for more and more laboratory tests." He indicates that cholesterol has been identified only as a "risk factor" that contributes to

heart disease, yet a book with the title, *The 8-Week Cure for Cholesterol*, enjoys wide sales.

Almost all of us are brainwashed to believe, in his opinion, that disability and even death lurk behind every step we take and every morsel of food we eat. He believes that the pursuit of fitness and health should not become a national obsession or an irrational response to manipulation by the health industry. He has the "uneasy feeling that the blood pressure clinic at the supermarket or shopping center may be more for pecuniary than salutary gain." Consumers must learn to question the health news and advertising they see and read.

Do you agree with Dr. Wassersug's position? Why or why not?

on marketers. The concern is with marketing's supposed ability to persuade people to buy things that they would not otherwise buy or do not need. For social marketers, several pointed questions are raised in Exhibit 9–3. First, the worthiness of the cause or idea itself needs to be questioned. For example, "drink milk," "eat beef," "right-to-life," "right-to-bear arms," and "save the whales," have all been marketed as positive social causes and perceived as instances of beneficial social marketing. But for at least some segments of the population, the acceptance of these ideas can cause economic, physical, or emotional problems. For example, both eating beef and drinking most kinds of milk can raise blood cholesterol levels. For other issues, the opposing viewpoints are also seen as valid. For instance, to many Japanese the whaling industry is an economically important and ethically defensible endeavor.

Still another question is whether success in marketing certain social ideas can lead to unworthy secondary results. For instance, does the promotion of breast-feeding to poor, single mothers lead them to want more children? Do anti-cocaine campaigns lead to more alcohol abuse? Do smoking cessation programs lead to eating disorders? Does condom usage lead to more promiscuity? These are very difficult questions to answer, but certainly social marketers must grapple with them. Assessing all significant and forseeable consequences is part of the discovery process of intended and unintended side effects.

The final question relating to manipulation refers to judging competing wants. Put another way, what are the opportunity costs of social marketing? The age-old economic argument is that consumers have insatiable wants. Even in the social marketing sphere, consumers probably want too much of a good thing. Does the active promotion of one cause or idea lead to the neglect of others? Each social marketer—whether a blood center, church, or social service organization—believes that its cause is most important. Aggressive marketing and promotion may persuade consumers to place an undue priority on one cause over another. One advantage of umbrella organizations such as the *United Way* is that it attempts to balance the needs of various social agencies in a systematic fashion.

Marketing Is Wasteful

The problem of wastefulness is another that plagues marketers. The concern here is with the question of how expensive it is to differentiate between product offerings that are often similar and to communicate persuasive messages about them through the mass media. The questions in Exhibit 9–3 should be considered by social marketers who have to confront this problem. The expenditure of marketing dollars to promote social causes has long been a criticism levied at this type of marketing. Health care providers have resisted marketing for this reason. Some critics contend that *beneficial* causes, such as drug abuse counseling and proper nutrition during pregnancy, may not need to be systematically marketed, but should instead be left to counselors and social service agencies. A related question is how much a social marketer should spend in order to convert "reluctant consumers" to "users" of the service or idea. Some individuals will simply never fasten their seat belts, go for blood pressure checks and cholesterol testing, or undertake other behavioral changes that social marketers advocate. High levels of marketing effort may then be wasteful, and the money could be more effectively spent in other endeavors or not spent at all by the organization.

Perhaps an even more fundamental question (in Exhibit 9–3) to ask is whether the status of a particular cause is better off after it has been marketed. Several good examples of *protest* social marketing can be found in the social causes of the 1990s. Pro and con groups exist for smoking rights, gun control, and abortion. Nonprofit organizations sometimes raise the ante on the cause with modest marketing efforts and thereby incur the ire of the affected industry or its lobby. For example, gun control advocates face a formidable task in combatting the National Rifle Association and gun manufacturers. Self-interest then takes over, and all the resulting, conflicting messages possibly confuse consumers and may make them cynical toward the cause. We are not proposing that social marketers abstain from promoting their cause, but they should consider that certain emotionally charged advertising might not clarify very much for the public (e.g., the current abortion debate).

Marketing Plays Favorites

One of the hallmarks of marketing is the use of market segmentation strategies. At times, this focus on potentially profitable markets ignores or gives second-class treatment to less promising consumer segments—minorities, the poor, and the elderly. Many marketing organizations such as auto dealerships, shopping malls, and financial service institutions are generally located in the more affluent areas to serve lucrative market segments. Professionals (e.g., physicians and attorneys) often employ similar segmentation approaches in their practices.

Social agencies are usually more egalitarian in nature and find such segmented favoritism too extreme. Some social agencies do practice segmentation to a gross degree in order to, for example, serve the poor or attract donations from those who are likely contributors. However, in adopting a marketing orientation social marketers must decide how much to segment. The questions listed in this section of Exhibit 9–3 pose classic utilitarian trade-offs. For instance, is the benefit of a marketing campaign to help teenage mothers worth the cost of allowing other segments (older, but yet indigent pregnant women) to go underserved? In programs to aid the education of native Americans, how much should be spent to overcome the problems they have experienced for many years? Similar questions may be asked about new immigrants to the United States. How much should and can be done for them at the expense of longer standing and equally deserving constituencies?

In social marketing, there is a potential danger of only catering to the most demanding and strident segments of the market. Some elderly and certain minority groups are afraid to ask for help even when they need and deserve it. How can social marketers overcome this tendency toward favoritism and reach the large needy population? For example, who will speak for those both elderly and poor?

Marketing Is Intrusive

The final bank of questions shown in Exhibit 9–3 deals with marketing's intrusive nature. The statement "marketing is everywhere," which is sometimes heard, reinforces this point. The first question concerns whether the cause being marketed is promoted using "good taste." Family planning agencies must be sensitive to the need to promote condoms or other birth control methods tastefully, without being overly offensive to the beliefs of some market segments. Similarly, health care organizations must also make sure that they meet or exceed societal standards of proper taste. For example, smoking cessation programs may want to avoid calling smokers "butt-heads," and breast self-examination programs should be careful about the gratuitous use of nudity.

Those engaged in marketing research for social causes should be cognizant of ethical issues that they may face over and above those experienced by commercial marketing researchers. Thus, the second question pertaining to intrusiveness in Exhibit 9–3 deals with what information is reasonable and appropriate. Marketing researchers need to be aware that some information that they seek is very sensitive. Topics such as past sexual history, recent charitable donations to social causes, and even membership in social clubs come to mind. And if this information can be gathered, the researcher has an ethical responsibility to fearlessly protect the confidentiality of the results. Difficult ethical questions arise, for instance, when the respondent to a questionnaire is identified as a very young teenager who is sexually active or an employee who is a drug abuser. Is the duty to the parent or company stronger than the individual's right to privacy? We refer the reader to the ethical theory discussion in Chapter 2 for guidance.

Emerging Ethical Concerns in Social Marketing

Social marketers have been faced with the ethical issues for some time. In addition, we see a few new ethical concerns emerging from the use of social marketing that will be important during the 1990s. Several of them arise from the growth of cause-related marketing as well as the increased marketing of controversial ideas by nonprofit organizations.

Cause-related marketing has been defined as the process of formulating and implementing marketing activities that involve the contribution of specified amounts of money to designated causes when customers engage in revenue-providing exchanges (i.e., when they use the service or buy the product that is being marketed).[9] For example, Coca-Cola Company was the major sponsor of the Hands Across America campaign and raised $5 million for the fight against hunger. The dollars that Coke contributed were based on the amount of Coca-Cola products consumers purchased during a specified period of time. Ideally, both the commercial marketer and benefactor gain from this partnership. Although companies such as Campbells has long redeemed soup labels for school equipment, the "cause-related marketing" label originated in 1983 with the American Express usage-based contribution to the restoration of the Statue of Liberty.[10]

One ethical issue that occurs here is the possible conflict of interest between the cause and the sponsoring organization. For example, an ad campaign that ran in 1988 stated that for each purchase of Bud or Bud Light beer during a specified period of time, a donation would be made to the Muscular Distrophy Association (MDA). Ethical questions seem to arise over whether the goals of Anheuser Busch and the MDA are the same and whether the MDA wants to be associated with a product that has many potentially detrimental side effects.

Another emerging ethical issue relates to the *promotion* of controversial ideas, such as drug and AIDS testing in the workplace. The risk to companies and organizations of not testing is great in terms of lost time from work and ineffective employees. However, those advocating the widespread use of involuntary testing must surely recognize that the right to privacy might be violated. The larger issue, of course, is the dilemma of the common good versus individual rights. In other words, is it ethical to force an individual to undergo drug or AIDS testing in order to protect an organization's integrity or work environment? The courts have supported the usage of drug testing for certain categories of workers, such as pilots and air traffic controllers.

Ideas for Ethical Action

Ethical issues should be at the top of a social marketer's priority list when developing marketing and advertising campaigns. First, *social and nonprofit marketers should develop clear guidelines as to what their product and promotional policies will be. This should be driven by their strategic plan, not by opportunistic schemes to increase their cash flow.* Boards of directors as well as chief administrators of nonprofit agencies should answer the question: *What* is our business? This answer should not change with the whim of administrators and should not necessarily include products that are tangential to the major thrust of the organization. For example, some universities may have stepped across the ethical line when they sponsored commercially oriented ventures, such as genetic engineering firms that compete with for-profit businesses.

Second, *the advertising posture of social and nonprofit organizations should be clearly delineated.* Too often it seems that nonprofit organizations think advertising and marketing will solve all their problems. The managers of nonprofit organizations may abdicate some of their oversight responsibility to their advertising agency. We believe that clear advertising guidelines need to be spelled out by the board and management team before an agency is selected. For example, a hospital might pre-specify that it wishes to eschew fear inducing ad campaigns like the example discussed in scenario 1. Similarly, the work of the agency should be reviewed from a moral as well as a business standpoint. (See Chapters 6 and 10 for more detailed discussions of similar positions.)

Third, *professional and trade organizations need to monitor their members' compliance with their code of ethical conduct.* These codes should obviously be more than window-dressing. Codes of ethics are a beginning, and some associations are just in the early stages of evaluating the ethical conduct of their members. These codes should have appropriate sanctions for violations. For instance, some colleges contend that the admissions offices of some of their competitors are not "playing fair." (See Exhibit 9–5 for a discussion of this problem.) Certain organizations, such as the Graduate Management Admissions Council (see Appendix 9A) and the National Association of College Admissions Counselors, do have detailed codes.

Marketing by Professionals

In contrast to the relatively recent discussion of ethics in social marketing, ethical issues are a more longstanding concern in the professions. It is common practice to mention the "professional obligation" of certain practitioners to behave ethically. Examples of such professional duties are the obligations of medicine to provide health, of law to provide justice, and of the clergy to provide spiritual guidance. Another, almost universal characteristic of the professions is the presence of formal codes of ethics and the existence of enforcement mechanisms for

---

EXHIBIT 9–5   Are Elite Colleges Guilty of Price Fixing?

During the 1950s selective Eastern colleges began meeting in the spring to end a bidding war for good students by determining how much a family could contribute to their child's education. The other purpose was to encourage students to make their college selection on educational quality and not economics. This practice continued until recently with twenty-three colleges participating. All but one of the Ivy League schools (Brown, Columbia, Cornell, Dartmouth, Harvard, Pennsylvania, and Princeton) and many other prestigious Eastern colleges (Amherst, Colby, MIT, Smith, Wesleyan, and Williams, etc.) belonged to this group.

The financial aid officers of these colleges met to compare notes on over 10,000 common applicants seeking financial aid. Before the meeting, the schools sent their records to Harvard, where a for-profit firm, run by some of Harvard's admissions personnel, compiles lists of applicants who are seeking financial aid at more than one school. The schools have given the innocuous label of "financial aid overlap" to their annual meeting. The evaluation process determined how much the family can pay yearly for their child's education. The Ivy subgroup tried to match the mix of aid between grants and loans and it allows institutions to adjust offers (often upward) before they are sent out to applicants.

Critics of this process contend that it is out-and-out price fixing. *The Wall Street Journal* wrote that "the Ivy Schools are part of a price fixing system that OPEC might envy." Another criticism revolves around the issue of "fairness." Critics feel that this process is unfair, because it often denies a student the potential of more financial aid, from at least one school. A third criticism, and one mentioned by admissions people at other schools, is that it saves these schools not only money but also grief from students and parents. In this way they don't have to fight bloody financial battles. A final criticism is that others have suggested this practice may be inconsistent with the "Principles of Good Practice" of the National Association of College Admissions Counselors to which many of the elite schools belong. The code of this group states that members will agree to "refrain from changing the financial aid awards to match those of the students' other college choices."

The schools defended the practice by stating that the meeting is primarily intended to exchange information. As one financial aid officer said, "there is no agreement that we agree" on a family's contribution amount. Another participating financial aid officer states that "we are not matching awards," but a closely similar award "may be the result" of the meeting although "it is not the intent or purpose."

Is this practice ethical? Why or why not?

these codes.[11] We focus here, though, mostly on ethical questions revolving around the marketing and advertising techniques used by professionals such as accountants, dentists, lawyers, and physicians.

The use of marketing and advertising by professionals is an emotional and controversial topic. Since the Supreme Court decisions in 1976 (*Virginia State*

Board of Pharmacy v. Virginia Citizens Consumer Council) and in 1977 (*Bates v. State Bar of Arizona*) that struck down prohibitions on such advertising, this issue has generated much debate in various professional communities. Feelings run deep on both sides, as exemplified by the following comment by former Chief Justice Warren Burger: "The public should never, never, never employ a lawyer or doctor who finds it necessary to advertise." His statement can be contrasted with one by an FTC official who said, "At bottom, the prejudice against advertising is that it creates pressure to compete."[12] Some feel that advertising will place undue emphasis on price at the expense of the provider's quality of service. Others contend that consumers generally seem much more favorably disposed to the use of advertising than many professionals.[13]

In this section, we review the forces that have caused professionals to increase their marketing and advertising expenditures. We summarize the arguments for and against the use of these techniques. Then, we examine specific ethical issues relating to accountants, lawyers, and the medical community. We conclude with ideas for ethical action that may help advertising and marketing by professionals to remain on a high ethical plane.

Forces Stimulating Marketing by Professionals

A number of developments in the last two decades have moved professionals out of their traditional mode of operation. The ones we believe to be the most important are emerging legal developments, growing competition, and marketing's applicability to professional practice in areas such as new service development and franchising.

Legal Developments

Historically, most state and national professional organizations had prohibitions against advertising in their codes of conduct. The outcome of the *Virginia Board of Pharmacy* case ruled unconstitutional a Virginia statute declaring that advertising of prescription drug prices by any pharmacist constituted unprofessional conduct.[14] The *Bates v. State Bar of Arizona* case challenged the state bar association's ban on publicizing legal fees. The case was appealed to the Supreme Court, which ruled in 1977 that attorneys have First Amendment freedom of speech rights to advertise fees for routine services, and consumers have the right to receive such information. But the Supreme Court did not foresee major changes in the way that lawyers and other professionals practiced. They wrote, "We suspect that with advertising, most lawyers will behave as they always have. They will abide by their solemn oath to uphold the honor and integrity of the profession and the legal systems."[15] The major professional associations followed the edict of the court and relaxed advertising restrictions for dentists in 1977 and for the accounting, legal, and medical professions in 1978. These decisions, then, set in motion the marketing and advertising of the professions.

Growing Competition

The world of the 1990s is much more competitive for everyone, including professionals. There appear to be three reasons for this growing level of competition. First, law, architecture, dentistry, and several other professions have become overcrowded by the number of new professionals entering the field. Professional schools continue to graduate large numbers of students every year. This means that their newer professionals especially must use marketing and advertising techniques to attract clients.

Second, the mentality of most professionals toward promotion has also changed. They have moved from the traditional "country club" contact method of publicizing their service to a more comprehensive marketing perspective. This is partially due to the changing legal climate, but also because professionals see marketing as a viable mechanism to compete effectively in this changing environment. Competition probably will not diminish in the future, and most professionals (some reluctantly, however) have recognized that marketing and advertising will continue to play a major role in this competitive world.

A third competitive development is the growth in different types of professional providers. Medicine and dentistry were dominated by individual practitioners who did not view themselves as competing directly with each other. Now, in medicine for example, these individual providers are competing with clinics, group practices, and health management organizations (HMOs) as well as hospitals. In the accounting field, the so-called Big Six (reduced from eight) are not only competing with one another, but also with smaller firms, consulting organizations, and specialty companies that provide highly specialized services (e.g., auditing for health care organizations). The pressure then is currently on all types of professional service providers to market themselves more aggressively against their new forms of competition. Much less room now exists for gentility on either side.

Marketing's Applicability to Professional Practice

Some professionals have found that marketing concepts such as branding, new service development, alternate delivery mechanisms, and franchising can be applied quite usefully to their situation. If the professional wants to meet the needs of the time-conscious and mobile consumer of the 1990s, such new approaches must be explored. Just as Burger King has found consumers to be loyal to its "brand," Humana, the hospital chain, has found that its "brand" of medicine is preferred by some consumers. The use of brand or corporate names has made it much easier to franchise legal, dental, optical, and medical clinics. Such retailing of the professions began even before the Bates decision, and gained popularity during the 1980s. Dental World, Omnidentix Systems, Nu Vision Centers, and Sterling Optical are some of the best known professional services franchises.[16]

Even the more traditional professional practices have expanded their product line and altered their distribution network. For instance, ambulatory surgery, alcoholic rehabilitation, psychological counseling, personal injury law, and management consulting by public accounting firms are recent additions to the product portfolio of service providers. Furthermore, professionals have begun using immediate care medical centers, satellite offices, and expanded hours to appeal to time conscious consumers. These developments often necessitated some type of advertising to inform consumers of the change in services offered by the professional.

The Status of Advertising by Professionals

Though fifteen years have passed since the *Virginia Board of Pharmacy* and *Bates* decisions, the use of marketing and advertising by professionals is still a controversial topic. We now review some of the strongest arguments on both sides of the issue.

The Case for Advertising by Professionals

Several arguments can be advanced. Probably the strongest is that consumers demand such information. Individuals are in need of information about legal, medical, optical, and dental services. They are used to getting information about other products and services via the newspaper and television. At minimum, consumers want to know the location of the provider and the range of services offered. Word of mouth is still the most trusted information source for all products, but dissatisfied consumers, newcomers to an area, the poor, and those experiencing a problem for the first time (likely younger people) may not have access to it. Consequently, advertising offers them an easily accessible vehicle for gaining information about professionals. From an ethical standpoint, it is argued that according to the principle of distributive justice, the poor, elderly and market illiterates are more likely to be served if advertising of these services is permitted.[17]

A second argument, and the one that legal decisions are mostly based upon, is the First Amendment right of free speech. Professionals should be able to communicate with consumers in any nondeceptive manner that they choose. Critics view advertising as "undignified," but Justice Blackmun noted in the majority opinion of *Bates* that "the assertion that advertising will diminish the attorney's reputation in the community is open to question. Bankers and engineers advertise, and yet these professions are not regarded as undignified."[18]

Third, proponents contend that the costs to consumers are lower when advertising is present. This is an extension of the competition argument that states that more information in the marketplace will have the effect of driving down prices. In the absence of advertising, professionals may collude and keep prices artificially high. The Federal Trade Commission (FTC) has used this argument extensively and did find in one study that in cities where lawyers advertised intensively, legal fees had declined by 5–13 percent.[19] When the FTC analysis is combined with the consumer information argument, the evidence suggests that advertising contributes to the efficient functioning of the marketplace.

A final reason to support increased marketing by professionals is that it allows a new entrant to gain access to the market more easily. In the absence of advertising, it may take years for a new lawyer or accountant or a new type of practice to make enough contacts to attain a thriving business. A specific example is Hyatt Legal Services, a legal services chain with over 200 offices nationwide employing over 600 attorneys. Hyatt spent several million dollars on TV ads using CEO Joel Hyatt to build its client base. Although this firm is one of the most successful, undoubtedly many more professionals received at least modest aid from advertising.

The Case against Advertising by Professionals

The critics of marketing and advertising by professionals articulate a number of variations on a common theme. Namely, it is unprofessional for individuals who consider themselves to belong to a professional community to lower themselves to use *common* business practices. The logical extension of this argument is that advertising undermines the relationship of trust that exists between a professional person and a client.[20] One accountant perceives that the best way to build a practice is to get involved in one's community, and that the emphasis should be on "quality control, not marketing concepts."[21]

A similar sentiment was expressed by a lawyer who felt that advertising contributes to the negative image of their profession. A Florida bar association survey found that professionals are very conscious of their image with the public, and some believe that the "dignity" of the profession is compromised with the use of mass market advertising. The view that marketing by professionals has an impact on all practitioners, not just those who advertise, is well articulated by a Florida lawyer: "Advertising is a broad brush, which stains all lawyers. We tend to be perceived as greedy, self-interested people who do not care about our clients and are only interested in making a buck."[22]

Another view expressed by critics of marketing and advertising is that the focus has shifted away from the professional's major job of healing, advising, and counseling toward an emphasis on an issue of lesser importance—generating a profit. They ask whether consumers want to shop for the lowest price for a dentist or chiropractor as one would for a used car? Probably not. Certainly there are some unethical professionals who do use advertising unscrupulously. Furthermore, consumers are interested in more than price. Most want a competent, knowledgeable practitioner who can solve problems; price is secondary in importance.[23] In the final analysis, however, the Supreme Court has affirmed the right of professionals to market and advertise their services.

It should be noted that many, if not most, current professional marketing examples involve little more than aggressive advertising and pricing of fees. This is not *real* marketing, which would also consider other product and distribution variables in the strategic menu. Ethical issues should apply to all elements.

Ethical Issues in Marketing by Accountants

Accountants were also reluctant to embrace marketing and advertising concepts. Times changed dramatically during the 1980s. Many accounting firms both developed advertising campaigns and employed staff people in a marketing capacity. Some of the largest ones, like Arthur Andersen, initiated consulting divisions that engaged in extensive marketing efforts. Consequently, questions regarding the ethics of these marketing practices became more prevalent (recall the discussion in scenario 2).

The definitive position on advertising in the accounting field is contained in Section 502 (Advertising and Other Forms of Solicitation) of the Code of Professional Conduct of the American Institute of Certified Public Accountants (AICPA). The emphasis in the code is on informational advertising. Section 502 delineates what is prohibited by the code, as well as what is considered ethical in advertising by accountants. For example, past experience is acceptable to mention in advertising as well as the Certified Public Accountant (CPA) designation. However, the advertiser cannot use self-laudatory statements unless they are based on verifiable facts.[24] Certain advertising of the largest CPA firms (Deloitte & Touche and Price Waterhouse) has been contested on ethical grounds.[25] Accounting firms that are concerned about the ethical posture of their advertising need to develop guidelines that delineate what is expected. For example, Arthur Andersen has a detailed book outlining the firm's position on "Ethical Standards/Independence," which includes the complete AICPA code as an appendix. The AICPA has also emphasized the association's commitment to ethics in its advertising (see Exhibit 9–6 promoting the "new P/E ratio," i.e., the relationship between profits and ethics).

Ethical Questions Regarding Lawyer Advertising

Some law firms have openly embraced marketing. As one CEO of a prepaid legal service commented, "We don't have attorneys that sit in the office and practice. We market law. That's all we do."[26] The law firms that have most extensively used advertising are those specializing in personal injury, medical malpractice, immigration law, or divorce. Lawyers now spend over $50 million on advertising, a ten-fold increase since 1980. The percentage of lawyers who advertise has increased from 3 percent to 32 percent over those years.[27]

The American Bar Association (ABA) has developed both a Model Code of Professional Responsibility and Model Rules of Professional Conduct. The state bar associations follow one of these two documents to serve as the official standard of conduct for lawyers. Appendix 9B shows Rules 7.1, 7.2, and 7.3 that govern the ethics of legal services marketing. Several of the clauses are quite similar to those governing accountants. Alleged violations are reviewed by a state bar committee, which can recommend reprimand, suspension, or disbarment.

There are many other potential ethical issues stemming from attorney advertising and marketing. Exhibit 9–7 lists some pertinent questions that could be asked about potentially unethical legal advertising, including fear generating TV

EXHIBIT 9–6　AICPA Ad Campaign

THE NEW P/E RATIO

A strange way to measure a company? Not really.

These days the push to improve the bottom line has put new pressures on the way companies behave.

To the point where some have gotten the idea that higher profits and ethical behavior are mutually exclusive.

Of course, this isn't true. Nor has it ever been.

This "new" P/E Ratio simply reaffirms the proven axiom that...

Good conduct is good business.

By voicing a clear code of conduct from the top, a company can eliminate misunderstanding and clarify the responsibilities of each employee.

Taking the lead in this way will raise morale and productivity, while reducing the potential for fraud and legal jeopardy.

CPAs who are members of the American Institute of CPAs know the value of a rigorous ethical code.

They work for companies of all sizes, as managers, accountants, independent auditors and consultants. In fact, a Louis Harris poll named CPAs the most ethical of all professionals.

The leaders of the accounting profession—members of the AICPA—recently voted to strengthen their Code of Professional Conduct even further. The new code defines proper conduct in terms of integrity, objectivity and independence—all to protect the public interest.

Members of the AICPA believe that every company should have an ethics code. Not to limit profits, but to enhance them.

The measure of excellence.

AICPA

AMERICAN INSTITUTE OF CERTIFIED PUBLIC ACCOUNTANTS
1211 Avenue of the Americas, New York, NY 10036-8775

IN AN INCREASINGLY COMPLEX WORLD, AICPA MEMBERS —
MORE THAN 260,000 CPAs IN PUBLIC PRACTICE, INDUSTRY, GOVERNMENT AND EDUCATION —
PROVIDE QUALITY SERVICE IN THE PUBLIC INTEREST.

Source: Reprinted by permission of the American Institute of Certified Public Accountants, Inc.

ads dramatized with sirens, and ads that vow to help you "collect cash." An in-depth study of law practice marketing concluded with the following admonition: "Inevitably, the standards which will govern all of lawyer business-getting activity will be those of honesty and fairness."[28]

EXHIBIT 9–7   Some Ethical Questions about Lawyer Advertising

"The principal difficulty, though, lies in determining just what is, for instance, misleading, or unfair, or dignified. Consider the following:

- A personal injury ad says, 'no recovery—no fee.' Is this misleading or deceptive for failure to mention the client may be responsible for litigation costs?
- Is a '24-Hour Legal Hotline' dignified?
- 'Real People, Not a Professional Corporation or Legal Clinic.' Is this misleading to the public and unfair to other lawyers?
- An ad seeking drunk driving cases shows a liquor bottle, a wrecked car, and a drunk. Is this dignified?
- '20 Years of Successful Criminal Practice.' Is this self-laudatory, does it contain information about past performance, and does it create an unjustified expectation?
- 'Low Rates.' Is this sufficient fee information, or deceptive?
- In an advertising circular, 'Bring this coupon in for a Free Consultation.' Is this dignified or deceptive?
- 'The Worst Injury of All May Be Not Being Properly Represented.' Is this misleading or unfair?
- 'Full Compensation for your Injuries.' Does this create unjustified expectations?
- 'Everyday our lawyers are in court representing innocent people charged with crimes they didn't commit.' Is this potentially fraudulent or deceptive?
- A TV ad for personal injury cases shows an accident, flashing lights, and injured persons being loaded into ambulances. Is this dignified or deceptive? Does it appeal to anger, fear or greed?
- 'We took the fear out of legal fees.' Is this deceptive? Is it telling the public to be fearful of lawyers and legal fees?
- A lawyers referral service sells all referrals from certain counties to lawyers for a monthly fee. The service advertises an '800' phone number in the yellow pages, with a nationwide answering service based in Tennessee. The service has been approved only by a local bar association in California. Does this meet the letter and spirit of Rule 7.3?"

Source: *Res Gestae*, August 1988, 63. Reprinted with permission of the Indiana State Bar Association.

Ethical Issues Facing Medical and Dental Marketing

Of all the professions, medicine has resisted marketing and advertising most vehemently. Survey results indicate that physicians are more skeptical than other professionals toward the benefits of marketing.[29] It may be that they perceive marketing to be primarily a selling activity and far removed from their view of the responsibilities contained in the Hippocratic Oath. Although the medical community was covered by the *Bates* decision, the American Medical Association was charged by the FTC with conspiring with state and local medical societies to suppress all forms of medical advertising. The Supreme Court handed down another decision in 1982.[30] It affirmed the right of physicians to advertise in a truthful, nondeceptive manner.

The majority of medical advertising is undertaken by clinics, HMOs, and hospitals. A number of codes developed by various associations exist to help insure ethical advertising. Appendix 9C contains the Advertising Guidelines of the Council of Medical Specialty Societies. Its thirteen points stipulate that the use of incomplete information, heavy fear appeals, and misleading claims are unacceptable. Many of these ethical guidelines should hold for the advertising of any product.

One especially ethically charged medical area is cosmetic surgery. It is heavily advertised in some parts of the country, such as California. A number of ethical hazards of advertising cosmetic surgery have been noted by critics, including the possibility of creating oversimplified expectations. A worst-case scenario is where ads manipulate individuals to demand services that are downright unhealthy. (Suction-assisted lipectomy, i.e., fat suction, for example, is an especially controversial procedure.) Another issue pertains to promoting the professional qualifications of individuals performing cosmetic surgery. Some physicians advertise themselves as specialists without the proper training or certification—a morally, medically, and legally dubious practice. Defenders of cosmetic surgery have noted three reasons why advertising such surgery may be ethically justifiable: (a) medicine should serve human wants and one's appearance may improve an individual's quality of life, (b) patients demanding this surgery are not sick and are more free to "shop around" and find the best deal, and (c) the surgical costs are voluntarily borne by the consumer.[31]

Ideas for Ethical Action

The three interested parties—professional associations, practitioners, and ad agencies—must all work together to insure that advertising by the professions is on the highest ethical plane. We propose a specific suggestion for each of them.

Professional associations must continue to place emphasis on advertising and marketing issues through updated codes and guidelines, enforcement of codes, and conference sessions devoted to the topic. Professional societies in law, accounting, medicine, and dentistry have had to change their posture toward advertising. As one practitioner aptly noted, "The question is thus not whether but how physicians shall be permitted to advertise their services."[32] It is in this spirit that associations should look at their role to assist and guide, but *not discourage,* advertising by their professionals. For example, the Indiana State Bar Association Lawyer Advertising Committee has recommended that the association publish articles outlining changes in rules governing legal advertising, and prepare a brochure to be disseminated to the public so that they can be better protected from false and misleading advertising.[33] Professional organizations need to scrutinize the marketing programs of their members, keep ethical questions in the limelight, and hold sessions that discuss such questions at association meetings. Furthermore, sanctions must be enforced so that violators know they will be prosecuted.

Professionals who employ advertising agencies must hold them to high levels of integrity and continuously monitor the messages they develop. Professionals need to be careful in the type of agency they select to do their advertising. One recommendation would be to monitor other noncompeting professional ads and find out what agency prepares the ads that have high integrity and credibility. Just because an agency contends that they are an "expert" in legal or medical advertising does not make them an acceptable choice. Professionals can further monitor the effect of the ad on clients by asking their impressions of it and doing some informal research.

Advertising agencies and marketing consultants who wish to serve professionals should be sensitive to the unique needs of the professional community. Many agencies and consultants see the growing professional advertising market as an extension of their regular business. This is possibly a mistake. Professionals are different in their orientation. Taking the high road in marketing and advertising is not just an ideal, it is a necessity. Therefore, marketers should develop campaigns and programs that are unquestioned in terms of integrity. Understanding the philosophical perspective of a professional is more than a semantic challenge. For example, the two accountants in scenario 2 might be advised to steer clear of marketing gimmicks like those discussed.

Political Marketing

The marketing of political candidates is a major force in US electoral politics. Since the publication of the best seller, *The Selling of a President 1968,* the effectiveness of marketing in packaging and promoting candidates for local, state, and national office has been widely recognized.[34] The ascendency of marketing in political campaigns specifically has to do with the use of communication techniques outside the control of traditional political parties and includes advertising as a major element.

Old-style politics relied heavily on party controls, use of local contacts, and heavy personal campaigning by the candidate. When market communications counsel was brought into a campaign, it contributed balloons and pamphlets for rallies, yard signs and bumper stickers for campaigners, and "tombstone" newspaper ads such as "Sally Doe/Democrat/State Senator." In contrast, the so-called *new politics* utilizes professional advisors, staged appearances, and mass media (especially television) advertising campaigns with significant production costs, e.g., a TV ad showing the environmentalist candidate tramping through the wilderness in a flannel shirt. During the 1988 presidential campaign, the central role of political "handlers," "sound bites," and "spin control" brought the use of political marketing to new highs or lows, depending on one's perspective.[35] These increasingly popular political marketing techniques are playing a central role in the 1992 Bush–Clinton campaign for the US presidency.

The campaigns of many political candidates use all the accepted marketing techniques and strategies. These include sophisticated information systems featuring extensive opinion polling and monitoring of swing voter segments, product development viewed in terms of the benefits offered to various voting groups, pricing in terms of financial and psychological costs, a distribution strategy that includes personal appearances and media coverage, and finally, promotion—especially television advertising, rather than the "factory gates handshaking" type of personal selling.[36]

The issue is whether the growing use of marketing techniques during political campaigns has led to more ethical problems. Critics believe that the marketing of candidates often presents distorted pictures of the politicians and their opponents. The cries have become louder during campaigns in the 1980s and 1990s, but they surfaced long before that. This portion of the chapter examines the ethical issues involved with the advertising of political candidates and the growing use of unethical and negative advertising. We conclude with several ideas for ethical action that could lead to more ethical marketing of political candidates.

The Supreme Status of Television Advertising

One of the central developments in the "new politics" of campaigning is the heavy reliance on TV advertising. Most major political campaigns, for better or worse, are waged on the television screen. As in the advertising of commercial products, the use of broadcast media (especially television) produces the most intense ethical questions. In fact, the comments shown in Exhibit 9–8 indicate that these questions have been asked for over two decades. Below, we examine some of the reasons for the growth in TV advertising before turning our attention to the arguments against this development.

The Case for TV Advertising[37]

There are three major arguments that can be advanced for televised political advertising. The first, and possibly the strongest, is that it is a form of free speech, subject to First Amendment protection. Political advertising is the contemporary version of the whistle-stop rally, stump speech, or town hall meeting. In a number of legal cases, the Supreme Court has affirmed political advertising as a legitimate form of marketing communication, fundamentally different from commercial speech, and deserving protection.

Second, advertising for political candidates on television is a distinctly contemporary method of campaigning. It is consistent with the strategic approach to the management of campaigns, part of an overall marketing strategy that candi-

---

EXHIBIT 9–8   Comments over the Years on TV and Political Advertising

Year	Quotation
1970	"Television seems particularly useful to the politician who can be charming but lacks ideas. Print is for ideas. Newspapermen write not about people but ideas . . . On television it matters less that he does not have ideas. His personality is what the viewers want to share . . . Style become substance. The medium is the message and the masseur gets the votes."[1]
1979	"The question with President Carter is whether he can do anything well except sell himself as a presidential product. . . . Ever since elections became advertising campaigns such questions have become largely irrelevant. Advertising's first question is, 'How can I sell it?' If the product happens to be demonstrably superior, the ad man is lucky. Most often, as with beer, it's all pretty much the same nowadays, and he has to play tricks on your psyche."[2]
1986	"Television advertising has resulted in the transformation of the electorate into an audience of passive spectators."[3]
1988	"The growing political problem is found where the degeneration of political parties intersects with the rise of television advertising, continuous polling, media consultants and consent-massaging election operatives."[4]
1988	He [Bush] owed it [campaign victory] in important part to his paid handlers, the cosmeticians who had made a mild man look hard and the armorers who had made a genteel man sound like a schoolyard bully; no recent President had been, or been presented as, so completely an artifact of packaging and promotion.[5]

1. J. Mc Ginniss, *The Selling of the President 1968* (New York: Pocket Books, 1970), 29.
2. Russell Baker, "Campaign Ads Outdo the Product," *The Milwaukee Journal* (October 25, 1979), Part 1, 23. Copyright © 1979 by the New York Times Company. Reprinted by permission.
3. Arthur Schlesinger, Jr., "Election Aftermath: Money and Meaning," *The Wall Street Journal* (November 18, 1986), 36.
4. Walter Dean Burnham, "Don't Blame Registration in Low Voter Turnout," *The New York Times* (November 24, 1988). Copyright © 1988 by the New York Times Company. Reprinted by permission.
5. "The Surge That Failed," *Newsweek* (November 21, 1988), 146.

dates and advisors develop to get elected. This argument can be supported by additional observations on television's power and efficiency.

TV is especially important in cultivating a positive candidate image. A media presence must be developed and nurtured by any candidate for office in the 1990s. For example, former President Reagan used television as an effective vehicle, both in his campaigns and during his tenure as president.

Television is the central communication vehicle of our time. TV advertising is the key medium for reaching adult Americans, especially the populous baby boomers, who are the eldest of the current TV generation. US voters are attuned to receiving messages in the thirty second bursts of information popularized by commercials. In fact, the 1992 presidential election made heavy use of sound bites that were packaged for use on the network news programs and appeared to be closer to a commercial than to hard news in content.

Television reaches voters quickly and with impact. A central contention for the growth in TV advertising is that it is an efficient medium for reaching many voters in a short time. Compared to print media, TV advertising speeds the flow of information to voters, thereby promoting an exchange of views concerning issues and candidates. (This point is often debated and we will turn our attention to it later.)

A final argument that can be made for televised political advertising is that it motivates voters. TV advertising is thought to reach and vitalize individuals who otherwise might not participate in the election. The ease with which information can be acquired is thought to help voters in their evaluation of candidates. However, recent voter turnout statistics, which continue to show decline for presidential elections, and the view that television is a "low involvement" medium seem to undermine this position.

The Case Against TV Advertising

One of the strongest arguments against the heavy reliance on television for political advertising is that the emphasis is on image and not issues. Some even argue that it trivializes the complexity of the whole process (see the quotes in Exhibit 9–8). One former National Republican Congressional Committee member cynically remarked, "It is image that sells. The substance is not worth a damn out there."[38] Television is also blamed for reducing some campaigns to single or limited issue affairs because so little information can be transmitted in a typical TV commercial. Although exactly what image-oriented TV advertising does to the flow of information in a political campaign still remains to be determined, the critics continue to strenuously voice this argument.

A second line of reasoning against political ads on television is that they are overly negative, i.e., they largely attack opponents. Critics charge that television places a premium on negative, emotional appeals thereby subverting the ideal of "rational" voter choice. TV advertising grew throughout the 1980s and, many believe, reached its nadir in the 1988 presidential election when a then mild-mannered, Vice-President Bush continuously attacked his opponent. Others contend that the very nature of a thirty second TV spot does not allow for much substantiation of charges against an opponent. Thus, the message can easily be distorted. We return to this point later.

Third, some observers believe that extensive use of TV advertising by candidates creates voter turnoff, which manifests itself in reduced turnout and increased public skepticism toward the electoral process. The cynical voter does not believe that the candidate can be as good (or the opponent as bad) as the TV ad claims. Voter turnout continues to decline in US elections and was especially low in recent senatorial campaigns, many of which were also dominated by negative advertising. A number of experts see reduced voter participation as one of the most significant consequences of the "new politics."[39]

Finally, political advertising on television is viewed by some as *ethically dubious* by its very nature. This is an explicit conclusion to some of the arguments made above as well as a new point. That is, because of its advocacy nature, political advertising is thought to damage the reputation of all political marketers by reinforcing the notion that they are hired guns. And this may harm the candidates' reputations as well. Studies have found that many persons perceive ethical concerns as more substantial when marketing social issues (such as a political candidate) than when marketing commercial goods and services.[40] One of the strongest statements against political advertising was made by David Ogilvy. He is one of the most respected elder statesmen in the advertising field and never allowed his own agency to take on a political candidate as a client. He said, "In a period when television commercials are often the decisive factor in deciding who shall be the next president of the United States, dishonest advertising is as evil as stuffing the ballot box. Perhaps the advertising people who have allowed their talents to be prostituted for this villainy are too naive to understand the complexity of the issues."[41]

Unethical and Negative Political Advertising

Despite the vociferous comments of the critics, we believe that most political advertising is reasonably ethical. It does convey useful information to large masses of voters on a variety of topics. This type of advertising also allows candidates to get their messages across to people who would not take the time to go to a campaign speech or even read a pamphlet containing the candidate's political agenda. In general, advertising that seeks to inform or remind the voter about a candidate's positions should be considered ethical. However, when the message moves to the persuasive end of the continuum (see Chapter 6 on advertising) and appeals to the raw emotions of the voter or attempts to proselytize a particular viewpoint utilizing psychological appeals, the likelihood of its being considered unethical increases.[42] Similarly, one type of persuasive advertising—negative advertising—has received a lion's share of the criticism for being unethical.

Exhibit 9–9 depicts a list of ten "cues" that political marketers can use to determine if an ad is unethical. In marketing, cues are stimuli (e.g., a brand name, a product attribute such as color, etc.) that convey information to the receiver. The

EXHIBIT 9–9   Ten Cues to Judge Potentially Unethical Political Advertising

"**Cue 1:** *The advertisement associates the candidate with a single issue* (e.g., 'Stop Nuclear Power Plants: Vote Johnson'). The rationale for this cue is that for national level elections (Congress, State, and President) the elected post would require the candidate to make decisions on a variety of issues ranging from the domestic budget to foreign policy.

"**Cue 2:** *The advertisement stresses some dimension of candidate integrity without supporting information* (e.g., 'For honesty in government, vote Johnson'). The rationale for this cue is that it seems dubious for a candidate to try to associate himself with laudatory personal characteristics (such as honesty) without providing a scintilla of evidence.

"**Cue 3:** *The advertisement stresses that the candidate's opponent lacks integrity along some dimension without supporting facts* (e.g., 'End Governor Smiths' foolish plunge toward State bankruptcy.'). The rationale for this cue is to call attention to some of the 'mudslinging' that has been the bane of certain recent campaigns.

"**Cue 4:** *The advertisement associates the candidate exclusively with the benefits of his/her party* (e.g., 'Vote Johnson, to enhance the Democratic clout in the Legislature'). The rationale for this cue is that some candidates may attempt to ride the coat-tails of their party rather than elaborate upon the issues.

"**Cue 5:** *The advertisement stereotypes the opponent with the evils of his party unsupported by facts* (e.g., 'Oppose Smith and the disastrous foreign policy his fellow Democrats have wrought'). This is the political party version of Cue 3, i.e., attack the opponent's political affiliation rather than his person. The problem here of course is not in disagreeing with the opposition but rather in not attempting to support the charges made.

"**Cue 6:** *The advertisement utilizes value-laden terminology (without supporting data) in characterizing the candidate's policy* (e.g., 'Johnson, a man for Liberty and Freedom'). The most typical manifestation of this practice involves associating the candidate with general and patriotic terms such as liberty and freedom.

"**Cue 7:** *The advertisement utilizes fear of scare tactics* (e.g., 'Vote Johnson, to stop the rush to nuclear Armegedon'). The rationale for this cue is that fear campaigns can degenerate into a cheap use of emotion which often polarizes the campaign into a single issue 'either-or' debate. Perhaps the classic case of this approach in recent political history at the national level was Lyndon Johnson's 'little girl and the daisy-mushroom cloud' commercial as a commentary on the perceived 'war-monger' tendencies of opponent Barry Goldwater during the 1964 presidential elections.

"**Cue 8:** *The advertisement makes exaggerated claims or promises* (e.g., 'Support Congressman Johnson and balance the Federal budget'). This cue refers to tactics which go beyond political puffery. The rationale for this cue is that while freedom of political speech is guaranteed, the public should be made aware of promises or claims made by the candidate which have no basis in reality.

"**Cue 9:** *The advertisement exceeds the bounds of good taste* (e.g., 'Johnson—he'll stop the butchering of thousands of human beings in public financed

Continued

EXHIBIT 9–9   *Continued*

abortion'). Perhaps this is the hardest of the cues to operationalize and justify since [w]hat constitutes 'good taste' is so subjective. The political slogan, 'Hey, hey LBJ how many babies did you kill today' was largely acceptable to crowds in Madison and Berkeley during the Vietnam era, but probably would have constituted 'bad taste' in Lukenback, Texas.

"Cue 10: *The advertisement panders to racial or ethnic stereotypes* (e.g., 'A vote for Sanchez, is a vote against the real America'). While it might be naive to assume that voters don't use racial, religious, and ethnic prejudices in voting, nevertheless it is ethically incumbant upon the candidates to avoid the use of such labels in their advertising."

Source: Clarke L. Caywood and Gene R. Laczniak, "Unethical Political Advertising: Decision Considerations for Policy and Evaluation." In *Marketing Communications—Theory and Research*, eds. M. J. Houston and R. J. Lutz, 38–39 (Chicago: American Marketing Association, 1985).

list of cues shown here is not comprehensive, but rather illustrative of the types of situations that *may* lead to unethical political ads. We also believe that if only one of the ten cues is present, this does not necessarily mean that the ad is definitely unethical. However, if the elicited cue is a serious violation, such as telling lies about one's opponent, it would be considered unethical. Furthermore, the presence of multiple cues (as in the case of some recent senatorial and presidential campaigns) indicates that the advertising is probably unethical. This listing can be productively utilized by political advisors in evaluating the ethical content of their own promotional campaigns.

Marketers should use these cues as an evaluative tool in the recognition that an increasing presence of such cues across all political advertising could be an indication that the public's fragile sense of a well running democracy is becoming tattered. That is, if growing segments of the public *perceive* elections can be decided on images projected by marketers, as indicated by the presence of these cues in advertising a growing dissatisfaction and alienation from the system may occur. This would result in a disenfranchised citizenship, lower voter turnout, and irreparable damage to the US tradition of participatory democracy.[43] Therefore, we believe that an "ethics check" needs to become an integral part of political marketing in the future.

One type of political advertising that increased in usage during the 1980s is the negative campaign. This type of comparative advertising seeks to evoke negative images of the sponsor's opponent. While comparative advertising in the commercial sector identifies a competitor for the purpose of claiming superiority, negative advertising in the political arena names the competitor "for the purpose of imputing inferiority."[44] The hoped-for outcome is the establishment of the unworthiness of an opponent. Negative advertising is more prevalent in political campaigns than in product promotion. The reason becomes clear when one real-izes that there is much more to gain when there are only two or a few (as in the primaries) competitors in the political marketplace. Thus, sinking or temporarily damaging an opponent can mean victory by default.

Negative advertising is growing in popularity, despite the cries of protests from targeted candidates and social critics. Many candidates, such as Randy Rome in scenario 3 heading the chapter, at least consider using the technique. Some early reports listed the percentage of all advertising that could be catego-rized as negative at about one-third.[45] Two recommendations by individuals who have studied negative advertising are the following: (1) there are serious doubts about the value of negative advertising, especially when used by a minor party candidate; and (2) a candidate is best advised to use negative advertising to attack the opposition only as a last resort.[46]

Ethical questions have arisen both in presidential campaigns and in many campaigns for lower offices. As a partial solution, we now offer the following ideas for political marketers who want to take the "higher road" in campaign-ing.

Ideas for Ethical Action

First, *the code of ethics developed by the American Association of Advertising Agencies, "Political Campaign Advertising and Advertising Agencies," should be followed in all political campaigns.* The code is shown in Exhibit 9–10. It was developed in 1968 and revised in 1982. The AAAA was stimulated to revise the code because the 1982 political campaigns were described as reaching an "all-time low ethical level."[47] It appears that the code was largely ignored in the 1984–1990 elections. Part of the problem is that the code is voluntary and that it pertains only to advertising agencies. Many campaigns have their own advertising staff, rather than hiring an agency, and do not feel compelled to follow these guidelines. If presidential and congressional candidates agreed to follow them, it is quite possible the trickle-down effect would influence state and local elections as well.

Second, *opposing candidates might* voluntarily *(due to First Amendment issues) permit mutually agreed upon neutral judges to preview or review advertising copy according to proposed standards.* This approach should reduce the number and severity of negative ads. If candidate and staff knew that the competitor could appeal the statements made in the ad, much more care would be taken in devel-oping accurate positions. The ideal would be to preview all ads so that flagrant violations would not reach the marketplace. Alternately, a review procedure (similar to the one used by the National Advertising Review Board) after the ad has aired might work almost as well. Even if the much discussed attack ads in the 1988 election had been shown only a few times and then pulled off, the effect would not have been as pronounced as they were, given their heavy use in the campaign. At the national level, trade and media self-regulatory groups could

**EXHIBIT 9–10   AAAA Code of Ethics for Agencies
Involved in Political Campaigns**

American Association of
Advertising Agencies
CODE OF ETHICS
for Political Campaign Advertising

The advertising agency has become an increasingly important factor in the conduct of American political campaigns. Just as the political candidate must observe the highest standards of fairness and morality in his campaign, so must the advertising agency operate under a code that reflects the finest values of our political system rather than any unethical temptations that arise in the heat of battle.

The advertising agency should not represent any candidate who has not signed or who does not observe the Code of Fair Campaign Practices of the Fair Campaign Practices Committee, endorsed by the A.A.A.A.

The agency should not knowingly misrepresent the views or stated record of any candidates nor quote them out of proper context.

The agency should not prepare any material which unfairly or prejudicially exploits the race, creed or national origin of any candidate.

The agency should take care to avoid unsubstantiated charges and accusations, especially those deliberately made too late in the campaign for opposing candidates to answer.

The agency should stand as an independent judge of fair campaign practices, rather than automatically yield to the wishes of the candidate or his authorized representatives.

The agency should not indulge in any practices which might be deceptive or misleading in word, photograph, film or sound.

Adopted by the
Board of Directors of the
American Association of
Advertising Agencies
February 22, 1968
Endorsement Reapproved by
A.A.A.A. Board July 20, 1982
Endorsed by
Fair Campaign Practices Committee
and League of Women Voters.
Endorsement Reapproved
August 12, 1982.

Source: Copyright © American Association of Advertising Agencies. Reprinted by permission.

advise candidates that certain advertising does not meet their ethical standards. At the local level, good-government groups could use this method under various institutional frameworks.

Third, *the media should play a more active role in pointing out unethical campaign advertising and controlling manipulation by campaign advisors.* When candidates concentrate on using ads that merely attack the opponent, the press should ask them why the candidate doesn't have something positive to say. The press could also be more rigorous in its examination and verification of charges made in TV ads. The media must be careful to make sure they are not controlled by the candidates' handlers. Newspeople should be objective in their reporting. They should not let the sound bite dominate the news about a candidate. The staff of the political candidate too often controls the information that reaches the voter through the network news, which is supposed to be an objective source. Consider the following telling comment about the 1988 election: "Somehow, it is acceptable for the reporters to say who is making hay, but not who is making sense. . . . Fear of seeming slanted overcame any interest in reporting the larger truth."[48] The media need to look closely at their procedures to insure they are not helping fuel unethical campaign practices.

The good news is that several respected publications during the 1990s congressional and presidential campaigns followed this approach. For instance, the *Washington Post*, the *Miami Herald*, the *Sacramento Bee* and the *Los Angeles Times* all started new columns devoted to fact-checking and critiquing political commercials. The outcome was to make candidates and their advisors more careful and conscientious. As one observer stated, "I think as the scrutiny gets tougher, the carefulness gets greater."[49] No one, however, was claiming that the use of negative ads had significantly decreased.

Advertising Age carried the following headline in a story about the 1990 campaign: "Let Voters Take Warning: Political Advertising Is a Travesty." One innovative suggestion was to use stars as in the well accepted movie and restaurant rating system to evaluate political ads. *Advertising Age* also went so far as to call for the following disclaimer to be placed on every campaign ad:

> This has been a paid political announcement. This station (or newspaper) is compelled by law to run it, but we have no right and no means to verify its accuracy or truthfulness. We encourage you to seek other sources for more complete information. WARNING: POLITICAL ADVERTISING CAN LEGALLY DISTORT THE TRUTH.[50]

Conclusion

This chapter has covered much territory. The discussed areas of emerging importance—social marketing, marketing by professionals, and political marketing—are significant for the field of marketing. We believe that ethical concerns associated with them will not go away. Rather, marketing practitioners in these areas need to consciously build ethical sensitivity into their decision-making process and examine larger society issues. We believe the directions and ideas provided here can move social, professional, and political marketers to a higher ethical plane.

Appendix 9A

Graduate Management Admission Council Code

Principles of Professional Conduct

Members of the Graduate Management Admission Council have agreed upon a set of principles of professional conduct relating to recruitment and selection of students to which its member schools and their representatives adhere. These principles of professional conduct include the following obligations:

I To adhere to established principles and standards of the organization, including the following:

· *Guide to the Use of GMAT Scores*

· Professional standards as enumerated in this document

· Any other principles or standards mutually agreed to in the future

II To maintain confidentiality of information about individuals which is obtained in the course of the admission process. Access to confidential data must be safeguarded in interactions with

· faculty, administration, and other colleagues within the institution;

· colleagues and peers from other institutions;

· placement officials within the institution and outside corporate recruiters and representatives.

III To pursue the establishment and use of sound selection criteria that promote equitable treatment of applicants.

1. A set of admission policies that relate to the educational objectives of the program must be developed and clearly described.

2. A clearly stated set of admission criteria for each academic program must be developed and applied in a non-discriminatory manner that insures fair and equitable treatment of all applicants.

3. The appropriateness of particular admission criteria must be validated periodically through the use of a statistical study that relates selection criteria to academic success, such as the Validity Study Service.

4. Applicants must be notified of their admission status in a timely manner.

IV To engage in ethical promotion, recruiting, and marketing practices.

1. Insure that all statements and representations about the program are clear, factually accurate, and current.

2. Insure that all recruiting, promotional, and marketing practices are fair, ethical, and equitable.

3. Insure that applicant recruitment is conducted by well-informed individuals who do not misrepresent employment opportunities, corporate recruitment of graduates, program costs, other institutions considered by the applicant, academic requirements to complete the program, or statistical data on the program applicants and enrolled students.

V To maintain ethical relationships with competing programs, including not misrepresenting the nature of the other programs.

VI To pursue personal and professional development in order to provide competent services to relevant constituencies.

1. Member institutions shall provide admission staff members time for professional and educational activities.

2. Admission staff members shall pursue professional and personal development to remain current with new developments and issues pertaining to the use of test scores, and other selection variables; enhance professional skills required in the field of admissions; and contribute to the knowledge of the field by sharing experience and knowledge with colleagues and peers.

Source: Graduate Management Admission Council. Reprinted by permission.

Appendix 9B

American Bar Association Model Rules of Professional Conduct

Rule 7.1   Communications Concerning a Lawyer's Services
A lawyer shall not make a false or misleading communication about the lawyer or the lawyer's services. A communication is false or misleading if it:

a. contains a material misrepresentation of fact or law, or omits a fact necessary to make the statement considered as a whole not materially misleading;

b. is likely to create an unjustified expectation about results the lawyer can achieve, or states or implies that the lawyer can achieve results by means that violate the rules of professional conduct or other law; or

c. compares the lawyer's services with other lawyer's services, unless the comparison can be factually substantiated.

Rule 7.2   Advertising
a. Subject to the requirements of Rule 7.1, a lawyer may advertise services through public media, such as a telephone directory, legal directory, newspaper or other periodical, outdoor, radio or television, or through written communication not involving solicitation as defined in Rule 7.3.

b. A copy or recording of an advertisement or written communication shall be kept for two years after its last dissemination along with a record of when and where it was used.

c. A lawyer shall not give anything of value to a person for recommending the lawyer's services, except that a lawyer may pay the reasonable cost of advertising or written communication permitted by this rule and may pay the usual charges of a not-for-profit lawyer referral service or other legal service organization.

d. Any communication made pursuant to this rule shall include the name of at least one lawyer responsible for its content.

Rule 7.3   Direct Contact with Prospective Clients
A lawyer may not solicit professional employment from a prospective client with whom the lawyer has no family or prior professional relationship, by mail, in-person or otherwise, when a sigificant motive for the lawyer's doing so is the lawyer's pecuniary gain. The term "solicit" includes contact in person, by telephone or telegraph, by letter or other writing, or by other communication directed to a specific recipient, but does not include letters addressed or advertising circulars distributed generally to persons not known to need legal services of the kind provided by the lawyer in a particular matter but who are so situated that they might in general find such services useful.

Appendix 9C

Advertising Guidelines of the Council of
Medical Specialty Societies (CMSS)[1]

According to the guidelines, ethical advertisements can include physician specialty, specialty residency, fellowships, professional society memberships, specialty board certification, and hospitals to which a physician admits patients. It can also state office hours and after-hours coverage, appointment requirements, office location and telephone number, a description of services, ranges of fees for specific services and tests, acceptance of Medicaid, Medicare and credit cards, and languages spoken. The CMSS cautions that this list is illustrative and does not exclude other relevant information consistent with ethical guidelines.

The Council is concerned that some physicians may unintentionally mislead the public by using misunderstood statements. The guidelines include several cases in which advertising is considered false, fraudulent, deceptive, or misleading:

1. When it contains a misrepresentation of fact or omits a material fact necessary to prevent deception or misrepresentation.
2. When it contains a picture or facsimile of a person promising relief or recovery unobtainable by the average patient by the methods described.
3. When it contains a testimonial pertaining to the quality or efficacy of medical care that does not represent the typical experience of other patients.
4. When it is intended or is likely to create false or unjustified expectations of favorable results.
5. When it contains a claim that the physician possesses skills or provides services superior to those of other physicians with similar training, unless such claims can be factually substantiated.
6. When it takes improper advantage of a person's fears, vanity, anxiety, or similar emotions.
7. When it contains a claim that is likely to deceive or mislead the average member of the audience to whom it is directed.
8. When it contains a false or misleading prediction or implication that a satisfactory result or a cure will result from performance of professional services.
9. When it states or implies that a physician is a certified specialist unless he is certified by a board recognized by the American Board of Medical Specialties.
10. When it describes the availability of products or services which are not permitted by law.
11. When it is likely to attract patients by the use of exaggerated claims.

[1]Source: "CMSS Develops Guidelines for Physician Advertising," *Annals of Emergency Medicine* (December 1981), 100.

12. When it is not identified as a paid advertisement or solicitation, unless it is apparent from the context that is a paid announcement or advertisement.
13. When it contains a statement of the fees charged for specific professional services but fails to indicate whether additional fees may be incurred for related professional services which may also be required.

Endnotes

1. Philip Kotler and Sidney J. Levy, "Broadening the Concept of Marketing," *Journal of Marketing* (January 1969), 10–15 and Philip Kotler and Gerald Zaltman, "Social Marketing: An Approach to Planned Social Change" *Journal of Marketing* (July 1971), 3–12.

2. Richard T. De George, *Business Ethics*, 2nd ed. (New York: Macmillan, 1986).

3. This section is adapted from Patrick E. Murphy and Paul N. Bloom, "Ethical Issues in Social Marketing." In *Social Marketing*, ed. S. Fine, 68–78 (Boston: Allyn & Bacon, 1990).

4. Philip Kotler, "The Elements of Social Action." In *Processes and Phenomena of Social Change*, ed. G. Zaltman, 169–190 (New York: John Wiley, 1973).

5. Patrick E. Murphy, Gene R. Laczniak, and Robert F. Lusch, "Ethical Guidelines for Business and Social Marketing," *Journal of the Academy of Marketing Science* (Summer 1978), 195–205.

6. Gene R. Laczniak, Robert F. Lusch, and Patrick E. Murphy, "Social Marketing: Its Ethical Dimension," *Journal of Marketing* (Spring 1979), 29–38 and Robert F. Lusch, Gene R. Laczniak, and Patrick E. Murphy, "The 'Ethics of Social Ideas' versus the 'Ethics of Marketing Social Ideas.' " *Journal of Consumer Affairs* (Summer 1980), 156–164.

7. Seymour H. Fine, "Social and Nonprofit Marketing: Some Trends and Issues." In *Advances in Nonprofit Marketing*, 2nd ed., ed. R. Belk, 71–98 (Greenwich, CT: JAI Press, 1987). See also Patrick E. Murphy, "Ethical Issues Facing Hospitals in Their Advertising," in *Ethical Issues in Healthcare Marketing* (St. Louis: The Catholic Health Association, 1989), 61–77.

8. Seymour H. Fine, "The Starving Baby Appeal." In Fine, 154–159 (see note 3 above).

9. P. Rajan Varadarjan and Anil Menon, "Cause-Related Marketing: A Coalignment of Marketing Strategy and Corporate Philanthropy," *Journal of Marketing* (July 1988), 59–74.

10. Patricia Caesar, "Cause-Related Marketing: The New Face of Corporate Philanthropy," *Business & Society Review* (Fall 1986), 15–19.

11. Andrew Abbott, "Professional Ethics," *American Journal of Sociology* 88 (1983), 855–885.

12. "Is Dignity Important in Legal Advertising?" *ABA Journal* (August 1, 1987), A1 and A2.

13. Robert E. Hite and Cynthia Fraser, "Meta-Analyses of Attitudes toward Advertising by Professionals," *Journal of Marketing* (July 1988), 95–105.

14. For a summary of the major points in the *Virginia Board of Pharmacy* and *Bates* cases, see Burton M. Leiser, "Professional Advertising: Price Fixing and Professional Dignity versus the Public's Right to a Free Market," *Journal of Business and Professional Ethics* (Spring/Summer 1984), 93–110.

15. See note 12 above.

16. Christine Dugas, "Marketing: The Prescription for Professional Practices?" *Ad Forum* (February 1983), 42–44.

17. Ruth Macklin, "Commentary on Leiser," *Journal of Business and Professional Ethics* (Spring/Summer 1984), 114.

18. Irwin Braun and Marilyn Braun, "Following a Decade of Advertising: Professionals Still Face Restraints," *Marketing News* (August 14, 1987), 21.

19. See note 18 above.

20. For an elaboration on this argument and others both for and against advertising by professionals in the United States and United Kingdom, see David C. Stafford, "Advertising in the Professions," *International Journal of Advertising* 7 (1988), 189–220; and in Canada, see Benjamin D. Singer, "Who Should Advertise? Ethical Issues for Professionals," in *Advertising & Society* (Don Mills, Ontario: Addison–Wesley Limited, 1986), 172–184.

21. William J. Walsh, "CPAs and Advertising: Another Voice," *Journal of Accountancy* (November 1986), 178–180.

22. Larry Stewart, "Advertising: The Need for a Strong ATLA Policy," *ATLA Advocate*, (July 1989), 2, 4.

23. See note 18 above.

24. "What Forms of Advertising Are Permissible under the Ethics Code?" *Journal of Accountancy* (November 1986), 98–99.

25. "Major CPA Firms Accused of Violations of Professional Conduct," *The Practical Accountant*, (April 1986), 43–44.

26. Sterling North, "Lawyers in the Age of Advertising," *New England Business* (August 3, 1987), 22–25.

27. See note 26 above.

28. Frederick C. Moss, "The Ethics of Law Practice Marketing," *Notre Dame Law Review* 61 (1986), 601–696.

29. Sherman Folland, R. Parameswaran, and John Darling, "On the Nature of Physicians' Opposition to Advertising," *Journal of Advertising* 18 (1989), 4–12 and see note 16 above.

30. See note 29 above, p. 4.

31. E. Haavi Morreim, "A Moral Examination of Medical Advertising," *Business & Society Review* (Winter 1988), 4–6.

32. See note 31 above, p. 6.

33. "Lawyer Advertising—Marketing, Professionalism, the Future," *Res Gestae* (August 1988), 59–64.

34. Joe McGinniss, *The Selling of the President 1968* (New York: Pocket Books, 1970).

35. Louis M. Seagull, "A Critical Review of the Broadened Concept of Marketing: The Case of Political Marketing." Paper presented at the fourteenth Annual Macromarketing Seminar, Toledo, Ohio, August 1989.

36. Clarke L. Caywood and Gene R. Laczniak, "The Marketing of Political Candidates: Current Tactics and Future Strategies." In Fine, 233–257 (see note 3 above) and Phillip B. Niffenegger, "Strategies for Success from the Political Marketers," *Journal of Consumer Marketing* (Winter 1989), 45–51.

37. The next two sections are excerpted from Gene R. Laczniak and Clarke L. Caywood, "The Case For and Against Televised Political Advertising: Implications for Research and Public Policy," *Journal of Public Policy & Marketing* 6 (1987), 16–32.

38. Margaret K. Latimer, "Political Advertising for Federal and State Elections: Images or Substance?" *Journalism Quarterly* (Winter 1985), 861–868.

39. Walter Dean Burnham, "The Turnout Problem." In *Elections American Style*, ed. James A. Reichley, 97–133 (Washington, DC: The Brookings Institution).

40. Gene R. Laczniak, Robert F. Lusch, and William A. Strang, "Ethical Marketing: Perceptions of Economic Goods and Social Programs," *Journal of Macromarketing* (Spring 1981), 49–57.

41. David Ogilvy, *Ogilvy on Advertising* (New York: Vintage Books, 1983), 213.

42. Clarke L. Caywood and Gene R. Laczniak, "Unethical Political Advertising: Decision Considerations for Policy and Evaluation." In *Marketing Communications—Theory and Research*, eds. M. J. Houston and R. J. Lutz, 37–41 (Chicago: American Marketing Association, 1985).

43. See note 42 above, p. 39.

44. Sharyne Merritt, "Negative Political Advertising: Some Empirical Findings," *Journal of Advertising* 13 (1984), 3: 27.

45. Larry J. Sabato, *The Rise of Poltical Consultants* (New York: Basic Books, 1981).

46. See notes 36 and 44 above.

47. "4A's Len Matthews Calls for Ethics in Political Advertising," *Broadcasting* (December 19, 1983), 84.

48. Jonathan Alter, "How the Media Blew It," *Newseek* (November 21, 1988), 24.

49. Joanne Lipman, "Newspapers Dissect Negative Political Ads," *The Wall Street Journal* (July 27, 1990), B3.

50. Bob Garfield, "Let Voters Take Warning: Political Advertising in This Country Is a Travesty," *Advertising Age* (November 5, 1990), 29.

Chapter 10

Implementing and Auditing Marketing Ethics

Scenario 1

Jan Jones, vice president of marketing for Ommen Company, received word from the controller that the expense accounts of the firm's marketing executives appeared to be padded with apparently unnecessary expenses. Jan called for her executive assistant and asked him to locate the company's code of ethics. **"Don't we have a written, precise policy that prohibits this type of behavior?"** she asked.

Scenario 2

Fred Miller, CEO of Ace Widgets, had just returned from his thirtieth class reunion at St. Isadore's College. During the Monday meeting with his executive committee, he spoke glowingly of an ethics seminar he attended at the reunion. "I think we need to sensitize our employees more to the ethical issues they face." He turned to Jim Stone, the marketing director, and said, "why don't we start with our sales force since they are our largest employee group. **Could you get back to me in a couple weeks with an outline of an ethics program for our salespeople?"**

Scenario 3

Rod Taylor had just taken over as international marketing manager for the Thunderbird Corporation. He felt guidelines should be developed to standardize procurement and marketing policies, wherever possible. Rod mentioned to Beth Smith, his student intern, "It would be a good idea to come up with a series of questions that we might use to insure that our company is treating its suppliers and customers fairly and similarly throughout the world." **He assigned Beth the task of finding out if other companies employed such procedures.**

These scenarios illustrate how ethics may be *implemented* in the day to day operations of an organization. We believe marketing managers working in the areas examined previously (product, distribution, advertising, international, etc.) need guidance from their firm to deal with ethically troublesome issues. *Corporate codes, ethics training programs,* and an *ethical questions checklist,* all alluded to above, can provide that direction. The crucial question addressed here is: how can companies incorporate the ethical dimension into their marketing decision making?

In this chapter we outline several avenues to instill ethical values into marketing organizations. First, we suggest formal corporate policies, such as ethics statements (i.e., codes or credos) and ethics programs for managers and employees. These structural mechanisms can enhance ethical decision-making. We then encourage the development of a corporate culture that places a premium on ethical action. This is a further approach to implementing ethics in businesses. Third, we envision that all these steps would include an audit involving "check" questions to assure routine considerations of ethical issues. Finally, we provide several ideas for ethical action and close with comments to spur future thinking about ethics in marketing.

Organizing for Marketing Ethics Implementation

Implementing marketing ethics entails both establishing policies that promote ethical decisions *and* creating a corporate culture conducive to ethical behavior. Managers should then follow through to insure these policies are carried out and an ethical culture is nurtured.[1] In practice, enacting ethical marketing policies includes several responsibilities in managing product, price, distribution, and promotion. Exhibit 10–1 presents a summary of these elements. We first turn to the issue of formal corporate policies and their role in improving organizational ethics.

Formal Corporate Policies

Companies that are models of sustaining concern for marketing ethics have instituted a number of formal policies ensuring that this topic is regularly discussed. The most prevalent approach is a corporate ethics statement. Such statements are important because they are public manifestations of an organization's commitment to ethics. Two possible types of ethics statements are commonly used.

Corporate Credos
The first is a corporate credo—a one-page (or less) document that lists values and responsibilities to stakeholders. Because of its brevity, a credo works best in firms

EXHIBIT 10–1   Implementing Marketing Ethics

Organizing For Ethical Marketing Policies

Structure:
The Formal Organization

Corporate Credos

Corporate Codes
  Communicated
  Specific
  Pertinent
  Enforced
  Revised

Ethics Training Programs

Culture:
The Informal Organization

Open and Candid

Family Values

Principles

Atmosphere/Ambience

- -

Enacting Ethical Marketing Policies

Implementation
Responsibilities

Leadership

Delegation

Communication

Motivation

Implementation
Tasks

Product Alteration

Price Negotiation

Place Determination

Promotion Presentation

Source: Adapted from Patrick E. Murphy, "Implementing Business Ethics," *Journal of Business Ethics* (December 1988), 908. Copyright © 1988 Kluwer Academic Publishers. Reprinted by permission.

with a cohesive corporate culture where a spirit of uninhibited communication exists. This approach may be less useful for multinational or recently merged companies. In addition to the acclaimed Johnson & Johnson credo (see Exhibit 1–6), several other exemplary credos exist.

The oldest corporate credo is "The Penney Idea" of J. C. Penney Company. It was originated in 1913 and is shown in Exhibit 10–2. In fact, the initial corporate name that founder J. C. Penney selected for his retail outlets was the "Golden Rule Stores." Why? He believed strongly that the application of and adherence to the Golden Rule concept should pervade his company's business decisions. The

---

EXHIBIT 10–2   The Penney Idea[1] (Adopted in 1913)

1. To serve the public, as nearly as we can, to its complete satisfaction.
2. To expect for the service we render a fair remuneration and not all the profit the traffic will bear.
3. To do all in our power to pack the customer's dollar full of value, quality, and satisfaction.
4. To continue to train ourselves and our associates so that the service we give will be more and more intelligently performed.
5. To improve constantly the human factor in our business.
6. To reward men and women in our organization through participation in what the business produces.
7. To test our every policy, method, and act in this wise: "Does it square with what is right and just?"

A former CEO of Penney's, Donald V. Siebert, made the following observations about the importance of ethics.[2]

I believe that the more energy corporate America devotes to examining its ethical standards, the freer executives will be to make the tough decisions that reflect the longer view and the stronger they will be to resist questionable actions for a quick fix. As a result, their corporate conduct will more consistently reflect their company's ethical standards. . . .

The vast majority of today's executives are ethical and honest. Yet, sometimes we can become so occupied with fretting over our mathematical models, sales projections and quarterly earning statements that it is difficult to keep in mind one of the most basic truths of successful business—in the long run, the best business decision is that which is founded on the most ethical judgments.

---

1. Reprinted by permission of J. C. Penney Company, Inc.
2. Quoted in "Corporate Ethics Makes Cents," *The Milwaukee Journal* (January 14, 1984), Section 1, 8. Reprinted by permission.

Penney Idea principles still serve as guideposts for company operations.[2] A more recent example involves Champion International. This company reports that its seven-year-old credo helped guide it through a recent restructuring. The firm decided to honor the credo's policy of commitment to employees and let no one go.[3] (See Appendix 10A for a stakeholder-focused corporate credo developed by Security Pacific.)

Codes of Ethics

Codes of conduct (or ethics) are a second, and more prevalent, type of ethics statement. Almost half of all firms and 90 percent of Fortune 500 companies have a formal ethics code.[4] These address such issues as conflicts of interest, treatment of competitors, privacy, gift-giving, and political contributions. According to a survey of executives, codes of conduct are perceived as *the* most effective way to encourage ethical corporate behavior.[5] However, many observers believe codes are really only public-relations documents—nothing more than "motherhood and apple pie statements" that fail to address significant managerial issues.[6]

We think that codes are useful but need to be tailored to critical marketing functions. That is, codes should go beyond platitudes and delve into substantive marketing issues facing the particular firm. Some companies have a consumer relations section in their codes, but few have sections on marketing. IBM is an exception. Its "Business Conduct Guidelines" concentrates primarily on selling issues, since at its core, IBM is a marketing and sales organization. The six major sections of the code detail the type of activities IBM expects of its sales representatives. For example, the code prohibits making misrepresentations, disparaging competitors, and using IBM's size for unfair advantage.[7]

For companies contemplating a marketing code of conduct, we offer the following suggestions.[8] (Another list of considerations in developing an effective code is shown in Exhibit 10–3.) Any marketing code of ethics should be:

Communicated. To be understood and appreciated, the code should be publicized to the entire firm. New employees are usually asked to read and sign off on the code during their orientation. However, the code is quickly forgotten if it is never mentioned again. Firms should regularly communicate with marketing personnel about the code and promote it in departmental memos and meetings. Some companies, including Michigan National Bank, require that employees read

---

EXHIBIT 10–3 Improving the Usefulness of Codes

"First, codes should be written in a manner designed to give the reasons for each order. In some areas it probably is necessary to use negative injunctions which are still the pithiest way of imparting moral judgments.

"Second, codes need beginnings and perhaps conclusions which try to secure support of the corporation or bureau team in a cooperative effort to keep the organization's actions strictly "above board."

"Third, codes would be more welcome if they included provisions which recognize the responsibilities of management as well as the responsibilities of employees. Too many codes are devoted soley to the employees' responsibilities to the company.

"Fourth, as codes become better means of ethical education, they should be publicized more, especially in areas near company factories or administrative headquarters; the interested public will learn to appreciate the organization more.

"Fifth, the usefulness of the code depends on boards of directors and top management who want to keep their organizations ethical. If the board chairman or chief executive officer distributes the code with a note of strong endorsement, the results will be better."

Source: George C. S. Benson, "Codes of Ethics," *Journal of Business Ethics* (May 1989), 317–318. Copyright 1989 Kluwer Academic Publishers. Reprinted by permission.

and affirm their commitment to the code on an annual basis. In addition to being communicated internally, the code should also be disseminated *publicly* to a firm's stakeholders. We are aware of several codes (including those of large firms) that are exclusively internal documents. If the code is worth having, it should be made widely available, or it gives the impression that the firm has something to hide.

Specific.   To avoid vagueness, the code should offer (wherever possible) detailed guidance to sales and marketing executives. The code should not use words such as "nominal," "token," or "modest value" when dealing with the giving and receiving of gifts. For example, Waste Management Company tells employees that gifts "should not exceed $100 in aggregate annual value," and Donnelly Mirrors' code says, "If you can't eat it, drink it or use it up in one day, don't give it or anything else of greater value." See also Security Pacific's guidance on gifts in Appendix 10A.

Pertinent.   To have maximum effectiveness, the code should deal with issues central to the industry for which the code is written. Each organization has certain areas that are particularly susceptible to ethical abuse, and these concerns are ones on which the code should focus. For instance, toy companies must make special provisions for protecting the safety of children. Mail order firms should address their return policies and how they handle merchandise damaged in shipping. Companies that spend millions of dollars on promotion and advertising need to detail their advertising philosophy, as well as what program vehicles or media they will or will not use.

Enforced.   To gain the respect of managers and their subordinates, the code of marketing conduct must be enforced. Sanctions should be specified and punishments meted out. Particular sanctions for given violations depends on their severity. For example, padding an expense account for the first time may result in a salesperson losing commissions temporarily, while a manager who induces employees to use bait-and-switch tactics might be dismissed. Specifically, Baxter's (formerly Baxter Travenol) code states that violators' employment will be terminated. Exhibit 10–4 shows an excellent list of questions that companies should answer in developing enforcement policies. In one survey of marketing managers, an alarming 30 percent of the respondents stated that their firm had *no* sanctions in place to deal with ethical code violations.[9]

Revised.   To remain current, credos and codes should be revised periodically. They need to be living documents to reflect changing worldwide conditions, community standards, and evolving organizational policies. For example, Caterpillar has revised its code four times since instituting it in 1974. Johnson & Johnson held a series of meetings in the late 1970s to challenge the company corporate credo. What emerged from the meetings was that the document in fact

---

EXHIBIT 10–4   Questions for Proper Enforcement of Ethics Codes

Questions a company needs to address concerning compliance monitoring and enforcement of the code include the following:

Who will have ultimate responsibility for enforcing the code?

By whom may alleged violations be brought to the attention of the person or committee responsible for enforcement?

What provisions will the company make to protect the confidentiality of employees who report apparent misconduct?

By what procedures will the allegations be evaluated and resolved?

What penalties will apply to violations of the code?

What procedure will there be, if any, for appealing the decisions, and before whom would such an appeal be made?

What additional "due process" will be afforded those against whom allegations have been made?

Source: Ethics Resource Center, *Creating a Workable Company Code of Ethics* (1990).

functioned as intended. A slightly reworded, but substantially unchanged, credo was re-introduced in 1979.[10]

Ethics Training

Another ethics-enhancing corporate policy involves the development of ethics training programs (see Exhibit 10–1). They can provide more specific direction than credos or codes. Such programs can range from a modest effort, such as having a speaker or panel at a dealer meeting or corporate conference, to a day-long, "in-house" conference. Polaroid has employed this more robust approach.[11] A few companies have gone even further in assisting their managers through a formalized ethics education program. For instance, a market research conference sponsored by the Drackett Company (a Bristol Myers subsidiary) included an ethics module. Participants at the meeting submitted, in advance, their responses to sixteen ethical scenarios. During the meeting, small groups discussed the three situations that had generated the greatest disagreement. According to the manager who led this exercise, it was enthusiastically received. Many of the researchers were surprised by their colleagues' ethical judgments and learned about analyzing these issues from the interchange.

Chemical Bank and McDonnell Douglas are two other firms that have engaged in extensive corporate-wide ethics training. Chemical's innovative program, "Decision Making and Corporate Values" is a two-day, off-site, seminar aimed at the vice-presidential level. Its purpose is "to encourage Chemical's employees to weigh the ethical or value dimensions of the decisions they make and to provide them with analytic tools to do that." Discussion centers around ethically charged cases such as credit approval, branch closings, foreign loans, and insider trading—all developed from interviews with Chemical's own person-nel.[12] We would suggest an approach like this one for Ace Widgets' sales force discussed in scenario 2 at the beginning of this chapter.

The McDonnell Douglas program involved distributing three ethics books to all employees of the company. Their revised code and other material followed the five previously mentioned points for a well constructed code. The firm also instituted a company-wide ethics training program for both white and blue collar employees. It was supervised by a seven person ethics committee.[13] Even though McDonnell Douglas undertook this extensive ethics program, some of its executives were subsequently implicated in a defense contractor scandal.

Thus, there are no guarantees that formal corporate policies will institution-alize ethics within a firm and its marketing department. Formal efforts alone—printed policies and training—do not by themselves ensure a corporate environment that both encourages ethical conduct *and* discourages misdeeds. To achieve that, we need to look at the informal aspects of corporate life—culture, values, and even managerial style. Additionally, policies and structures that frame issues such as compensation and employee control will shape the "charac-ter" of a company, its managers, employees, and dealers. Thus, we now turn to corporate elements that may provide more continual and longer lasting guidance.

Corporate Culture: The Informal Organization

Corporate culture can be a pervasive informal policy for instilling better ethics in a company. It is one of the major focal points of organizational analysis in recent times. Although many definitions of corporate culture exist, one offered in the marketing literature seems to capture it well.

> Corporate culture is the pattern of shared values and beliefs that help indi-viduals understand organizational functioning and thus provide them norms for behavior in the organization.[14]

Several organizational analysts have explicitly linked corporate culture with eth-ics, in the sense that cohesive and strong cultures tend to reinforce ethical be-havior.[15] Open communication, a sense of organizational values and their relationship to family values are hallmarks of such ethically oriented cultures. It is the role of the CEO and top marketing executives to insure that such character-istics exist.

A major dimension of corporate culture refers to organizational *values*. They are universally held core attitudes of the firm's members. Exhibit 10–5 lists Bechtel Corporation's values and refers to them as the "bedrock of our corporate culture." One logical way to examine a corporation's values is to liken the obliga-tions of members of an organization to familial ones.[16] Exhibit 10–6 shows a comparison of typical family values with possible organizational values. These two sets of values are strikingly similar. This analogy may ease the understanding

EXHIBIT 10–5   Bechtel's Goals and Values

Bechtel's Goals

Goals provide the objectives which we strive to meet in order for the business to compete successfully, reward our people, and recognize their contributions.

Maintain our reputation for excellence:

- Be the best at what we do.
- Be entrepreneurial and encourage innovation.
- Stay at the leading edge of computer/automation/telecommunication applications to our business.
- Set the standard for quality of performance in our industry.
- Maintain our reputation for providing a full range of services at a cost appropriate to value.
- Continue upgrading our capabilities and improving our performance and responsiveness.

Adapt to a changing marketplace:

- Develop a consistently profitable fixed price capability.
- Increase our competitiveness in ideas and costs.
- Simplify and reduce our internal controls and procedures.
- Improve our flexibility and quickness in response to changing market conditions and new opportunities.

Improve our marketing skills and effectiveness:

- Improve effectiveness of our approach to domestic and international business, including regional strategies that positively address the issue of nationalism.
- Develop and apply new technologies, new services and develop new business lines to meet client needs and create market opportunities.

Build teamwork and enhance job fulfillment with our employees:

- Improve our employee relations and internal communications, emphasize leadership and create a friendly, open work environment.
- Provide interesting, challenging and rewarding work for our people that will fully utilize their potential.
- Improve mutual trust and confidence and develop the spirit of teamwork.
- Provide enhanced training and career development opportunities.

Bechtel's Values

Values are the bedrock of our corporate culture, and reflect the organization's personality characteristics. They represent our corporate character reflecting the attitude of all the people of Bechtel.

Bechtel strives to perform our work in a manner which is:

- Responsive to our clients
- Quality and value minded
- Performance oriented

Bechtel people should continue to be:

- Ethical, reliable and fair
- Innovative, competitive, versatile and self-starting
- Professional, dedicated and loyal

Our methods of performing our work should encourage:

- Sensitivity to the needs and aspirations of our people
- Teamwork
- Mutual trust
- An open and communicative environment
- Accountability
- Flexibility

Source: Management Memo from Steve Bechtel, Jr., Vol. 19, No. 7, (November 20, 1987).

EXHIBIT 10–6   A Comparison of Organizational with Family Values

Basic Family Values	*Basic Organization Values*
Caring for nuclear family members (i.e., husband, wife, children if any)	→ Caring for organizational family (i.e., employees, management, stockholders)
Caring for close relatives (e.g., grandparents, aunts, uncles)	→ Caring for integral publics (e.g. customers, creditors)
Being a helpful and friendly neighbor	→ Being a helpful and friendly corporate neighbor
Obeying the law	→ Obeying the law
Being a "good" citizen in the community	→ Being a "good" citizen in the community, the nation, and the world
A portion of the family budget is allocated for philanthropic purposes	→ A portion of the organizations budget is allocated for philanthropic purposes
Protecting and caring for the family's home and land	→ Protecting and caring for the physical environment on which the organization has an impact

Source: Donald P. Robin and R. Eric Reidenbach, "Social Responsibility, Ethics and Marketing Strategy: Closing the Gap between Concept and Application," *Journal of Marketing* (January 1987), 51. Reprinted by permission of the American Marketing Association.

---

and integration of ethics into a familial management style. One writer appropriately stated: "As in family life, corporate ethics begins at home, and a corporation that emphasizes ethical behavior within the organization is probably going to insist on ethical behavior and a positive impact on the outside community as well." [17] There are limits to this metaphor, however. For example, an organization will necessarily terminate members for breaching policies and require documented expense reports.

Other components of corporate culture relate to the *principles* espoused by firms. Principles refer to the articulation of the atmosphere and ambience of a company. For example, Dow Corning and Champion International have a statement of corporate principles. However, for most firms the ethical principles are implicit, i.e., the values have become part of the culture rather than having been included in formal corporate policies. Exhibit 10–7 discusses four principles often followed by firms that place a high value on ethics.

It is also important to note that managers can suffer from "moral stress" if ethical issues are never discussed in their firm. To alleviate this problem, a two-pronged approach was proposed: "articulation and communication of an explicit managerial ideology" and the "facilitation of discussions and agreements on moral questions among all organization members."[18] The first component—*communication about ethics*—is achieved by removing ambiguity about the firm's ethical priorities; that is, top management has the responsibility to let its manag-

---

EXHIBIT 10–7   Principles for the High-Ethics Firm

After studying twenty-five firms that are recognized for both their economic and ethical performance, Mark Pastin proposed the following four principles for the high-ethics firm. They are the following:

Principle 1. High-ethics firms are at ease interacting with diverse internal and external stakeholder groups. The ground rules of these firms make the good of these stakeholder groups part of the firm's own good.

Principle 2. High-ethics firms are obsessed with fairness. Their ground rules emphasize that the other person's interests count as much as their own.

Principle 3. In high-ethics firms, responsibility is individual rather than collective, with individuals assuming personal responsibility for actions of the firm. These firms' ground rules mandate that individuals are responsible to themselves.

Principle 4. The high-ethics firm sees its activities in terms of a purpose. This purpose is a way of operating that members of the firm value. And purpose ties the firm to its environment.

Source: Mark Pastin, *The Hard Problems of Management: Gaining the Ethics Edge* (San Francisco: Jossey-Bass, 1986), 221–225.

ers and employees know exactly where they stand on key ethical issues, such as dealing with suppliers and promotional policies. The second point—*discussion of ethics*—is accomplished by examining specific moral questions during employee training sessions. Such exchanges may ultimately lead to a consensus on what constitutes morally appropriate behavior for particular situations. The first communication component is prescriptive and directive, while the second is participative and nondirective; yet they are equally important.

A candid and ethical corporate culture exists when communication flows freely within the organization. In such a culture, managers are open to questions by subordinates; two way communications must be encouraged and supported. One writer persuasively argued for a candid corporate culture.

> The perceived threat or fear of embarrassment must be removed and replaced by the belief that sincerity and forthright communication will be encouraged and rewarded. Once this belief is accepted by members of an organization the new norms of behavior will be reinforced and a candid culture will be created.[19]

Corporate culture is an elusive concept. In its broadest sense, culture refers to the "corporate air one breathes." And it is important to recognize that organizational culture and ethics are very closely related. Pressures encouraging unethical behavior by marketing employees can often be explained by examining the corporate culture. For example, certain appliance superstores place their employees in an atmosphere of high-pressure selling aimed at consumers and pit them against fellow salespeople; sometimes commissions are based on sales of service contracts of dubious value. Yet, these retailers wonder why morale is low and customers are dissatisfied. On the other hand, Cummins Engine of Indiana has a long-standing culture of commitment to employees in terms of outplacement and training. Even though its financial performance has been uneven in recent years, commitment to the firm has remained high. This example illustrates that marketing managers who want ethics to be a central theme of their organization must make the long-term commitment to instituting and reinforcing a culture where this objective, ethical concern, is a reality.

Enacting Ethical Marketing Policies

Exhibit 10–1 also shows the two components of actually performing marketing ethics implementation. It is not enough to have a structure and culture that support ethical decision-making. These organizational dimensions must be combined with implementation responsibilities and tasks, so that managers act ethically when they carry out marketing strategies.[20]

Implementation Responsibilities

Although four managerial responsibilities are listed in Exhibit 10–1, the overarching one in establishing ethical concern is *executive leadership*. There is truth to the view that American corporations are often over-managed and under-led. Leadership is important in all aspects of the business, but critical in the ethics area. Examinations of CEO characteristics typically list integrity as an indispensible ingredient.[21] For instance, top management at Johnson & Johnson had managers evaluate their corporate credo—and the swift product recall and sensitive reaction to the infamous Tylenol poisonings are often credited to these efforts. Basically, the steps taken by Johnson & Johnson reaffirmed the company's longstanding commitment to ethical business practice. Several additional illustrations are provided in the Business Roundtable publication on exemplary corporate ethics programs (recall Exhibit 1–2). The introduction to the book highlighting these programs made a cogent observation on the importance of leadership.

> Effective leadership by the management of corporations is the best way to support and advance the cause of private enterprise. Basic to such leadership is the insight that corporate ethics is a strategic key to survival and profitability in this era of fierce competitiveness in a global economy.[22]

Delegation is a second necessary managerial responsibility and it follows from leadership. To effect ethical sensitivity, middle and lower level marketing managers must not be placed in difficult ethical situations where their ethical responsibilities are unclear. Ethical guidance, delegated "down the line," is critical. A way to describe delegation is through trust. See Exhibit 10–8 about trust at Johnson & Johnson. Just as integrity is integral for leadership, trust seems inherent in effective delegation.

Delegation can also have a negative interpretation. Statements such as "I don't care how you do it, just meet or beat your quota," or "Ship more to that customer this month than you did last," or "Find a way to make that person quit" often give subordinates the impression that any tactics can be used to reach organizational objectives. For example, a sales manager who continually raises the quota or reduces territory size of a top performing salesperson puts increasing pressure on the individual to engage in unethical activities like lavish gift-giving or overselling to accomplish the sales objective. If the delegation responsibility is to be dispatched properly, executives must be more explicit about what practices are acceptable.

Communication is a third managerial characteristic if ethical marketing policies are to be implemented effectively. For communication to occur, the watchword should be openness between and among marketing managers and their subordinates. This communication can occur "formally" in many ways, including through the ethics code as well as through ethics seminars and training programs. For example, new employees of many companies are asked to read, reflect upon, and then sign the ethics code upon their employment. In many instances, however, little communication follows the initial exposure. To overcome this potential problem, Caterpillar requires its managers to report annually about the implementation of the code within their division or department. As noted previously, Michigan National Bank stipulates that employees affirm their compliance with the ethics code every year. This communication is most effective if combined with concrete actions by top marketing managers about ethics.

"Informal" communication is also a potentially effective implementation mechanism. The grapevine can disseminate information that formal channels cannot. For instance, the fact a couple of salespersons lost a commission for

---

EXHIBIT 10–8   Decentralization and Trust at Johnson & Johnson

"Decentralization also implies certain ethical values which are fundamental to the Credo. The greatest of these is trust: trust in an individual manager's ability to make the right decisions from both a business and moral point of view. . . .

"The real issue, says [former CEO James] Burke, is not ethics. It is trust. . . .

"'But the overriding value,' according to Burke, 'is that we all make sure that you (the consumer) can trust that we are going to deliver on what we say, package by package.'"

Source: Laura Nash, "Johnson & Johnson's Credo," in J. Keogh, *Corporate Ethics: A Prime Business Asset* (New York: Business Roundtable, 1988), 80, 92, 93.

padding their expense account may not lend itself to discussion in the company newsletter. However, "word" can get out through informal channels and thereby influence future behavior. This might be a possible technique to deal with scenario 1 heading this chapter.

The last, but certainly not the least important managerial responsibility for successful ethics implementation, is *motivation*. If companies are to be successful in enacting ethical marketing policies, individuals must be rewarded for doing things "right" and penalized for doing them "wrong." This means that higher level executives must look closely at how performance is measured. There are many illustrations of recognizing and promoting excellent (e.g., ethical) behavior in the book *In Search of Excellence*. For instance, managers at Hewlett–Packard and Tupperware provide positive reinforcement for ethical actions.[23]

The negative side of motivation—*punishment*—should also not be ignored. For example, marketing personnel who engage in exorbitant entertainment of clients or who informally practice racial or sexual discrimination should be reprimanded (or fired) for these activities. One partial explanation of the Wall Street insider trading scandals was that top managers did not look closely at the huge sums their associates were earning, because they were generating large profits for the firm. How did such commissions materialize? Unfortunately in many cases, we now know the answer. Employees are motivated by the expectations communicated by higher level executives. If generating client activity, and hence commissions, is the sole object, ethical issues will receive only limited consideration.

Implementation Tasks

The implementation of ethics in marketing ultimately requires relating ethical policies to specific functional areas (e.g., product, price, distribution, and promotion). Because marketing deals with the external firm and customer relationships, many ethical issues occur during the implementation phase. Exhibit 10–1 (lower right column) lists some of the relevant tasks stemming from implementation of a marketing program. This list is illustrative, but by no means exhaustive.

Product alteration is intended to enhance product value and get the consumer to make the intended purchase. Ethical questions emerge when minor product adjustments are promoted as being significant. For example, some recent food products are labeled as "light" or "reduced calorie" while the reductions are very modest. The Food and Drug Administration has developed guidelines for the use of such terms. Furthermore, the introduction of "me-too" products raises additional ethical issues. For example, how many flavors of toothpaste are really needed? Another product alteration issue relates to the position of product manager. Several questions come to mind. For example, do these fast track individuals make necessary long-term modifications to a brand to insure its marketplace staying power, regardless of the short term financial performance? Or, do they simply undertake cosmetic modifications to improve next quarter's market share or profit picture?

Price negotiation is often at the heart of marketing implementation. Marketing managers who can effectively negotiate on price win many contracts. An ethical problem occurs in this process when one of the participants has more leverage than the other. For example, several years ago a large Midwestern department store chain which dealt with a small candy producer told the company that they would pay 70 percent of the earlier negotiated price and the small firm could keep the account. Or the larger firm would pay the full amount of the invoice, but the small manufacturer would lose the account. This approach was little more than extortion. The issue of slotting allowances discussed in Chapter 5 is another good illustration. Some of these practices, while bordering on being unethical or possibly illegal, are nonetheless quite common. They might be mitigated somewhat by the small firm taking its case to the top echelon of the company that made the threat.

In this era of single sourcing, manufacturers often look at their suppliers as partners rather than adversaries in price negotiation. The emphasis is placed on consistent product quality and timely delivery, instead of price. For example, while many US distributors were once skeptical of Japanese manufacturers, their high-quality products and service responsiveness quickly won the Americans over.

Distribution determination refers to getting the product where it is demanded in an expeditious manner. Sometimes marketers promise more than they can deliver. For instance, certain suppliers assure one week delivery, but commonly ship in ten days. It becomes an ethical issue when there is economic or psychological harm to the client/consumer. In health care or other life-threatening situations, distribution "as promised" is critical. Overpromotion by these organizations may heighten the ethical problems they face. Furthermore, some manufacturers (see the Benetton example in Chapter 5) may treat some of their retailers unevenly simply to meet their objectives in getting products to the most desirable markets.

Promotional presentation is another primary function of marketing. Both selling and advertising have persuasive, informative, and reminder components. Persuasive promotions are most often associated with ethical abuses. In selling, ethical problems often arise when persuasion is too intense or competitors are unscrupulous in their appeals. What ethical salespersons should do is insure that buyers are making decisions on the most relevant evaluative criteria. For instance, if the competitor is stressing price and the salesperson knows that product quality in terms of failure or breakage rates is the most important criterion, the buyer should be informed of this fact. If unethical marketers cannot deliver on their promises, the ethical firm has a good chance to gain the business.

Even if the business is lost, when principles are not compromised, an opportunity may occur to gain it back later. For example, a communications consultant submitted a proposal to a defense contractor, but found the defense company's sole intention was to procure the consulting firm's valuable list of newspaper editors. The consultant determined that he would not meet such terms and "walked out. Several months later he got a $50,000 contract from the same defense contractor."[24]

In striving to be ethical, some companies even identify in their code of ethics types of acceptable sales tactics. For instance, Automatic Data Processing (ADP), a computer software company, states, "Aggressive selling should not include defamation of competition, malicious rumors or unsupportable promises." IBM's code makes a similar point: "It has long been the company's policy to provide customers the best possible products and services. Sell them on their merits, not by disparaging competitors."

The advertising area is one where persuasion is often criticized for being unethical. (Recall our discussion in Chapter 6.) If the message includes puffery (exaggerated praise for the product) but not deception (which is illegal) it falls into an ethically gray area. One type of advertising that continues to receive growing criticism is advertising to children, especially for war toys and highly sugared products. Furthermore, the current debate about advertising beer and wine on television pits free speech against the potential negative effects of consuming such products, especially when their desirability is enhanced by the lifestyles portrayed in these commercials.

In examining a number of codes of conduct, we were surprised to find that very few recommend guidelines for ethical advertising. An exception is Ford, which provides specific policies for utilizing comparative advertising. Consumer products marketers, who spend millions of dollars every year on advertising, should consider developing explicit guidelines for their advertising. Some firms have *ad hoc* policies regarding sponsorship of shows dealing with sensitive subjects or containing large amounts of sex and/or violence. But more thought should be given to what constitutes an appropriate advertising message and, perhaps, what media should be used.

The Concept of an Ethical Audit

The dictionary defines an audit as an official examination of records. The purpose of an accounting audit is to examine the financial health of an organization, and is standard practice in most companies. The objective of a marketing audit is to similarly assess the marketing function. It too has become more widely accepted. Proponents of this method recently remarked

> . . . the marketing audit is now a fairly standard tool that can be objectively applied to evaluate whether a company's total marketing posture and resources are best positioned to take advantage of its evolving opportunities.[25]

An *ethical audit* for marketing, then, possesses some of the same characteristics as these more traditional audits. It gauges the ethical health of the marketing department and its activities. Like a marketing audit, it should be comprehensive, systematic, independent, and periodic. That is, all major marketing decisions should be evaluated through an orderly sequence of steps in an objective fashion every few years. Some management experts believe it is appropriate to use internal auditors to survey the ethical posture of the organization.[26] However, we believe that the marketing ethics auditor usually should be someone from outside the firm who nevertheless has the necessary expertise and whose background is above reproach. Possibilities for an ethics auditor include a retired marketing executive, an outside director, or a member of the board's audit committee.[27]

Types of Ethical Audits

Philosophical, functional, and cultural audits are the three major thematic variations used in conducting a marketing audit. The *philosophical* approach involves asking questions about the duties to stakeholders in a marketing decision and asking whether the decision violates any written or unwritten obligations to these parties. Additional philosophical considerations entail the consequences of marketing decisions. That is, what are the costs and benefits of any marketing action? An assessment of the positive and negative impacts on consumers, employees, and other stakeholders should be conducted. In the final analysis, the company must decide if more people are better or worse off because of the marketing action.[28]

A second type of ethical audit pertains to the *functional* decisions that marketing managers make in devising and implementing marketing strategies. This audit does not explicitly draw on philosophical theories, but reflects them through a battery of questions. These questions are discussed in further detail later and are shown in Appendix 10B, Part IV. A third possible audit evaluates the corporate context or *cultural* characteristics of the organization in which individuals work. A representative list of questions that can help determine the firm's marketing culture is:

Do you consider your relationship with your immediate peers to be primarily one of competition or one of cooperation and mutual trust?

Does your organization have "heroes?" Who are they, and what are their virtues? (Any notable vices?)

Do you generally work under pressure? Do you ever feel pressured to do more or achieve more than you believe is reasonable or possible? Where does this pressure come from?

Do you feel pressured by your organization to act contrary to your own moral judgment? (If so, how seriously, and at what risk, etc.?)[29]

Company Examples of Ethical Audits

A number of companies, including Johnson & Johnson and General Mills, conduct periodic surveys of employees to seek their guidance concerning the status of the company code and its implementation. Such general surveys, while useful, are not as comprehensive as a full-blown audit nor do they typically focus on the marketing function. Obviously, several approaches to conducting a comprehensive ethical audit exist. For example, a company with one of the longest and most complete ethical audit programs is Dow Corning. The firm started using face-to-face audits at its plants worldwide over a decade ago. Their process works as follows.

The number of participants in these four to six hour audits ranges from five to forty. The auditors meet with the manager in charge the evening before to ascertain the most pressing issues. Actual questions come from relevant sections of the corporate code and are adjusted for the audit location. At sales offices, the auditors concentrate on issues such as kickbacks, unusual requests from customers and special pricing terms. The following is a sampling of these questions:

> Are there any examples of business that Dow Corning has lost because of our refusal to provide 'gifts' or other incentives to government officials at our customers' facilities?
>
> Do any of our employees have ownership or financial interest in any of our distributorships?
>
> Have our sales representatives been able to undertake business conduct discussions with distributors in a way that actually strengthens our ties with them?
>
> Do you believe our distributors are in regular contact with their competitors? If so, why?
>
> Which specific Dow Corning policies conflict with local practices?[30]

The manager of corporate internal and management communications heads this effort and believes that the audit approach actively discourages employees from consciously making unethical decisions. Over twenty of these meetings are held annually. A Business Conduct Committee oversees the audits and then prepares a report for the Audit Committee of the board. In the view of the manager who heads the ethics audit, there are no shortcuts to implementing this program because it requires much time and extensive interaction with the people involved.

This audit procedure might be a useful vehicle for Mr. Taylor in scenario 3 to consider. For companies without the resources or inclination to conduct such an extensive audit, we postulate in the following section a "generic" ethical audit that can be used for marketing.

An Ethical Audit for Marketing

Appendix 10B lists questions to be answered in an ethical audit for marketing. This type of audit should put primary emphasis on the integrity of the organization relative to customers and society-at-large. The questions pertain to all marketing activities within a firm. They are based on our assessment and study of the marketing function and not, unfortunately, on existing audit documents because none are available. Although there are undoubtedly more qualified and complete possible answers to the questions, at minimum a "yes-no" format is recommended to allow managers to compare their answers quickly with their subordinates. For a more in-depth examination, a range of answers (e.g., always, usually, sometimes, rarely, never) could be used.

The audit is divided into four sections roughly corresponding to the major phases of marketing implementation. The first section deals with the formal organizational structure. Second, questions about the culture of the marketing department are asked. Overall implementation responsibilities are covered in the third section. Tasks relating to each of the marketing mix variables are reflected in the final and most extensive bank of questions.

Questions on Formal Corporate Structure

Part I measures the presence of formal corporate ethical policies. The existence of a code/credo or values statement is one manifestation of a commitment to ethics. Even more important, any code must be revised periodically to take account of new issues in each industry. As mentioned earlier, general codes that merely provide platitudes are probably not worth much taken by themselves.[31] Enforcement is also necessary if the code is to be considered seriously. Finally, ethics implementation through special training programs or existing strategy sessions add ways of integrating ethics into the marketing function.

Questions on Informal Corporate Culture

Most observers consider the culture of the marketing department to be very important in promoting ethical organizational conduct. The first five questions in Part II deal with candor and honesty in communication. If a marketing department does not have open and forthright discussions about areas of disagreement, an ethical culture probably does not exist. The next three questions pertain to the symmetry between family and corporate values shown in Exhibit 10-6. We believe there is a distinct parallel between the values necessary for family cooperation and those required for a healthy organizational climate. The final four questions are formulated from the recommendations about the principles followed by highly ethical firms.[32] This series of questions, while not exhaustive, permits the marketing manager to gain insights into whether the corporate culture in the department can be characterized as ethical or not.

Questions on Implementation Responsibilities

The questions on implementation responsibilities revolve around basic marketing management issues discussed above—executive leadership, delegation, communication, and motivation. The questions are similar to, yet different from, those listed in the corporate culture section. It is imperative that the top marketing executives take seriously their role in implementing marketing ethics. If they can answer positively the audit questions posed in Part III about their roles in creating an ethical environment, the firm should be well on its way to meeting its ethical objectives. As the questions indicate, leadership and other ethical responsibilities need to be demonstrated both orally and in writing.

Questions on Implementation Tasks

The most extensive list of audit questions is contained in Part IV. This section details questions regarding the functional areas of marketing. The first bank of questions addresses product issues. Not all of these questions are relevant for every company, but they typify questions that product and marketing managers should consider. For example, marketers of consumer packaged goods should pay particular attention to the nature of their product offering. Bankers or investment brokers need to explain the core product (e.g., is the financial information consumers receive on a new service purposely vague?). Nonprofit marketers such as hospitals and universities should be aware of ethical ramifications of their service decisions. The marketing of ideas through cause-related marketing also needs evaluation as these few questions attest.[33] In sum, ethical questions regarding the viability and configuration of the organization's product assortment should be answered in a straightforward way.

The second section of Part IV on implementation tasks deals with pricing issues. The way prices are arrived at often has ethical overtones. The setting of pricing objectives can be legal but not ethical. For instance, a large firm may try to undercut a smaller competitor by just enough to damage the firm, but not enough to cause legal recourse. In other words, the *intent* is predatory even when the action may not be provable *de jure*.

The third section of Part IV pertains to the channel of distribution. Issues such as coercion within the channel and the markups charged by wholesalers and retailers are ones that commonly come up in evaluating channel members. The marketing manager needs to examine the relevant channel issues and decide how ethical the firm is in its relationships with other channel members. Of course, the ethical posture reinforced by the corporate culture will probably have much to do with how these and other questions dealing with the marketing mix are answered.

The final section in this portion of the audit deals with promotional questions. Promotion is the most visible area in marketing. Consequently, ethical questions tend to abound. The inherently persuasive nature of certain promotional vehicles means that some consumers will find these selling efforts unethical (see Chapters 6 and 7 for a discussion of ethics in advertising and selling). For example, the growth of telemarketing (telephone sales) is found to be too intrusive by some critics. Others find the whole business of automobile selling fraught with ethical concerns.

Using the Ethical Audit

The easiest way to employ our ethical audit is to compile the "yes" and "no" answers and calculate percentages in each category. Questions that are not relevant to a particular organization can be eliminated. Companies should strive for 100 percent "yes" answers, or at least more than 90 percent. If the final percentage of yes answers falls below 70 percent, the company should definitely reevaluate the ethics of its marketing program. (We use the 70 percent figure somewhat arbitrarily; we want to create some debate and that percentage is the common passing grade.) We realize that no firm, however, is perfect, and there are undoubtedly areas where even the most ethical companies can improve. The audit instrument can help a firm pinpoint those practices where there are concerns about its ethical position.

More than one person's views should be sought in answering these questions. Everyone in a department or division may be asked to fill out the audit and the answers could be compiled by the independent auditor. The areas of largest departure (i.e., where the "no" answers dominate) could be discussed at a follow-up meeting of the department. For instance, members of the sales force may believe that they are being encouraged to use very aggressive sales tactics to meet sales quotas while the sales managers might not interpret their instructions in this manner. A thorough audit evaluation would allow such differences to surface.

The audit should ideally be undertaken every year or two. If too long a time elapses, the culture and strategy of the firm obviously can change. Several months after a new manager or parent company takes over would also be a good time for an ethical audit. If the audit is conducted too soon after a change, the new environment will not have had enough time to emerge. As in the case of a financial or marketing audit, the ethical audit should normally not be undertaken only in a time of crisis. For example, just after a law suit or court case has been brought by a competitor or customer is not the best time for an ethical audit. Such an audit approach has been the knee-jerk reaction of several companies in the investment banking community after being confronted with ethical violations.

Ideas for Ethical Action

Marketing organizations should put a formal structure in place to promote ethics. In addition, steps should be taken to develop an informal culture that enhances ethical decision making. Specific guidelines for accomplishing these endeavors are sketched above. In conducting an ethical audit, it is more important to develop and discuss provocative questions than to seek right (i.e., perfect) answers. We agree with two observers who remarked:

Ethics is not a coherent set of answers but a coherent set of questions.

Ethical judgment consists not in getting the right answer all the time, but in consistently asking the right questions.[34]

Marketing managers should institute or evaluate current ethics policies. We suggest a number of possibilities in this chapter. We assume that most firms have ethical policies in place, but they are not the Ten Commandments chiseled in stone. Every several years, the corporate code, training programs, and ethical audit mechanisms need to be reviewed. We advocate that ethics documents that pertain exclusively to the marketing department be developed, if they do not already exist.

For the smaller or new firm, the CEO and chief marketing officer can develop ethical guidelines from scratch. Several models are suggested in this chapter. There is no best way to implement ethical policies, but care should be taken that the unique aspects of the firm receive consideration. One possible approach that parallels our thinking is suggested in Exhibit 10–9. Here one executive has provided a good roadmap to instituting ethically sensitive corporate policies.

The ethical component of corporate culture should be assessed. One of the early writings on corporate culture labeled the central values of an organization as spiritual values.[35] While we do not attribute undue religious significance to this, it does capture the fact that values encompass the issue of justice in business operations. Surprisingly little attention has been paid to the corporate culture and its ethics linkage. Marketing managers should be aware of the fact that the culture of their firm can enhance or impede ethical decision making by subordinates.

There are ways for executives to make this tie between ethics and culture explicit. For instance, those implementation responsibilities of leadership, delegation, communication, and motivation are really about creating a climate of trust and commitment within the firm. Top marketing managers can use many methods to nurture the ethical component of their corporate culture. Specifically, Joseph Pichler, CEO of Kroger, listed several pithy points about how to create a moral corporate culture (see Exhibit 10–10).

An ethical audit for marketing should be conducted regularly. One barometer of a company's ethical position is an ethical audit. Our comprehensive audit questions are shown in Appendix 10B. The cautions expressed earlier should be followed. Just as accounting or marketing audits are useful for isolating problems in these functional areas, an ethical audit can provide needed information about troublesome issues. For example, the ethical audit of a firm might pinpoint major differences of opinion between upper and middle management on openness of communication and goal setting. We suggest that the ethical audit instrument (in some form) is a vehicle whose time has come.

EXHIBIT 10–9   Are You an Ethical Manager?

Robert Goddard, an executive at Liberty Mutual Insurance Group based in Boston, proposed the following six-step process for managers to follow in creating a more ethical climate in their firm.

1. Identify ethical attitudes critical to your operation. High technology firms may value loyalty to maintain the security of their scientific know-how. Security firms may stress honesty, or a drug manufacturer may conclude that responsibility is essential to ensure product quality. Determining these unique attitudes are a crucial first step for developing a positive work-related environment.

2. Select employees with desired attitudes. Construct interviewing questions that probe a candidate's ethical values. The answers provided will give a sense of the potential employee's ethical attitudes toward integrity, responsibility, and other factors. Information given on job applications and resumes should be verified. If they lie on these, they probably will lie on the job.

3. Incorporate ethics in the job evaluation process. Job performance criteria should influence employee work-related ethical attitudes. These may be covered in a code or other standards that detail the parameters of expected ethical behavior. It is probably best for the company to require managers to commit themselves, in writing, to the code.

4. Establish a work culture that reinforces ethical attitudes. Managers should build ethics into their recognition and reward systems, decision-making process, staff-meeting discussions, and orientation and training sessions. They can promote values such as trust by interacting equitably and respectfully with subordinates, delegating work that has real value, being reliable with assistance, fostering teamwork, and even maintaining a sense of humor in difficult situations.

5. Increase employee participation in decision making. Most employees will act differently when they have a stake in a decision, both as to how they approach the process and how they support the final decision. Substantive involvement in decision-making (including goal setting and problem solving) tends to unify individuals within the firm and promotes greater effort on the part of the employees.

6. Exhibit ethical leadership. Few observers deny that managers set the value systems of their work units. No group will be any more ethical than its manager demands. This is precisely why it is important for managers to exhibit ethical leadership in everything they do—every decision they make and every discussion they hold. Superiors must make it clear that employees who harm others, allegedly for the benefit of the company or department, will be sanctioned or disciplined.

Adapted from Robert W. Goddard, "Are You an Ethical Manager?" *Personnel Journal* (March 1988), 38–47. Reprinted by permission from *Personnel Journal*, Costa Mesa, California. All rights reserved.

Closing Comments

To conclude this chapter and the book, we offer several observations we hope will assist marketing managers in taking the "higher road" in the future. First, although we tended to use well-known and large companies for most of the illus-

---

EXHIBIT 10–10   Creating a Moral Corporate Culture

▲ Talk it [difficult issues] out and do it. Actions speak louder than words.

▲ You have to enforce it. Use the corporate code and spell out expectations.

▲ Play fair with violators. It is important to follow due process.

▲ Use *The Wall Street Journal* test. How will this decision read in the paper tomorrow?

▲ Listen carefully. Use both internal (audit staff) and external (outside directors) channels for communication about ethical issues.

▲ Manage by walking around. Buy the truck drivers a pizza and walk around the plants to find out what is going on.

▲ Give employees a sense of ownership. Create a stock option plan and incentive systems for all employees.

Source: Speech given by Joseph Pichler, president and CEO of The Kroger Company, March 7, 1990 at the University of Notre Dame.

trations in this book, we believe *ethical sensitivity is equally important in smaller firms.* The thrust toward entrepreneurial activity probably means there will be a growing number of small firms in the future. Therefore, more attention must be paid to ethical issues in smaller firms, particularly as they struggle to survive in the competitive climate of the 1990s. In these companies there is probably less need for the formal corporate policies discussed in this chapter because the employees work closely with the founder or owner. They know the values and ethical stance of the CEO. In hiring individuals in this environment, the manager should weigh ethical concerns heavily in the selection process. One manager of an entrepreneurial venture told us that she hires good people and does not feel that it is necessary to institute rules or policies for them to follow. However, hiring "good people" is probably not enough. At a minimum, ethical questions should be discussed with some regularity in all firms.

Second, *a new approach to codes of ethics seems needed.* From our examination of codes over the years, there appears to be too much of a boiler-plate approach to them. Nearly every code covers the same topics—relationships with employees and suppliers, conflicts of interest, bribery, insider information, and political activities and contributions. We sometimes get the sense that only the company names are changed. At minimum, codes in the future should possess the five characteristics outlined in this chapter—communicated, specific, pertinent, enforced, and revised.

Although few codes do stand out, Tandem Computers has been singled out. Their code is traditional in the sense that it covers the topic areas noted above. However, the code's statements are both thorough and concise, so that employees can understand the discussion. What is different is that for every point, there is a clear-cut explanation that gives the reason for the enactment of this policy.[36] Unfortunately, most firms do not tell us why they institute such policies within the code. Furthermore, companies should always publicize the code to outsiders. Stakeholders will then know the managers are proud of their ethical stance and not just covering themselves legally.

Third, *ethical issues facing companies in the future will likely require both a philosophical and technical analysis*. Most ethical issues are complex. Therefore, one reaction by many firms is to hire ethicists to help them deal with the issues and set up ethics training programs. However, this is probably not enough for the future. For example, many environmental and solid waste problems caused by consumer and industrial refuse require sophisticated technical advice on recycling vis-à-vis landfill disposal. Consumer packaged good companies are now examining the biodegradability of their packaging. These issues require engineering and scientific, as well as ethical advice. The "right" decision may not be clear until the scientific evidence (even if it is mixed) is factored in. Therefore, we advocate the use of both ethical and technical consultants to help illuminate the difficult choices ahead.

Fourth, *marketing's role in dealing with societal issues should be examined from an ethical standpoint*. Major social issues facing the United States include AIDS, illegal drug use, deteriorating primary and secondary education, racism, and the widening gap between the rich and poor. As we discussed in Chapter 9, marketing has been effectively if not always ethically used to promote a number of social causes. While we offered several observations regarding marketing's role there, we want to reaffirm that issues such as AIDS and drug testing, as well as support for education and social services, will continue to be major concerns throughout the 1990s. We believe that managers should view these areas as not just social issues, but ethical ones as well.

At minimum, more informed discussion and debate about social issues must occur, not only in the boardrooms but throughout entire companies. Solutions will not be forthcoming without commitment by large numbers of individuals acting within companies or in civic and religious groups. In addition, a more creative relationship between business and the government will have to be developed to find a way to share the costs of dealing with public welfare issues.[37] We do believe that marketing principles, such as market segmentation, positioning, and customer orientation, can be applied to alleviate some of society's major social ills. Ethics, however, should play a central role in evaluating all marketing techniques.

Finally, *a dynamic tension will always exist between ethics and competition*. This issue, in various forms, always comes up. Many opinions are expressed as to what energizes a marketplace economy, but certainly selfishness is there somewhere. Most everyone in our capitalistic system lauds competition and then spends much time and effort trying to find a shelter (i.e., sustainable competitive advantage) from it. Antitrust laws set the boundaries of the playing field for marketers, but there are many strategic (legal and illegal) avenues to get around competition.

Since competition is a most powerful force, we need to keep managers aware of its ethical ramifications so the dynamic tension is balanced. In other words, we are faced with a formidable task of creating a system where the selfishness of competitive aggression can create marketplace innovation, while at the same time tempering the ethical abuse that can come with the desire "to win at all costs." We need to rely on self-control and self-regulation, as well as some government but not too much. Otherwise, we create an inferior economic alternative (e.g., witness the failed planned economies of Eastern Europe). Our professional responsibility as marketing educators is to deal with the tension generated by competition and insure that ethics is always brought into the debate. If we succeed, the result should be a more vigorous and ethical marketplace should result where managers choose the higher road.

Appendix 10A

The Security Pacific Credo and Guidelines for Gifts[1]

The Credo of Security Pacific Corporation

Commitment to Customer

The first commitment is to provide our customers with quality products and services which are innovative and technologically responsive to their current requirements, at appropriate prices. To perform these tasks with integrity requires that we maintain confidentiality and protect customer privacy, promote customer satisfaction, and serve customer needs. We strive to serve qualified customers and industries which are socially responsible according to broadly accepted community and company standards.

Commitment to Employee

The second commitment is to establish an environment for our employees which promotes professional growth, encourages each person to achieve his or her highest potential, and promotes individual creativity and responsibility. Security Pacific acknowledges our responsibility to employees, including providing for open and honest communication, stated expectations, fair and timely assessment of performance and equitable compensation which rewards employee contributions to company objectives within a framework of equal opportunity and affirmative action.

Commitment of Employee to Security Pacific

The third commitment is that of the employee to Security Pacific. As employees, we strive to understand and adhere to the Corporation's policies and objectives, act in a professional manner, and give our best effort to improve Security Pacific. We recognize the trust and confidence placed in us by our customers and community and act with integrity and honesty in all situations to preserve that trust and confidence. We act responsibly to avoid conflicts of interest and other situations which are potentially harmful to the Corporation.

Commitment of Employee to Employee

The fourth commitment is that of employees to their fellow employees. We must be committed to promote a climate of mutual respect, integrity, and professional relationships, characterized by open and honest communication within and across all levels of the organization. Such a climate will promote attainment of the Corporation's goals and objectives, while leaving room for individual initiative within a competitive environment.

Commitment to Communities

The fifth commitment is that of Security Pacific to the communities which we serve. We must constantly strive to improve the quality of life through our support of community organizations and projects, through encouraging service to the community by employees, and by promoting participation in community services. By the appropriate use of our resources, we work to support or further advance the interests of the community, particularly in times of crisis or social need. The Corporation and its employees are committed to complying fully with each community's laws and regulations.

Commitment to Stockholder

The sixth commitment of Security Pacific is to its stockholders. We will strive to provide consistent growth and a superior rate of return on their investment, to maintain a position and reputation as a leading financial institution, to protect stockholder investments, and to provide full and timely information. Achievement of these goals for Security Pacific is dependent upon the successful development of the five previous sets of relationships.

[1]Source: Security Pacific Corporation, Code of Business Conduct.

To avoid the implications of any impropriety, it is important that each staff member decline any gifts, the acceptance of which would raise even the slightest doubt of improper influence. As a general rule, no gifts of significant value from present or prospective customers or suppliers should be accepted.

Security Pacific does recognize that situations may arise when it would be appropriate for a staff member to accept the benefit of another's expenditure. Such situations include:

Gifts of nominal value (not in excess of $50) given at Christmas, other holidays, or special occasions which represent expressions of friendship;

Reasonable entertainment at luncheon, dinner, or business meetings with present or prospective customers and suppliers when the return of the expenditure on a comparable basis is likely to occur and would be properly chargeable as a business expense;

Unsolicited advertising or promotional material (e.g., pens, calendars, etc.) of a value not exceeding $50.

Awards given by charitable, educational, civil or religious organizations for meritorious contributions or service; and

Gifts or bequests based upon family relationships.

Appendix 10B

Ethical Audit Questions for Marketing

	Yes	No

I. *Formal Corporate Policies*

Codes

	Yes	No
Does our company have a formal code/corporate credo or values statement?	_____	_____
Has it been revised in the last five years?	_____	_____
Is it specific in terms of guidance for marketing?	_____	_____
Are issues pertinent to our industry covered in it (e.g., mail order returns, toy safety, etc.)?	_____	_____
Is the code actively enforced?	_____	_____
Does the severity of the sanction/enforcement fit the ethical violation?	_____	_____

Programs

Has our company engaged in ethics training programs either for new employees or for experienced marketing executives?

Do ethical issues come up in sales meetings or other regular meetings of our marketing department?

II. *Informal Corporate Culture*

Interactions

Can the communication within our marketing department be described as open and candid?

Do superiors instill confidence, rather than fear, in their subordinates?

Are marketing managers supportive of disagreement and questioning from those who disagree with them?

Do managers reward truthfulness rather than just "good news" from subordinates?

Do managers encourage differing views from others in the department?

Family Values

Are the values of our marketing department similar to those of a family in that a caring atmosphere dominates?

Does our firm care about the health and welfare of our customers?

Is our company a helpful corporate neighbor?

Principles

Is our department obsessed with fairness?

Do our marketing personnel assume personal responsibility for actions of the company?

Are our marketing personnel comfortable interacting with diverse internal and external stakeholders?

Does our marketing department see its activities in terms of a purpose that members of the company value?

III. *Implementation Responsibilities*

Executive Leadership

Has our CEO or vice president of marketing pub-
licly stated their views on ethics in the last year?   _____ _____

Have they communicated to the marketing department in writing about ethics in the last year?   _____ _____

Delegation

Do the vice president and marketing managers
clarify how goals and objectives are to be accomplished in the field?   _____ _____

Are salespeople and lower level marketing personnel allowed to question upper level marketing executives on selling and advertising strategies and
other implementation techniques that may generate ethical problems?   _____ _____

Communication

Are marketing personnel required to sign off on the
ethics code/credo every year?   _____ _____

Are informal channels of communication used to
disseminate information about ethics?   _____ _____

Motivation

Do marketing managers reward employees for
making the "right" ethical decision?   _____ _____

Is performance monitored to make sure that high
achievers are not cutting corners?   _____ _____

IV. *Implementation Tasks*

A. Ethical Questions Relating to the Product
Core Product

Is there an underlying benefit to the product?   _____ _____

Are benefits accurately communicated?   _____ _____

Product Offering

Does the package adequately present the size or
components of the product?   _____ _____

Are the brand name and manufacturer clearly
spelled out on the label?   _____ _____

Does the label contain adequate amounts of information for safe consumer use? _____ _____

Is after-sale service promised with adequate provisions to deliver it? _____ _____

Is the warranty, including restrictions and requirements, clearly spelled out to consumers? _____ _____

Goods Marketing
Does the company inform the consumer about reductions in the quality or quantity of the product? _____ _____

Is responsible product use promoted? _____ _____

Services Marketing
Does the firm emphasize primarily "new" services, not those copied from a competitor? _____ _____

Are services salespeople instructed to be precise (rather than vague) in discussing the benefits or performance of the service? _____ _____

Nonprofit Marketing
Does the nonprofit organization refrain from using high pressure even though they are promoting socially beneficial products? _____ _____

Are nonprofit administrators willing to respond to consumer complaints (even when they feel they "know" what is best for the consumer)? _____ _____

Ideas Marketing
Are ideas marketers promoting the cause (not propaganda) in the name of marketing? _____ _____

Is the idea not embellished, rather than making it sound so good that consumers will accept it (and donate time or money) without reservation? _____ _____

B. Ethical Questions in Pricing
Pricing Objectives
Does the company consciously set pricing objectives to not damage competitors? _____ _____

Do marketers who convey a discount image do so accurately (i.e., try not to add expensive services and accessories that inflate the final price)? _____ _____

Pricing Methods

Is the price discrimination that the marketer practices always justifiable? (For example, do professionals avoid charging more to people they know can pay more?)

In competitive bidding, does the firm not attempt (by lawful means) to find out what another firm bid? Do they also avoid lowballing (bidding the first contract low in hopes of recovering on later contracts)?

In markup pricing, does the marketer promote only accurate sales percentages (e.g., refrain from advertising large, i.e., 50 percent, discounts from the normal selling price)?

Pricing Decisions

Does the marketer promote only one line as its highest quality (e.g., he or she does not try to differentiate on only cosmetic differences or a different package that distinguishes it from the middle price line)?

Does the firm always justify its flexible pricing (i.e., different prices for differing customers)?

Are loss leaders beneficial to consumers (rather than an expensive version of bait and switch)?

C. Ethical Questions in Distribution

Channel Questions

Do large channel members avoid coercing smaller ones in selling or pricing products?

Do manufacturers try to build relationships with their intermediaries rather than seeking new channels to force traditional channel members to take small markups?

Are smaller wholesalers or retailers banding together to influence public policy to protect them from larger channel members?

Wholesaling

Do wholesalers keep products in reserve for larger customers while not adequately serving smaller customers?

Do the services rendered relate to the quantity of products purchased?

    _____   _____

Retailing

Does the retailer avoid special (lower quality) merchandise used for sales?

Does the commission system discourage salespeople from using high-pressure sales tactics?

    _____   _____

Are salespeople instructed to "trade up" customers only when the buyers express interest in the more expensive product?

    _____   _____

Physical Distribution

Are cost minimization decisions arrived at in a manner equitable to all parties?

    _____   _____

Are transportation companies only asked to bid for contracts when price is not a major component of the cost?

    _____   _____

Are conservation and pollution considerations important in deciding among modes of transportation such as trucks, trains, planes?

    _____   _____

D. Ethical Questions about Promotion
Advertising (See Exhibit 6–13 on page 172)

Does advertising promise what it can deliver?

Is embellishment (i.e., exaggerated product benefits) discouraged?

    _____   _____

Do ads promote significant facts (as opposed to leaving them out) about the products?

Are claims based on unbiased research results?

    _____   _____

Sales Promotion

Are products properly represented at trade shows and exhibitions?

Are samples or premiums only promoted when they have significant value?

    _____   _____

Publicity

Do organizations rely on newsworthiness rather than influence to get publicity?

    _____   _____

Are only major product changes promoted to the
media as innovations?   _____   _____

Personal Selling

Does the organization discourage salespeople from
using high-pressure selling techniques?   _____   _____

Do salespeople avoid utilizing questionable psychological pressure to close the sale?   _____   _____

Sales Management

Do sales managers monitor expense accounts and
watch out for inflated expenses and padding of
these accounts.   _____   _____

Are territory quotas adjusted to economic condi-
tions rather than automatically inflated every year?   _____   _____

Public Relations

Does the public-relations department share valuable information with the media even if it is sometimes negative?   _____   _____

If negative stories about the organization appear,
does the public-relations department avoid retalia-
tion at a later time?   _____   _____

International Issues

See Exhibit 8–9 on page 229 for list of questions.

Endnotes

1. Portions of the following discussion are adapted from Patrick E. Murphy, "Implementing Business Ethics," *Journal of Business Ethics* (December 1988), 907–915.

2. Mary Ellen Oliverio, "The Implementation of a Code of Ethics: The Early Efforts of One Entrepreneur," *Journal of Business Ethics* 8 (1989), 367–374.

3. Todd Barrett, "Business Ethics for Sale," *Newsweek* (May 9, 1988), 56.

4. Center for Business Ethics, "Are Corporations Institutionalizing Ethics?" *Journal of Business Ethics* 5 (1986), 85–91.

5. Touche Ross, *Ethics in American Business* (New York: Touche Ross & Company, January 1988).

6. Ronald E. Berenbeim, *Corporate Ethics* (New York: The Conference Board Research Report 900, 1987) and Rick Wartyma, "Nature or Nurture? Study Blames Ethical Lapses on Corporate Goals," *The Wall Street Journal*, (October 9, 1987), 21.

7. For a more extensive discussion of this point, see Patrick E. Murphy, "Creating Ethical Corporate Structures," *Sloan Management Review* (Winter 1989), 81–86.

8. For another view on the topic of effective codes, see James Weber, "Institutionaliz-ing Ethics into the Corporation," *MSU Business Topics* (Spring 1981), 47–52.

9. Patrick E. Murphy and Mark G. Dunn, "Instilling an Ethical Dimension in Decision Making by Marketing Managers," Working Paper, 1989.

10. Laura L. Nash, "Johnson & Johnson Credo." In *Corporate Ethics: A Prime Business Asset*, ed. James Keogh, 93–104 (New York: The Business Roundtable, 1988).

11. Joline Godfrey, "Ethics on an Entrepreneurial Venture," *Training News* (June 1987).

12. See note 7 above.

13. For a more complete discussion of Mc Donnell Douglas, see note 1 above.

14. R. Deshpande and Frederick E. Webster, Jr., "Organizational Culture and Market-ing: Defining the Research Agenda," *Journal of Marketing* (January 1989), 3–15.

15. For discussions of corporate culture and ethics in the popular press, see T. J. Peters and R. H. Waterman, Jr., *In Search of Excellence* (New York: Warner Books, 1982); and Kenneth Blanchard and Norman Vincent Peale, *The Power of Ethical Management* (New York: William Morrow, 1988); and in the academic press, see W. Michael Hoffman, Jennifer M. Moore, and David A. Fedo, eds., *Corporate Governance and Institutionalizing Ethics* (Lexington, MA: Lexington Books, 1984).

16. William J. Everett, "OKIOS: Convergence in Business Ethics," *Journal of Business Ethics* (August 1986), 313–327 and Donald P. Robin and R. Eric Reidenbach, "Social Re-sponsibility, Ethics and Marketing Strategy: Closing the Gap between Concept and Appli-cation," *Journal of Marketing* (January 1987), 44–58.

17. Robert C. Solomon and Kristine R. Hanson, *It's Good Business* (New York: Athe-neum, 1985), 171.

18. James A. Waters and Frederick Bird, "The Moral Dimension of Organizational Culture," *Journal of Business Ethics* (January 1987), 15–20.

19. Roy Serpa, "Creating a Candid Culture," *Journal of Business Ethics* (December 1985), 425–430.

20. For an interesting discussion of ethical responsibility, which merges organiza-tional and individual factors, see Barbara Ley Toffler, *Tough Choices: Managers Talk Ethics* (New York: John Wiley, 1986).

21. Thomas R. Horton, *What Works for Me: 16 CEOs Talk about Their Careers and Commitments*, (New York: Random House, 1986).

22. James Keogh, ed., *Corporate Ethics: A Prime Business Asset* (New York: The Business Roundtable, 1988), 10.

23. See note 15 above, Peters and Waterman.

24. Jeffrey P. Davidson, "The Elusive Nature of Integrity," *Marketing News* (November 7, 1986), 24.

25. Philip Kotler, William T. Gregor, William H. Rodgers III, "The Marketing Audit Comes of Age," *Sloan Management Review* (Winter 1989), 62.

26. Peter Arlow and Thomas A. Ulrich, "Auditing Your Organization's Ethics," *The Internal Auditor* (August 1980), 26–31.

27. For a discussion of ethical consultants, see Richard H. Guerrette, "Corporate Ethical Consulting: Developing Management Strategies for Corporate Ethics," *Journal of Business Ethics* (May 1988), 373–380.

28. Donald P. Robin and R. Eric Reidenbach, *Business Ethics: Where Profits Meet Value Systems* (Englewood Cliffs, NJ: Prentice Hall, 1989), 138–141.

29. See note 17 above, 275–276.

30. David Whiteside and Kenneth E. Goodpaster, "Dow Corning Corporation: Busi-ness Conduct and Global Values (A)," Harvard Business School Case, 9-385-018, (1984),

Exhibit 7. For a discussion of why Dow Corning's ethics audit did not detect the breast implant safety problem, see John A. Byrne, "The Best-Laid Ethics Programs . . ." *Business Week* (March 9, 1992), 67–70.

31. Michael R. Hyman, Robert Skipper, and Richard Tansey, "Ethical Codes Are Not Enough," *Business Horizons* (March–April 1990), 15–22.

32. Mark Pastin, *The Hard Problems of Management* (San Francisco: Jossey–Bass, 1986).

33. Patrick E. Murphy and Paul N. Bloom, "Ethical Issues in Social Marketing," In *Social Marketing: Promoting the Causes of Public and Nonprofit Agencies,* ed. S. Fine, 68–78 (Boston: Allyn & Bacon, 1990).

34. Robert Reich quoted in Robert W. Goddard, "Are You an Ethical Manager?" *Personnel Journal* (March 1988), 38–47 and Tad Tuleja, *Beyond the Bottom Line: How Business Leaders Are Turning Principles into Profits* (New York: Facts on File, 1985).

35. Richard Tanner Pascale and Anthony Athos, *The Art of Japanese Management* (New York: Simon and Schuster, 1981).

36. George C. S. Benson, "Codes of Ethics," *Journal of Business Ethics* (May 1989), 305–320.

37. Laura L. Nash, *Good Intentions Aside: A Manager's Guide to Resolving Ethical Problems"* (Boston, MA: Harvard Business School Press, 1990), 234–237.

About the Authors

Gene R. Laczniak is Professor of Business in the Department of Marketing at Marquette University. Dr. Laczniak earned the Ph.D. in business administration at the University of Wisconsin—Madison. His primary research interests focus on the social influence of marketing activities on society as well as marketing strategy. Dr. Laczniak has published over eighty articles and papers. His works have appeared in the *Journal of Marketing, Journal of Public Policy & Marketing, Journalism Quarterly,* and *Long Range Planning.* He is active in the American Marketing Association and has worked as a marketing research specialist for the U.S. Treasury Department and a NASA Biomedical Applications Team.

Patrick E. Murphy is Professor and Chairman of the Department of Marketing at the University of Notre Dame. Dr. Murphy earned his Ph.D. in Business Administration from the University of Houston, an M.B.A. from Bradley University and a B.B.A. from Notre Dame. His primary research interests focus on ethical and public policy issues facing business. Professor Murphy has written numerous scholarly articles and is a frequent speaker on business and marketing ethics. He is the immediate past editor of the *Journal of Public Policy & Marketing* and serves on the editorial or advisory boards of *Annual Editions: Business Ethics, Business Ethics Quarterly, Journal of Marketing, Journal of Macromarketing* and *JPP&M.* Professor Murphy was previously affiliated with Marquette University and the Federal Trade Commission.

Name Index

Aaker, David A., 176, 237
Abbott, Andrew, 273
Achenbaum, Alvin A., 79
Agins, Teri, 120
Akaah, Ishmael, P., 78
Alter, Jonathan, 275
Altman, Henry, 141
Anderson, B. R., 206
Anderson, R. E., 200, 206
Andrews, J. C., 107
Aristotle, 51
Arlow, Peter, 310
Armstrong, Gary M., 177
Arrington, Robert, 176
Ashmore, Robert B., 51
Athos, Anthony, 311
Audi, Robert, 176
Avlonitis, George J., 108

Bagozzi, R., 108
Baker, Russell, 262
Barrett, Todd, 309
Bauer, Raymond, A., 176
Baumhart, Raymond C., 52
Bechtel, Steve, Jr., 285
Becker, Helmut, 237
Bell, Daniel, 148
Belk R., 273
Bellizzi, Joseph A., 196, 206, 207
Bentham, Jeremy, 51
Benson, George C. S., 281, 311
Berenbeim, Ronald E., 309
Berkowicz, E. N., 206
Bird, Frederick, 310
Bishop, Willard R., Jr., 140
Bitner, M. J., 141

Bivins, Thomas H., 176
Blanchard, Kenneth, 310
Blankenship, A. B., 78
Bloom, Paul N., 245, 273, 311
Blomstrom, R. L., 112
Boddewyn, J. J., 177, 237
Bone, P. F., 95
Bowie, Norman, 51, 141
Bradley, Peter, 115
Bradshaw, T., 237
Braun, Irwin, 274
Braun, Marilyn, 274
Brenner, Steve, 23
Brown, James R., 140
Brown, Patricia Leigh, 107
Brucks, Merrie, 177
Buck, Rinker, 177
Burnham, Walter Dean, 262, 275
Bush, A. J., 200, 206
Bushman, F. A., 207
Buskirk, F. A., 206, 207
Bussey, John, 108
Byrne, John, 311

Caesar, Patricia, 273
Cahill, M. F., 237
Carroll, Archie B., 22, 23, 108, 213, 237
Carson, Thomas L., 176
Castleberry, Stephen B., 74, 79
Caywood, Clarke L., 206, 207, 266, 274, 275
Chase, Marilyn, 131
Chiller, Zachary, 177
Chonko, Lawrence B., 153, 176
Christians, Clifford G., 176, 177
Churchill, Gilbert A., Jr., 207
Cicero, 37

Corey, R. J., 95
Cox, James E., Jr., 176
Crichton, John, 149, 176
Crisp, Roger, 176
Crosby, L. A., 141
Cross, Frank B., 107

Dagnoli, Jadann, 140
Dalrymple, Douglas J., 207
Darlin, Damon, 91
Darling, John, 274
Daslin, Damon, 107
Davidson, Jeffrey P., 310
Davis, Keith, 112, 139
Deal, Terrence E., 23
DeGeorge, Gail, 140
DeGeorge, Richard T., 176, 177, 273
Dempsey, W., 207
DeRose, Louis, 139
Deshpande, R., 310
Dholakia, N., 108
Dickie, R. B., 226
Dillon, Wiliam R., 77
Dommermuth, W. P., 193
Donahue, Christine, 140
Donaldson, Thomas, 238
Dubinsky, Alan J., 78, 124, 140, 206, 207
Dugas, Christine, 274
Dumaine, Brian, 78
Dunkin, Amy, 120
Dunn, Mark G., 310
Dunn, Watson, 237
Durvasula, S., 107
Duska, R. F., 141

El-Ansary, Adel I., 140
Elliot, Stuart, 169
Emamalizadeh, H., 176
Enis, Ben M., 51, 108, 111, 127
Enshwiller, John B., 106
Eovaldi, Thomas L., 107, 139
Everett, William J., 310

Fackler, Mark, 176, 177
Fannin, Rebecca, 140
Feder, Barnaby J., 96
Fedo, David A., 310
Ferrell, O. C., 52, 78
Fine, Seymour H., 245, 273, 311

Firat, A. F., 108
Firtle, Neil H., 77
Flax, Steven, 78
Flynn, Julia, 177
Folland, Sherman, 274
Ford, Neil M., 207
Forker, Laura B., 139
Fraser, Cynthia, 273
Frederick, William C., 23, 42, 112, 139
Freedman, Alix M., 106
Freeman, Edward R., 23
Freeman, Laurie, 140
French, Warren, 74, 79
Friedman, Hershey, 166
Fritzche, David J., 229, 237
Fromson, B. D., 23

Gaeth, Gary J., 161
Galbraith, John Kenneth, 148
Gamarekian, Barbara, 177
Garfield, Bob, 275
Garrett, Thomas, 172, 207
Gates, Roger, 78
Gatewood, Elizabeth, 108
Gellerman, Saul W., 13, 23
Gibson, Richard, 22, 140
Gifford, John B., 139, 141
Gilman, Hank, 140
Goddard, Robert W., 299, 311
Godfrey, Joline, 310
Goodpaster, Kenneth E., 23, 311
Goslin, D. A., 22, 51
Gratz, J. E., 176
Greenbaum, Thomas L., 79
Gregor, William T., 310
Gresham, L., 52
Greyser, Stephen A., 141, 176, 178
Guerrette, Richard H., 310
Guiltinan, Joseph P., 98, 139
Gundlach, Gregory T., 141
Guyon, Janet, 108

Haefner, James, 178
Hair, J. F., Jr., 200, 206
Hansen, Nancy L., 141
Hanson, Kristine R., 310
Harvey, Michael, 107
Hawkins, Del I., 64, 77
Heath, Timothy B., 161

Heilbroner, Robert, 148
Helsmich, Nanci, 108
Hinds, Michael deCourcy, 237
Hinge, John B., 141
Hite, R. E., 196, 207, 273
Hoffman, W. Michael, 310
Holbrook, Morris, 176
Horton, Cleveland, 78
Horton, Thomas R., 310
Hotchkiss, Joseph, 141
Houston, M. J., 266, 275
Hume, Scott, 140
Hunt, Shelby D., 52, 153, 176
Hyman, Michael R., 311

Ingersoll, Bruce, 108
Ingram, Thomas N., 189, 207

Jacobs, Richard M., 107
Jacobson, Granna, 107
Jacobson, Michael F., 108
Johnson, Robert, 139, 141

Kahneman, Daniel, 129
Kaikati, Jack G., 23, 237
Kalish, David E., 141
Kant, Immanuel, 51
Kehoe, William J., 136, 141
Kennedy, Allen A., 23
Keogh, James, 8, 23, 289, 310
Kiley, David, 141, 169
Kimmel, Allen J., 51
Kirkpatrick, Jerry, 176
Klein, Thomas, 141
Kleinfield, N. R., 33
Kluckhorn, Clyde, 237
Knetsch, Jack L., 129
Kohlberg, L., 22, 51
Korbin, Stephen J., 237
Koten, John, 141
Kotler, Philip, 237, 273, 310
Krugman, Herbert, 177

LaBarbara, Priscilla, 178
Label, Wayne A., 23, 237
Laczniak, Gene R., 23, 51, 52, 107, 136, 141, 206,
    207, 223, 229, 236, 242, 266, 273, 274, 275
LaForge, R. W., 189
Lambeth, Edmund B., 177

Landler, Mark, 177
Langley, Monica, 141
Lantos, Geoffrey, P., 176
Latimer, Margaret K., 275
Lawrence, Jennifer, 107
Lazier-Smith, Linda, 177
Lee, Kam-Hon, 176
Lees, Cristina, 214
Lehrman, Celia K., 141
Leiser, Burton M., 177, 273
Levitt, Theodore, 237
Levy, Michael, 111, 124, 140
Levy, Sidney J., 273
Liebman, Ronnie, 108
Lipman, Joanne, 177, 275
Logan, John Danier, 148
Lohr, Steve, 106
Lovelock, C. H., 77
Lusch, Robert F., 206, 242, 273, 275
Lusch, V. N., 206
Lutz, R. J., 266, 275

McCarrier, John T., 140
McCarthy, Michael J., 140
McDaniel, Carl, 78
McGinniss, Joe, 262, 274
McMahon, Thomas F., 43
MacIntyre, Alasdair, 51
Macklin, Ruth, 274
Madden, Thomas J., 77
Maher, Philip, 78
Mannes, Marya, 148
Marks, Leonard, Jr., 237
Martin, T. R., 11, 23, 223
Mason, J. Barry, 140
Mason, Kenneth, 226
Mason, Roger, 108
Mathews, W., 23
Mayer, Morris L., 140
Means, Kirsten J., 61, 78
Meier, Barry, 169
Mellow, Craig, 78
Menon, Anil, 273
Merritt, Sharyne, 275
Meyerowitz, Steven A., 9
Miles, Robert H., 238
Mill, John Stuart, 51
Miller, Cyndee, 61
Miller, William W., 61

Mitchell, Russell, 107
Mokwa, Michael P., 108
Molander, Earl, 23
Moore, Jennifer M., 310
Morgan, Fred W., 107
Morreim, E. Haavi, 274
Morris, Betsy, 22, 107
Morrison, Patt, 108
Moss, Frederick C., 274
Mulson, Steve, 22
Murphy, Patrick E., 23, 51, 108, 111, 127, 136,
    141, 151, 178, 206, 229, 237, 242, 245, 273,
    279, 309, 310, 311
Murphy, Thomas A., 237
Myers, John G., 176

Nagle, Thomas T., 139
Naor, Jacob, 236, 237
Nash, Laura L., 289, 310, 311
Neal, William D., 79
Nelson, James E., 57, 63, 78
Nelson, Philip, 176
Netemeyer, R. G., 107
Niffenegger, Phillip B., 274
Norris, Donald G., 139, 141
North, Sterling, 274

Oathout, John D., 107
Ogilvy, David, 176, 275
Oleksak, William, 40
Oliverio, Mary Ellen, 309
O'Reilly, Brian, 131
Ossip, Al, 79
O'Toole, John, 149, 176

Parameswaran, R., 274
Parasuraman, A., 77
Parsons, Patrick R., 177
Pascale, Richard Tanner, 311
Pastin, Mark, 287, 311
Peale, Norman Vincent, 310
Peters, T. J., 310
Pichler, Joseph, 176, 177, 300
Pine, Art, 237
Plank, R. E., 207
Pollay, Richard W., 148, 176
Porter, Michael E., 78
Post, James E., 23, 237
Potter, David M., 148

Pratt, Cornelius B., 178
Putka, Gary, 251

Quinn, Jane Bryant, 177

Radding, Alan, 140
Rawls, John, 51
Reece, Bonnie B., 178
Reich, Robert, 311
Reidenbach, R. Eric, 22, 45, 51, 286, 310
Richards, Jef I., 176
Riordan, Edward A., 78
Robin, Donald P., 22, 23, 45, 51, 286, 310
Rodgers, William H., III, 310
Roening, K., 51
Rose, Robert L., 22
Ross, Touche, 212, 309
Ross, William David, 36, 51, 74
Rotfeld, Herbert J., 177
Rothfeder, Jeffrey, 78
Rothschild, Michael L., 176
Rotzoll, Kim B., 176, 177, 178
Rouner, L. S., 226
Rudelius, W., 206
Ryan, Nancy, 177

Sabato, Larry J., 275
Sajko, Stephen, J., 141
Santilli, Paul C., 176
Schellhardt, T. D., 207
Schiller, Zachary, 177
Schlesinger, Arthur, Jr., 262
Schlossberg, Howard, 79, 164, 177
Schneider, Kenneth C., 57, 63, 78
Schoell, William F., 98, 139
Schultze, Steve, 82
Schurenberg, Eric, 244
Schwadel, Francine, 140
Schwartz, Marvin, 78
Seagull, Louis M., 274
Serpa, Roy, 310
Sethi, S. Prakash, 23
Sethuraman, Raj., 177
Shariff, S., 214
Sheth, Jagdish, 237
Siebert, Patty, 177
Singer, Benjamin D., 274
Skinner, Steven J., 78
Skipper, Robert, 311

Smart, Tim, 177
Smith, N. Craig, 108
Smith, Randolph B., 97
Smith, Timothy, 237
Solomon, Robert C., 310
Sottosanti, Vincent, 135
Stack, Bill, 140
Stafford, David C., 274
Stanton, W. J., 206, 207
Star, Steven H., 108
Steiner, George F., 237
Steiner, John F., 237
Stern, Louis W., 107, 139
Stertz, Bradley A., 140
Stewart, Larry, 274
Stipp, David, 177
Storholm, Gordon, 166
Strang, William A., 275

Tansey, Richard, 311
Taubes, Gary A., 107
Taylor, Herbert B., 220
Telander, Rick, 162
Tellis, Gerald, 177
Thaler, Richard, 129
Thayer, Lee, 149, 176
Therrien, Lois, 140
Ticer, Scott, 107
Toffler, Barbara Ley, 310
Trauk, James, 23
Tuleja, Tad, 311
Tull, Donald S., 64, 77
Tybout, Alice M., 78

Udell, Jon G., 107, 206
Ulrich, Thomas A., 310
Upah, Gregory D., 108

Vachris, L. A., 207

Varadarjan, P. Rajan, 273
Veblen, Thorstein, 99
Velasquez, Manuel, 147
Vitell, S., 52
Vogel, D., 237

Waldman, Peter, 107
Walker, Orville, C., 207
Walsh, William J., 274
Walton, Clarence C., 141
Warnock, G. J., 74
Wartyma, Rick, 309
Wasilewski, Vincent T., 149
Wassersug, Joseph D., 246
Waterman, R. H., Jr., 310
Waters, James A., 310
Weber, James, 42, 310
Webster, Frederick, E., Jr., 310
Weinburg, Charles, 77
Weinstein, Steve, 140
Weitz, Barton A., 111, 140
Wermiel, Stephen, 107
Wessel, David, 107, 186, 206
Whiteside, David, 311
Wilkie, W., 151, 155, 177, 178
Willett, Hugh G., 139
Williams, Oliver F., 51, 141
Winslett, Brenda J., 107
Wise, Jeff, 141
Wokutch, Richard E., 108, 176
Wollenberg, Skip, 177

Youman, Nancy, 107

Zaltman, Gerald, 78, 273
Zeltner, Herbert, 176
Zetmeir, Karl, 78
Zinkhan, G. M., 207

Subject Index

Absolute obligations, 55
Act utilitarianism, 30
Advertising to children, 33, 148, 158–160, 173, 292
Advertorial, 163
AIDS, 61, 249, 301
Air bags, 89
Alcoholic beverages, 59, 60, 88, 91–94, 100, 122, 165, 168, 216
All terrain vehicles (ATV's), 84–85
Amoral, 44, 66
Automobile safety, 127

Bait and switch, 113, 119, 122, 127, 174, 280
Beneficial social marketing, 241–243
Bid rigging, 130, 203
Biodegradable, 5, 94, 103, 169, 301
Bribery, 8, 112–113, 191, 199– 200, 210, 211–216, 222, 229, 300
Business Roundtable, 6, 7, 288

Categorical imperatives, 34, 36, 37, 56
Cause-related marketing, 249
Certified Public Researchers (CPRs), 74
Channel captain, 111
Channel of distribution, ethical issues, 110–113, 296
Cigarettes, 91–93
Cigarette advertising, 2, 67, 91–92, 154, 215
Clayton Act, 111, 127, 189
Codes of ethics, 7–8, 13, 18–21, 30, 40–41, 45–47, 55, 60, 64–65, 70, 73–77, 134–135, 165, 170, 202, 218–221, 225–226, 250, 256, 259, 267–268, 277–278, 280–284, 288, 292, 295, 298–300
Cooling off laws, 190

Competitive bidding, 130
Computerized data bases, 60–61, 68
Computerized random dialing, 55
Computerized selling messages, 185
Confidentiality, 18, 60, 63, 65, 69–70, 302
Conflict of interest, 19, 63, 65, 194, 199, 249, 280, 300, 302
Consequence based theories, 17, 28–34, 50, 223
Consequences test, the, 49
Consequentialist view, 152
Conspicuous consumption, 99
Consumer advocates, 14
Consumer boycotts, 9
Consumer Goods Pricing Act (1975), 127
Consumer Product Safety Commission, 85
Contingency model, the, 46–47
Conventional stage, 44
Core values, 218, 221, 225, 227
Corporate credos, 7, 15, 39, 278–280, 288
Corporate culture, 7–8, 13–14, 21–22, 41–42, 218, 220–221, 278–279, 284–288, 295–296, 298, 300
Corporate intelligence, 68–69, 72, 192
Corporate value system, 41
Cost-benefit analysis, 17, 50, 103, 228
Cost-plus pricing, 65
Crook, the, 11, 13, 106, 191
Cultural relativism, 211, 215

Deceptive practices, 56
Degree of disclosure, 83–84
Deceptive advertising, 128, 150, 152, 165, 175, 240
Deceptive pricing, 112, 174
Difference principle, 36–37
Direct mail ethics, 165

Duties test, the, 49
Deontological theories, 28, 34, 37
Developed ethical, 46
Duty-based theories, 28–29, 34–39, 50, 55, 93, 100, 112, 152
Duty of beneficence, 35, 49
Duty of fidelity, 35, 49
Duty of nonmaleficence, 36, 49
Duty of justice, 35, 49
Duty of gratitude, 35, 49
Duty to interdict, 93
Duty to inform, 93, 103
Duty to investigate, 93
Duty to self-improvement, 35

Ecological ethic, 220
Egalitarian principle, 37
Egoism, 28–30, 35
Embellishment, 154, 156
Emerging ethical, 45–46
Emotional appeals, 39, 41, 164, 263
Entertainment, 194–197, 199, 214, 230–231, 290, 303
Environmentally incompatible products, 5–6, 10, 14, 84, 94–96, 98, 103, 126, 169, 229
Equal Employment Act, 97
Ethical audit, 22, 292–298
Ethical culture, 21, 40, 42, 46
Ethical dilemmas, 4–5, 13, 27–28, 64, 203
Ethical ombudsman, 170, 202
Ethical questions checklist, 278
Ethical reasoning, 13, 26, 49
Ethical theory, 13, 27–42
Ethics codes. *See* Codes of ethics
Ethics committee, 22, 46, 284
Ethics education, 12, 13, 75
Ethics gap, 125
Ethics programs. *See* Ethics training programs
Ethics seminars, 13, 21, 277, 288
Ethics training programs, 277–279, 283–284, 288, 298, 301
Ethnocentrism, 218, 221
Exaggeration in advertising, 145
Exclusive dealing, 111
Exclusive territories, 111
Express warranty, 85–86
Externalities, 95
Externalities effect, 228
Extortion, 216, 229

Fear appeals, 26, 35, 41, 50, 239, 243, 256, 259, 265
Federal Hazardous Substance Act, 89
Federal Trade Commission Act, 111, 190
Firearms, 88, 91–92, 122
Flammable Fabrics Act, 88–89
Focus groups, 58–59, 64, 73, 192, 244
Foreign Corrupt Practices Act (of 1977), the, 6–7, 211, 225
Forward buying, 112, 116–117
Fraud, 216
Frugging, 57, 59

Geocentric, 218
Gift giving, 27, 35, 37–39, 112–114, 122, 135, 194–195, 199, 214, 230–231, 280, 282, 288, 294, 303
Golden Rule, the, 17, 152
Grease payments, 211–215
Green marketing, 96–97, 169
Green River Ordinances, 190
Greshman's Law, 244

Handlers, 260
Health claims, 85, 91, 104, 143
Hierarchy principles, 157
Host communities, 14

Implied warranty, 85–86, 89, 190
Industrial espionage, 68, 190
Infomercials, 168–169
Intelligence gathering, 56, 72
International ethics audit, 288
Invasion of privacy, 56, 193, 201
Iron law of responsibility, 112

Junk mail, 186
Justice test, the, 50

Kant's absolute duties, 39, 152
Kickbacks, 190, 197, 200, 202, 226, 294

Lanham Act of 1946, 90
Legalistic, 44–45
Legalists, 11–12
Legal test, the, 49
Liberty principle, the, 36, 85
Lowballing, 122
Lying to customers, 191

Magnuson-Moss Warranty Act of 1975, 86
Marketing by professionals, 240
Marketing to children, 84
Mergers, 111
Meritorious duties, 152
Misleading claims, 19, 35, 67–68, 101, 145, 190, 259
Misrepresentation of research findings, 55, 66, 76
Misrepresentation of research procedures, 58
Moral Development Model, the, 5, 43–44, 196
Moralist, 11–12
Moral reasoning, 12, 21, 27
Motives Test, the, 49

Negative political advertising, 240, 261, 264, 266–267
Nepotism, 216
"No Harm, No Foul" approach, 60
Nutritional labeling, 6, 95

Observational studies without informed consent, 60
Organizational Moral Development Model, the, 44–46
Overbilling the client, 63, 65
Overly personal questions and topics, 60
Overstatement of conclusions, 64

Padding expense accounts, 3, 18, 188, 191, 277, 282, 290
Peripheral values, 218
Persuasive advertising, 154–156
Planned product obsolescence, 96–99, 243
Political marketing, 260–269
"Power-responsibility equilibrium," 112, 119, 132
Preconventional stage, 43–44
Predatory pricing, 20, 127
Price deception, 127
Price discrimination, 117, 126–127
Price fixing, 20, 111, 126–127, 130, 240, 251
Price gouging, 65, 126, 128, 130
Prima facia duties, 34
Primary stakeholders, 14–15
Principled stage, the, 44
Principle of fairness, 128, 153
Product alteration, 290
Product counterfeiting, 84, 89–91
Product defects, 128
Product dumping, 126, 215, 221–222, 229

Product elimination, 105
Product fraud, 9
Products in poor taste, 84, 99–100
Product liability, 103
Product liability law, 85, 86–87, 89
Product misrepresentation, 100–102
Product package disposal, 5–6, 14
Product recall, 105, 122, 224, 288
Product safety, 49, 81, 84, 87, 91, 103, 200, 215
Product safety testing, 32, 35, 87, 89
Product tampering, 192
Professional ethic, the, 18
Program length commercials, 159–160
Projective technique, 60
Promotional warranties, 86
Proportionality framework, the, 203–204
Proportionate reason, 128
Protest social marketing, 241–243, 247
Public interest groups, 14–15
Puffery, 154, 156, 190, 200, 265, 292
Punitive damages, 87
Push money (P.M.s or Spiffs), 123

Rationalizers, 11–13, 200
"Rational person" approach, the, 47
Reasoned action model, the, 47–48
Relativism, 37, 39
Responsive, 45
Revolutionary social marketing, 241–243
Right of privacy, the, 59–62, 249, 280, 302
Rights of subjects, the, 55
Rights test, the, 50
Robinson-Patman Act, 111, 127, 189
Rule utilitarianism, 30

Sales chaplain, 201–202
Sales management ethics, 197–199
Sales quotas, ethics of, 199–200
Secondary stakeholders, 14
Seekers, 11–12
Sherman Act, 111, 127
Slack packaging, 101
Slotting allowances/fees, 1, 112, 116–122, 291
Smokeless cigarette, 93
Social audits, 228
Socially controversial products, 84, 91–102
Social marketing, 240–250
Sound bites, 260, 263, 269
Special obligations test, the, 49

Spin control, 260
Spying on competitors, 192
Stakeholders, 14–17, 21, 28, 30, 34, 44, 48, 49, 50,
    51, 56, 69, 73, 103, 125, 133, 221–222, 278,
    280, 282, 297, 301
Stakeholder concept, the, 14–17, 51, 95, 221, 222–
    223
Strict liability, 86–87
Subliminal advertising, 154–155
Sullivan principles, the, 218–220
Sugging, 57, 59

Teaching ethics, 5
Telemarketing, 71, 190, 193
Teleological theories, 30
Theory of negligence, 86
Tie-in-sales, 189
Tobacco Institute, the, 92
Tobacco products, 2, 88, 165, 168, 216, 248
Tort law, 86–88
Trademarks, 90
Trademark Counterfeiting Act (1984), 90
Truth in Lending Act, 127
TV Test, the, 18, 73

Tying arrangements, 111
Tylenol product recall, the, 15

U.S. Privacy Act of 1974, 59
Uniform commercial code, 190
Unit pricing, 6, 127
Unnecessary market research, 62–63
Unsafe products, 8, 215–216, 222
Utilitarian ethics. *See* Utilitarianism
Utilitarianism, 17, 28–34, 37, 50, 56, 89, 95, 126,
    128, 151–152, 158, 163, 248
Utilitarian test, the, 49

Valdez principles, 95–96, 103
Veracity principle, 157
Virtue ethics, 28–29, 39–42, 50, 72, 152

Warning labels, 28, 93–94, 103–104
Warranties, 35, 85–86, 102
Wheeler-Lea Amendment, 151, 190
Whistleblowing, 202
White collar crime, 3
Worldwide codes of ethics, 218–221